Rethinking Australia's Defence

Rethinking Australia's Defence

Ross Babbage

University of Queensland Press

© University of Queensland Press, St Lucia, Queensland, 1980

This book is copyright. Apart from any fair dealing for the purposes of private study, research, criticism, or review, as permitted under the Copyright Act, no part may be reproduced by any process without written permission. Enquiries should be made to the publishers.

Typeset by Press Etching Pty Ltd, Brisbane
Printed and bound by Southwood Press, Marrickville, NSW

Distributed in the United Kingdom, Europe, the Middle East, Africa, and the Caribbean by Prentice-Hall International, International Book Distributors Ltd, 66 Wood Lane End, Hemel Hempstead, Herts., England

National Library of Australia
Cataloguing-in-Publication data

Babbage, Ross Eden, 1949-
   Rethinking Australia's defence.

   Index
   Bibliography
   ISBN 0 7022 1486 8

   1. Australia - Military policy. 2. Australia - Defenses.
I. Title.

355'.0335'94

Contents

Figures   *vii*
Tables   *ix*
Acronyms and Abbreviations   *xi*
Acknowledgements   *xv*
A Note on Sources   *xvii*

Introduction: Why Rethink?   xix

Part I   **The Altered Strategic Environment**   1

       1   A More Qualified ANZUS   *3*
       2   The Revolution in Conventional Military Technologies   *23*

Part II   **New Imperatives for Change**   51

       3   A Broader Range of Potential Threats   *53*
       4   The Identification of Our Major Weaknesses   *76*

Part III   **Constraints on Change**   107

       5   Practical Constraints on Change   *109*
       6   Bureaucratic Resistance   *125*

Part IV   **Deriving Future Policy**   147

       7   Gaining a Sense of Direction   *149*
       8   Wider Strategic Options   *158*
       9   New Manpower Concepts   *184*

10 The Challenge of Appropriate
    Response *209*

Appendixes: **215**

Appendix A. The Shape, Size and Capacity of
             Australia's Current Defence Force: A
             Brief Summary *217*

Appendix B. The New Conventional Military
             Technologies: What They Are and
             What They Do *225*

             An Introductory Note to Appendixes
             C and D: Approaching Current
             Problems in Australian Security
             Planning *260*

Appendix C. Managing an Uncertain Threat
             Environment: Deriving Representative
             Scenarios *262*

Appendix D. Towards Coherent Security
             Planning *275*

Select Bibliography *295*
Index *303*

Figures

1 Defence outlay as a percentage of total government outlays and gross domestic product, 1965-66 to 1975-76   *118*
2 Simplified representation of a potential security planning process   *156*
3 Categories of expenditure as a percentage of the total defence budgetary vote, 1965-66 to 1975-76   *186*
4 Approximate cost substitution function between full-time conventional force personnel and latent conventional force personnel   *201*
5 Approximate cost substitution function between full-time conventional force personnel and latent territorial force personnel   *202*
6 Diagrammatic presentation of a means of deriving representative scenarios   *263*
7 Diagrammatic presentation of the threat evaluation process in Stage 3   *266*
8 Relating short-term financial input to long-term national security output   *281*
9 Programme and project relationship   *285*

Tables

1. United States: Objectives and levels of security assistance under the Guam Doctrine   7
2. United States: Expressed intentions and capabilities to assist Australia in a range of hypothetical situations   13
3. Australia: Imports and exports, proportions, by country of consignment or origin, 1952-53 to 1972-73   57
4. Australian attitudes to compulsory military training, 1942-73   114
5. Australian attitudes to two years' full-time military service, with possible overseas deployment, for a randomly chosen minority of men aged twenty, 1964-71   115
6. Comparative tabulation of civilian personnel strengths in defence establishments   192
7. Functional distribution of full-time defence manpower, 1976   193
8. Efficiency of specialized force structures   277
9. Efficiency of less-specialized force structures   278

Acronyms and Abbreviations

ADFA	Australian Defence Force Academy
AHAMS	advanced heavy anti-tank missile system
AIDATS	Army in-flight data transmission system
ALCM	air-launched cruise missile
ANOP	Australian National Opinion Polls
ANZUS	Australia, New Zealand and United States (Security Treaty)
APC	armoured personnel carrier
APFSDS	armour-piercing, fin-stabilized, discarding-sabot (tank-gun round)
APSA	Australian Political Science Association
ARM	anti-radiation missile
ARPA	Advanced Research Projects Agency
ASW	anti-submarine warfare
ATIGS	advanced tactical inertial guiding system
AWACS	airborne warning and control system
BCS	battery computer system (for artillery units)
C^3	communications, command and control
CAPTOR	encapsulated torpedo
CDFS	Chief of Defence Force Staff
CIWS	close-in weapons system
CLGP	cannon-launched guided projectile
CODAG	combination of diesel and gas (turbine) (i.e. capable of operating simultaneously)
CODOG	combination of diesel or gas (turbine) (i.e. only one type can power ship at any one time)
COMINT	communications intelligence
CSE	Central Studies Establishment
DARPA	Defense Advanced Research Projects Agency
DME	distance-measuring equipment
DMS	Defense Marketing Services
DoD	Department of Defence
DP	decision-point

ELINT	electronic intelligence
EW	electronic warfare
FAE	fuel-air explosive
FEBA	forward edge of battle area
FLIR	forward-looking infra-red (sensor)
FYDP	five-year defence programme
FYRP	five-year rolling programme
GPS	global positioning satellite (system)
GVN	Government of Vietnam (i.e. South)
HALO	high-altitude large optics (technology)
HARM	high-speed anti-radiation missile
HIMAG	high mobility and agility (programme)
HIMAT	high manoeuvreability aircraft technology (programme)
HOWLS	hostile weapons location system
HSM	hard-structure munition
IAC	Industries Assistance Commission
IBCS	integrated battlefield control system
ICBM	intercontinental ballistic missile
IISS	International Institute for Strategic Studies
ILAW	improved light anti-tank weapon
IRS	infra-red scan
JTIDS	joint tactical information distribution system
KE	kinetic energy
LRP	long-range plan
MAD	mutual assured destruction (doctrine)
MAGCOM	magnetic contour-matching (navigation technique)
MERDC	Mobility Equipment Research and Development Centre
MICRAD	microwave radiometric (technology)
MICV	mechanized infantry combat vehicle
MRBM	medium-range ballistic missile
MSS	moored surveillance system
NAP/TAWS	Naval Air Power and Tactical Air Weapon System (study)
NASA	National Aeronautics and Space Administration
NATO	North Atlantic Treaty Organization
OTH	over the horizon
OTH-B	over-the-horizon backscatter (radar)
PHM	patrol hydrofoil, missile-armed (programme)
PNG	Papua New Guinea
PRC	People's Republic of China
PRAM	propelled rocket-assisted mine

RAAF	Royal Australian Air Force
RAN	Royal Australian Navy
R & D	research and development
REMBASS	remotely emplaced battlefield sensor system
RPV	remotely piloted vehicle
SALT	Strategic Arms Limitation Treaty
SAM	surface-to-air missile
SEATO	South-East Asian Treaty Organization
SIAM	self-initiated attack missile
SIG-D	simplified inertial guidance-demonstration (programme)
SLBM	submarine-launched ballistic missile
SLCM	sea-launched cruise missile
SMEAC	scene-matching area correlation (navigation technique)
SOSUS	sonar surveillance system
SOTAS	stand-off target-acquisition system
SSBN	ballistic missile-firing nuclear (submarine)
SSLP	Secretariat for National Security and Long-range Defence Planning (Swedish Ministry of Defence)
SSN	nuclear-attack submarine
SURTASS	surveillance towed-array sensor system
SWATH	small waterplane, area-twin hull
TACTAS	tactical towed-array sensor
T-AGOS	tug-area general ocean surveillance [probable meaning]
TASS	towed-array surveillance system
TERCOM	terrain contour-matching (navigation technique)
TOS	tactical operations system
TRAM	target recognition attack multi-sensor
ULTRA	ultra lightweight transmissive array
V/STOL	vertical/short take-off and landing
WAAM	wide area anti-armour munitions (programme)

Acknowledgements

I am deeply indebted to a large number of people for their assistance in the production of this book.

The Australian National University, and the Department of International Relations in particular, were generous in their support of my field-work programme and in the provision of office accommodation and other facilities. I am also grateful to the Department of Defence for supporting my application for three years' leave without pay from the Public Service.

The assistance provided by my colleagues and academic supervisors at the ANU, Drs Robert O'Neill and Desmond Ball, was of very great value. Despite the pressures of other activities, they gave freely of their time and were prepared to share their extensive knowledge and experience in a generous manner. The three years spent as an active member of the Strategic and Defence Studies Centre "team" was a most valuable and enjoyable experience.

Finally, special mention should be made of the sacrifices made by my family. It is they who suffered most from the financial stringencies that were necessary to undertake this work. They also had to put up with my lengthy periods of absence on field-trips and with extended working hours on weekends and evenings. Their long-suffering support and encouragement largely made this project possible.

A Note on Sources

Rethinking Australia's Defence is an edited version of a Ph.D. thesis entitled "Australian Security Planning in a Changing Strategic Environment". This was written in its entirety while I was studying in the Department of International Relations at the Australian National University and on leave from the Australian Public Service.

Gathering the information required for this project was not easy. This was primarily because the processes of security policy-making in Australia are unusually "closed". In marked contrast to most Western countries, senior service and civilian officers rarely express their views publicly and in any detail on the broader issues of national security concern, nor does the Parliament hold regular or detailed committee hearings on the central issues of security policy. As a consequence, the number of people who are actively engaged in public debate on national security issues in Australia is relatively limited. Nearly all of those who are available to comment regularly and in depth, do so from a vantage-point outside the formal decision-making structure and many are motivated to plead the cause of particular interest groups.

The problems this situation presents to serious researchers are formidable. However, for this work, it proved possible to overcome many of these difficulties by drawing extensively upon the accounts and opinions of those who have been intimately involved in the processes of security decision-making in the recent past, those who have studied the existing system closely and those who have monitored the progression of Australian defence policy over an extended period. Although these informed external observers differ widely in their levels of experience, their political beliefs and their means of earning a living, they do largely agree on a wide range of important matters. This has made it possible to base a significant proportion of the argument and some of the conclusions in this book upon their evidence.

Another source of information and important perspectives was discussion and debate within the academic and broader national security communities in Canberra. Daily contact with the membership of the Strategic and Defence Studies Centre and the Department of International Relations at the Australian National University was particularly helpful. In addition, the regular meetings and seminars of the United Service Institution of the Australian Capital Territory provided valuable opportunities to share the insights of others and to subject my own views to informed and critical review.

No classified documents or materials were employed in the construction of this volume. However, it was possible to gain a significant amount of information on a wide range of matters that are veiled by secrecy within Australia by referring to overseas professional and trade journals and the documentation produced by foreign governments. United States Congressional hearings, and the publications *International Defense Review* and *Aviation Week and Space Technology* deserve particular mention in this regard.

In the final analysis, the views expressed in this book should be regarded as mine alone. They should not be attributed to either the Department of Defence (where I was formerly employed) or the Office of National Assessments (where I am currently employed).

Ross Babbage

Introduction

Why Rethink?

Dependence upon major power allies has dominated Australian security policy.[1] The isolation of Australia from the rest of the "civilized" world caused the first European settlers to regard themselves as a vulnerable outpost of Western society. They naturally sought to strengthen their security by fostering close links with the Empire and encouraging the presence of the Royal Navy. To bolster the Imperial relationship, the Australian colonies willingly deployed military forces to support British commitments in a number of foreign wars. Thus the concept of ensuring the nation's security through an alliance, maintained in part by the deployment in a subsidiary role of Australian forces overseas, became firmly established. The forward defence era was born.

This pattern of close co-operation in Imperial security affairs continued largely unaltered until the paucity of British forces in the Far East during the Second World War prompted Prime Minister Curtin to turn to the United States as the primary guarantor of Australia's security. But while the country's major ally changed, Australia's security strategy remained unaltered. Consequently, during the late 1940s and through the 1950s and 1960s, the United States was viewed as the prime source of Australian security and significant components of the Defence Force were again deployed overseas, to support major allied commitments and to foster the relationship.

However, by the late 1960s, Australia's traditional policy of forward defence was being undermined by the declining regional strength and interest of its traditional major allies. In the decade from 1967 Britain completely withdrew its military presence from the Far East, and the United States withdrew all its forces from Indo-China, all of its combat forces from Thailand, and commenced a phased withdrawal of ground combat forces from South Korea. During this period the United States also began to define more narrowly the form of assistance that would be made available to friends and allies than previously understood by them. In contrast to its continuing concern and involvement in Europe and the Middle

East, the United States relegated its security interests in more peripheral theatres, such as South-East Asia, to a much lower level than in the 1960s.

From time to time it is tempting for Australian politicians and others to suggest that nothing important has changed during this period and to publicly exaggerate the value and significance of the security tie with the United States. Undue prominence is sometimes given to the periodic co-ordination of sea and air surveillance with the ANZUS partners or to major joint exercises. But these activities should not disguise the fact that during the past decade United States inclinations and capacities to intervene militarily in South-east Asia and the Western Pacific have declined markedly. While this does not spell the end of ANZUS itself, the altered regional role of the United States effectively removes the essential basis of Australia's long-established strategy of forward defence. In simple terms, Australian security planners can no longer expect United States (or British) forces to become engaged in a variety of regional conflicts alongside, and in support of, Australian military units. Any future Australian commitments to support regional states would most probably need to be undertaken without the direct assistance and joint action of a major power. Clearly this type of deployment would represent a most perilous departure from the pattern of Australia's historical experience. In the absence of major allied support, Australia does not possess the military capacity nor the political will to undertake successfully many types of foreign intervention. The limited scale of the Australian Defence Force heavily restricts its capability to combat regional domestic violence, insurgency or intrastate conflict, either independently or with local support. Consequently it is likely that in the future significant components of the Defence Force will be deployed overseas only in very special circumstances, such as United Nations peacekeeping operations or the emergency evacuation of Australian citizens from a hostile environment.[2]

Because the forward defence concept is no longer viable, Australia's defence policy in the future is likely to be primarily concerned with the development of an independent capacity to secure the nation's immediate environment — the continent itself and its offshore islands and resources. This re-ordering of priorities represents a fundamental shift in policy direction.

During the past decade, there has also been a series of much broader changes in the international strategic environment. The Sino-Soviet split has become more complex; new centres of power have emerged in Japan, China, the Middle East and a more unified Europe; the super-powers have moderated somewhat the ideological character of their differences and engaged in extensive consultations on a wide range of matters; the tension between the industrial and developing countries regarding the distribution of wealth and the terms of trade has increased; and the world generally has become more interdependent — the industrial states have increased their reliance on external sources of raw materials and energy, and the developing states in turn have become increasingly reliant upon external sources of capital and technology.

During this period, a technological revolution has also become obvious in conventional military capacities. New surveillance, long-range targeting, ordnance delivery, precision-guidance and other technologies are being developed that promise unprecedented enhancements of military capabilities. The ground-rules of conventional warfare, of what is possible and impossible on the battlefield, have begun to alter dramatically.

This book argues that, in combination, these developments represent a fundamental transformation of Australia's strategic environment. In the future, Australia's armed forces may not only have to deploy and fight alone, but they may have to do so with very little warning and in a geographical environment that is quite different to the battlefields of the past. In addition, they will require a capacity to combat a much broader range of pressures and threats in the face of technologies, many of which are revolutionary in character.

The demands of this new environment are quite different to those of the past. Australia's security planners therefore are confronted with an urgent requirement to review the traditional policies and concepts inherited from the forward defence era. In the new strategic situation, it is necessary to question what types of contingencies Australia's security system should be prepared to meet, in the context of which geographical environment and within what time-span? What level of independent capacity is required? What should be the priorities in developing capabilities to meet the types of pressures and threats with which Australia may be confronted in the future? And what operational concepts, doctrines, technologies and force structures would most efficiently and economically provide the capabilities desired? The obsolescence of so much of the conventional wisdom in Australian security policy necessitates a thorough rethinking of Australia's defence.

Notes and References

1. In this volume, the term "security policy" is generally favoured over that of "defence policy". This is primarily because security policy can be defined in a

broad manner to encompass a wide range of diplomatic, political, economic, military, social and other pressures and threats to which nation states are potentially susceptible.
2. The prospect of significant portions of the Australian Defence Force being deployed abroad in the future is most frequently discussed in the context of a range of scenarios involving domestic violence, sub-national violence and regional interstate conflicts in Papua New Guinea (PNG). There is undoubtedly some potential for each of these possibilities to arise. However, because the Australian Defence Force is currently only capable of providing up to two battalions for a protracted external commitment, its capacity to contribute meaningfully to the support of indigenous capabilities through the provision of troops is extremely limited. Consequently, in nearly every conceivable situation, the primary burden of maintaining PNG security is likely to fall upon the local police and defence forces. This is not to imply that Australia would fail to provide any support to PNG in a security crisis. In the military sphere, increased quantities of equipment, supplies, technical assistance and training might be made available. In addition, diplomatic, economic and other avenues of support might be mobilized.

However, it is important to appreciate that, in the context of Australia's overall security responsibilities in the future, those involving the dispatch of forces to PNG are not of overriding significance. As a consequence, it is unlikely that contingencies in this category would be permitted to dominate Australia's future processes of security planning. These considerations are discussed at greater length by Robert O'Neill, "The Defence Relationship: Aid — When, Where, How Much and For How Long?" *New Guinea* 10, no. 4 (December 1976): 62-70.

Part 1

THE ALTERED STRATEGIC ENVIRONMENT

1
A More Qualified ANZUS

During the past thirty years, there has been a great tendency for Australians to over-value the international significance of their connections with the United States. Perhaps this is not very surprising. The scale of its resources has made it possible for the United States to play a highly visible and important role in many aspects of Australian society. Thus the United States has not only become Australia's major ally but many other things as well, including its largest source of foreign capital investment and its second-largest trading partner; taking 11 per cent of the nation's exports and providing 21 per cent of its imports.[1]

However, whilst the United States—Australian relationship is most prominent in Australian domestic affairs, its significance to the United States is quite peripheral and in no sense comparable. In the economic sphere, Australia supplies less than one per cent of United States imports and receives a bare 2 per cent of United States exports.[2] This overwhelming contrast in the scale of influence and power results in United States dominance of nearly every aspect of the relationship. As Dr J.M. Siracusa points out:

> Since the turn of the century, the United States could normally count on at least sixteen times the population and nineteen times the economic resources of Australia. This huge disparity in power, both real and potential, had thus one inevitable consequence. In any partnership, the United States had to be vastly more important to Australia than Australia could ever be to the United States. Any perusal of a documentary history or reader in Australian—American relations invariably bears ample evidence to the fact that Australian policymakers were necessarily thinking and talking about the United States far more than Americans were ever thinking and talking about Australia.[3]

Australian perceptions of the importance of the relationship have been magnified further by the very uneven flow of culture and sentiment across the Pacific. During and since the Second World War, Australian society has become very heavily influenced by the American mass media. Partly because of this, partly because of the developing United States global role and partly because of the growing security and economic relationship, many Australians have tended to identify closely with the United States, its values, culture, products, policies and actions. By contrast, Americans have been exposed to very little Australian culture and have limited knowledge of the country. As Robin Boyd pointed out, "communication is virtually one way along the Pacific axis".[4]

Identification with the United States also has been reinforced by the emphasis Australia's politicians have continually placed upon the broader aspects of the relationship when discussing national security affairs. For example, in his June 1976 posture statement, the Prime Minister, Mr Malcolm Fraser said:

> Of all the great powers with active interests and capabilities in the areas of critical concern to Australia, the United States is the power with whom we have the closest links. These links are based not merely on known common interests and in commitments to a peaceful stable world, but on common traditions of democratic institutions and values of respect for the individual.[5]

It is certainly true that the two countries have similar democratic institutions and ideals, are predominantly white, English-speaking and share a similar "frontier"-type history, but continued Australian reference to these matters and to the two countries' history of comradeship-in-arms has led to a very much stronger perception of the significance of the relationship in Australia than in the United States.

In American eyes, Australia is, at best, one of many middle-ranking powers. Yet Australia does occupy a significant position in the economic structure of the Western world and, in particular, plays a major part in supporting Japanese economic growth and stability. In addition, Australia's natural resources, her suitability for the siting of an array of military and scientific installations and her strategic location bordering the major transit routes between the South Pacific and the Indian Oceans are of positive value. Perhaps even more importantly, from the American point of view, the close relationship with Australia effectively denies an opponent access to all of these assets. Yet while these considerations may appear to be of considerable significance in isolation, they are quite peripheral in the context of the United States' overall global strategic concerns.

Few Australian descriptions of the relationship emphasize its limited utility to the United States. This is a consequence of the very great value that successive generations of Australians have placed upon alliance relationships. Heavy emphasis upon the maintenance of a close affiliation with major allies traditionally has been perceived as an ideal means of enhancing the country's security at a time when realistically it could not be performed independently. The enormous size, extreme inhospitability and relative isolation of the Australian continent, when considered in the light of the limited population and financial resources that have been available, always has served to make access to the resources of a major power ally, even if only in theory, an extremely attractive option. For instance, it has meant that national budgetary priority could be given consistently to the enormous, continuing and more politically appealing requirements of national development, social welfare and education, rather than to the provision of an independent national security capacity.

The gradual reduction of Australia's deeply held feelings of isolated vulnerability through the adoption of major power alliances has inhibited severely the development of strategic independence. Successive Australian governments have considered that the relationships with major allies have required continuous supportive activity. Apart from frequent declarations of affinity, the prime Australian means of establishing and maintaining these close security relationships has been participation in joint-force deployments overseas. Thus the process of sending forces abroad in support of major power allies accounts for almost all of Australia's military history. In professed loyalty to the Empire, Australians fought in the Maori Wars, the Sudan, served in the Boxer Rebellion and shared the frustrations of the Boer War. This experience largely continued through both world wars and since 1945, Australians have played further supporting roles in Korea, the Malayan Emergency, Indonesian confrontation and Vietnam. The cultural and structural impact of this on-going experience upon the Australian population and, most particularly, the Australian defence establishment, can hardly be overestimated. For the Australian defence structure, the primary effect has been to direct most of the country's scarce national security resources away from the requirements of developing a self-reliant defence capacity. Up until the late 1960s, the neglect of Australia's independent national security capacity could be justified by the then-perceived necessity of maintaining and developing an expeditionary capacity well-suited to participation in joint allied operations overseas, but during the past decade, this rationale has been undermined primarily as a result of a series of important changes in United States policy towards the Asian region.

When viewed in perspective, the trauma of the Vietnam experience appears to have had a very significant and enduring impact upon the propensity of the United States to maintain the strength of forces stationed abroad and to deploy them in support of regional allies.[6] United States national security policy is now reorientated much more directly towards those areas of the world that are of central significance in supporting United States interests in the global strategic balance (continental United States, Europe, the Middle East and North-East Asia in particular). In terms of the physical United States presence in Australia's proximity, this global reorientation has already had a significant impact. In recent years, United States force deployments in the Western Pacific have been reduced substantially. It is by no means clear how far or how fast these processes of United States withdrawal will proceed, but it is quite apparent that the military presence of the United States in the Western Pacific is declining in both absolute and relative terms, and it may continue to do so for many years.[7]

In addition to a reduced physical presence, the inclination of the United States to intervene in conflicts in the region has also declined. Successive American presidents and a large number of congressional leaders have expressed their desire to avoid any new commitment of ground forces to the Asian mainland. The most coherent and enduring expression of this view was made by President Nixon during an informal meeting with reporters at Guam on 25 July 1969. According to the official text, the following exchange took place:

> *Questioner* Mr President, sir, on the question of U.S. military relationships in Asia, if I may ask a hypothetical question: If a leader of one of the countries with which we have close military relationships either through SEATO or in Vietnam should say, "Well, you are pulling out of Vietnam with your troops, we can read in the newspapers. How can we know that you will remain to play a significant role as you say you wish to do in security arrangements in Asia?" What kind of an approach can you take to that question?
> *The President* I have already indicated that the answer to that question is not an easy one — not easy because we will be greatly tempted when that question is put to indicate that if any nation desires the assistance of the United States militarily in order to meet an internal or external threat, we will provide it.
>
> However, I believe that the time has come when the United States, in our relations with all of our Asian friends, be quite emphatic on two points: One, that we will keep our treaty commitments, our treaty commitments, for example, with Thailand under SEATO; but, two, that as far as the problems of internal security are concerned, as far as the problems of military defense, except for the threat of a major power involving nuclear weapons, that the United States is going to encourage and has the right to expect that this problem will be increasingly handled by, and the responsibility for it taken by, the Asian nations themselves.
> ... It will not be easy. But if the United States just continues down the road of responding to requests for assistance, of assuming the primary

responsibility for defending these countries when they have internal problems or external problems, they are never going to take care of themselves.[8]

This heavily qualified expression of United States policy towards the region and subsequent supporting statements and actions are of great significance for Australia. One of the most important implications is that, if American ground forces are not to be committed to the Asian mainland again, there is unlikely to be a further opportunity for the Australian armed forces to be committed in their support.[9]

However, this altered United States policy also impacts upon the future scope for co-operative or joint Australian—American operations in the defence of Australia itself. The Guam Doctrine and more detailed United States elaborations of it have explained consistently that the level of peacetime force structure integration with allied regional powers will be determined primarily by the nature of the threat with which they are confronted. This relationship is most clearly illustrated in Table 1, which summarizes a large part of the findings of a major Rand Corporation study into the implications of the Guam Doctrine.[10]

Table 1. United States: Objectives and levels of security assistance under the Guam Doctrine.

Objective	Level of assistance	Likely conflict	Degree of U.S. involvement
Total force planning	Combined force planning	Attack by USSR or PRC on U.S. friend or ally	Greatest
Regionalism	Complementary force planning	Attack by a minor communist power on U.S. friend or ally; attack by a Soviet client on U.S. friend or ally	
Self-reliance	Supplementary force planning	Conflict between U.S. friends or allies; communist-supported insurgency; Soviet client-supported insurgency	
		Home-grown insurgency	Least

It would thus appear that under current United States policy, unless Australia is threatened directly by the Soviet Union or China, the Australian government cannot expect to receive unqualified American support. In the circumstances of a regional dispute or crisis, it is by no means clear what type of support the United States might be prepared to supply its allies.

Primarily as a result of these policy changes, the limited utility of the relationship in United States eyes has become much more evident to the Australian national security community. The high levels of ambiguity and uncertainty that characterize the alliance are now being cited more frequently as an important element of the relationship. This is evidenced most clearly in the 1976 Defence White Paper:

> Remote from Europe, we now have one significant alliance — the ANZUS Treaty, with New Zealand and the US. Both countries are important to us; but it is prudent to remind ourselves that the US has many diverse interests and obligations. . . . Our alliance with the US gives substantial grounds for confidence that in the event of a fundamental threat to Australia's security US military support would be forthcoming. However, even though our security may be ultimately dependent upon US support, we owe it to ourselves to be able to mount a national defence effort that would maximise the risks and costs of any aggression.
>
> Short of this major, and improbable situation, we could face a range of other situations that we should expect to handle more independently. It is not our policy, nor would it be prudent, to rely on US combat help in all circumstances. Indeed it is possible to envisage a range of situations in which the threshold of direct US combat involvement could be quite high.[11]

A United Service Institution report on the alliance also emphasized the ambiguous nature of the relationship in describing the formal security connection:

> The ANZUS Treaty makes no guarantees, it entails no binding obligations. It depends on consultation and mutual consent. In the event of armed aggression on one of the member states the character of the assistance offered is not stated unequivocally; rather, the Treaty looks to a declaration of intent. ANZUS like all treaties depends ultimately on *trust*.[12] By their very character treaties cannot be "watertight"; they depend on the actions in the future of governments of men in as yet unknown situations.[13]

The central clauses of the ANZUS treaty state that:

> The Parties will consult together whenever in the opinion of any of them the territorial integrity, political independence or security of any of the Parties is threatened in the Pacific.

Each Party recognizes that an armed attack in the Pacific area on any of the Parties would be dangerous to its own peace and safety and declares that it would act to meet the common danger in accordance with its constitutional processes.[14]

However, in the absence of firm assurances concerning particular types of assistance in categories of situations, evaluations of the treaty's utility are, of necessity, very unclear. Certainly a high level of imprecision almost always has been a notable feature of treaty arrangements. This provides a basis for each party to declare general intent without unduly restricting future freedom of action. The fact that treaties rarely usurp governmental prerogatives or predetermine government actions enhances greatly their political acceptability. Such agreements certainly do not assure each partner the provision of defence resources from its allies in all situations. However, they do provide each party with a level of proxy deterrence, for while each partner to such a treaty may be unsure what action its allies may take in particular circumstances, those same types of doubts are also likely to arise in the minds of any intending adversaries.

For Australia, the Guam Doctrine represents the overlay of an unclear statement on top of an already imprecise treaty. President Nixon's briefing at Guam was deliberately blurred at the edges, with journalists, politicians and members of the President's staff encouraged to derive a variety of interpretations.[15] Its presentation provided a sophisticated level of ambiguity that apparently was intended to keep potential aggressors uncertain of future United States intentions while at the same time satisfying the demands of friends and allies.

For Australian security planners, the degree of uncertainty inherent in this type of alliance relationship makes long-term conceptual and structural planning of the Australian Defence Force extremely difficult. On the one hand, it can be argued that the Guam Doctrine is analogous to, and in reality as tenuous as, Dean Acheson's perimeter strategy.[16] In other words, the case can be made that, regardless of public pronouncements of United States intentions, it is practically impossible to predetermine the types of force commitments the United States may make some time in the future. It is quite conceivable, although of doubtful probability, that in the circumstances of some types of pressure against Australia, the United States might abandon or waive its current foreign policy principles and provide massive assistance to meet a regional threat. On the other hand, it can also be argued that virtually no assistance can be guaranteed from the United States under any circumstances and hence Australia must be prepared to develop an independent capacity to meet all conceivable threat categories. It is difficult to resolve these alternative views. Perhaps the best independent formulation of likely United State reactions was given by McGeorge Bundy, a former Assistant to the President for National Security Affairs. He stated that: "the American commitment anywhere is only as deep as the continued conviction of Americans that their own interests require it."[17]

If this is true, can Australian policy be made to impact upon the evaluation by the United States of its own interests? Certainly there are some factors that, in the circumstances of any future crisis involving Australia, would have a major influence upon United States decision-making and which are, to some degree, under Australian control. The formal treaty itself, the state of the diplomatic linkage, the strength of economic connections, the significance the United States government places upon the Australian continent and the installations upon it, the capacity of Australia to act in her own defence, the number of United States citizens resident in Australia, the number of United States citizens who have visited Australia, the state of United States sentimental ties with Australia, etc., can all be structured to some degree from Australia to maximize the probability of a favourable United States response. However, in a crisis situation, even though an Australian government may use its full influence to stimulate, encourage, cajole or even coerce a favourable United States response, in the final analysis, the decision on whether or not forces would be committed to support Australia can be expected to be made by the United States government of the day in the light of its full range of domestic and world-wide interests.

The nature of the problem confronting those who are tasked with the long-term planning of Australia's security capacity can be elaborated to some degree by examining more closely expressed United States intentions in the circumstances of particular types of crises. For instance, the Guam Doctrine indicates that the level of security assistance Australia can expect to receive from the United States will not be related necessarily to the seriousness of the threat that arises to Australia's security. Rather, it will tend to be related much more closely to current United States perceptions of the indirect threat to the United States itself of Australia being attacked by the country concerned. Thus if a major power mounts a heavy attack upon Australia, the United States response will not be conditioned primarily by the severity of the assault and its implications for Australian security and survival, but rather by United States perceptions of the impact that the conflict and the possible outcome will have upon United States regional and global interests. If the country attacking Australia happens to be a super-power rival of the United

States, it can be concluded that the United States would almost certainly wish to respond vigorously. However, even in this relatively clear-cut situation, the desire to assist Australia may not be converted automatically into the physical provision of the level of aid the Australian government may request. Most particularly, if such an attack took place in the context of global super-power conflict, the United States may be distracted by higher priority commitments of a pressing nature elsewhere and be unable to render significant assistance.

In other circumstances, if the country attacking Australia happens also to be allied to the United States, or possibly non-aligned, the United States may not necessarily perceive its interests to be best served by heavily supporting Australia. It may provide a minimum of supplies; it might support both sides; it may decide to stand aloof and mediate; or in some circumstances, it might favour Australia's opponent. Even in circumstances where the United States Administration in fact may wish to assist a hard-pressed Australia and would appear not to be diverted elsewhere, there still might be significant difficulties for Australia in actually receiving the assistance it might desire. For instance, the United States inventories of specialized armaments or highly critical spare-parts might run low. Because of a heightening of global tensions, the United States might be concerned not to run down its immediate supplies of some war materials, for fear of rendering itself vulnerable to more serious attacks elsewhere. In addition, in some circumstances, there might be an impasse between the legislative and executive branches of the United States government, which could serve to delay or even prevent the provision of assistance.[18]

These major uncertainties in the alliance relationship serve to make Australian national security planning extremely difficult. They generate a large grey area of doubt and uncertainty within which long-term judgements must be made as to what Australia can *plan* on receiving from its great-power ally in given situations. These assessments obviously must be made in a conservative manner, for if in a given scenario, Australia plans on receiving much more than the United States is either willing and/or able to provide in those circumstances, the country's complete defence structure may be undermined. With this requirement for caution in mind, it is important to note that the assumptions that were made in the 1960s concerning the circumstances in which the United States could be expected to support heavily an Australia under threat can no longer be considered valid. For example, in 1969, Dr T. B. Millar wrote:

> Darwin remains the most vulnerable point. It is closer to Djakarta than it

is to Sydney. It is a small, isolated and only lightly-defended base, from which any air attacks, pre-emptive or retaliatory, on Indonesia would presumably be launched if coming from the Australian mainland. (Malaysia, where Australian bomber and fighter squadrons are stationed, is of course very much closer.) A sudden, well-planned combined attack on Darwin might appear to have a good chance of success, especially if linked with an assault on Tindal [an airfield 360 km south of Darwin, near Katherine.] Yet strategic warning of such hostilities should enable extra defences to be located in the Northern Territory. And we must assume that if the ANZUS Treaty means anything, any attack of this kind would entitle Australia to invoke the Treaty with near-certainty that the United States would come to our aid, as it would in any of the other situations mentioned.[19]

In the 1980s, this type of presumption no longer can be supported by declared United States policy. It is now clear that, in the specific hypothetical circumstance of a limited Indonesian attack upon Australia, the United States would expect Australia to provide the main forces for its own defence. The type of support Australia might receive in these circumstances would almost certainly be limited to military supplies, intelligence and possibly diplomatic support. However, as was discussed above, the provision of even this type of assistance could not be guaranteed under all circumstances. Thus for national security planning purposes, this assistance would best be regarded as a welcome bonus to, rather than an anticipated central element of, Australia's response capacity.

Attempting to perceive in advance the likely United States response to a series of hypothetical situations is a highly speculative type of forecasting. As has been emphasized above, this question continues to be hedged about by a very large number of imponderables. However, bearing these difficulties in mind, it is possible to summarize, in a tentative fashion, likely United States responses to a variety of threats to Australian security by drawing upon stated United States government intentions and elaborations of them made by United States government-funded research bodies. This is attempted in Table 2.

From this discussion, it is clear that the criteria to be employed in designing Australia's national security capacities to deter and meet regional pressures and threats will need to be quite different to those of the past. Australian ground forces are unlikely to be deployed again in the South-East Asian region, except possibly for small-scale specialized operations of short duration. But more importantly, because the role of the United States in Australia's security concerns has declined substantially, it is highly desirable that the limited national security resources now available be allocated almost exclusively to the priority requirements of conducting operations independently in Australia's immediate environment.

Table 2. United States: Expressed intentions and capabilities to assist Australia in a range of hypothetical situations.

Type of crisis	Expressed U.S. intentions	Likely U.S. capability to assist
1. Isolated attack by a super-power rival of the U.S.	Full support would be provided	Likely that full support would be forthcoming
2. Attack by a super-power rival of the U.S. in the context of a super-power conflict	Full support would be provided within capabilities	Unlikely to be able to divert significant resources away from the major effort
3. Heavy attack by a non-aligned major power	Unclear; may supply equipment, intelligence and diplomatic support	If this attack did not take place in the context of a major global conflict, the U.S. could assist to the extent of its intentions
4. Heavy attack by a major power allied to the U.S.	Unclear; may supply some equipment, intelligence and diplomatic support to both parties; may try to mediate; may favour Australia's opponent	As above
5. Heavy attack by a neighbouring power	Expects Australia to be self-sufficient; may assist with heavy equipment supplies, particularly if attacking neighbour receives heavy support from a super-power rival	As above
6. Other attacks by a neighbouring power	Australia expected to be self-sufficient	As above
7. Resource crises confronting Australia	As above	Australia might receive priority treatment if the U.S. controlled scarce resource supplies
8. The effects of foreign wars and resource conflicts	As above	As above

This represents a change of fundamental importance. The psychological crutch of the great-power alliance that has been the basis of Australian security policy for well over a century has been weakened severely and is now of doubtful reliability. No longer can Australia's security planners assume that the country's traditional allies will provide substantial forces for Australia's defence. As a consequence, if the country is to be insured against the wide range of potential pressures and threats that may arise in the future, this will need to be done primarily with Australia's own resources. Developing a national security structure that possesses the required level of independent capacity is a task that is quite new in both nature and scale.

The full implications of this major shift in Australian national security policy for the continuing Australian—American relationship are difficult to determine. The re-ordering of Australia's security priorities does not, of itself, serve to degrade severely the importance of many of the broader aspects of the relationship. Certainly the value of the ANZUS alliance for the deterrence of proxy warfare is likely to remain of considerable importance to Australia. Very significant value will continue to be placed upon co-operation and exchanges in the fields of intelligence, defence science and technology, training and the development of tactical doctrine and operational procedures. However, because Australia will be seeking a heightened degree of independent operational capacity and will be concentrating far more than in the past upon tasks within its immediate security environment, the direct value of many of these areas of exchange can be expected to decline. In contrast to most of Australia's military history, the design criteria for the country's force structure and operational concepts, in the future, may differ much more significantly from those of its major-power ally.

The Global Strategic Dimension of ANZUS

It is important to realize that because the United States is a superpower, the bounds of the ANZUS relationship extend beyond the local and regional dimension and into world-wide strategic affairs.

In an overall sense, the general mutuality of global interests between the alliance partners is well established and is likely to remain no matter which major political party is in power on each side of the Pacific. It is certain to remain in Australia's interests for the United States to retain sufficient strength at least to act as a balancing counter-weight to the Soviet Union. In the past, Australia has been willing to contribute to this balance where it has been possible for it to do so. This basic desire to assist in the maintenance of the global strategic balance is likely to remain indefinitely. However, because of the increasingly dynamic nature of global strategic developments, and particularly those of a technological character, the potential for Australia to lose effective control over activities with a global strategic significance undertaken within or supported from Australia under the aegis of the alliance is rising. The propensity for this loss of effective control to take place can be illustrated by reference to the debate concerning the presence of United States and joint American—Australian-controlled defence facilities on Australian territory.

When the Australian government originally sanctioned the construction of these facilities in the early 1960s, the officials and politicans who were intimately involved appeared to harbour little doubt that the facilities were stabilizing in the global strategic sense and hence a positive contribution to the maintenance of the super-power balance.[20] As an added bonus, these facilities were also perceived, and still are by some commentators, to be a major means of binding the United States to Australia, thus ensuring that a high level of assistance would be forthcoming to Australia should it be threatened by a regional power.[21] However, because of a large number of developments in the strategic technological environment, both of these assumptions, which have long been part of the conventional wisdom in the Australian defence community, are now the subject of considerable doubt.

There are currently eleven "scientific" and defence installations and facilities in Australia of which the United States has partial or complete control.[22] Several critics have argued that the facilities at North-west Cape, Pine Gap and Nurrungar not only have a capacity to support the mutual assured destruction (MAD) doctrine,[23] but in addition, play a significant role in providing the United States with a nuclear-war fighting capability.[24] They reason that the United States acquisition of this capability not only increases the likelihood of some types of nuclear war but it also provides the United States with a strategic advantage that the Soviet Union and China cannot match because of the geographical constraints that limit their ground-station siting options. Thus the critics conclude that the North-west Cape, Pine Gap and Nurrungar facilities are a destabilizing influence in the global nuclear balance.

Whether this particular argument is accepted or not, it is beyond question that in the period since approval was given for the construction of these facilities, the capabilities of strategic military systems, and especially space-based systems, have been transformed. The implications of these rapid advances in strategic technologies and the accompanying changes in doctrine may have altered substantially the strategic significance of the facilities in

Australia. As a consequence, it should not be assumed automatically that the ramifications for Australian security of hosting the United States facilities are the same now as they were perceived to be in the early 1960s.

The argument that the presence of American and jointly-controlled defence installations would serve to bind the United States to an Australia threatened by a regional power is also highly questionable. There is abundant evidence to show that the United States places a very high value upon space-based systems generally, and those facilities in Australia that support space-based systems in particular.[25] There is little doubt that the presence of these facilities in Australia is supportive of the general Australian—American relationship as a whole. Thus to the extent that their siting in this country increases United States perceptions of a friendly relationship with Australia and strengthens sentimental affinity, they may be important. However, this should not be confused with an expectation that the presence of the facilities will trigger automatically a favourable United States response to an Australia threatened by a regional power.

By way of precedent, it is interesting to note that during the Turkish invasion of Cyprus in 1974, the presence of important United States and NATO intelligence-gathering facilities, especially on Mt Olympus, did not stimulate an open American response to ensure their security.[26] Certainly the invading and defending forces were both allied to the United States: it is quite conceivable that an understanding was reached at an early stage with both sides concerning the inviolability of the installations. But in the event of a non-nuclear threat to Australia, or attack upon it some time in the future, could not similar arrangements be made by the United States with attacking forces? In the circumstances of a regional-power threat, harassment or even lodgement upon Australian territory, the United States government, in many circumstances, may prefer to reach an understanding with Australia's opponent concerning the facilities, rather than be committed automatically to assist Australian forces in their defence.[27]

Hence it does appear that at least some of the considerations that were cited originally to support the case for constructing these facilities may no longer be valid. This discussion is not to suggest that the impact of these changed technological and strategic circumstances necessarily renders the continued presence of the facilities undesirable. This is a much broader question. However, this illustration does serve to emphasize that the current pace of technological and strategic change may have already altered in a fundamental manner the national security significance of an established aspect of the alliance relationship. Moreover, there are indications that this phenomenon can be expected to recur more frequently in the future. This is primarily because both the United States and Australia are expanding greatly the physical capacities and technical sophistication of their military structures. Many developments in U.S. military technology and operational doctrine possess the potential to change the significance of a wide range of institutionalized arrangements.[28] At the same time, Australia's acquisition of new technological capacities, particularly involving long-range surveillance systems, provides potential for the employment of such systems not only for national and regional purposes but also for global alliance functions.[29] In combination, these technological and strategic developments hold the potential to transform the alliance partnership by providing a completely new meaning and a wide range of new ramifications to already established procedures, processes and agreements.

If the Australian government is to possess a capacity to regulate the impact of these developments on the ANZUS relationship in anything but a limited negative sense, the changing trends in strategic technologies and their implications for the alliance will need to be monitored continuously and in considerable detail. The relatively benign and comparatively undynamic strategic and technological environment of the 1950s and early 1960s scarcely made this necessary.

Notes and References

1. These figures are for the financial year 1977—78 and appear in: Australian Bureau of Statistics, *Overseas Trade (Preliminary) 1977—78 Part 1 — Exports* (Canberra: Australian Government Publishing Service, 1978), p. 87; and Australian Bureau of Statistics, *Overseas Trade (Preliminary) 1977—78 Part 2 — Imports* (Canberra: Australian Government Publishing Service, 1978), p. 227.
2. These figures are calculated from those for 1977 appearing in *Direction of Trade Annual 1971—77* (Washington, DC: International Monetary Fund, 1978), p. 267.
3. J.M. Siracusa, "Further Reflections on United States Interests in Australia", *Australian Outlook* 30, no. 3 (December 1976): 475.
4. Cited by F.S. Hopkins, "The American Image of Australia", in *Pacific Orbit: Australian American Relations Since 1942*, ed. N. Harper (Melbourne: Cheshire, for the Australian—American Association, 1968), p. 221.
5. Australia. House of Representatives, *Debates*, Thirtieth Parliament, 1 June 1976, p. 2738.
6. In reality, a large number of influences have encouraged a reassessment of U.S. commitments abroad, although most are related either directly or indirectly to the very great domestic and international political and social costs that were incurred during the Vietnam debacle. Other specific factors include the processes of rapprochement with China, the growing pressure to employ military

manpower more efficiently as a result of the abolition of the draft, the increasing role of Congress in the generation and conduct of U.S. foreign policy, etc. These matters are discussed at length in Leslie H. Brown, *American Security Policy in Asia* (London: International Institute for Strategic Studies, 1977), Adelphi Paper 132, pp. 1—9.
7. It is interesting to compare U.S. force levels in Europe and Asia both before and after the major phase of the Vietnam War and before and after the introduction of all-volunteer U.S. armed forces.

United States force levels in Asia and Europe, 1963-76 ('000s)

	1963	1973	1976 (January)
Korea	57	42	41
Japan) Ryukyus)	91	57	48
Philippines	14	16	14
Taiwan	4	9	2
Vietnam	14	-	-
Thailand	4	42	11
Afloat	38	32	21
Total Asia	222	198	137
Total Europe	380	300	303

Source: Brown, *American Security Policy in Asia*, p. 7.

Manpower is not the only determinant of military capacity, but in this case it is the indicator concerning which information is most freely available. The International Institute for Strategic Studies first started listing deployment strengths for U.S. forces in the West Pacific in 1974. Since that time, tactical fighter squadrons have been reduced from 11 to 9. Aircraft carriers deployed with the Seventh Fleet have been reduced from 3 to 2 and other surface combatants from 25 to 18. See *The Military Balance 1974—1975* (London: International Institute for Strategic Studies, 1974), p. 7; and *The Military Balance 1976—1977* (London: International Institute for Strategic Studies, 1976), p. 7. It could be argued that these numerical reductions may be at least partially offset by qualitative improvements. However, as is argued in Chapter 2, in the new technology environment, increased concentration of military capacities normally also implies increased vulnerability.
8. "Informal Remarks with Newsmen. July 25, 1969", in *Public Papers of the Presidents: Richard M. Nixon, 1969* (Washington, DC: U.S. Government Printing Office, 1970), pp. 548—49. An almost verbatim account also appears in "Excerpts from Unofficial Account of President Nixon's Meeting with Reporters", *New York Times*, 26 July 1969, pp. 28 ff.
9. T.B. Millar has argued that the apparent cessation of joint force commitments is likely to reduce greatly the strategic significance of the ANZUS treaty to Australia.
It seems extremely unlikely that the United States will be engaged in war in Southeast Asia during the remainder of this century. If this is so, it will have little need of Australia, and the ANZUS Treaty will become increasingly a formality, an excuse for occasional rhetoric, and unfortunately also a

specious rationalization for continued Australian reluctance to come to terms with its environment.
See T.B. Millar, "From Whitlam to Fraser", *Foreign Affairs* 55, no. 4 (July 1977): 871.
10. G.J. Pauker, S. Canby, A. Ross Johnson and W.B. Quandt, *In Search of Self-reliance: U.S. Security Assistance to the Third World Under the Nixon Doctrine* (Santa Monica: Rand Corporation, June 1973), R−1092−ARPA, p. 13.
11. *Australian Defence*, a White Paper presented to Parliament by the Minister for Defence, the Hon. D.J. Killen, November 1976 (Canberra: Australian Government Publishing Service, 1976), pp. 2, 10.
12. The emphasis here is in the original text.
13. *The United States/Australia Alliance − Problems and Prospects* (Syndicate Research Reports) (Canberra: United Service Institution of the Australian Capital Territory, 1976), p. 3.
14. The full text of the ANZUS security treaty is published as an appendix to Claire Clark, ed., *Australian Foreign Policy: Towards a Reassessment* (Melbourne: Cassell, 1973), pp. 243−45. It is interesting to compare the phrasing of the ANZUS treaty with that of other major U.S. written commitments. This is discussed at length in R.A. Paul, *American Military Commitments Abroad* (New Brunswick, N.J.: Rutgers University Press, 1973), pp. 14 ff.
15. This is discussed by J.L.S. Girling, "The Guam Doctrine", *International Affairs* 46, no. 1 (January 1970): 48.
16. On 12 January 1950, the U.S. Secretary of State, Dean Acheson, said: "The defensive perimeter runs along the Aleutians to Japan and then goes to the Ryukyus... to the Philippine Islands... So far as the military security of other areas of the Pacific is concerned, it must be clear that no person can guarantee these areas against military attack." Such a guarantee is "hardly sensible or necessary". Despite the fact that Korea was clearly placed outside this "defensive perimeter", within six months U.S. forces were heavily committed there. This is cited by Girling, ibid., p. 48.
17. Quoted in United Service Institution of the Australian Capital Territory, *United States/Australian Alliance*, p. 3.
18. In recent years, the U.S. Congress has involved itself far more intimately with foreign and military policies. One of the more notable features of this development has been the War Powers Resolution of 1973. Its relation to and significance for the ANZUS alliance are discussed in F.A. Mediansky, "United States Interests in Australia", *Australian Outlook* 30, no. 1 (April 1976): 144−45; and also in Siracusa, "Further Reflections on United States Interests in Australia", p. 479.
19. T.B. Millar, *Australia's Defence* (Melbourne: Melbourne University Press, 2nd edn, 1969), pp. 172−73.
20. This case has been made in a variety of forms. See, for example, "Barwick Explains Agreement on U.S. Radio Base", *Sydney Morning Herald*, 10 May 1963, p. 6; and also "Opening of the US Naval Communication Station at North-west Cape, Western Australia", roneoed (Speech by the Prime Minister, Mr Harold Holt, 16 September 1967), p. 2.
21. This point is made in "Strategic Basis of Policy", Department of Defence, *Defence Report 1965* (Canberra: Commonwealth Government Publishing Service, 1965), p. 8. The case is argued at greater length in Michael Leifer, "Living with Terror", and Ian Turner, "The Exmouth Base: Opting Out", *Bulletin* (Sydney) (27 April 1963): 25−26.
22. This information is provided in the reply to a Parliamentary Question posed by Mr. W. Hayden, H. of R., *Debates*, Thirtieth Parliament, 2 November 1976, p. 2255.

23. The MAD Doctrine is the notion that each super-power can be deterred from initiating a nuclear war by the realization that such action would trigger a massive automatic retaliatory response from the other side. This contrasts markedly with the concept of developing a nuclear war fighting capacity. Such a capability provides the potential to fight a nuclear war in a carefully controlled, phased manner. Limited nuclear exchange options are an integral part of this concept.
24. This case is argued in detail by Desmond Ball, "American Bases in Australia: The Strategic Implications", *Current Affairs Bulletin* 51, no. 10 (March 1975); and also by Andrew Clark, "US Bases Here Give Pentagon a Disturbing Nuclear Advantage", *National Times*, 9—14 September 1974, p. 8.
25. For example, the former U.S. Secretary of Defence, Donald Rumsfeld, stated in his congressional testimony that:
    > As space technology matures space-based systems will play an even more important role in support of US and Soviet military operations. In the future dependence on these systems may increase to the point where their loss could materially influence the outcome of a conflict.

    See the posture statement of the Secretary of Defence, Donald H. Rumsfield, *Department of Defense Appropriations for 1977* (hearings before a Subcommittee of the Committee on Appropriations, House of Representatives, 4 February 1976), p. 311.

    One extract from what is purported to be the Australian Defence Department's 1975 Strategic Basis document states that "the US has repeatedly made clear the value it attaches to the defence facilities it maintains in Australia". See Alan Reid, "Top Secret: Our Defence Planning", *Bulletin* (Sydney) (12 June 1976): 19.

    The Defence White Paper also raises the point briefly:
    > Our co-operation, which includes the joint maintenance of defence related facilities on Australian soil, is also, despite the disparate strength and resources of the two countries, of value to the US.

    See *Australian Defence*, p. 11.
26. This is discussed in "An Eye on the Enemy Over the Horizon", *New Scientist* (7 November 1974): 420—23.
27. Alternatively, the United States would have the options of destroying and evacuating the facilities or removing them to another location. There were press reports that the Ford Administration considered the latter option late in 1975. See Andrew Clark, "In a Politically Unstable Country (Like Australia) America's Pine Gap Base is a Risk", *National Times*, 17 November 1975, p. 3; and also "One For Rumsfeld", *Boston Sunday Globe*, 28 December 1975, p. 4.
28. Perhaps the most notable instance in this regard is the potential that modern developments in military technology display to alter greatly the implications of continuing to provide hitherto uncontroversial assistance to U.S. forces in the form of aircraft staging and refuelling facilities. The United States has conducted major exercises to test the concept of employing long-range, land-based aircraft, B-52s, P-3s, F-111s, etc., with multiple in-flight refuelling on long-range, over-ocean, sea-control missions. See, for example, the testimony of General D.C. Jones, Chief of Staff of the U.S. Air Force, before the Committee on Armed Services, U.S. Senate, *Fiscal Year 1977 Authorization for Military Procurement, Research and Development, and Active Duty, Selected Reserve and Civilian Personnel Strengths*, Part 2, 18 February 1976, p. 985. During the course of his testimony to Congress, Admiral Gayler, the former U.S. Commander-in-Chief in the Pacific, expressed strong support for the employment of this mode of operations in the Pacific-Indian Ocean region. See Hearings before the Subcommittee on Manpower and Personnel of the Committee on Armed Ser-

vices, U.S. Senate, *Fiscal Year 1977 Authorization for Military Procurement, Research and Development, and Active Duty, Selected Reserve and Civilian Personnel Strengths*, Part 7, 1 March 1976, p. 4070. The concept of the long-range aerial task force has been discussed at length in the United States. For example, see "Navy Cool to Land-based Aircraft Study", *Aviation Week and Space Technology* 105, no. 15 (18 October 1976): 91; Major-General W.J. Ellis, "Air Mobility and Flexibility", *Flight International* 110, no. 3519 (21 August 1976): 432; and W.C. Moore, "Time for Aerial Task Forces?" *US Naval Institute Proceedings* 101, no. 112/874 (December 1975): 79-80.

It appears that originally the U.S. Department of Defence intended to deploy long-range aircraft fleets through the Indian Ocean, from Guam or the Clark Air Base in the Philippines, as soon as the 3658-metre runway on Diego Garcia was completed in October 1977. This strip is adequate to handle fully-loaded KC-135 aerial tankers on a regular basis and to act as an emergency landing-ground for B-52s. See testimony of General G.S. Brown, Chairman, Joint Chiefs of Staff, before the Committee on Armed Services, U.S. Senate, *Disapprove Construction Projects on the Island of Diego Garcia*, 10 June 1975, p. 61; and also *Australian*, 15 April 1977, p. 7.

In April 1977, a decision was announced to "shelve indefinitely" long-range flights into the Indian Ocean by B-52s. However, it is interesting to note that the primary cause given for this decision was rivalry between the Air Force and Navy, although it was also compatible with President Carter's proposal for "mutual military restraints". See "America Stops Plan for B-52s in Indian Ocean", *Australian*, 15 April 1977, p. 7.

The clear implication for Australia is that support for aerial task forces, in either the Pacific or Indian Oceans, through the refuelling of transitting aircraft, and particularly KC-135 tanker aircraft, would be a proposition with quite different implications to those of current arrangements. The likely reactions of regional and other powers to such activities and their implications for Australian foreign policy would need to be examined thoroughly prior to the provision of diplomatic clearance for task force aircraft to land in Australia.

There are, in addition, other areas where changing U.S. technological capacities offer the potential to alter fundamentally the nature of established aspects of the Australian-American relationship. For instance, the rapidly expanding U.S. capacity to perform all its major military functions without reliance upon installations situated on the territory of foreign states may affect U.S. perceptions of the strategic value of Australia.

29. There are a number of systems that, if procured by Australia, could have a major impact upon Australia's role within the alliance. For instance, if the experimental over-the-horizon backscatter (OTH-B) radar system, called Jindalee, proves to be successful and is operationally deployed, it is quite possible that much of the target tracking and regional high-frequency signals intelligence information obtained may be passed to the United States for use in its global strategic surveillance network.

Similarly, if and when Australia deploys fixed long-range sonar surveillance systems, the information gained may be used not only to support Australia's regional defence effort but also to feed into the U.S. global anti-submarine surveillance system. The same can be said of information that might be gained from advanced long-range towed-array sonar systems. The American FFG-7 Patrol Frigates will be fitted with the very advanced tactical towed-array sensor (TACTAS). Presumably, the four Australian Patrol Frigates will also be equipped with TACTAS at some stage, but if so, would the information gained be passed automatically to the United States?

If fixed and mobile units of the Australian Defence Force routinely feed air, surface and undersea surveillance information into the United States global command and control network, these Australian systems *and* their support bases might well be regarded as legitimate and valuable targets by the Soviet Union in the event of some types of nuclear exchange. If this is so, naval and air bases within and adjacent to Australia's major population centres may well be targeted for nuclear attack by the Soviet Union. The statement of this possibility is not to argue that such intimate Australian-American co-operation should necessarily be avoided, but merely to point out that the alliance implications of current technological developments are far-reaching and deserve thorough examination prior to any such procurement decision. Further details of the systems mentioned in this note are discussed in Chapter 2 and Appendix B.

2
The Revolution in Conventional Military Technologies

The nature and speed of recent technological developments and the impact they are having upon the conventional military battlefield is a second area of fundamental change in Australia's strategic environment. Dr G.H. Heilmeier, the recently retired Director of the United States Defense Advanced Reseach Projects Agency (DARPA), summarized the current situation in the following terms:

> I really do believe this is a unique time. I cannot remember a time in the last decade, or perhaps the decade before that, where there were so many technology initiatives on the horizon that could make a major difference to the national security. I think that in this case, the payoff is very, very large. We are not talking about incremental changes to the way we do things today. We are talking about radically different concepts, things that can make a big difference.[2]

As Dr Heilmeier implies, the pace of technological change affects much more than simply the performance of the items of equipment with which armed forces are supplied. In some fields, completely new capacities are being developed. Strategies, doctrines, tactics and force structures are all being subjected to increasing pressures for change. The nature of conventional warfare as it has been known in the past is being altered fundamentally. In a real sense, the realms of what is possible and impossible on the conventional battlefield are in a state of flux that is unprecedented in both scale and scope.

What are these revolutionary technological capacities that are having such an impact on warfare as we have known it in the past?[3]

1. First, there is a whole host of *highly accurate precision-guidance capacities*. By using various terminal homing techniques, it is now possible to direct rockets, bombs, artillery rounds, mortar rounds and other types of ordnance to impact with great precision upon targets of small dimensions, whether they are stationary or mobile. Thus if a target can be distinguished from its background environment or its location accurately determined, it is becoming much

more likely that it will be hit by the first round of ordnance directed against it.

2. The second major area of advance concerns the development of a wide range of *more efficient propulsion systems*. The main effect of these is to provide both weapons themselves and weapons carriers (or "platforms") with much greater range, speed and fuel efficiency, while at the same time frequently reducing their sound, heat, radar and other media signatures. Thus on the tactical operational level, when the new propulsion systems are combined with the new terminal guidance technologies, it becomes possible to hit accurately any target that can be acquired and identified, even at very long range. On the strategic level, much of the traditional tyranny of distance, in the sense of isolation, is being replaced by a new tyranny of military accessibility.

3. The third major field of technological advance is the development of *much more effective conventional warheads*. Minelets and bomblets of "fist" size, fuel-air explosives and multi-stage hard structure munitions are the most significant areas of progress in this arena. The primary consequence is that if a target can be hit (and that is becoming increasingly easy), the resulting destruction is likely to be far greater for a given warhead volume and weight than has been the case in the past.

4. The fourth major area of advance has been in the capabilities of *long-range surveillance and target-acquisition technologies*. New types of underwater sonar sensors and satellite, aircraft and ground-based radar systems are making it increasingly easy to acquire and track targets at long range, particularly those in the air and sea environments.

5. There has also been *a proliferation of short-range battlefield target-acquisition and identification systems*, some of which employ completely new technologies. An important consequence of this has been the stimulation of an intensive counter-effort to reduce the optical, radar, acoustic, infra-red and other signatures of a wide range of targets.

6. A sixth major area of advance is the development of *increasingly sophisticated communications, command and control (C^3) systems*. Primarily through the exploitation of greatly expanded automatic data-processing capacities, a wide variety of area-surveillance, target-acquisition, classification and locating systems, as well as weapon systems themselves, are being tied together electronically. In practice, it has been found that this degree of automatic system integration can significantly multiply the battlefield effectiveness of a total force.

7. New technology has also produced some *completely new weap-*

ons concepts. Modular glide-bombs, new types of tank-gun rounds, sensor weapons, including self-launching torpedoes and anti-aircraft missiles, and even high-powered laser weapons (a form of "ray" gun).

8. There is also an array of *new weapons platforms* under development. Various types of vertical, short take-off and landing (V/STOL) aircraft, very large multi-purpose aircraft, hybrid helicopter/conventional aircraft, robot or remotely piloted aircraft, large sea-going hovercraft and hydrofoils, and new types of small and highly manoeuvrable tanks are some of the most important programmes in this field.

It is really very difficult to summarize the implications for Australian security of these developments. On the one hand, the new technologies provide greatly increased scope for long-range surveillance, particularly in the sea and air environments. Targets now can not only be detected, identified and tracked at long ranges, but they also can be destroyed at great distances, frequently with the expenditure of a single round. The task of developing a capacity to control activities on Australia's land mass and in its sea and air approaches could be simplified greatly by the application of a carefully chosen mix of these new technologies.

However, Australia's adoption of new technological options is no panacea. It is important to realize that recent technological advances also have made possible a wide range of new and very effective counter-measures, many of which could be made available to Australia's potential opponents. For instance, most types of long-range surveillance, target-identification and tracking systems and many types of weapons systems can be confused or jammed and some can be easily destroyed. As a consequence, battlefields of the future are certain to be characterized by an intensive technological tussle of ploy and counter-ploy.

There is at least one other important consequence of these recent advances in military technology. It is important to realize that while Australia certainly could enhance its security by exploiting imaginatively the potential of the new technologies, there will also be great scope for regional opponents to take advantage of the new developments, to generate completely new levels of threat to Australia. For example, a regional opponent's acquisition of long-range terminally guided cruise missiles could successfully threaten many of Australia's concentrated and unprotected defence facilities and infrastructure targets: airfields, ports, C^3 centres, bridges, tunnels, transport nodes, etc. Similarly, Australia would face major difficulties were an opponent to develop a capacity to insert large numbers of small, well-trained raiding parties equipped with the new generation of light, man-portable precision-guided munitions. The implications of this are obvious. The benefits to flow from the introduction of new technology systems cannot be expected to automatically enhance Australia's security.

It is also clear that the future balance of regional military technological capacities will depend upon a wide range of non-technical variables. The state of domestic financial, political, bureaucratic and social forces and the level of super-power involvement will obviously influence the rate at which new technology systems will be acquired, both in Australia and in other countries in the Asian region. The actual impact that these systems will have upon operational capabilities will depend heavily upon the capacities of local security personnel to recognize the potential of the new developments, to choose selectively from the greatly expanded range of technological options, to operate effectively those systems that are procured, to service and maintain them efficiently and to derive strategies, tactics, structures, doctrines and operational procedures that exploit fully the potential of the new systems.

Primarily because of the number, complexity and variability of these factors, it is very difficult to predict the overall impact of the new military technologies upon Australia's strategic environment in the years ahead. However, it is possible to identify a series of broad consequential trends, which should be of assistance in planning Australia's security. It is to an elaboration of these that the remainder of this chapter is devoted.

Some Important Implications of New Technological Developments

Trend 1 The Increasing Vulnerability of Large and Obvious Weapons Platforms and the Degradation of their Cost-effectiveness

Because of the very great advances in long-range surveillance and target-acquisition technologies, military platforms that have large radar, magnetic, heat, acoustic, electronic or other media signatures are becoming much easier to detect, identify and acquire as targets. Once acquired as a target, the new precision-guidance, propulsion and warhead technologies are increasing greatly the ease with which objects can be attacked and destroyed at both short and long ranges.

These developments have two important consequences. First, large and obvious weapons platforms are becoming increasingly easy to destroy on the modern battlefield, i.e. they are subject to increasing rates of *active attrition*.

However, this greatly increased capacity for physical destruction represents only a portion of the total impact of the new technologies. A second major consequence is to force large and obvious aircraft, surface ships and armoured vehicles to adopt expensive defensive equipment fits and elaborate defensive operational tactics in attempts to maintain their survivability on the modern battlefield. These defensive reactive measures are very complex and expensive, and many imply a very great degradation in total system cost-effectiveness in the performance of traditional functions. In combination, these less-obvious effects of the new technological developments can be termed the processes of *passive attrition*.

Active and Passive Attrition in the Air

In intense battlefield environments, aircraft are now subjected to a wide array of advanced ground-based defensive systems. New generation light, man-portable surface-to-air missile (SAM) systems not only possess a greater range capacity and more effective warheads than their predecessors but they are also capable of attacking a target from any direction — even head on.[4] Mobile radar-controlled gun systems are likely to retain important battlefield functions.[5] Similarly, larger vehicle-mounted short-,[6] medium-[7] and long-range missile systems[8] can be extremely effective in providing a high level of twenty-four-hour all-weather security against air attack. However, it should be noted that the greatly increased lethality of ground-based air defences is not due simply to the vastly increased performance capabilities of individual systems. In order for the effectiveness of ground-based anti-aircraft defences to be optimized over the tactical battlefield, it is necessary to co-ordinate a mix of several different types of surface-to-air system, each of which is very effective in performing its specific air-defence function (i.e. a mix of systems effective against low-, medium- and high-altitude targets).

The vastly increased lethality of co-ordinated anti-aircraft defences has forced tactical aircraft to adopt a wide range of measures to improve their survivability and maintain their mission effectiveness. The response of many Western European air forces is to fly through such areas at extremely low altitudes and very high speeds. This tactic has been designed so that aircraft can penetrate below the coverage of most ground-based surveillance and target-acquisition sensors. The speed of penetration gives the few ground-based systems that can acquire targets flying at that altitude insufficient time to react effectively. However, mission profiles requiring high-speed flight at low levels effectively limit range and encourage aircraft designs that are not optimized for the secondary task of air-to-air combat at low and medium altitudes.[9]

A second response, which is most notably practised by the United States Air Force, is to fly at medium altitudes within the coverage of enemy area air defences where necessary, but to do so only with the assistance of large numbers of air-superiority fighter aircraft and also specialized electronic warfare and defence suppression systems. This involves a direct air-superiority confrontation. Specialized fighter aircraft cover the fighter-bomber formations and engage in air-to-air duels where this is necessary. In attempts to foil anti-aircraft surveillance, tracking and guidance systems, parts of fighter-bomber weapon loads are frequently sacrificed to permit the carriage of defensive underwing electronic counter-measure pods.[10] In some intense battlefield environments, supplementary aircraft are required to perform specifically the task of confusing or jamming enemy surveillance and weapon-guidance radars. In addition, in areas where air defences are well co-ordinated and controlled, it is frequently necessary for attacking or specialized supporting aircraft to concentrate first upon the destruction of the opponent's surface-to-air systems before the primary targets can be attacked with an acceptable degree of security. The gradual addition of a large number of essential supporting aircraft to those required to make close support or interdiction strike missions in the intense European environment has prompted one prominent United States defence analyst to describe planned United States Air Force operations as air convoys.[11] The complexity and expense of mounting this type of operation is clearly much greater than that which was required to perform a similar function in the past.

A third type of air force response to the growing lethality of integrated ground-based anti-aircraft networks involves a partial abandonment of the traditional close air support function and its replacement by strengthened ground-based tube and rocket artillery systems. Under this concept, where air-delivered ordnance is still required in intense battlefield environments, it is delivered at extended ranges by stand-off air-launched precision-guided munitions. However, in practice, this does not overcome all of the difficulties associated with traditional types of close-air support operations. The acquisition of many categories of ground target from tactical strike aircraft is extremely difficult at stand-off ranges. In order to overcome this problem, at least partially, extensive support technologies are required (normally ground-based or in other aircraft), to provide a remote target acquisition and designation capability. A second major difficulty of stand-off precision-guided munition delivery into intense battlefield environments is that weapon launch-points may not always be placed beyond the range of components of an enemy's integrated air defence system. As I have argued elsewhere, the fluidity of intense modern battlefields may make the accurate identification of secure launch areas extremely difficult.[12]

Following the Middle East War of October 1973, General Chaim Herzog, a prominent Israeli military correspondent, reflected on the significance of these developments:

> The role of the plane in war has changed, and new strategies and uses of air power will have to be evolved. To a degree air power will obviously not be as influential as it has been and will affect the battlefield less than it did. The proliferation of light, portable missile launchers in the front line means that close support will be the exception to the rule in the future, with the air force being forced to concentrate on isolating the field of battle, maintaining supremacy in the air and destroying the forces in or near the battlefield.[13]

Active and Passive Attrition at Sea

The new military technologies are also increasing greatly the vulnerability of large and obvious surface ships. They too are becoming easier to acquire at long range and are much more vulnerable to a wide range of anti-ship weapon systems. William H. Pickering, Head of the Naval Studies Board of the United States Academy of Sciences and a former Director of the Jet Propulsion Laboratory, outlined the two major themes in surface ship passive attrition in the following terms:

> As the world moves into an era of widespread, inexpensive precision-guided weapons, the vulnerability of all ships increases. This will require either that the Navy develop an effective defense to protect a small number of high value ships or else deploy large numbers of low value ships to perform the same mission.[14]

In response to the increasing anti-shipping threat, most modern navies have concentrated their resources on a five-element programme,[15] to enhance the security of their major surface platforms. The overall effectiveness of this effort is, however, the subject of serious doubt.

The first element of the programme is to seek to destroy weapon-launch platforms before weapons are released. If the defending naval unit, task force, convoy or fleet contains an aircraft carrier, it may be possible for its aircraft to strike cruise missile-equipped patrol craft, surface shipping and aircraft at short and medium ranges before weaponry can be launched. However, for a variety of reasons, this might not always be possible. Firstly, carrier aircraft may not always be available to perform this function. Secondly, even if they are available, they may not be authorized to launch this type of pre-emptive attack.[16] Thirdly, even if carrier aircraft were on regular patrol, it seems likely that in many environments enemy aircraft and surface vessels could approach undetected within the maximum range of their weaponry. Fourthly, even if such a strike were authorized and effectively carried out, that still would not ensure the survivability of major surface shipping. Hostile submarines and mobile ground-based systems could still launch anti-ship missile and torpedo attacks. The capacity of surface shipping and their accompanying aircraft to attack submarine and ground-based platforms is limited in most environments. Thus it can be concluded that it is unlikely that all anti-ship systems will be destroyed before they can be launched in any particular conflict, unless some special circumstances apply.[17]

The second element of the surface naval ship's defensive capability also involves the use of carrier-borne aircraft. Naval airborne warning and control systems (AWACS) and fighter aircraft would attempt to destroy anti-ship missiles in flight. This capability assumes the propitious air deployment of naval AWACS and advanced fighter aircraft with a look-down, shoot-down capability at the time and in the area of missile flight. Even if all of these systems were deployed in advance in appropriate locations and were not saturated by a large number of incoming cruise missiles, they would still be ineffective against very high altitude Mach 2+ missiles[18] and against submarine-launched torpedoes. Again it seems that only in very particular circumstances could it be expected that anti-ship strikes would be defeated at this point.[19]

The third element of the surface ship defensive concept is to employ long-range ship-borne missiles to destroy approaching anti-ship weapons. Clearly there is no practical means of intercepting long-range self-homing torpedoes, although it may be possible for them to be spoofed. Wire-guided torpedoes[20] could be thwarted only if the launching-platform's sensors or control systems could be confused or destroyed prior to launch or during running time. This, however, would be extremely difficult to achieve in practice.

The destruction of anti-ship missiles by long-range ship-borne systems would be possible, although still not easy, if the incoming weaponry flew at medium-altitude and moderate subsonic or transonic speed. However, in the more likely instance of a missile flying at a very low altitude, it would be extremely difficult for it to be acquired and tracked, since most sea-skimming missiles have a very small radar cross-section and would need to be detected against the "clutter" of the sea's surface.[21] However, for the purpose of this discussion, if it can be assumed that advanced radar techniques and a high state of crew alertness largely resolve the clutter problem, there would still be serious difficulties arising from the very limited reaction time that would be available. If the incoming missile were detected the instant it broached the horizon (which seems highly improbable), and if it were travelling at between Mach 1 and 2, between 1¼ and 2½ minutes would remain before impact. If the ship were in a high state of alert, long-range weaponry probably could be fired within that time, but even then, directing the interception of a very fast missile, which may well be taking evasive countermeasures and could be at least partially obscured by a confused sea, would be extremely difficult. Even if this were possible, specialized proximity fuses would be required to be fitted, to prevent premature missile detonation in response to the interference of the sea's surface. The problems, of course, would be compounded in the event of a simultaneous, multi-directional attack by several weapons. The long-range interception of very high-altitude anti-shipping missiles presents yet another series of extremely complicated problems. The success of a ship-borne defence system against this type of threat would depend upon the attacking weapon's speed, the ease with which it could be detected at long range and a wide range of other factors.

The fourth element of the surface naval ship's defence is its electronic counter-measure capability. Some active radar homing missiles can be spoofed with chaff[22] and electronic jamming; some infra-red homing systems can be decoyed with flares; electro-optical systems can be disrupted with smoke screens; laser designation systems can be foiled by aerosols and smoke; and some magnetic and acoustic homing torpedo systems can be defeated by trailed decoys and jammers. However, it should be noted that some wire and inertial guided weaponry is not susceptible to the normal types of electronic counter-measures. Moreover, the incorporation of many counter-counter-measurers in anti-ship weaponry is reducing greatly the effectiveness of a wide range of current ship-borne electronic warfare (EW) systems. Frequency-agile homing radars, infra-red tuning, infra-red imaging, improved data links, multi-sensor terminal guidance and many other techniques are being employed to decrease anti-ship missile susceptibility to electronic warfare.

The final defence element available to surface shipping is that of close-in weapons systems (CIWS). Against submarine-, coastal- or aircraft-launched torpedo systems, guns and short-range missile systems are completely ineffective. In order to provide surface ships with a "last-ditch" defence against anti-ship missile attack, the

United States has developed the Phalanx automatic gun system and Britain the Sea Wolf short-range missile system. However, senior United States officials have admitted openly that even against some types of existing anti-ship missiles, the Phalanx system will not be effective.[23] The Sea Wolf system, on the other hand, appears to suffer from a relatively long reaction time.[24] For a very short-range system that may be confronted with co-ordinated multiple supersonic missile attacks, this time delay may be critical.

While in one-only non-manoeuvring or jamming target situations, the capacity of both Phalanx and Sea Wolf appears credible, they are both potentially susceptible to external jamming, spoofing[25] and decoying. Further, because of the very short-range nature of these systems, many of the intercepts they have achieved, even in ideal circumstances, have taken place at ranges of 500 metres or less.[26] It should be noted that if an anti-shipping missile carrying a 550 kg third-generation fuel-air explosive warhead is detonated at 300 metres range, the blast effect would be sufficient to destroy most types of ship-borne radio, radar, EW and other external antennae.[27] This would effectively render a ship defenceless to a following missile attack. If detonation occurred at 170 metres or less, the blast effect would be sufficient to sink a moderately sized ship.[28]

Thus despite the fact that all of the major naval powers have expended very large sums of money on anti-ship missile defence systems of various sorts, their effectiveness in realistic wartime multiple-attack conditions is highly questionable. By far the most sophisticated, elaborate and expensive anti-ship missile defence system in existence is the American Aegis system. In February and March 1975, the first complete and fully tested Aegis system, which is mounted on the USS *Norton Sound*, was subjected to simulated wartime operations for a continuous period of six days. At the end of this period, the Aegis system's project manager and the Naval Systems Technical Representative could not report that the ship's systems had "defeated" all simulated attacks. The best that they could state was that none of the manned aircraft raids had penetrated within missile range undetected.[29]

In an even more candid statement of surface ship vulnerability, the former United States Director of Defence Research and Engineering, Dr Malcolm Currie, pointed to the extreme difficulty of providing an effective defence even against currently deployed anti-ship missile systems. When discussing the capacity of the new Soviet aircraft carrier *Kiev*, he stated that it was not so much its V/STOL aircraft that made the ship so formidable:

> rather that it is so heavily armed [with] SS-N-12's, a supersonic cruise missile that can come in [at various] angles and ... from a naval point of

view — not a strategic nuclear point of view — is next to impossible to defend against.[30]

The technology struggle between offence and defence on and above the surface of the sea is likely to intensify further. On the one hand, high-energy laser point defence systems might be available to supersede Phalanx and Sea Wolf by the late 1980s. On the other hand, there are already Mach 2+ integral rocket/ramjet sea-skimming cruise missiles under development in both Europe and the United States, and torpedo-carrying surface skimmers may be developed to avoid close-in weapons systems altogether.[31] In this environment, the survivability of major surface ships in the face of modern multiple anti-ship missile and torpedo attacks appears by no means assured.

In addition, it should be realized that the increasing vulnerability of large and obvious surface shipping and the defensive reactive measures that have followed have caused a severe degradation in the operational effectiveness of individual vessels performing their primary assigned roles. In some cases, self-defence considerations have driven the elaboration and expansion of originally simple ship designs into larger and more complex platforms. Yet even when these extremely sophisticated ships are deployed into high-threat environments, they must be operated in closely co-ordinated teams if their survivability is to be maximized. However, this tactic serves to reduce their capabilities to perform most of their originally intended functions to an even greater degree, be they anti-submarine warfare, convoy escort, shore bombardment, the attack of surface shipping or some other task.

As a result of these accumulating pressures of active and passive attrition, a second and more long-term reaction to large surface ship vulnerability is now beginning to display itself in a definite shift away from the largest, most elaborate and expensive types of ship. Where the sponsoring nation's economy can afford to replace aging large surface naval platforms, they are frequently being superseded by larger numbers of smaller, less conspicuous and less expensive craft. In many instances, this represents a deliberate attempt to reduce the wartime possibility of losing rapidly a significant proportion of a navy's total capability with the destruction of a small number of ships.[32]

Submarine survivability varies greatly, depending upon a large number of factors. Older, large, metallic submarines, which are poorly shaped and emit great amounts of noise, are much more easily detected than new, smaller, tear-drop-shaped submarines, which are constructed primarily of non-magnetic materials and employ laminar-flow[33] technology to reduce drag and water disturbance. Current types of conventional submarines retain an additional source of vulnerability because of their requirement to cruise for significant periods with their snorkels above the surface of the sea. New types of non-nuclear propulsion systems are likely to reduce this requirement greatly.

The second major determinant of submarine survivability is the intensity with which their area of operations is seeded with passive sonar sensors and patrolled by opposing anti-submarine warfare forces. There is a far higher probability of submarines of all types being detected, targeted and in a wartime situation, destroyed, in the North Atlantic and the Sea of Japan than in the Antarctic or the southern Indian Oceans. In the future, the balance of the offence/defence struggle in this field is likely to depend heavily upon the ocean environments within which submarines are deployed.

Active and Passive Attrition on the Ground

The vulnerability and cost-effectiveness of traditional major items of defence equipment in the ground environment is also in a state of flux. The immediate reaction of many countries' armoured units to the proliferation of light, highly accurate and inexpensive anti-tank weapons has been an intensification of combined arms tactics. As a consequence, it seems extremely unlikely that in the future armoured units will manoeuvre and attack fixed positions in isolation, as occurred during the first hours of the Yom Kippur War. Rather, infantry will travel in close proximity to tanks in mechanized infantry combat vehicles (MICVs) or open-topped armoured personnel carriers (APCs), spraying likely anti-tank missile team vantage-points with machine-gun and mortar fire. In addition, self-propelled rocket and/or tube artillery will travel in strength in reasonably close proximity, so as to be able to add weight to the curtain of suppressive fire. If enemy surface-to-air systems can be suppressed in the local region, close air-support aircraft can be expected to operate in co-ordination. The final integrated component of the modern all-arms ground battlefield team is a mobile gun and/or missile anti-aircraft capability. Thus in order for modern armoured forces to be effective and survivable, a large number of supportive systems are required to act in co-ordination in most environments.

The second major reaction of armoured units to the proliferation of light anti-tank weaponry has been to improve standards of armoured protection. Vehicles equipped with conventional solid armour (AMX 30, Leopard I A1 and I A2, M-60, T-62, etc.) are likely to remain susceptible to a very large number of ground- and air-launched anti-tank weapon systems. Those vehicles that are equipped with spaced armour (e.g. Leopard I A3, Chariot) gain a degree of protection from the smaller, man-portable shaped-charge weapons. However, Chobham "special" or layered armour, which is currently being fitted to XMI, Leopard II and the latest Chieftain tanks, offers a much greater degree of protection. This armour effectively resists all but the largest artillery and air-launched shaped-charge warheads and most currently deployed tank-gun rounds. The most effective ground weapon penetration against this new armour appears to have been achieved by a British experimental, very high velocity, 120 mm, armour-penetrating, fin-stabilized, discarding-sabot (APFSDS), kinetic energy (KE) tank-gun round and a United States experimental very high velocity 105 mm, KE depleted uranium (Stabiloy) tank-gun round.[34]

The implications of these new developments in armour-plating are very great indeed. It appears that because Chobham armour is not excessively expensive, it may eventually be deployed widely on a variety of armoured vehicles. This, in turn, will impact heavily upon the types of anti-armour weaponry that will be effective in the future. In terms of warheads, there appears to be the option of either very large shaped-charge[35] or very fast KE penetration rounds. As is discussed in Appendix B, the United States is developing a 75 mm anti-tank gun that fires very high velocity APFSDS rounds. As yet, it remains to be seen whether this medium-calibre weapon can generate sufficient penetrator velocity to be effective against Chobham armour.

Another consequence of the widespread introduction of new armour is that it may be extremely difficult to develop an effective new-generation man-portable anti-tank system. The size of the shaped-charges needed would almost certainly require vehicles to transport a missile system as a whole. Another alternative might become available if the terminal accelerator technology developed for air-launched runway penetration bombs can be extended and applied in the anti-tank field.[36] This would require the development of an extremely rapid flight-acceleration capacity for a light man-portable or vehicle-mounted KE round. American experimentation with self-forming forged fragmentation warheads may provide such a capacity in the mid-1980s.[37]

The vulnerability of major ground battlefield weapons platforms in the future will depend at least partly upon the extent of Chobham armour deployment and the speed with which effective ground-launched direct-fire anti-tank systems can be developed and deployed. However, it should be realized that, even before new types of anti-tank systems are developed, all tanks, regardless of the composition of their armour-plating, will remain vulnerable to many air- and artillery-launched precision-guided munitions, fuel-air explosives and anti-tank mines and minelets.

There appears to be a clear, identifiable trend emerging from the nature of the battlefield situation that is confronting large and obvious weapons platforms. Although the offensive capabilities of large surface ships, aircraft and conventionally armoured vehicles are rising, they are also becoming increasingly easy to detect, target and destroy on technologically advanced battlefields. Many of the weapons systems that can effectively damage and destroy these platforms are relatively cheap to buy and it is perhaps not surprising that some are already being procured by a number of states in South-East Asia.[38] Thus in a future conflict in Australia's region, these large and obvious concentrations of defence capital may be subjected to multiple co-ordinated attacks by new generations of anti-systems. In order to enhance their survivability, aircraft, ships and tanks now require the support of increasing numbers of supplementary systems and technologies, and the development of more protective and elaborate operational tactics and doctrines. But even with such heavy supportive technologies and tactics, there are now some tasks that are extremely difficult and expensive for traditional platforms to undertake at all.[39] Thus the overall impact upon large and obvious weapons platforms performing their traditional battlefield functions is to degrade their survivability, stimulate a quantum jump in their costs and, in many cases, cause a drastic reduction in their operational effectiveness.

Trend 2   The Increasing Utility of Small Units

Because large and obvious weapons platforms are being subjected to higher levels of both active and passive attrition in intense battlefield environments, it is becoming increasingly desirable to disperse military capacities. It is becoming preferable to force an enemy to try to find and destroy many relatively inexpensive platforms rather than a few high-value ones. This development is being reinforced by the fact that the range capabilities of many small weapons platforms are being extended greatly and most forms of effective guided firepower are becoming increasingly light and compact. In combination, these factors are having the effect of making small units viable for a much wider range of tasks than has hitherto been the case. Small units are not only able to threaten and destroy larger units in more situations, but they themselves frequently have a better chance of surviving because of their lower all-media signatures and their high level of natural agility. Add to this the relatively low cost of these small units and it becomes clear that in many battlefield environments in the future, small unit proliferation will be a major feature.

The proliferation of small, relatively independent military units will have a large number of secondary implications for military structures. Most notably, research and development and procurement priorities will need to change. It will also be necessary to modify tactical doctrines and operational procedures if the potential offered by the new technologies is to be exploited fully. One specific change likely in tactical doctrine will be a reduced requirement for the highly vulnerable close concentration of military units in many environments. Concentrations of precisely directed firepower launched from remote locations will be able to provide much of the capability that in the past has been available only from closely deployed forces in the immediate battlefield area. However, it is important to appreciate that force dispersal over large areas will increase reliance upon high-capacity command, control and communications facilities. In many situations, it will also mean that the span of effective command is reduced severely. This, in turn, will place greatly increased authority and responsibility in the hands of small unit commanders. Personnel training systems will need to be adjusted to ensure that military personnel filling key positions within this type of structure are equipped adequately to meet the intense demands that may be made upon them in battlefield situations.

Trend 3   The Increasing Importance of Remaining Untargeted

Because in the new technology environment it is becoming increasingly easy to hit a target once acquired, and a target hit is more likely to be destroyed, it is obvious that the capacity to remain untargeted is becoming an increasingly central determinant of battlefield outcomes. As has been discussed above, this is stimulating a high level of force dispersal, but it is also encouraging the rapid development of a wide array of stealth technologies and tactics. In terms of equipment, it means the extensive deployment of visual, radar, sound, heat and electronic suppression and camouflage systems. In the field of tactical doctrine, the primary effect is to accentuate the requirement for dispersed and co-ordinated movement undertaken under the cover of vegetation, built-up areas, darkness and poor weather. Where a battlefield function regularly requires a high level of battlefield visibility, remotely controlled or remotely emplaced automatic systems are likely to provide the most desirable means of task performance.

Trend 4 The Increasing Importance of Target Detection, Identification and Localization System Survival

In order to ensure that target acquisition sensor systems remain untargeted by the enemy, it will be important for defence decision-makers to select systems that can operate in as covert and passive a manner as possible. Thus in the ground environment, intensified activity is already apparent in the development of advanced acoustic, seismic, optical and imaging infra-red systems. Imaging infra-red scanners already can provide a completely passive 24-hour medium-range target acquisition and tracking capability.[40] New generations of remotely emplaced passive surveillance sensors are also under development for both ground battlefield and maritime applications. Where active radiation-emitting target-acquisition sensors are necessary, it is highly desirable that they be mobile and/or operated as far away from intense battlefield environments as possible. Hence airborne target-acquisition radars of various types are designed to be operated mainly from areas well behind the forward edge of the battle area (FEBA). Over-the-horizon (OTH) radar transmitters are also likely to be sited at remote locations and, in the future, may be provided with a degree of mobility.

Trend 5 The Accelerating Pace of Tactical War

Because a large number of new technology systems are being employed either to replace or assist the human eye to perform target-acquisition and weapons-guidance tasks, much of the security hitherto derived from darkness, bad weather and light camouflage is being removed. The gradual lifting of this target-acquisition constraint is having the effect of making modern tactical war a more intense and an almost non-stop round-the-clock operation. This has different implications for different people in different situations, but on the general level, it has obvious significance in purely human-endurance terms. Patterns of sleeping, eating and general human activity are likely to be far more subject to modification to fit the new military requirements. Various forms of drugs may be dispensed to improve peak efficiency, extend human endurance or assist personnel to rest and sleep, even in noisy and uncomfortable environments.

Trend 6 Changing Logistics Requirements

The non-stop nature of modern war and the proliferation and wide dispersal of mobile small units will necessitate the development of a new logistics support concept. The delegation of a larger amount of authority to lower command levels on this type of continuously active battlefield, in many environments, could be expected to stimulate an increased rate of ammunition expenditure. On the other hand, because of dramatically improved weapon accuracies and warhead efficiencies, far less ordnance should be required to destroy a given number of acquired targets than has been the case in the past. The balance between these competing factors is likely to vary considerably according to operating doctrines and the nature of the local battlefield environment.

In those battlefield situations where it is possible for small units to be withdrawn in a modular fashion from the major areas of intense battlefield activity at 48- or 72-hour intervals, it may be sufficient for the logistics system to concentrate upon refurbishing forces at these locations. However, it can be anticipated that the practical difficulties of this concept will necessitate the provision of a large amount of logistics support directly into intense battlefield areas. In most situations, this is likely to be provided by conventional means of transport. However, in very intense environments in the future, it will be possible to deliver relatively compact high-value goods in simple, re-usable terminally guided rocket-powered canisters. These could be ground-, sea- or air-launched to home on to the desired location and be restrained in the final seconds of flight by an integrated parachute system.

In an overall sense, conventional components of battlefield logistics systems are likely to become much more vulnerable to direct attack. Roads, bridges, railways, tunnels, storage and transit areas are likely to be relatively easy for an enemy to acquire and destroy, even if they are located deep behind the FEBA. As a consequence, centres and routes of logistics support will need to be concealed where possible, but certainly duplicated and dispersed. It thus will become increasingly important for logistics support vehicles to possess an off-road rough-terrain capability.

Trend 7 The Increasing Vulnerability of Large, Fixed, Obvious and Unprotected Base and Support Areas

Unless base structures are designed, constructed and maintained in a highly dispersed, camouflaged and covert fashion, their acquisition for targeting is normally relatively easily undertaken in times of peace from public documents, through diplomatic channels or foreign agents. However, despite the ease with which they can be acquired as targets, base structures and essential elements of the national infrastructure are highly vulnerable only if precision-guided weapons can penetrate to the areas in which they are located. As long as an effective and moderately-priced anti-ballistic missile system is not developed, intercontinental ballistic missiles (ICBMs) can probably reach any target on the earth's surface. However, because of their technological complexity and great expense, in the future ICBMs are likely to be possessed by only a few major powers. Cruise missiles, on the other hand, represent a much simpler technology, which will be significantly less expensive to acquire and proliferate. The new surveillance and target acquisition technologies should make the detection of cruise missile-carrying platforms (aircraft, ships, submarines, etc.) feasible in many environments, even at long range. However, the detection, identification, localization and interception of long-range cruise missiles in flight may be a much more difficult proposition. Large, relatively unsophisticated cruise missiles possess many of the signature characteristics of conventional aircraft and hence should be detected relatively easily by satellite sensors and OTH and AWACS radar systems. However, the stealth technologies employed in the latest cruise missiles (e.g. the United States sea-launched cruise missile (SLCM) Tomahawk and the air-launched cruise missile (ALCM)) effectively reduce the radar signature of these systems to a degree where it is comparable to that of a seagull.[41] It has yet to be demonstrated conclusively whether these missiles can be detected and tracked consistently by the new generation long-range surveillance systems.

A country's capacity for intercepting incoming cruise missiles also would depend heavily upon the length of cruise missile flight from an undetected launcher to the target. For example, it is unlikely that satellite, OTH radar or AWACS-vectored air defences would be capable of preventing a surprise cruise missile attack upon coastal installations from an undetected submarine cruising close offshore. However, if cruise missile flight time to target was in the order of twenty minutes or more, it is possible that this might permit successful interception by fighter aircraft stationed nearby.[42] The essential point to be made here is that in some environments, it may be possible to provide a defence against some types of long-range cruise missile attacks. However, such defences would be vulnerable to saturation in the circumstances of a multi-missile attack and they would be very sensitive to the degradation or destruction of the long-range defensive vectoring capability, whether this is provided by satellite sensors, OTH radar, AWACS, an elaborate ground-control intercept radar system or a combination of the four. Extensive efforts would be required to ensure the survival of this essential command and control capacity in the face of a wide range of potential threats.

Given that effective defences against long-range cruise missiles and precision-guided weapon-equipped strike aircraft may not be available or effective in all circumstances and in all environments, there will be an expanding requirement for the vulnerability of base and support facilities to be reduced. The vulnerability of military support facilities can be decreased by dispersing and hardening[43] facilities within local base areas. However, it should be realized that in an era of precision-guided fuel-air explosives and hard-structure munitions, local dispersal and sheltering alone may not provide a very effective solution. Moreover, the vulnerability of military facilities represents only a proportion of the total problem. There are many elements of national economic infrastructures — bridges, factories, warehouses, railways, tunnels, etc. — that play central roles in supporting military capacities. Because of the scope of military support vulnerability, both inside and outside immediate base areas, this particular problem is not amenable to any single, simple solution. Rather, a variety of measures is likely to be required if a high degree of endurance is to be provided to overall military capacity. Many types of military operational systems can be dispersed and concealed to prevent targeting. Some can be made mobile and prepared with alternative operating sites.[44] However, factories, transport networks, power-stations and other key facilities are difficult to conceal and many are expensive to construct underground or otherwise protect. In these categories, it may be necessary to design selectively and construct a degree of system redundancy to ensure the provision of services that are vital in wartime situations. The most sophisticated and expensive defence equipment is of very limited value in military terms if its base and operating support system is highly vulnerable to attack.

Trend 8   The Increasing Scope for Surprise Attack

If there is a means by which a country's long-range surveillance and target-acquisition sensors can be degraded or destroyed in an effective manner, then that country will become increasingly vulnerable to powerful surprise strikes. If, in addition, that country has not concealed, dispersed and protected key elements of its defence structure, then new generations of precision-guided weapons will make it increasingly susceptible to rapid and decisive defeat. If ships, aircraft, armoured vehicles, artillery pieces, communications, command and control facilities and other units of defence capital are grouped in unconcealed and unprotected concentrations, it is becoming very easy for them to be targeted and destroyed by long-range terminally guided weaponry.

However, if long-range surveillance and target-acquisition sensors are concealed, dispersed, protected and, where possible, duplicated and made mobile, it will be extremely difficult for an opponent to mount a surprise attack. Further, if key elements of the defending country's support base and national infrastructure are also concealed, dispersed, protected and provided with a degree of system redundancy, this will serve to greatly enhance defensive endurance in a manner not likely to be sensitive to an opponent's development of new conventional military capacities.

Trend 9   The Increasing Necessity for Total Defence Planning

One consequence arising from developments in long-range missile, remotely piloted vehicle (RPV) and conventional warhead technologies will be to increase greatly the ease with which large numbers of countries will be able to target and, if they wish, attack the economic infrastructures of opposing states from bases within their own national boundaries. Consequently, modern conventional warfare, even between relatively minor states, is likely to threaten the existence of all aspects of the societies involved. It seems probable that many states will strive to reduce the vulnerability not only of key elements of the national infrastructure that support the military defence effort in the most direct sense but also a much wider array of targets, including the major centres of population. These broad national security considerations are likely to surface as a significant influence in many aspects of national development policy and planning.

Trend 10   The Rising Costs of Many Military Systems

In the case of many new and improved conventional military systems, unit costs are rising rapidly.[45] This is particularly the case regarding complex multi-purpose systems that involve numerous integrated technologies. For instance, Desmond Ball estimates that the costs of United States fighter aircraft increased between 50 and 80 times from 1940 to 1975.[46] S. J. Dudzinsky and James Digby support this general view by arguing that the costs of United States aircraft carriers doubled in real terms in the decade to 1975 and that the average unit costs of United States main battle tanks rose by a comparable proportion.[47]

Certainly the operational capacity of almost all of the new technology systems surpasses that of their predecessors by a significant margin. Because of this, the cost-effectiveness of some of the new systems in some operational environments is difficult to dispute. For instance, while a guided glide-bomb may cost thirty times that of an unguided iron bomb, in effect, it may be able to accomplish tasks that otherwise would require hundreds of iron bombs, multiple aircraft sorties and greatly increased risks to both aircraft and air crews.

Cost/performance trade-offs in terms of high/low technology mixes are already accepted practice in many national security structures.[48] However, the magnitude of the current capital equipment cost expansion is likely to place even greater pressure upon the processes of selecting new technology elements in total force structures.

Trend 11 The Increasing Cost-effectiveness of Medium-technology Defensive Structures

Whereas most current defence structures are designed to perform both offensive and defensive functions, this situation may change as a consequence of new technology developments. In particular, there is now increased scope for the development of relatively inexpensive specialized structures for tactical defence.

The most desirable selection of defensive technologies is likely to vary greatly according to local conditions. However, in many countries, it should be possible to procure a small number of carefully selected high-technology early-warning, identification and long-range target-detection systems and a large number of medium-technology weapons systems which, when structured into appropriate military units, should provide a highly survivable capacity to defend in depth.

In practice, the selective exploitation of the potential that the new technologies provide is likely to have the effect of enhancing greatly the deterrence and tactical defensive capacity of a wide range of states. Their impact on the balance of forces on the Korean Peninsula, in the Middle East and in the Scandinavian/Baltic region is already quite noticeable. For countries whose potential enemies are equipped substantially with new technology weaponry, the utility of war, as distinct from the threat of war, will be reduced greatly. However, it should be noted that if a small or medium state is confronted by a major-power opponent, its possession of advanced defensive technologies, while greatly increasing its power of deterrence and tactical defence, will do little to increase the effectiveness of that country's strategic defences (i.e. to protect its total economic infrastructure).

Trend 12 The Enhanced Capacities of Terrorist Groups

Although national governments will retain a clear superiority in conventional military power, the increasingly light and compact nature of guided firepower will provide stateless groups with a means of inflicting violence in a highly discriminating manner from stand-off ranges. Terrorist groups armed with modern anti-aircraft, anti-tank and anti-shipping weaponry will pose a threat of quite a different type to that of the past.

Trend 13 The Partial Replacement of Tactical Nuclear Weapons by Precision-guided Munitions

The effectiveness of advanced precision-guided weapon systems of various types against small hardened and large unhardened targets will make them a viable alternative to tactical nuclear weapons in the performance of many battlefield functions. The precision accuracy of these weapons serves to reduce greatly the requirements for the enormous quantities of firepower that only nuclear weapons can effectively provide. Hence precision-guided 'munition equipped forces of moderate size can effectively deter major powers on the tactical level, and if deterrence fails, they can effectively destroy attacking forces, their immediate support and in many environments, important parts of their national domestic infrastructures. As a consequence, precision-guided munitions may be substituted for tactical nuclear weapons when major powers wish to destroy major enemy forces, when major powers wish to enhance a client's defensive capacity or when an independent state wishes to enhance greatly its self-defence capacity.

Nuclear weapons (as well as chemical and biological weapons to some degree), because of their unsurpassed destructive capacity, are likely to retain a level of deterrence potential that exceeds that of any conventional munition. The requirement for this level of deterrence, as well as the prestige and other incentives that are always likely to accompany the possession of tactical nuclear weapons, most probably will thwart attempts to reduce non-super-power holdings of nuclear weapons. However, because the strictly military requirement for this type of highly expensive, large, hard-target destructive capacity is becoming more limited in most environments, pressure for the acquisition of tactical nuclear weapons may be decreased in many countries.

Trend 14 Multi-party Mutual Deterrence

One significant consequence of the wider distribution of accurate long-range bombardment capacities is likely to be the development of a complex web of mutual deterrence. Even where neighbouring states are in conflict over serious matters, if their long-range precision-guided munition capacity is comparable, it seems probable that in many situations, each will be constrained from unrestricted deep infrastructure attack by the prospect of heavy retaliation.

It is clear from this discussion that forthcoming developments in conventional military technology are of far greater significance than anything experienced in a comparable period in the past. Australia's defence bureaucracy faces a major challenge if it is to exploit fully the potentialities offered by these advances.

The processes of adjusting to the new technology environment will be extremely complex. As Dr Malcolm Currie points out, appropriate adaptation involves much more than the simple placement of new technology items on defence equipment shopping-lists:

> I want to make the point that technology *per se* is not enough ... Equally important to technology is its innovative use in the overall military context. That is why I believe that the development of tactics is every bit as important as hardware and must be made an explicit and implicit part of the design evolution and development process.[49]

Hence the task confronting Australia is not only to decide the most appropriate mix of new technology systems to buy: it is of comparable importance that a major effort be made to devise tactics, doctrines and structures that fully exploit the potential of the new technologies in satisfying Australia's priority security requirements. This will not be easy. The independent defence of Australia and its vital interests poses a unique set of problems. The range of threats that Australia requires a capacity to meet, the country's physical geography, its climatic pattern, its population distribution and its economic structure all differ substantially from those countries with which Australia is normally compared. As a consequence, the lessons that might be available from the experiences of others can be expected to provide only a general guide to local requirements. In these circumstances, the most effective method of exploiting the potential of the new technologies would be to initiate an intensive process of analysis and evaluation. Through an ongoing round of studies, field trials and experiments, the Australian defence structure could become much more familiar with the battlefield potential of a broad cross-section of the new technologies. Dr Robert O'Neill has suggested making trial purchases and perhaps even leasing or hiring a selected range of precision-guided munitions, advanced detection systems, remotely piloted vehicles and electronic warfare systems.[50] This would facilitate the type of dynamic experimentation required to demonstrate the capabilities and limitations of each type of system in the Australian environment.

However, awareness of those technologies most suited to

Australia's requirements would only solve part of the problem. Military concepts, structures, strategies, tactics and operational procedures also would need to be thrown open for question. The sorts of issues needing to be addressed would include the following:
- the tactics of force dispersal and concentration in a high-technology environment;
- optimal unit and sub-unit sizes and armament in various phases of warfare;
- means of achieving high levels of mobility while minimizing exposure to enemy detection;
- the most effective means of concealing personnel, vehicles, aircraft, ships and fortifications;
- the most survivable and efficient means of basing aircraft and ships;
- the most suitable C^3 systems to cope with the requirements of rapid dispersal and concentration;
- the potential to exploit new electronic warfare capacities;
- the utility of surprise and the scope for its achievement in the presence of new types of detection systems;
- the most appropriate procedures for servicing and supplying highly dispersed units, etc.

From these ongoing investigations, it is possible that many existing ideas would be upheld, but it is also likely that a wide range of new concepts, structures and tactics would emerge. Certainly a much clearer picture would be generated of the types of ground vehicles, aircraft and ships best suited for the defence of Australia. The enormous potential of such an effort would appear obvious and irresistible.

In any society, the instigation of such a fundamental process of reassessment is certain to arouse the resistance of military, bureaucratic and political vested interests. While these influences cannot be ignored, they must be overcome. As Dr Currie has argued:

> [we] ... must ... tear down the barriers of tradition, of bureaucratic inertia and thinking, of service roles and missions, of familiar scenarios projected from the experience of the past. The world is changing fast. The opportunities are there and our failure to perceive them first could be fatal.[51]

Australia cannot avoid the technological challenge of the future. If our defence structure proves sufficiently flexible to accept the requirement for change and to launch a determined effort to exploit the potential of the new technologies, the security of Australia will undoubtedly be enhanced substantially. On the other hand, if a decision is made to remain with that which is comfortable and familiar, and the security structure is not subjected to a thorough process of review, Australia's security will suffer a relative decline. There can be no doubt that in the future, national security structures that have not mastered the new technology environment will become increasingly vulnerable to those that have.

Notes and References

1. Dr Malcolm Currie, the former U.S. Director of Defence Research and Engineering, was one of the first and most prominent commentators to describe recent advances in conventional military technology as a "revolution": "A remarkable series of technical developments has brought us to the threshold of what I believe will become a true revolution in conventional warfare." Cited by Phil Stanford, "The Automated Battlefield", *New York Times Magazine*, 23 February 1975, p. 14.
2. Testimony before the Research and Development Subcommittee of the Committee on Armed Services, U.S. Senate, *Fiscal Year 1977 Authorization for Military Procurement, Research and Development, and Active Duty, Selected Reserve and Civilian Personnel Strengths*, Part 11, 9 March 1976, p. 5859.
3. The major technological developments outlined on the following pages are detailed in much greater length in Appendix B.
4. Examples of this type of system include Blowpipe, Stinger and RBS-70.
5. Examples of this type of system include the Soviet ZSU-23-4 Shilka, the West German Gepard Flakpanzer and the American Divads.
6. Examples of this category of SAM include Roland, Rapier and SAM 8.
7. Examples of medium-range SAMs include Advanced Hawk and SAM 6.
8. The most advanced long-range SAM systems are the Soviet SAM 10 and the American SAM-D Patriot.
9. This concept of air operations is described at length by Steven L. Canby, *Tactical Airpower in Europe: Airing the European View* (Santa Monica: Technology Service Corporation, 1976). It also should be noted at this stage that those U.S. squadrons equipped with A-10 aircraft are being trained to employ similar low-level terrain-following flight profiles in attacks involving shallow penetrations of enemy airspace. For a detailed elaboration of A-10 tactical doctrine, see Donald E. Fink, "A-10 Survivability in Attack Role Shown", *Aviation Week and Space Technology* 106, no. 25 (20 June 1977): 88-93.
10. Pods are cylindrical or "bomb"-shaped structures that can be attached to aircraft weapon pylons, under the wings or fuselage. They frequently contain specialized electronic systems designed to confuse or jam enemy radar or communication signals in the vicinity of the aircraft. Other types of pods carry reconnaissance systems with special types of cameras, infra-red scanners, etc.
11. This point is made by Canby, *Tactical Airpower in Europe*, p. 37.
12. See this argument elaborated in R. Babbage, "The Implications of Changing Technology for the Future of Manned Tactical Aircraft", in *The Future of Tactical Airpower in the Defence of Australia*, ed. Desmond Ball (Canberra: Strategic and Defence Studies Centre, Australian National University, 1977), pp. 32-33.
13. Quoted by B. Latter, "Lessons for NATO from the Yom Kippur War", *Royal Air Forces Quarterly* 16, no. 4 (Winter 1976): 385.
14. Quoted in *Aviation Week and Space Technology* 105, no. 18 (2 November 1976): 19.

15. Describing naval reaction in terms of such a five-phase programme involves a large degree of over-simplification. Many other areas of naval activity, in reality, may have been changed in response to the increased anti-ship missile threat — training programmes, operational procedures, etc. However, for the purposes of this discussion, it is sufficient to argue mainly within the bounds of these five elements.
16. These types of availability constraints also might confront attackers. For example, the attacking forces simply might not have either the weapons platforms or the weapons themselves ready when enemy shipping approaches; but for them, the issue would not be nearly so critical because their survival would not be at stake. In most environments, the attacking forces would largely retain the prerogative to select the time, place and mode of attack. Obviously, these choices could be made in the light of any existing availability constraints.
17. Special circumstances may include an opponent's possession of very few anti-shipping weapons, their carriage in a few large, obvious and highly vulnerable platforms, and missile system malfunctions preventing the launching of the attack, etc.
18. This is the flight profile of the Soviet SS-N-12. See C.A. Robinson jun., "Soviets Make New SALT Bid", *Aviation Week and Space Technology* 104, no. 5 (2 February 1976): 13, 15.
19. It should be noted that the operational capabilities of the latest naval carrier AWACS (E-2C) have been overrated by many commentators. See the account of an E-2C operator in *U.S. Naval Institute Proceedings* 103/3/889 (March 1977): 82.
20. Wire-guided torpedoes are directed by guidance commands passed from the launcher vessel (e.g. a submarine) down a thin wire, which is dispensed from the torpedo as it travels.
21. For the flight profiles of all Soviet-designed anti-ship missiles, see Robinson, "Soviets Make New SALT Bid", pp. 13-16.
    This part of the argument also assumes that the defending ship will be operating with its surveillance radar system actively emitting. Operating in this manner makes targeting of the ship very easy, since it can be identified and located from very long range. However if the ship's surveillance radar is not operating, an incoming missile may not be detected at all, unless it emits an active radar signal during the terminal homing phase. New types of highly sensitive ship-borne infra-red scanning systems may provide a passive missile detection system for surface ships in the 1980s.
22. "Chaff" and "window" are terms used to describe minute slithers of radar-reflecting aluminium or metal-impregnated fibreglass. The operational concept is to fire clouds of chaff into the air, to decoy or confuse an opponent's surveillance, target acquisition and weapon-borne radars.
23. See the testimony of Commander G.R. Meinig, the U.S. Navy's Phalanx Project Manager, before the Subcommittee on Tactical Air Power of the Committee on Armed Services, U.S. Senate, *Fiscal Year 1977 Authorization for Military Procurement, Research and Development, and Active Duty, Selected Reserve and Civilian Personnel Strengths*, Part 10, 17 March 1976, p. 5570.
24. For details, see "Seawolf/GWS25, the Royal Navy's Anti-missile Missile System", *International Defense Review* 9, no. 5 (October 1976): 792.
25. "Spoofing" is a term frequently used in electronic warfare circles as a synonym for deception.
26. Ibid.; and see also the testimony of Commander G.R. Meinig, the U.S. Navy's Phalanx Project Manager, before the Subcommittee on Tactical Air Power of the Committee on Armed Services, U.S. Senate, *Fiscal Year 1977 Authorization*

for Military Procurement, Research and Development, and Active Duty, Selected Reserve and Civilian Personnel Strengths, Part 10, 17 March 1976, p. 5574.
27. See this elaborated by Desmond J. Ball and Steven J. Rosen, "Fuel Air Explosives for Medium Powers", *Pacific Defence Reporter* 3, no. 10 (April 1977): 18.
28. Ibid.; and see also G. Johannsohn, "Fuel Air Explosives Revolutionise Conventional Warfare", *International Defense Review* 9, no. 6 (December 1976): 995-96.
29. See Rear-Admiral W.E. Meyer and Captain B.D. Mura, "Aegis", *US Naval Institute Proceedings* 103/2/888 (February 1977): 95. The very great expense of the Aegis system and the cancellation of the CGN-38 strike cruiser programme now means that Aegis probably will only be deployed aboard the DDG-47 class. The implications of this for U.S. fleet air defence are elaborated by Arthur D. Baker in "Aegis", *US Naval Institute Proceedings* 103/7/893 (July 1977): 87-88.
30. Quoted by E. Ulsamer, "The New Five-year Defense Plan", *Air Force Magazine* 60, no. 1 (January 1977): 63.
31. See *Aviation Week and Space Technology* 105, no. 11 (13 September 1976): 71 ff.; and *International Defense Review* 9, no. 6 (December 1976): 1024.
32. The U.S. Navy's move in this direction is outlined by E.H. Kolcum, "Navy Request Stresses Shift to V/STOL", *Aviation Week and Space Technology* 106, no. 4 (24 January 1977): 18 ff. A comparable trend is noted in the Soviet Navy by J. Erickson, "Soviet Military Operational Research: Objectives and Methods", *Strategic Review* 5, no. 2 (Spring 1977): 65.
33. Laminar-flow technology uses a variety of techniques to reduce the drag and the water disturbance induced by minor indentations in the hulls of vessels.
34. For details, see *International Defense Review* 10, no. 1 (February 1977): 21.
35. A shaped-charge is a cone-shaped explosive warhead that, when it detonates, directs a stream of very hot gases on to a small portion of the target's surface. The effect on armour-plating is to leave a small hole and project the fragments melted in the process of boring the hole into the space beyond.
36. See this technology described in *NATO's Fifteen Nations* 21, no. 2 (April-May 1976): 97, with regard to the Thomson—Brandt 100 mm tactical-support bomb; and in R.T. Pretty, ed., *Jane's Weapon Systems 1975* (London: Jane's Yearbooks, 1974), p. 502, with regard to the Durandal penetration bomb.
37. For details of American experimentation with self-forming forged fragmentation warheads, see R.D.M. Furlong, "WAAM: The U.S. Air Force's Next Generation of Anti-armour Weapons", *International Defense Review* 11, no. 9 (1978): 1378-79.
38. For details of weaponry purchased by particular states in South-East Asia, see *The Military Balance 1978-79* (London: International Institute for Strategic Studies, 1978).
39. For example, it is becoming extremely difficult and expensive for tactical aircraft to perform close air support tasks in intense battlefield environments. The same can be said of large surface ships performing conventional gunfire support missions adjacent to coastlines occupied by well-equipped enemy forces.
40. For details, see Stefan J. Geisenheyner, "Optronics for Gun-laying and Surveillance", *Asian Defence Journal* (January 1977): 14.
41. The radar cross-section of SLCM [Tomahawk] is said to be the equivalent of a seagull's, while the Navy is attempting to reduce it to that of a sparrow by the use of surface coatings which at low altitudes would break the typical Soviet ground radar's ability to lock on.

Cited from J.P. Geddes, "The Sea Launched Cruise Missile", *International Defense Review* 9, no. 2 (April 1976): 201.

42. This assumes, of course, that the AWACS or OTH radar systems can actually detect incoming cruise missiles that incorporate stealth technologies and also that fighter aircraft radars and other systems are sufficiently sensitive to make close-range interception feasible. This may be extremely difficult, especially if the cruise missiles are flying low and hence are heavily camouflaged by ground clutter from some types of downward-looking sensors.
43. A "hardened" target is one that is specifically strengthened to resist destruction. Common "hardening" techniques include the placement of facilities underground, their protection by concrete and/or steel structures, etc.
44. Air, naval and army base refuelling and rearming facilities can be given a large degree of protection in this manner. European practice is most notable in this regard. See, for instance, *The Defence Forces of Switzerland* (a supplementary booklet published by the *Army Quarterly and Defence Journal*, Tavistock, U.K., 1974), pp. 29-30; and D. Chopping, "In Fighting Trim — The Swedish Air Force", *International Defense Review* 6, no. 3 (June 1973): 303 ff.
45. For a detailed discussion of the costs of an array of new weapons technologies, see J.P. Large, "Notes on Costs", an appendix to S.J. Dudzinsky jun. and James Digby, *Qualitative Constraints on Conventional Armaments: An Emerging Issue* (Santa Monica: Rand Corporation, 1976), Paper R−1957, pp. 87-91.
46. See the discussion in Desmond J. Ball, "Australia's Tactical Air Requirements and the Criteria for Evaluating Tactical Aircraft for Australian Procurement", in *Future of Tactical Airpower in the Defence of Australia*, ed. Ball, pp. 61-65.
47. See their argument in S.J. Dudzinsky jun. and James Digby, "The Strategic and Tactical Implications of New Weapons Technologies", in *The Defence of Australia: Fundamental New Aspects*, ed. Robert O'Neill (Canberra: Strategic and Defence Studies Centre, Australian National University, 1977), pp. 49-56. This case can also be substantiated by reference to the cost escalation of a number of other weapons platforms and systems. For example, with regard to attack aircraft, see William D. White, *US Tactical Air Power: Missions Forces and Costs* (Washington, DC: Brookings Institution, 1974), pp. 55-59.
48. The concept of a high/low cost equipment mix has been the subject of an intense debate in the United States ever since the original proposals of this type were made for the U.S. Navy by Admiral E.R. Zumwalt. For an elaboration of the issues involved, see the article by him entitled "High-Low", *United States Naval Institute Proceedings* 102/4/878 (April 1976): 46; and also the discussion in subsequent issues of the same journal.
49. Quoted in *Aviation Week and Space Technology* 104, no. 21 (24 May 1976): 56.
50. This suggestion is made in "The Influence of Recent Developments in Conventional Weapons Technology in Strategic and Tactical Doctrine: Consequences for Australia" (paper presented to the United Service Institution of the Australian Capital Territory, Canberra, 5 May 1976), p. 3.
51. Quoted in *Aviation Week and Space Technology* 104, no. 21 (24 May 1976): 56.

Part 2

NEW IMPERATIVES FOR CHANGE

ns new security
3
A Broader Range of Potential Threats

It is clear from the discussion in the first two chapters that the nature of Australia's strategic environment has changed fundamentally during the past decade. Primarily because of the altered United States regional role, it is unlikely that Australian forces again will be deployed to support the commitments of major power allies in foreign countries. But more importantly, if Australia is threatened directly in the years ahead, the United States will be available to provide the assistance Australia requires only in very special circumstances. As a consequence, the nation's prime security function is now to develop a capacity to defend the vast Australian continent and its maritime surrounds with a high level of independence. This is a quite different and much more demanding task from that of the forward defence era.

One of the most important features of Australia's new security situation is also the source of a major planning problem. Because Australia must now provide the prime forces for her own defence in nearly every conceivable circumstance, the nation's security system must be designed to deter and, if necessary, meet a very much wider range of pressures and threats than has been required in the past. This complicates greatly the task of planning Australia's security, for in practice, it is extremely difficult to select a series of threats from the vast array of possibilities to provide a firm basis for force structure design.[1] It is simply impossible to predict the precise character of the pressures and threats that may arise to confront Australia in the period ahead.

A partial solution to this problem is to attempt to reduce the effects of planning uncertainty by building high levels of flexibility and adaptability into the Australian security structure. But in order to provide rational design parameters for the development of the force structure, it is still necessary somehow to rate, or order, the full array of potential pressures and threats. One of the most valuable means of gaining insights into the relative priority of various threats is to examine systematically the breadth of Australia's susceptibilities, for it can reasonably be assumed that, in general terms, those pressures and threats to which Australia is most vulnerable are also those that most demand a deterrence and response capacity.

It is in this context that the examination of Australia's natural vulnerabilities in this chapter should be viewed. In order to clarify the discussion that follows, the full spectrum of international pressures and threats to which Australia might conceivably be subjected is divided into three categories:

1. *The pressures of peace.* These concern the mostly non-violent but also the sub-national violent pressures that are a product of the stresses and strains implicit in the world environment in the absence of open conflict between states.

2. *The pressures of international crises.* This category concerns the pressures that might be felt in Australia as an indirect result of a conflict or war overseas in which Australia is not directly involved.

3. *The pressures of international aggression.* This category includes those types of pressure that might be applied by an external state mounting a direct attack upon Australia, employing economic, political, psychological and/or military means.

Of course, some pressures are more likely to arise than others. The pressures of peace are manifested in many types of activity that occur daily. The pressures of international crises, while not currently affecting Australia in a significant sense, have done so on several occasions during the post-war period (e.g. during the Korean War, 1950-53; Indonesian Confrontation, 1963-66; the 1973-74 oil crisis, etc.). However, assigning a high level of relevance to the pressures of international aggression, especially concerning those threats that are very demanding in their response requirements, is far more difficult in the Australian environment. This is partly because of the limited historical precedent for this type of high-level threat to Australia, but it is also caused by the fact that the current regional and global situation is structured in such a manner that it would be difficult for such threats to arise quickly. Dr Robert O'Neill has argued that at least one of three major changes in the international environment would be necessary, although not of themselves sufficient, prior to the presentation of a major threat to Australia:

 a. The superpowers change their attitudes to each other to the point where one or both consider the risk of a serious clash to be acceptable . . .

 b. World class struggle sharpens a great deal while at the same time Australia conducts herself in a manner which is viewed as extremely irresponsible by the less privileged nations . . .

 c. Regional and great power actors acquire both a high degree of military capacity for aggressive action at a long range and a high degree of strategic freedom to pursue selfish interests at the expense of others.[2]

This is not to say that major international changes of these types could not take place rapidly. In some conceivable circumstances, they could, but the sheer scale of the change that would be required serves to limit the potential for high-level threats arising against Australia. Excepting possibly the circumstances where a superpower becomes Australia's opponent, much more change would be required in the international environment than a simple alteration of a single actor's intentions.

Despite the relative improbability of major direct threats arising against Australia in the short term, this does not negate the value of their study and serious consideration. If such a threat actually did arise, the implications for Australian national security clearly would be of a much higher order of magnitude than those of the lower-level threat categories.

While it is difficult to speculate about the probability of major threats arising against Australia, something can be stated about their timing. For a high-level threat to develop against Australia, a large amount of change would be required in the international environment. Where the change required is primarily that of perceptions and/or intentions, a major threat could develop quickly. However, where the change required in the international environment involved not only an alteration of intentions but also a substantial development of military capacities, the threat could not readily arise in a short period.

A similar argument can be made concerning the development of medium-level threats. However, in their case, a lesser amount of change is required in the international environment in order for them to arise. Again, where this change does not involve a significant alteration of military capacities but merely a change in intentions, in some circumstances such threats could arise very quickly.

In the light of this preamble, it is now appropriate to analyse Australia's susceptibility to the full range of potential pressures and threats.

1. The Pressures of Peace

Diplomatic channels provide avenues for a wide range of low-level pressures. These can range from the very casual, off-the-cuff ambiguous remark made at a cocktail party to a much more formal comment, suggestion, expression of opinion or protest. Most international actors,[3] including the Australian government, engage in elaborate and almost continuous processes of bargaining and negotiation over a very wide set of issues, such as relations with neighbours, international economic aid, disarmament measures, United Nations-related activities and sea-bed boundaries, to name just a few. From time to time, these forums are used for minor trials of strength and for the management of disputes that threaten an escalation of tension.

Low-level pressure can also be applied through a range of economic measures and to some of these Australia is unusually vulnerable. Because the normal peacetime economy is oriented towards very high levels of international trade, the variation by other countries of tariffs, import and export quotas, quality restrictions, currency values, foreign investment holdings and a host of other variables can affect the prosperity of many sectors of Australian industry to a marked degree. The major consumers of Australia's export products are probably best placed to cause disruption in this regard. As can be seen from Table 3, Japan, the United States and the countries of the European Economic Community acquire nearly two-thirds of Australia's export product. Their restriction of imports, by whatever means and whether with the intention of applying pressure or merely attempting to solve domestic economic or political problems, can have a significant impact upon Australia.[4]

The potential for applying low-level pressure through the disruption of imports to Australia is much more restricted. The Australian economy is self-sufficient in essential foods and most basic materials required for its short-term sustenance.[7] Moreover, the range of commodities that Australia does import, although increasing substantially,[6] is available from a number of intensely competitive alternative suppliers. Hence although a variation in imports by a major supplier such as the United States, Japan or the United Kingdom could cause severe inconvenience to particular sectors of the economy, Australia is not susceptible to long-term disruptive activities of this type undertaken by a single international actor. Australia's vulnerability to these pressures would only increase significantly if a number of commodity producer states combined to enforce trading restrictions. However, even this extreme action probably only would have a major and immediate impact upon Australia if the commodity involved were oil.

There are some low-level international pressures to which Australia is vulnerable that could be applied with or without the sanction of a foreign government. For example, in the economic sphere, disruptive activities initiated by foreign-owned or multinational corporations could be the cause of serious difficulties in some

Table 3. Australian exports and imports, proportions, by country of consignment or origin, 1952-53 to 1972-73 (Percentages).

Country	Exports			Imports		
	1952-53	1962-63	1972-73	1952-53	1962-63	1972-73
Arab Republic of Egypt	0.39	0.10	0.66	0.18	0.01	0.00
Austria	0.07	0.14	0.07	0.23	0.31	0.31
Bahrain	0.04	0.06	0.22	2.90	0.02	0.73
Belgium-Luxembourg	3.69	2.16	0.99	1.07	0.65	0.89
Brazil	0.05	0.02	0.08	0.18	0.12	0.23
Canada	0.99	1.77	2.66	3.80	4.25	3.26
China, People's Republic of	0.08	6.01	1.01	0.27	0.52	1.21
Denmark	0.08	0.06	0.09	0.10	0.32	0.38
Finland	0.01	0.03	0.18	0.17	0.52	0.59
France	8.72	4.92	3.03	1.80	1.64	1.83
Germany, Federal Republic of	2.57	3.18	3.28	2.64	5.42	6.99
Greece	0.09	0.16	0.49	0.00	0.06	0.09
Hong Kong	0.56	1.88	1.53	0.10	0.71	1.94
India	1.97	1.73	0.60	2.85	1.67	0.77
Indonesia	0.58	0.29	1.20	4.19	2.71	0.33
Iran	0.04	0.18	0.42	0.06	1.78	0.45
Iraq	0.04	0.04	0.03	0.03	0.09	0.50
Italy	5.13	4.09	2.15	1.02	1.81	2.10
Japan	9.64	16.09	31.10	0.91	5.98	17.93
Korea, Republic of	(a)	0.30	0.85	(a)	0.02	0.25
Kuwait	(a)	0.20	0.25	(a)	1.76	0.73
Malaysia	(a)	1.38	1.56	(a)	1.58	0.93
Nauru	0.06	0.15	0.08	0.25	0.28	0.29
Netherlands	0.93	0.67	1.03	1.16	1.27	1.35
New Caledonia	0.29	0.23	0.31	0.02	0.06	0.02
New Zealand	3.29	6.09	5.24	0.78	1.64	3.15
Norway	0.08	0.24	0.21	0.47	0.33	0.29
Pakistan	0.52	0.66	0.11	0.44	0.53	0.11
Papua New Guinea	0.70	1.79	2.17	0.92	0.68	0.60
Philippines	0.06	0.58	0.79	0.01	0.07	0.19
Poland	0.42	0.58	0.88	0.01	0.05	0.09
Saudi Arabia	(a)	0.17	0.22	(a)	1.85	0.49
Singapore	1.47	1.57	2.12	1.14	0.32	0.97
South Africa, Republic of	0.42	0.88	1.53	0.60	0.75	0.50
Spain	0.02	0.47	0.36	0.13	0.21	0.49
Sri Lanka	1.69	0.60	0.18	1.90	0.79	0.23
Sweden	0.33	0.30	0.36	1.32	1.66	2.01
Switzerland	0.25	0.08	0.12	0.79	1.31	1.60
Taiwan	0.08	0.19	1.12	0.01	0.05	1.32
Thailand	0.14	0.34	0.58	0.01	0.04	0.17
United Kingdom	41.23	18.66	9.68	41.76	30.45	18.63
United States of America	6.64	12.35	12.21	16.57	21.27	20.87
U.S.S.R.	0.19	1.36	1.99	0.14	0.05	0.07
Yugoslavia	0.05	0.55	0.80	0.02	0.02	0.02
Other countries	6.40	6.00	5.36	8.98	4.27	3.60
'Foreign orders' and country of origin or destination unknown	..	0.72	0.08	0.06	0.10	0.46
Total	100.00	100.00	100.00	100.00	100.00	100.00

Note: [a] Comparable figures not available.

Source: Australian Bureau of Statistics, *Official Yearbook of Australia 1974* (Canberra: Australian Government Publishing Service, 1975), p. 324.

circumstances. The domination by these organizations of a series of key Australian industries[7] and their vast capacity to transfer funds, technologies and ultimately productive capacity and jobs between countries does impose a significant constraint upon governmental prerogatives.

There are other types of government-sponsored or non-government pressure to which Australia is particularly vulnerable because of its size, the length of its uninhabited coastline and the difficulties of maintaining effective control over activities in remote regions. Incursions by foreign fishing vessels into national territorial waters or declared sovereign fishing zones, illicit offshore mineral and oceanographic exploration and fishing surveys, coastal landings by individuals carrying contagious diseases, the introduction of diseased animals or destructive plant parasites, the landing of illegal immigrants and the smuggling of narcotics, bullion and native fauna are of particular concern. During the past decade, Australia has been subjected to many of these pressures and there appears to be little reason to suspect that they will not be the source of further problems in the future.

In normal peacetime conditions, military capacities rarely dominate as a means of applying pressure. However, they can exert a very significant background influence upon the manner in which diplomatic, economic, political and other activities are undertaken. For example, if the Australian government and Australian officials feel that the country is greatly inferior in military terms to an international actor or country with whom they are negotiating a sensitive issue, they may perceive that their freedom of action is limited for fear of unintentionally provoking the other actor to escalate the dispute into the military or some other media in which Australia is relatively weak. In some circumstances, the possession of military strength may be the only effective means of deterring a rival from escalating a dispute into a higher level of conflict. Thus the possession of military strength can have a significant moderating or restraining influence upon the behaviour of international actors, even though it may not be exploited deliberately for this purpose. Australia may be particularly susceptible to the indirect pressures arising from perceived military inferiority because of the population's long and deeply held feelings of isolated vulnerability.[8]

2. The Pressures of International Crises

(a) Global or Regional Resource Crises

As major industrialized countries of the world gradually exhaust local supplies of raw materials and many centres of world population become increasingly dependent upon external supplies of food, energy, fertilizers and other basic materials, increasing pressure is being brought to bear upon resource suppliers. The relative geographical concentration of a variety of key resources provides potential scope for the artificial regulation of supply by producers acting in concert.

International crises over resource supply and distribution may not necessarily involve Australia directly. If as a result of regional or global action, the flow of imports to Australia is restricted, this is likely to cause serious damage to the economy in a direct and immediate sense only if petroleum products are involved. However, it is possible that in an indirect manner, the impact of restrictions upon the flows of some basic raw materials may be more severe. Many of Australia's major trading partners are likely to be affected very heavily by an artificial restriction in their capacity to import fuels and other key raw materials. International shipping and air transport might be disrupted. As a result, the capacity of several of Australia's major trading partners to pay for, transport and consume Australian exports may be reduced significantly.

It would thus appear that while the survival and basic well-being of the Australian population is likely to be secure during the course of any international resource crisis, those sectors of Australian industry that depend heavily upon international trade for their prosperity may be vulnerable to severe reverses. A continuation of this type of indirect international pressure over a protracted period would be likely to imply a major reduction in Australia's living standards.

(b) Regional or Global Conventional Conflict with Australia not Participating as a Combatant

A serious regional conflict, perhaps in North-East Asia, on the Sino-Soviet border or in Korea, would be likely to have a significant impact upon Australian security. Depending upon the nature and scope of the hostilities, international sea and air transport might be disrupted severely. As was explained above, this could directly and indirectly affect the prosperity of those sectors of the Australian economy that are import- or export-oriented.

If regional hostilities were extended to, or initiated in, areas much closer to Australia, there probably would be heightened demands upon the Australian Defence Force to deter and, if necessary, resist violations of national sovereignty. Advanced methods of surveillance and air and sea patrolling of offshore possessions and the long coastline could be expected to be at a premium in this type of situation.

If conflict were to escalate to a global or major bloc level, the impact upon Australia would probably be greater, but not necessarily more damaging. For example, while most of the world's shipping might be expected to be transferred to satisfy wartime requirements, the combatants on one or both sides of the conflict might seek to draw upon Australian agricultural, mineral and perhaps also secondary industrial resources to help meet their needs. In other words, it is possible that this type of conflict could actually serve to boost the Australian economy, as was the case during the Korean War.

3. The Pressures of International Aggression

(a) Demands and Threats directed against Australia and supported by Political, Military and/or Economic Measures

Demands and threats can be made in a highly specific manner, outlining detailed diplomatic, economic, political and/or military consequences of particular activities. Alternatively, they can be introduced in vague and ambiguous terms, in an effort simply to lend weight and draw attention to a nation's strongly held views on a particular matter. For whatever motives they are issued and whatever form they may take, the receipt of a demand or threat is normally followed by an intensive evaluation of its significance. What factors prompted the demand to be made? What are the chances that the threat will be carried out if the dispute continues? Exactly what type of action is most likely? How vulnerable is the recipient? Can any support be gained in the circumstances, either domestically or abroad? How do the possible gains from the dispute compare with the possible consequences in the light of the new developments? The answers to these and other related questions will depend essentially upon assessments of the comparative power, past practices and perceived intentions of the actors concerned in those fields that are considered most critical.

The issuing of demands and threats is not without its risks and costs. Unless a threat is issued in secret and with some kind of guarantee that it will never become the subject of international discussion, the threatening actor's credibility will be affected by the reaction and the outcome. If a demand or threat is widely held to be clumsy, the nation's or the government's reputation for finesse may decline and subsequent threats given little credence. If a threat is widely regarded as unjust or illegal because of some kind of international convention or agreement, again reputations may suffer. It is also possible that the delivery of a demand or threat may stimulate retaliatory action, possibly in a series of counter-threats. If a demand is made in specific terms, the risks of it being defied have also to be considered. The very act of defiance may do damage to the threatening state's reputation. In addition, the problem would remain of facing the costs of carrying out the threat, with whatever consequences that may imply, or having its credibility suffer further damage by simply accepting that its bluff has been called. The risks implicit in the issuance of threats, at least those expressed in specific terms, tends to reduce their diplomatic utility to well-planned psychological campaigns and to situations where they are seen as alternatives to the initiation of the threatened action.

The issuing of a series of demands and threats may signal the adoption of a strategy of confrontation. The objective here normally is to wear down, by a process of diplomatic, political, economic and/or military measures, the willpower of the opponent concerning a particular issue. Because of the relatively open nature of its society, Australia might prove to be vulnerable to this kind of pressure, particularly when the issue at stake is regarded as being of marginal significance by a large proportion of the population. In such circumstances, an opponent may be able to conduct a sustained campaign of subversion to weaken national willpower. It probably would be relatively easy for an external actor to introduce propaganda into the processes of internal debate in such a way that it would be difficult for it to be distinguished from legitimate internal criticism. The problem of discerning hostile propaganda that is externally sourced from legitimate internal debate that is simply exploited by outside powers would be very difficult to solve in the Australian environment.

If the external actor initiating the confrontation campaign wished to apply further pressure through a campaign of organized violence, it would be extremely difficult for any ambiguity or disavowability to be retained. Even if a small portion of the Australian population sympathized with the external actor's cause, it seems improbable, in current circumstances, that they would be prepared, of their own volition, to take up arms and attack their fellow citizens and government employees. As a result, it would be difficult for an external actor to attempt to disguise a rash of sabotage, hi-jacking, bomb attacks and isolated violent assaults as being merely an expression of internal support for its cause or a sign of extreme inner social tension.

Because Australia is an island continent, any external agitators or terrorists would have to be transported by some means across the surrounding water barrier. If air, sea and under-sea surveillance and patrolling of these regions is undertaken in a sufficiently thorough manner and international civil transport is monitored closely, the task of penetration may itself be difficult. However, once this has been achieved, many targets would be presented. On Australia's remote periphery, along the coast and on offshore islands, a large number of relatively isolated small population centres are within easy reach of airborne and/or seaborne attackers. Communications lines, microwave links, telecommunication cables, road bridges, etc. are readily accessible in the more remote parts of the continent and their systematic destruction would be an effective means of applying a large amount of pressure at little risk and cost.

The economic and military implications of this type of violent harassment would be immense. Certainly the normal pattern of life in remote parts of the continent and on offshore islands would have to alter and economic productivity could be expected to decline significantly. An enormously disproportionate Australian military response would be required in order to patrol the coastal and continental expanses that might be involved. In addition, and at the same time as attempts were made to prevent attacks and violent incidents, the installations damaged or destroyed would have to be replaced or supported by additional facilities. The economic drain upon the national economy, even of these very direct response requirements, could be expected to impact heavily upon the national budget. Yet in most circumstances, this would be, in effect, but one of the forms of pressure applied by an external actor in this type of confrontation. The overall design of the campaign most probably would be structured to incur the maximum possible theatrical value from the effort. By a wide variety of means and over an extended period, a large amount of publicity might be gained, the authorities may be discredited, the security forces may be provoked to take excessive counter-measures and large portions of the population may be demoralized and even terrorized. Over a protracted period, when the issue at stake was of marginal significance to the nation as a whole, it might be expected that Australian willpower and resilience could be gradually eroded to a point where major compromises would be politically feasible.

It is possible to conceive of circumstances in an external confrontation situation where, because of a foreign actor's limited success or its impatience with very low-level violent harassment activities, it may decide to escalate the pace and scope of attacks. The character of the operations might continue to be similar to those elaborated above, but they may be expanded in number and scope, they may be better planned and perhaps also be executed in a more professional manner by regular military forces. The depth of penetration of this type of force would probably be significantly greater than that achievable by irregular harassment forces. In addition, the higher standards of training and technical skill that could be expected probably would mean that the new generations of light and compact, but extremely accurate, high firepower weaponry could be made available to enhance greatly the destructive capacity of these small units. The targets for this type of campaign also might be expanded to include not only isolated population centres and their lines of communication but also centres of Australian reactive capacity, airfields, base structures and perhaps portions of Australian industry. In addition to violent raids, pressure also might be exerted by deploying small bodies of troops to demonstate temporary control of relatively remote positions of high political, economic or strategic importance — for example, one of the islands in the Torres Strait, Cocos Island, or perhaps even the joint United States—Australian communications facility at North-west Cape.

It should be noted, however, that if an external actor maintained an intransigent negotiating stance and at the same time escalated the level of conflict, it seems improbable that any Australian government would be content merely to maintain a defensive position. In the international sphere, for instance, it can be anticipated that efforts would be made to mobilize the diplomatic support of allies and others to pressure the opponent to compromise. The United Nations and other international forums almost certainly would be used in attempts to arouse world-wide opposition to the opponent's action. In addition, Australia could move to discriminate against the state concerned in its trading relationships and also might be able to organize broader regional economic, diplomatic and other sanctions. The success of these retaliatory activities cannot be expected to be very great in all circumstances because the opposing state and its international supporters almost certainly would be attempting similar strategies which, depending upon the issue at stake and the relative balance of forces, could more than offset Australia's capacity in this field.

An escalation of violent activities by Australia's opponent also may stimulate an offensive military response. Air or surface raids of various types could be launched in reply, subversive activities could be fostered and dissident groups within the opposing state might be encouraged and actively supported from Australia. Depending upon the nature of the country concerned, these counter-offensive activities may present an even worse disproportionate response problem for the opponent than it is capable of inflicting upon Australia.

There is one other major category of influence that might be employed by external actors to support demands and threats: that of economic pressure. Variations in tariffs, quotas, investment rules and even wholesale embargoes and sanctions might be employed, but as was mentioned earlier in this chapter, unless Australia's opponent happened to be a major trading partner, or alternatively, if Australia's major trading partners supported the opponent's cause, any restrictions of this kind most likely would be marginal and manageable. Even if Australia's opponent were able to coerce some major trading partners to apply sanctions, unless petroleum products were involved, the effects would fall primarily upon non-essential export sectors of the economy. The major implication of this situation would be a reduction in economic prosperity, which would threaten national security only in so far as it reduced Australia's capacity to respond to other pressures.

(b) Economic Warfare against Australia

In a situation where a foreign country or group of countries decided to conduct economic warfare against Australia, tariff and quota regulations, embargoes, sanctions and a range of other weapons would be available. Australia's vulnerability to this type of pressure has already been discussed.

Any attempt to use a military blockade to isolate the Australian economy would offer doubtful potential gains and be extremely difficult to implement in practice. The country's relative self-sufficiency implies that while major disruptions to its trade flows would affect national prosperity seriously, they would not represent, in themselves, an extreme threat to national security. The prospects of an external actor gaining substantial rewards from the imposition of a blockade would appear to be limited.

The physical difficulties that would be experienced by an opponent who attempted to blockade Australia would be considerable. Firstly, because of the country's geographic position, there is a large number of alternative approach routes to Australian ports. In order for an external actor to mount a distant blockade against the country, all of these approach routes would have to be controlled effectively, or at least threatened. In reality, it would be extremely difficult, if not impossible, for any power to undertake such a task at the Cape of Good Hope, Suez, the Strait of Hormuz, the Indonesian Straits, in the Coral Sea and across the expanses of the Pacific and Antarctic Oceans. Even if this level of surveillance were achieved, for it to be effective in the facilitation of a traditional form of blockade, each ship passing through these areas, which are some of the busiest in the world, would have to be boarded so that her manifests could be inspected. However, even if this were done, there would still be major problems — for example, an obvious and immediate counter-measure would be to forge the ship's manifests.

Historically, blockades have mainly been used by major maritime powers or alliances of maritime powers against significant adversaries and in the course of major wars.[9] An attempt to blockade Australia from distant narrows and waterways would be an instance of a power, or group of powers, attempting to isolate a relatively minor state in the course of a limited dispute and in several of the world's most heavily travelled seas. The danger and nuisance to innocent shipping could be expected to evoke resistance from the great powers, particularly if the hindrances persisted over many months.

The difficulties of attempting to blockade Australia from distant transport "choke" points and the almost innumerable alternative approach routes to the country would appear to make the option of blockading from close inshore a relatively attractive proposition. This option, in addition, would possess potential for the disruption of Australian coastal shipping. However, this type of action would necessitate the stationing of large numbers of ships at very long distances from their home bases, to cover the numerous and widely spaced Australian ports. Minefields might be laid directly outside ports or in their entrance channels as part of the campaign, but these would have to be protected, to prevent clearance by helicopters or mine-clearance counter-measure vessels operating from the ports concerned.[10] This close patrolling would almost certainly make effective Australian counteraction a simple proposition. Blockading ships could be attacked directly by land-based artillery and missile units, by short-range attack aircraft and by a variety of light coastal defence vessels.[11]

The problems, difficulties and expense of attempting to impose a total blockade against Australia, either from a distance or from close inshore, would appear likely to more than offset the possible gains in terms of the impact upon the Australian economy. However, it should be noted that in fact there may be alternative, more cost-effective means of applying severe pressure on Australian trade and international transport. For instance, the surveillance problem could be reduced by employing modern technologies, satellites, high-flying long-range remotely piloted vehicles and towed and fixed long-range passive sonar arrays.[12] The scope of the problem also could be narrowed by concentrating attention upon vessels leaving Australian ports. This might mean that attempts would be made to intercept only the small numbers of ships known, with a high degree of certainty, to be involved in trade with Australia. In this type of campaign, the resources required would be relatively limited and its effectiveness would depend more on the deterrent effect created by uncertainty in the minds of ship-owners and neutral actors than on the physical severence of all lines of seaborne communication. This type of campaign also might lend itself to extension in the form of harassment attacks upon aircraft and air transport facilities involved in trade with Australia.

Thus it does appear that in some circumstances short of a major conflict, the volume of Australian trade could be reduced significantly and at limited costs to an opponent by a carefully orchestrated application of economic warfare techniques. However, they almost certainly would not take the form of an attempted water-tight blockade. A more attractive option might bear more resemblance to a well-designed and co-ordinated terrorist or pirate campaign against international transport carriers and facilities.

(c) Assault with a Limited Objective

This type of operation could take the form of an extended raid involving no more than one or two hundred troops or, at the other end of the scale, it could concern a multiple division assault aimed at permanent occupation of a major geographic section of the continent. Such an assault thus could be defined to be limited either in the sense of the scale of the geographic area occupied, the time period of occupation or the magnitude of the assault's underlying political objective.

In one sense, as there is no land barrier for armies to walk or drive across, any assault upon Australia is difficult. Ships and/or aircraft are an essential prerequisite for any assault. The resources currently held by several regional powers would be sufficient, at least in theory, for an assault very limited in scale and/or length.[13] However, no power in Australia's region currently possesses a capacity to deploy division-sized forces on to Australian territory.[14] The acquisition of such a capability presumably would be readily detectable by Australia's intelligence organizations.

Australia offers a wide variety of targets. Those most commonly mentioned in the context of this type of attack include areas of the north and north-west coasts and various offshore islands — for example, the Pilbara, the Northern Territory, Cape York and various islands in the Barrier Reef, Torres Strait, Gulf of Carpentaria, Arafura Sea and the Indian Ocean.[15] However, other conceivable objectives have occasionally been mentioned. For instance, Dr O'Neill has suggested that Tasmania could represent an attractive target for a high-technology major power, perhaps prior to an invasion of the mainland itself.[16]

The scale of any assault could be expected to vary primarily according to the size of the area to be attacked and the length of time it is to be held. Some of the offshore islands probably could be assaulted and then defended by a force of one or two battalions. However, any attempt to attack and hold the Pilbara, the northern half of the Northern Territory or Cape York certainly would be a multiple-division operation.

The achievement of surprise, in many circumstances, would be a prerequisite for the success of such an operation, for if an assault were contested seriously during the initial crossing of the sea/air gap, it might fail completely. Even if the assaulting forces arrived at their objective relatively unscathed, they still would be vulnerable to continuous interdiction of their lines of communication and supply across the water gap. Short of major preliminary attacks upon Australia's reactive capacity, an opponent mounting this type of operation would have no simple means of providing a high level of security to these links.

Once landed on any objective along or adjacent to Australia's northern coastline, an enemy would be confronted with a naturally inhospitable environment. The weather pattern throughout Australia's tropical north is monsoonal. During the summer "wet", cyclones are common and frequently cause extensive damage. Overland travel during this season is extremely difficult and the human efficiency rating falls to very low levels. Because almost all of the annual rainfall is concentrated into a relatively short season, the vegetation cover on nearly all of the western and northern coasts is open woodland. During the dry season, water can become very scarce in some areas and dust clouds tend to betray any vehicle movement.

In the north of the continent, transport resources are rudimentary, except in the immediate Darwin area, the east coast south of Cairns and on a few of the offshore islands. While there are many airstrips, few are sealed and most are not supplied with fuel. Almost all of the major round-Australia highway is sealed with at least one trafficable lane, but with very few exceptions, other roads are simply graded from the natural earth. General-purpose port facilities in a developed form exist only at Townsville and, to a lesser extent, Cairns and Darwin. However, in addition, there are many specialized port facilities serving mining installations. The most notable of these are at Dampier, Karratha, Wickham, Port Hedland, Gove and Weipa.

In general, then, it can be said that if surprise is achieved, at least in timing, it should be possilbe for a small assaulting force to cross the sea/air gap and occupy a localized area. On the assumption that such an assault were made in isolation, it would be vulnerable to rapid air and naval counter-strikes and the disruption and possible severance of its lines of communication. However, if the assaulting force were reasonably self-contained and protected, it might well be able to maintain its position until major Australian land forces were mobilized and deployed for a direct confrontation.

In the case of a much larger assault, the achievement of surprise probably would be far more difficult. But if it could be assumed that surprise could be gained and a relatively secure air and sea crossing of the water gap were possible, an extensive range of objectives would be available for an enemy's consideration. Once landed, the relative paucity of local facilities in most areas would be a major liability and the continued vulnerability of supply and communications lines an ongoing problem. As pointed out above, assuming that Australia's air and maritime strike forces were not destroyed in an initial co-ordinated attack, any foreign landing could be bombarded and harassed at an early stage. But the distances involved and the openness of terrain in much of the northern continent most probably would mean that an assaulting force would not be confronted by major Australian land forces for several weeks at least. This might mean that the invading forces would have sufficient time to methodically prepare extensive ground-defence positions. However, Australian air, sea and small-scale land harassment almost certainly could preclude the full-scale exploitation and export of major on-site resources.

(d) Full-scale Invasion

Similar considerations to those discussed above would apply to any country attempting a full-scale invasion through the north or west of the continent. Achieving surprise in the landing of the massive forces that would be required for this type of operation would be very difficult. Assuming that Australian air and maritime strike forces survived any initial attack, the invading forces would be extremely vulnerable if their initial crossing of the sea/air gap could be intercepted. This would be the stage at which the assaulting forces would be most susceptible to attack, i.e. when they are packaged in a highly concentrated form aboard large and relatively vulnerable ship and aircraft platforms. When landed and relatively dispersed, they almost certainly would be less vulnerable, but still susceptible to aerial bombardment and to the interdiction of their lines of communication and supply.

The difficulties of moving large land forces across the long and, in most places, relatively open expanses of the continent also could be expected to severely inhibit the expansion of invasion bridgeheads in isolated areas. The distances are immense and in most areas the routes available for rapid advance are restricted and predictable. Even without a well-coordinated Australian ground, sea and air harassment of enemy forces, the logistics problems of a major force advance across the continent would be immense.

With these considerations in mind, a very attractive option for a major power high-technology invader might be a direct assault upon the south-eastern coast of Australia. This type of operation would demand the allocation of very substantial ground, naval and naval-air forces. Because such a combined force would need to operate from bases in the archipelago to Australia's north, the north-west Pacific Ocean or the Indian Ocean, its passage to the southern coast of the continent would necessitate long transit routes adjacent to, although probably a substantial distance from, the Australian coast. This might provide Australia's maritime strike forces with an extended opportunity to extract a heavy rate of attrition, should they survive to do so. However, if an invader could successfully thwart such plans, by mounting a preliminary surprise strike against Australia's reactive capacity, this type of direct assault would hold great potential for the conduct of a rapid and decisive campaign.

(e) Australian Involvement in a Global or Regional Nuclear, Biological or Chemical Exchange

The escalation of a super-power conflict into a nuclear exchange, even if it were on a limited restrained level, would present a very high degree of danger for Australia. The presence of several important United States defence facilities on Australian territory could make some parts of the country vulnerable to direct attack at an early stage. The immediate implication is that, in the event of a limited or an unlimited nuclear exchange, the populations of Alice Springs and Exmouth, which are situated close to Pine Gap and North-west Cape respectively, may be subjected to a nuclear assault. Depending upon the nature of the weapons used, the manner in which they are detonated and the pattern of the weather at the time, a much larger proportion of the Australian population might be threatened by the subsequent fallout.

In the event of a general uninhibited global nuclear exchange, as long as further installations on Australian territory were not targeted by the major combatants, the prospects for the survival and continued well-being of the Australian population would appear to be favourable. As in this situation most of the nuclear weapons would be detonated in the northern hemisphere, the world weather pattern would ensure that Australia would be relatively free from fall-out contamination.[17] Other conceivable effects, such as a diminution of the ozone layer in the stratosphere, in time may affect the entire globe, but current research indicates that Australians would certainly be better placed to survive these indirect effects than populations situated in the northern hemisphere.[18] For similar reasons, the effects of chemical and most types of biological warfare attacks that might take place in the northern hemisphere are also likely to be concentrated within that half of the globe.

Finally, it should be noted that because of the country's high level of population and industrial concentration, Australia is extremely vulnerable to any form of nuclear, chemical or biological bombardment on these centres. The identification of various categories of super-power and regional state motivation for this type of attack has been undertaken by various writers. However, it is extremely difficult, if not impossible, to evaluate the potential or probability of these kinds of attack.[19]

The overall conclusion to be drawn from this discussion is that some potential pressures and threats could conceivably be deterred by Australia's independent actions. If Australia can prevent serious pressures and threats arising, this is clearly preferable to reliance upon purely defensive measures. However, many potential pressures and threats are likely to be beyond Australia's capacity to deter. This applies most notably to many of the pressures of international crises and some of the more demanding pressures of international aggression. Australia's capacity to prevent these types of threat arising in the flow of world-wide events, in nearly every conceivable circumstance, would be marginal at best. Hence if Australia is to have a security option in these types of situations, the limited coverage of ANZUS means that it has little choice but to develop an independent capacity to respond to a wide spectrum of pressures and threats.

This broadened defensive requirement must be evaluated in the context of the limited resources Australia can afford to devote on a full-time basis to national security tasks in times of peace. A significant multiplication of the current full-time military and diplomatic resources maintained by Australia is not politically feasible in the absence of a clear and obvious major threat, but even if this type of force expansion were possible, it is doubtful that it would be an effective means of meeting many of the types of pressure and threat with which Australia may be confronted in the future. A large number of the pressures and threats that have been identified in the discussion above are primarily economic, political, social and psychological in character. Their effect upon Australia would not necessarily heavily involve the military and diplomatic sections of the community. Many pressures and threats would impact far more directly upon much broader sectors of the total community, rural and secondary industry, and, in the case of the more demanding pressures and threats, the total community may be directly threatened, if not with destruction, by a substantial reduction in living standards.

The increasing complexity of modern societies, such as that in Australia, serves to increase their vulnerability to serious disruption should normal peacetime international interactions be disturbed. New possibilities are being provided for international actors to pressure and threaten advanced countries through the exploitation of these susceptibilities. Certainly the dangers from military pressure and threat are still present and in some areas may be increasing, but in order to have a capability to deter effectively and, if required, meet the full range of potential pressures and threats, it may be necessary to extend national security preparations beyond the long-institutionalized military and diplomatic spheres to involve much larger sections of Australian society.

Notes and References

1. While it is very difficult to manage the enormous number of potential pressures and threats, it is argued at some length in Chapter 7 and Appendix C that means are available to largely resolve the problem for the purposes of planning Australian security.
2. Dr Robert O'Neill, "Changes Required in the International Environment for the Development of Extreme Threats to Australia" (paper prepared for seminar entitled "The Potential for Extreme Threats in the International Environment and Australia's Response Options", held by Strategic and Defence Studies Centre, Australian National University, Canberra, 3-4 March 1977), pp. 5-7.
3. International actors may be defined to include nation states, interstate organizations, multinational corporations and sub-national groups such as terrorist organizations. However, during the course of this discussion, references primarily refer to nation states.
4. Probably the most notable examples of this influence in recent years have been the quotas on beef imports into the United States and Japan, and the much broader restrictions on a wide range of primary products being imported into the Europen Economic Community.
5. Australia's dependence on imports is at present limited to a relatively small, although increasing number of commodity areas. At present, the list primarily comprises liquid fuels and lubricants, an array of chemical materials, some pharmaceutical products and a wide variety of medium- and high-technology manufactured goods: machine tools, transport equipment, motor vehicle components, etc. The table reproduced below provides an indication of the quantities involved.

Australian imports of merchandise, by economic class, 1970-71 to 1972-73.

Purpose	Value ($'000 f.o.b.)			Proportion of value of imports of merchandise (%)		
	1970-71	1971-72	1972-73	1970-71	1971-72	1972-73
Producers' materials for use in:						
Building and construction	146 947	135 533	167 084	3.6	3.4	4.1
Rural industries	45 383	40 768	47 880	1.1	1.0	1.2
Manufacturing:						
Motor vehicle assembly[a]	288 100	256 379	228 760	7.0	6.5	5.6
Other[b]	1 297 846	1 257 555	1 269 279	31.7	31.8	31.2
Total producers' materials[b]	1 778 276	1 690 234	1 713 002	43.4	42.7	42.1
Capital equipment[c]:						
Producers' equipment	981 930	915 335	855 892	24.0	23.2	21.0
Transport equipment						
Complete road vehicles and assembled chassis	155 285	159 533	193 853	3.8	4.0	4.8
Railway equipment, vessels and civil aircraft	137 780	90 072	69 382	3.3	2.3	1.7

Food, beverages and tobacco	157 234	165 121	171 073	3.8	4.2	4.2
Clothing and accessories	57 108	76 438	88 180	1.4	1.9	2.2
All other[d]	580 210	628 298	736 561	14.2	15.9	18.1
Total, finished consumer goods[d]	794 552	869 857	995 814	19.4	22.0	24.5
Fuels and lubricants[e]	61 495	69 406	68 933	1.5	1.8	1.7
Auxiliary aids to production[f]	99 823	100 515	93 505	2.4	2.5	2.3
Munitions and war stores	89 419	59 824	81 530	2.2	1.4	2.0
Grand total	4 098 560	3 954 775	4 071 911	100.0	100.0	100.0

Notes: [a] Owing to insufficient information, it is not possible to treat unassembled tractors and other machinery in a similar manner to motor vehicles, and all such machinery and replacement parts therefor are treated as capital equipment whether imported in an assembled or unassembled condition. [b] Excludes a percentage for piece-goods to be sold at retail and paper to be used solely for wrapping, which are recorded in Finished consumer goods, All other; and Auxiliary aids to production respectively. [c] See footnote a. [d] Includes a percentage for piece-goods to be sold at retail; see footnote a. [e] Excludes petroleum, which is included in Producers' materials. Manufacturing Other. [f] Includes a percentage for paper to be used solely for wrapping; see footnote b. [g] The class fuels and lubricants consist of goods "Simply transformed", and the classes Capital equipment and Munitions and war stores entirely of goods "more elaborately transformed". The class Auxiliary aids to production is about equally divided between goods "simply transformed" and "elaborately transformed".

Source: *Official Yearbook of Australia 1974*, p. 322. A much more detailed classification of Australian imports appears on p. 319 of the same publication.

6. In recent years, many areas of Australian secondary industry have declined in the face of greatly increased competition from imported products originating principally from newly industrialized Asian countries. This phenomenon is discussed at length in the report to the Prime Minister by the Committee to Advise on Policies for Manufacturing Industry, *Policies for Development of Manufacturing Industry*. (Jackson Committee Report), Green Paper (Canberra: Australian Government Publishing Service, 1975), vol. 1.
7. Most notably, the petroleum, motor vehicle, chemical, pharmaceutical and cosmetic industries.
8. This is a consistent theme in national opinion polls conducted in Australia on defence and security questions. For example, in the *Australian Public Opinion Newsletter* I, no. 1 (September 1971): 20, the question was asked, "What is the *one thing* you fear most in Australia's development over the next ten years?" The second most popular response (after economic instability), on the very long list of answers, was "war and invasion".

   On page 23 of that same survey, the question was asked, "Do you think that Australia will be threatened from outside its borders in the next fifteen years?" 45 per cent of the respondents answered no; 42 per cent answered yes; and 13 per cent were unsure.

   In the Sydney *Bulletin* (8 January 1977): 41, an International Gallup Poll table was published that showed that among the populations of thirteen comparable countries, Australians gave the second most pessimistic response to a question that asked whether they expected 1977 to be a peaceful or troubled year. The most pessimistic response came from Spain, which at least partially might be explained by disturbances that accompanied domestic political changes at that time.
9. For a background analysis of this subject in a different geographical context, see S.J. Rosen, "Military Geography and Military Balance in the Arab-Israel Conflict" (seminar paper presented at Strategic and Defence Studies Centre, Australian National University, Canberra, 22 April 1976).
10. This argument assumes that these mine clearance forces are available in the Australian Defence Force.
11. This argument assumes that coastal attack forces are available.
12. These surveillance systems are discussed in greater length in Chapter 2 and Appendix B.
13. For details of the air and sea transport capacities of regional states, see *The Military Balance 1976-1977* (London: International Institute for Strategic Studies, 1976), pp. 53 ff.
14. It should be noted that several regional states possess multi-divisional armies, but none possesses the air and/or naval capacity to readily transport and support their deployment on to the Australian continent. See ibid. For a discussion of the numbers of ships and aircraft that have been required to transport major military forces across sea/air gaps during recent history, see R. Babbage, "A Strategy for the Continental Defence of Australia" (unpublished M.Ec. thesis, University of Sydney, 1974), pp. 22-23.
15. See discussion on these geographical targets by Colonel J.O. Langtry, "Ground Defence of the Australian Continent", and Robert O'Neill, "Australia As a Target for International Violence", *United Service* 28, no. 2 (October 1974): 55, 12.
16. See O'Neill, "Australia As a Target for International Violence", p. 12.
17. See L. Machta and R.J. List, "The Global Pattern of Fallout", in *Fallout: A Study of Superbombs, Strontium 90 and Survival*, ed. J.M. Fowler (New York: Basic Books, 1960), pp. 26-35.

18. For details, see Committee to Study the Long-term World-wide Effects of Multiple Nuclear Weapons Detonations, *Long-term World-wide Effects of Multiple Nuclear Weapons Detonations* (Washington, DC: National Academy of Science, 1975), p. 44.
19. Possible motivations for nuclear bombardment are discussed in Desmond Ball, "American Bases in Australia: The Strategic Implications", *Current Affairs Bulletin* 51, no. 10 (March 1975): 16-17.

4
The Identification of Our Major Weaknesses

It is clear from the previous chapter that in the future, the range of security problems that might conceivably require a response from Australia will be much broader, and in many respects more demanding, than that of the forward defence era. Many potential pressures and threats might be met most properly and effectively through the employment of resources and capacities that have not normally been engaged in the past for national security functions. Moreover, even in those instances where the more traditional types of military and diplomatic responses would be appropriate, the nature of the new requirements in terms of scale, timing and type is likely to impose demands of quite a new character.

Yet despite the greatly altered nature of Australia's strategic environment, the security concepts and structures currently employed are primarily those that have been inherited from the forward defence era.[1] Thus it is perhaps not surprising that, in the context of the new environment, they are characterized by a series of fundamental weaknesses and contradictions. In the discussion that follows, those established security concepts and structures that appear to be most directly challenged by the new requirements of Australia's changed strategic situation are discussed in turn.

1. Inadequate Strategic Guidance

Because of the nature of Australia's historical experience, it has never been necessary for the nation's security planners to construct a completely independent strategic policy, concept and structure. Almost all of Australia's military history involves single service operations, with comparable allied units in foreign environments. Thus in the past, Australia has been heavily dependent upon allies for commitment decisions, operating doctrines, tactics, many types of procedures, equipments and logistic support services. Consequently, there never has been a need to independently develop, test and modify a complex national security strategy and structure to meet the specialized requirements of defending the Australian continent and its vital interests. However, now, with a wide range of environmental factors changing the fundamental nature of Australia's security problem, there is a clear requirement for the nation's security policy, strategy and structures to be constructed independently from first principles.

The general nature of Australia's changed strategic environment has been recognized by both the present government and the opposition. However, the strategic assessment and planning system inherited from the forward defence era appears to be incapable of the level of adaption that the new environment requires. The underlying problem appears not to be one of personal failings or intellectual weakness on the part of those government employees involved in this area of policy development: rather, the most serious planning difficulties have arisen as a result of the retention of the established system and structure to perform functions of a much more complex and demanding nature than those for which they were originally designed and intended.

The basic foundation for all current security planning is a document entitled *The Strategic Basis for Australian Defence.* As an official explanatory paper expresses it, "the genesis of all significant defence decisions is the Strategic Basis".[2] A former Defence Minister, W. L. Morrison, elaborated the significance of the document in the following terms:

> Within the Department, the Strategic Basis paper is used as a reference document in the preparation of the Force Capabilities paper which informs policy proposals on force levels and weapons procurement.[3]

However, there appears to be a general recognition both inside and outside the Defence Department that the Strategic Basis paper is an imperfect means of performing this task. For instance, Admiral Sir Anthony Synnot, the Chief of the Defence Force Staff, has stated that in his opinion:

> At a time of low or intermediate threat, strategic guidance [in the form of the Strategic Basis] cannot be expected to be sufficiently specific to enable us to determine the force structure; if there were a clear threat this problem would of course be much easier.[4]

Mr Morrison appears to support this view:

> The Strategic Basis paper read in the light of the Government's response forms the parameters of defence policy. What it really amounts to is an informed account of the current situation and a useful perception of future trends. It is not an immutable major premise from which to deduce all manner of policies.[5]

Certainly a great deal can be learnt from the type of systematic analysis of foreign actors' economic, social, political, technological and military capacities contained in the Strategic Basis paper. Studies such as these can be used to extrapolate present trends into the future, but in the absence of knowledge concerning the long-term intentions of foreign actors, the further one attempts to predict events, or even the development of trends, the less credible the process becomes. No matter how skilled the analysts may be, and no matter how many analysts may be available for the task, this type of predictive study is incapable of providing, on its own, a sufficient basis for coherent long-term security planning in the Australian environment.

Many of the weaknesses of the Strategic Basis document are a direct consequence of the processes of its formulation.

> The draft [of the Strategic Basis] is prepared in the Strategic and Force Development Organization drawing on the information and judgments of the Department of Foreign Affairs, the assessments of the Joint Intelligence Organization which in turn drawns on US and UK intelligence sources, the military judgement of the CDFS [Chief of the Defence Force Staff] and the Chiefs of Staff and the technological advice of its defence scientists. The draft is considered and finalized by the Defence Coordination Committee, comprising apart from the Defence component, the Secretaries of the Departments of Prime Minister and Cabinet, Foreign Affairs and Treasury. The Strategic Basis is certainly derived from the best advice available and assessed by experienced people. It represents the best judgement that can be made at the time. But by its nature it is a committee document and has all the failings of such a document, particularly as it represents a consensus and necessarily involves compromises. Furthermore it deals with perceptions of future trends and is subject to the uncertainties, unknowns and variables of prognostication.[6]

As a consequence, it appears from the accounts of experienced obervers that the final document lacks the precision and clarity required for detailed security planning.[7] According to Dr F. A. Mediansky:

> A common complaint about the present Strategic Basis is that it is too vague and too generalised; that it is written so as to mean all things to all men. As such, it is of little use to defence planners.[8]

In support of this view, Dr Robert O'Neill has written:

> The Strategic Basis document is one obvious source of general guidance but, in the light of what has appeared recently in some newspapers purporting to be extracts from earlier versions of this document, one hopes that more precise guide-lines have been generated and disseminated in some other form.[9]

The consequences of this apparent absence of clarity, coherence and direction in the basic foundations of defence planning are far-reaching and of very great significance. The shortcomings of the Strategic Basis documents produced in recent years impact directly upon the quality and integrated nature of nearly every important aspect of Australia's processes of strategic analysis — security planning, the generation of operational requirements and procurement options, judgements concerning the security significance of civil industries and other components of the national infrastructure, the options considered in the processes of manpower planning, the development of doctrines, tactics, operational procedures, etc.

The fundamental weakness and inappropriate nature of the existing system can best be illustrated by citing the accounts of a number of experienced observers concerning specific system failures. For example, in discussing the reasons for the apparent lack of clear procurement priorities, Dr O'Neill has stated:

> If there currently existed clear policy guidelines, setting forth priorities in the light of threat assessments and required response strategies, one could be optimistic.
>
> However to the best of our knowledge such clear guidelines do not exist as a formal policy.
>
> No doubt they exist in different forms in the minds of different individuals at senior levels within the Department of Defence but much remains to be done.[10]

Dr Desmond J. Ball has cited an instance where the weakness of the current security-planning system has seriously inhibited long-term decision-making in Australia's defence-related industries:

> In 1974, for example, during the Industries Assistance Commission's inquiry into the Australian aerospace industry, a number of the principal aircraft manufacturers, whose forward planning depends upon a clear statement of such a policy, in their submissions frequently lamented "the lack of any real policy guidelines...from the Government" regarding defence procurement. The IAC report itself states that the Department of Defence was unable to provide any specific list of Australian defence equipment requirements. And a study by a Defence (Industrial) Committee Panel which provided much of the detailed background material for that IAC inquiry noted that the panel had sought guidance on the relevant strategic considerations, but that "authoritative guidance could not be given by the Department of Defence".[11]

T. P. Muggleton points out that the absence of clear strategic guidance also has had the effect of undermining seriously the Defence Department's own analytical research:

The consequences of such a vacuum on the economic efficiency of subsequent analyses of a force structure are marked. First, analytical groups develop their own operational scenarios which may, or may not represent the most likely future threat environments. The validity of subsequent analyses rests therefore on dubious premises. The Naval Air Power and Tactical Air Weapon System study, completed in mid-1975, provides an example of the possible adverse effects of inadequate guidance. The NAP/TAWS study was relevant only as long as the seven scenarios on which it was based were relevant. These scenarios however were not created by the higher defence machinery but by CSE [the Central Studies Establishment] itself. The scenarios are in fact no longer legitimate reflections of the most probable future states of the world. Thus just fourteen months after its completion, " . . . the general feeling in the Defence Department is that the NAP/TAWS study is now invalid". As the NAP/TAWS study incorporated the equivalent of fifty man-years of analysis, a lack of guidance leads to a wastage of analytical resources on projects of doubtful relevance and to a misallocation of resources.[12]

The inappropriate nature and basic weakness of the present system can be elaborated further by examining the manner in which the Strategic Basis document is used within the Department of Defence. According to official explanatory papers:

> The Force Development and Analysis Division of the DoD derives from the Strategic Basis, the Defence (as opposed to Service) Capabilities Guidelines Paper which is issued to the Services for assessment. From this paper the Services prepare their individual Service Capabilities Papers which "indicate areas in which the present capabilities are least consistent with guidance". The individual Capabilities Papers are synthesized by Defence Central into a single Defence Capabilities Paper. It is by this process of articulating endorsed guidelines that Defence Central directs and integrates Service planning efforts.[13]

Although this statement clearly describes the formal structural processes, because the Strategic Basis documents have proved to be generally unsatisfactory for defence planning purposes, the manner in which they are actually employed appears to be quite different. As Muggleton points out, in practice:

> Services develop their own long term force structure philosophies. The Army, for example, has produced a "Basis for Army Development" paper which is a perspective document aspiring to a twenty-year validity. It is at present only in a draft form but its existence is indicative of the Services belief that a strategic guidance vacuum does exist in areas in which it should not. Whereas the Services in theory should justify any bid for a weapons system in terms of the Strategic Basis, because the Strategic Basis is too general a document, . . . the Services in practice

develop their own conceptions of what the force posture should be. The Services disjointed programmes are then submitted to higher defence committees. Defence Central has therefore accepted the limited role of arbiter...[14]

Some of the more obvious difficulties arising from this situation have been raised by Dr K. J. Foley:

> But although those [strategic] assessments explicitly recognized change, they have been so scant, general and qualified that, for reasons different from those prevailing in the past, the planner has remained without a basis for rational selection of roles, missions and weaponry. In those situations the Defence Department, Army, Navy and Air Force have been in a position of virtually "writing their own scenarios".[15]

In these circumstances, it is perhaps not surprising that Muggleton can quote middle-ranking Service officers as saying that the Strategic Basis is "not a professional military document", is "irrelevant for force-structure decision-making" and that "the Strategic Basis can be used to justify the procurement of any weapon system".[16]

It appears that, on the evidence of many of those who are active participants in the system, as well as on that of a number of experienced external observers, clear strategic concepts, planning objectives and guidelines have not been derived. One of the most important consequences of this structural failure has been that the performance of the current security system and of possible future alternatives cannot be tested and evaluated. As Muggleton points out:

> The ultimate measure of defence expenditure utility is how well it achieves strategic objectives, however, given little operationally meaningful articulation of strategic objectives utility has no basis for measurement.[17]

Dr Foley supports this view: "Without explicit objectives... no management group can have meaningful evaluative criteria or performance indicators."[18]

Thus primarily because "Australia's basic national security policy is too vacuous and inchoate",[19] realistic input-output analysis is impossible. Morrison elaborates this point further:

> The purpose of program and performance budgeting is not simply what forces cost, but also what they do — to measure outputs as well as inputs. To do this effectively there must be program categories which are largely mission-oriented and whose purposes are defined. This is not an easy task, which to a large extent explains why it has not been attempted. It involves a much clearer concept of roles and missions and will cut across individual Services. Maritime surveillance could be a pro-

gram involving as it does both Naval and Air Force inputs. The output is not merely measured in terms of nautical miles steamed or flying hours achieved but in results such as the apprehension of vessels illegally fishing, interception of smugglers or the role that the program plays in inhibiting such activities. By teasing the data, judgements could be made as to the desirable mix of air and surface operations. This type of analysis has not, as the Tange Report reveals, been carried out.[20]

From this discussion, it appears to be clear in the minds of several of those who have been directly involved and who have studied the present system closely that it has not only failed to conduct any meaningful input-output analysis but it also has proved to be incapable of deriving any clear strategic concept, preferred national security structure or long-term planning criteria.

Morrison once described his view of a departmental manager as one who "muddles through purposefully".[21] In the view of many critics, the present system is one that encourages muddling through, with the purpose and direction varying from time to time according to the relative power and influence of the bureaucratic actors involved with the issue at stake.[22] To many external observers and to at least some participants, the system appears to be distinguished by a long succession of loosely structured *ad hoc* decisions, which almost always involve a perpetuation or supplementation of existing processes, structures and programmes. Dr Foley and others have claimed that this essential characteristic of the system is clearly evident from the Defence Department's public documents:

> The recent White Paper (Australian Defence), in spite of its pathbreaking character and substantial stimulus to public debate, does little to allay the concern of those who argue that planning for Australia's defence lacks coherence and as a result more closely approximates a model of disjointed incrementalism than one of rationality.[23]

It is notable that Muggleton summarizes his extensive work by emphasizing this same characteristic:

> The principal conclusion is that although rejecting in theory a strongly pragmatic approach to decision-making the DoD has, in practice, adopted a permutation of the pragmatic approach, namely, disjointed incrementalism ... individual weapon systems are evaluated not in terms of how they contribute to the preferred force structure, as no such force structure exists, but simply as additions or alterations to the existing force structure.[24]

He continues by quoting Derek Woolner:[25]

> "our planning processes are biting around the edges". The NAP/TAWS study, for example, limited the scope of its analysis to a consideration of only those option elements that were possible "future additions to the

current force structure". Analysis in Australia is not being utilized to determine a preferred force structure ... Analysis in the Australian DoD is in fact a constraint on rational decision-making as it has been used extensively within a framework consistent with a disjointed incremental planning philosophy.[26]

It would appear from this discussion that the security analysis and planning system inherited from the forward defence era is unsuited to, and possibly incapable of the task of developing and testing an independent security structure appropriate for Australia's new strategic environment. However, although the requirement for major change is appreciated widely, it is not recognized universally. The last major reassessment of the system's efficiency was conducted in 1973, by the then Secretary of the Department of Defence, Sir Arthur Tange. In his discussion of the current system, he failed to mention the existence of any serious problem:

> In the reorganization it is important to preserve and preferably improve the processes by which the strategic assessments are made for the Government. There appears to be no need to change the basic machinery.[27]

As a primary consequence of Australia's changed strategic environment, it would appear that the judgements of 1973 now deserve thorough re-examination.

Australia requires a coherent and integrated system of strategic analysis, assessment and both long- and short-range planning. The detailed complexities and practical difficulties of developing such a system are discussed at some length in Chapter 7 and Appendices C and D. However, it is important to note at this stage that the primary function of such a system would be to evolve strategies, structures, technologies, tactics, doctrines and operating procedures to employ the limited resources that can be allocated consistently to the national security task in the most efficent manner possible.

The basic foundation for this type of extremely complex and demanding process of security planning would need to be a clear expression of strategic goals or objectives. In practical circumstances, these necessarily would be determined, or at least agreed to, by the government of the day.[28] However, in order to simplify the discussion in following chapters, it is desirable that a series of primary goals for national security doctrine be tentatively defined at this point.

1. To prevent the development of pressures and threats.
2. To deter pressures and threats.[29]
3. To attempt to defer those pressures and threats that are not easily deterred.

4. To provide a national capacity to withstand non-deterrable pressures of peace and pressures of international crises in such a manner that their impact upon the total society is minimized.
5. To provide a capacity to defeat regional power attacks at short notice.
6. To deprive a great power of the potential for rapid victory.
7. To assist other government agencies in the apprehension of persons or vehicles infringing Australian territorial rights in a manner that does not constitute an attack.[30]

The determination of a firm series of doctrinal goals for the national security structure would provide a basic foundation for strategy formulation and evolution. From this beginning, it should be possible to evolve a planning process within which alternative strategies and force structures could be tested, modified and retested, with effectiveness being judged according to the degree of goal achievement. Eventually, the characteristics of an optimizing strategic concept and force structure might be determined. This, in turn, would make it possible to derive clear priorities in operational tasks and provide a rational basis for the allocation of total national security resources. Alternative means of technical task performance then could be evaluated. Manpower, equipment, technology and other choices could be made so as to optimize not only individual task performance but also the efficiency of the total national security structure.

Many of these processes of conceptual testing and experimentation could be expected to be on-going. Not all questions would be amenable to rapid or simple solutions. In the military sphere, new technologies, equipment, tactics, procedures and structures would require testing, modification and retesting in the search for optimal solutions.[31]

These processes of system re-evaluation, strategy and concept reassessment and thorough restructuring would be extremely complex and demanding. Dr O'Neill described the personal qualities of those required for this type of task when discussing the means by which adaptation must be made to new technology developments:

> This process of experiment should be carried out in a rigorous and daring manner, by people who have a burning desire to master the challenges of the new technologies, who are fruitful in their own ideas and whose imagination can lift them out of the groove of their past experience without forgetting what that experience has taught them along the way. Otherwise we might as well not bother. Feeble or timid experimentation is unlikely to bring in any knowledge that we do not already have.[32]

Similar personal characteristics are likely to be required at all levels of the structural reassessment, strategy formulation and evaluation process. If this task were to be performed in a half-hearted fashion, or perhaps not undertaken at all, it would be likely that the security assessment and planning structure inherited from the forward defence era would be retained with only minor alterations, to meet the requirements of Australia's new strategic environment. This would imply a willingness to permit the suitability of the country's national security system for the requirements of the 1980s and 1990s to be left more to chance than design.

2. An Inadequate Mobilization Capacity

Australia's current "core force" rationale, depending heavily upon small numbers of regular service personnel, made considerable sense when Australia's forces were designed primarily for deployment in support of major ally commitments overseas.[33] In that situation, although the expanded forces were frequently required urgently, the direct physical security of Australia was never heavily dependent upon the speed and efficiency of core force expansion. The Australian government was always in control of the timing in the expansion process. It largely determined the rate at which force expansion was attempted and decided exactly when Australian units would be deployed to the war zone. In peacetime, there thus has never been an overriding incentive to adopt unusual measures to optimize force expansion (surge) capacity. But now, with the Australian government needing to accept prime responsibility for the defence of the continent and its territories, there may be little choice as to whether and when Australia's armed forces are committed to undertake defensive operations. Far more than in the past, that basic decision-making prerogative will be dependent upon the opponent's activities. Thus if, in the future, Australia is vulnerable to a certain type of attack with little warning, the Defence Force will have to be designed to react effectively within the same time-span. In such situations, a rapid force expansion capacity is likely to be crucial.

However, it is extremely doubtful whether the present core force structure has the capacity to expand fast enough to meet effectively the types of threats Australia may face in the future. If one were to attempt to justify the retention of the present core force structure to meet the demands of the new environment, a range of highly questionable assumptions would need to be accepted. For example, in the area of army manpower, it would be necessary to accept that for *any* scenario requiring the response of an Australian army larger than 150 000 men, between 2½ to 5 years would need to be available from the time of the mobilization order to the commencement of hostilities (i.e. defence preparation time would be 2½-5 years). Similarly, it would need to be assumed that for any scenario requiring the response of an Australian army larger than 250 000 men, between 4 and 8 years' defence preparation time would be available.[34] It is important to realize that this defence preparation time would only *begin* when the government perceived the existence of a specific threat *and* ordered the full-scale mobilization of Australia's resources in response. Several important evaluative decision-making processes would have to be completed before any government could take such extreme action.

Firstly, political, diplomatic and perhaps military pre-warning signals would have to be received by the country's intelligence services, but actually perceiving such signals as pre-warning indicators may be very difficult against the background of a confused international environment, especially if, as must be assumed, the potential enemy attempts to disguise or conceal its real intentions. The meaning of the pre-warning signals, even if they are correctly identified and perceived, is almost always open to alternative explanations. The consistently accurate interpretation of these signals to deduce the goals and intentions of other countries at the pre-warning stage is extremely difficult, if not impossible.[35] However, if we assume here that the Australian intelligence services do perceive the pre-warning signals and accurately interpret them, they would need to be convinced and united on the matter for it to be taken to the Cabinet. But again, assuming the most favourable outcome, Cabinet then would have the choice of deciding whether to wait and study the matter further or, alternatively, of making a decision to institute some type of preliminary or precautionary military response. Even if the latter course were decided upon, a wide range of possibilities would be open, such as the ordering of greater numbers of long lead-time equipment items, the strengthening of domestic defence industries or ordering the partial expansion of the manpower strength of the armed forces, to name just a few. It is implicit in the expansion theory concerning the present core force that not only all of the early pre-warning decisions are made in a positive manner by all of the parties concerned, but that when the matter is actually taken to Cabinet, a decision is made to order a *full national mobilization* to meet the threat as it is then perceived. Defence preparation time can only *begin* at the successful conclusion of this long and complicated chain of decisions. The length of time that lapses between the initial perception of pre-warning signals by members of the intelligence community and the Cabinet decision to mobilize may well be weeks, months or perhaps even years. And yet, even when a decision to mobilize is taken, it must currently be assumed that no threat requiring an army response greater than 150 000 men could arise within 2½ to 5 years and that no threat requiring an army response greater than 250 000 men could arise within 4 to 8 years.

What type of threat would require the response of an Australian army of these dimensions? Certainly an army of 150 000 men would not be required to meet normal peacetime surveillance, maintenance of sovereignty, civil-aid and rescue tasks, nor would it be required to meet and defeat isolated low-level terrorist attacks. But if a well-organized campaign of widespread terrorist attacks against scattered and remote installations and population centres were organized by a subnational organization, with or without the direct support of a foreign government or a small section of the Australian population, the present Australian Army could find itself overstretched. When it comes to a foreign national organization or a foreign government conducting an intensive campaign of small-scale raids on a continuing basis throughout large parts of the continent and against offshore territories and coastal shipping, an army of at least 150 000 and possibly 250 000 might well be required.[36] If the raids were intensified further and were conducted by battalion-sized units, the response requirement would probably heavily press a 250 000-man army.[37] Certainly if an attacking state undertook a limited land-grab or lodgement operation with multiple brigade or division-sized forces co-ordinated with widespread raids, a response capacity of over 250 000 is likely to be required. If multiple lodgement or larger, more numerous sustained enemy operations of various types were considered, it can be assumed that the manpower requirements of an effective Australian response are likely to be even greater.[38]

But can it be assumed realistically that *none* of these terrorist, raid, confrontation or lodgement threat possibilities could arise and physically confront Australia less than 2½ to 8 years from the government's decision to mobilize to meet such a threat? In other words, can it be taken for granted that Australia's intelligence organizations will receive preliminary warning signals; that these will be interpreted correctly; that the Cabinet will be alerted; that Cabinet will then decide to order general mobilization; and that, even at that stage, there will still be 2½ to 8 years' time to prepare a response before an enemy could attack?

If an analysis is made of the major conflicts that have occurred during and since the Second World War, the precise length of perceived governmental warning time and defence preparation time is, in many instances, difficult to determine exactly. However, it can be concluded that in *only one instance* brought to the author's attention has defence preparation time exceeded seventeen months.[39] In most instances, it was well under twelve months, and in many instances it was under three. Is there any reason to expect that in the future Australian defence planners can anticipate effective defence preparation time of an order of magnitude five to twenty-five times greater than that available to others in the recent past?[40] There have been those who have argued that Australia's remoteness from the major world centres of power would serve to insulate it, to some degree, from strategic surprise.[41] They tend to argue that, for a nation to attack over such long distances, extensive preparations would be required, which could be detected many years in advance. This would depend very much upon the characteristics of the country concerned and the nature of the attack intended. For example, it would certainly take considerable time for a close regional neighbour to develop the armed forces, transport and logistics capacities that would be required to mount a conventional multiple-division over-the-beach assault against continental Australia. Sections of that country's domestic economy would need to be mobilized and extensive foreign assistance would be required. All of these preparations would be readily detectable by Australia's intelligence services. However, it must not be assumed that the detection of a neighbour's developing capabilities would imply a rapid and automatic Australian mobilization in response. The regional state's long-term intentions may be far from clear. If, in reality, they are detrimental to Australia's interests, they are almost certain to be concealed in an elaborate disguise. In order to decoy Australia, a dispute might be fostered with a relatively minor regional power. Alternatively, newly raised and equipped forces may be exercised in quashing a series of artificially stimulated internal revolts. Diplomatic assurances of all types might be freely available. In this sort of environment, despite the development of a clearly superior regional military power, the reactive response of Australian politicians may be very limited. It is quite conceivable that full-scale Australian mobilization would be ordered only when the regional state's intentions were unambiguously identified. It is difficult to judge at what stage before the mounting of an assault a potential enemy's intentions would be sufficiently clear to justify a mobilization order.[42] However, it is an implicit assumption of the current Australian national security structure that from the time that full mobilization is ordered, between 2½ to 8 years still would be available before a regional opponent could attack. The validity of this type of institutionalized presumption ought to be the subject of considerable scepticism.

In discussing this subject, there are a number of related matters that should not be taken for granted. For instance, it ought not to be assumed that in order for Australia to require the response of a 150 000- or 250 000-man army, it would be necessary for an opponent to transport forces of a comparable size on to Australian territory. On the contrary, in the circumstances of a regional dispute stimulating armed confrontation, Australia may need to deploy forces of this size in order to meet satisfactorily the threat posed by forces that number less than 20 per cent of their own strength.[43] The length of time that would be required by the regional state concerned to prepare to mount an extensive confrontation campaign of raids and possibly local bombardment and mining operations against isolated Australian installations and population centres might be a matter of days, weeks, or at the most, a few months. The degree of warning and, more importantly, the length of active defence preparation time that Australia might recieve in these circumstances conceivably could be limited to a few days. In this type of situation, Australia obviously could not afford to wait 2½ to 8 years for appropriate response forces to become available. Either significant concessions or losses of sovereignty would have to be accepted or, alternatively, major escalations in the scale of conflict would have to be made.[44] Both options would be inimical to Australia's short- and long-term national security interests.

The warning times likely to be received prior to the onset of many types of threats are also being affected heavily by new developments in technology. As was discussed in Chapter 2 and is elaborated in Appendix B, there is a major trend developing in weaponry and transport technologies towards the effective reduction of the significance of distance as a constraint upon the rapid application of force. The proliferation of jumbo aircraft, remotely piloted vehicles and long-range precision-guided munitions is having the effect of cutting deployment times for powerful units of military capability over long distances in a dramatic fashion. Hence the capability of major powers to project rapidly different types of force in a precise fashion over long ranges is being transformed. At the same time, their capacity to supply this potential to client states at short notice is also increasing markedly. In this highly dynamic strategic environment, Australia's retention of the national security response concepts of a previous era is difficult to justify.

If Australia is to maximize its capacity to deter and defer the development of threats and, at the same time, optimize its capacity to meet a wide range of potential security problems, it needs to develop a surge capacity that can produce satisfactory force levels within the minimum warning times for particular threats. This is not an argument for the simple multiplication of the current regular manpower force structure. Such a proposal would be politically and economically unrealistic. However, there are several alternative means of expanding surge capacity.[45] The changed nature of Australia's strategic environment serves to increase greatly the desirability of seriously considering their adoption.

3. An Over-dependence on Allied Intelligence

Australia's national security interests will not always coincide with those of its great power allies. Hence reliance upon foreign intelligence services for significant components of the country's priority requirements is highly undesirable. Institutionalized dependence upon foreign sources of intelligence may render Australia vulnerable to a large number of potentially damaging influences. To illustrate the point, there is considerable scope in this type of relationship for the dispensing country to regulate or modify the flow of information in its own interests. Disinformation might be supplied either unintentionally or otherwise. It must be anticipated that in addition to flows of valuable objective information, foreign countries will channel their own value judgements, interests, philosophies and concepts into senior levels of the national security structure. Over an extended period of time, this influence could have a significant impact upon the attitudes and reactions of Australia's national security decision-makers. Further, in some types of situations, foreign sources of information could be suspended arbitrarily or made the subject of bargaining pressures that would not be in Australia's interests.

The policy implications of these misgivings were expressed clearly in Justice Hope's Third Report of the Royal Commission on Intelligence and Security:

> Australia's intelligence interests do not and cannot coincide with those of any other country. Therefore, although we can and should benefit from exchanges of information and views with friends and allies we need our own intelligence collection and assessment capabilities. We also need constantly to re-assess the benefits to Australia from intelligence relationships with other countries against the costs.[46]

From Australia's point of view, one of the continuing enticements of close intelligence relationships with major power allies is likely to be that those countries alone will be able to afford the full range of sophisticated intelligence collection and analysis facilities.[47] The heavily restricted and constrained passage of material from these sources is likely to be of continuing interest to Australia. However, it should be noted that in the context of Australia's reorientated national security requirements, most of these highly specialized areas of allied intelligence activity are likely to become relatively less important. As Australian intelligence organizations restructure their activities to meet the requirements of the new security environment and strategic concepts, an increasing proportion of high-priority information should be available from indigenous intelligence-gathering facilities based on Australian territory. Some increased intelligence-gathering capacity may be gained as a consequence of long-range surveillance systems of various types being deployed primarily for other purposes.[48] Other more specialized methods and means of intelligence collection are likely to be required if a high degree of autonomy and self-sufficiency is to be gained and these will require special attention and funding.

An expansion of Australia's independent intelligence-gathering capabilities would need to be matched by a more sophisticated capacity for intelligence analysis and interpretation. This area is highly complex and difficult. The derivation of meaningful intelligence assessments from the almost overwhelming background "noise" of spurious information in the international environment requires the employment of advanced techniques and high levels of technical skill. In the key area of interpreting and foreseeing foreign actor intentions, the experience of several foreign countries suggests that the intelligence assessment structure should be designed in such a manner as to facilitate the expression of alternative opinions.[49] The suppression of dissenting views in the normal decision-making processes of a conventional bureaucratic structure serves to generate and perpetuate theories, views and concepts that become conventional wisdom within the structure, but that, on several occasions, have proved to be misleading, inaccurate or incorrect in important respects.[50] The structural incorporation of alternative assessment staffs, at least in key areas, would provide an important means of encouraging the expression of non-conformist views and potentially a method of sharpening the value of the total intelligence assessment staff.

The changed nature of Australia's security strategy is likely to impact directly upon the tasking of the intelligence services. Much greater attention will need to be given to intelligence likely to be of specific significance to Australia. Perhaps most importantly, very close monitoring will have to be maintained upon all variables relating to pressure and threat lead and warning times.[51] It would be upon the basis of detailed material in this field that many important characteristics of Australia's response capacity could be determined.

Another important consequence of Australia's strategic reorientation will be a much greater requirement for detailed "general intelligence" relating to Australia's immediate security environment.[52] Much of the Australian continent has yet to be mapped in detail and large portions of Australia's coastal and offshore waters have been charted only in the most generalized manner.[53] If Australia's security forces are to have the capacity to operate effectively in all parts of the continent and its surrounding environment, much more detailed information will be required on terrain, weather patterns, vegetation, land-use, human occupation, man-made structures, etc.

On the local level, a great deal might be gained from a more active involvement of the local population in the collection of routine tactical intelligence: the sighting of unusual shipping and aircraft movements, the presence of strangers acting in a suspicious manner, etc. This type of activity could be expected to be particularly valuable and generally accepted in the more remote parts of the country, where it might conceivably be co-ordinated by local police forces.[54]

Australia's requirements for intelligence in the 1980s can be expected to differ considerably from those of the past. Many types of information relating to Australia's immediate environment can be expected to gain increased significance. There is also likely to be a broadened intelligence requirement in non-military national security areas concerning economic, social, political and other developments. It is clear that it would be preferable for all areas of intelligence that are centrally important to the national security structure to be satisfied in the future from purely indigenous means of collection, processing and assessment. This cannot be expected to be a simple or inexpensive task. However, it is unavoidable if Australia's national security structure is to be provided with independent intelligence assessments that are relevant, timely and of high quality.

4. An Inappropriate Communications, Command and Control (C^3) Framework

One major consequence of Australia's changed security environment is a greatly increased requirement for its security forces to prepare for operations on and from Australian territory. The Australian continent, its offshore islands and maritime approaches need to be considered, for long-term planning purposes, a potential battle zone. This has major implications for the Australian C^3 structure.

At present, the Australia armed services exist as three separate organizations. They are organized internally on functional principles, consisting of an operational element — the Fleet, the Army Field Force Commmand and the RAAF Operational Command —

and one or more support elements. As Dr Robert O'Neill has pointed out, this structure is not well suited to the requirements of operating flexibly and at short notice in Australia's immediate environment:

> Each service can... readily make contributions to a joint force if required to do so. However, the joint force structure into which such contributions would have to be fitted does not exist and so if the Australian services are to be used jointly to defend Australia, there would be appreciable delays until the framework was set up. Given that the Department of Defence is now integrated, that the post of Chief of Defence Force Staff has been created giving its incumbent command over the three services, it seems only logical that a joint service force structure should be established also.[55]

Dr O'Neill has argued in detail the case for a command structure more appropriate for the requirements of security operations in Australia's immediate environment.[56] Probably the simplest type of system would involve the establishment of regional Maritime Defence Commands comprising air and naval forces and regional Continental Defence Commands comprising ground and air forces. For instance, there might be two Maritime Defence Commands, one for the east and one for the west of the continent. The continental land mass adjacent to each of the maritime commands might best be divided for the purposes of command into two, in such a manner as to produce a North-East and a South-East Continental Defence Command adjacent to the Eastern Maritime Defence Command, and a North-West and a South-West Continental Defence Command adjacent to the Western Maritime Defence Command. The ideal boundaries for each command area are not easy to identify. It is notable, however, that overseas experience testifies to the great advantages of closely co-ordinating military command boundaries with those already existing for state and local community administration. This facilitates meaningful civil-military co-operation of all types and at all levels.[57]

Ideally, the military support structure might be divided into a logistics command, a training command and a reserve command, each of which would have centralized and regional tri-service and single-service elements. However, in addition to this military support structure, there would be a requirement for a small co-ordinating body to communicate centrally determined national emergency priorities with the broader sections of the total community — a range of federal government departments, state and local governments, civil defence organizations, industry, trade unions, medical authorities, the media, churches, social-welfare agencies, etc. Peacetime planning in this field would need to be comprehensive, with ultimate authority resting at the highest levels of national government.

Inevitably, this level of change to the national security command structure would disturb Australia's military establishment during the period of transition. However, the compensating advantages would be of very great value. Most importantly, this type of regional tri-service command structure would provide a suitable basis for rapid reaction to security problems of all types in Australia's environment. For the military sector, it would encourage a degree of regional specialization that, when combined with increased familiarity with local terrain, weather, population and other factors, could be expected to increase greatly the efficiency of local operations. Additional economies of effort might be forthcoming from the regional integration of service activities and particularly support facilities. Tri-service operations would become daily practice and operational procedures, doctrines and tactics could be tested regularly and inexpensively in the areas of likely future operations. Finally, it can be noted that the institution of an integrated regional command structure would entail a significant degree of geographical dispersion. Depending upon the effectiveness of supporting concealment, mobility and hardening measures, this level of dispersion should have the effect of increasing significantly the potential survivability of the total command structure. This in turn may serve to encourage further efficiencies through the integration of service communication systems.

An efficient, reliable and secure communications, command and control capability is crucial to the credibility and effectiveness of the total national security structure. Much remains to be done if Australia's capacity in this field is to be optimized for the new strategic environment.

5. The Inadequate Support Capacity of Domestic Industry

The need for greater self-reliance impacts upon the industrial sector's capacity to support national security policy in three categories of situation: in meeting peacetime requirements, in meeting the pressures of international crises and in meeting the pressures of international aggression.

In normal periods of peace, the first requirement is likely to be for industry to supply equipment and support to meet those specialized requirements that cannot be met by systems already in low-cost production overseas. The second peacetime requirement is likely to be for industry to produce high-usage ordnance and parts for the large range of equipments held in the existing national security structure. The third and, most probably, increasingly important peacetime requirement will be for Australia's civil industrial sector to develop a capacity to be able to produce a wide range of national security requirements in crisis situations.

In the face of pressures of international crises, Australian industry almost certainly will be expected to reduce the vulnerability of the total society. In practice, this would involve the institution of active measures to compensate for those areas of essential resource and commodity production that Australia currently lacks.[58] Some critical resources may have to be stockpiled in advance and, in other instances, alternative means of production may have to be established to substitute for critical imports.

When confronted by the pressures of national aggression, it would be important to safeguard a proportion of Australia's industrial capacity so as to secure a continuing supply of essential civil and military commodities. Ensuring the survival of essential components of industry in the face of a wide range of pressures and violent attacks could not be expected to be easy. Some production capacities may need to be dispersed and others of very high priority may need to be duplicated, concealed and physically protected. However, it must be recognized that, even if it were highly survivable, Australian industry in its present state could not be expected to provide all the support requirements of the current security structure, nor would it be easy to expand industrial capacity in such a way as to provide a capability to support fully a mobilized version of the current force structure. Even with heavy stockpiling of imported raw materials, equipment components and fully built-up pieces of equipment, the very wide variety of systems currently deployed in the service structure would make long-term support extremely difficult.

In order to increase Australia's independent operational capacity in serious crises of international aggression, a degree of equipment rationalization may be required. One approach might be to adopt a carefully calculated high/low technology mix of military equipments. In the case of large, very high-technology equipments — advanced combat aircraft, large sophisticated warships, main battle tanks, etc. — it may be possible to retain a capacity to produce high-usage parts and to undertake minor overhauls and repairs from purely indigenous resources. However, the capacity to replace or heavily modify this type of equipment without extensive foreign support needs to be recognized as being beyond Australia's current capabilities.[59] In a crisis situation, the development of an indigenous capacity to undertake these demanding tasks would be technically impossible in some areas and extremely difficult and expensive in others. In the absence of a major peacetime government initiative to encourage large-scale high-technology developments in a significant number of industrial sectors, it may be preferable to withdraw from all but the production of a very carefully selected number of small high-technology systems, high-usage parts and the general support of large high-technology equipments.

If local aspirations to produce large warships, advanced combat aircraft and main battle tanks in emergency situations were foregone, this would serve to weaken the Australian security structure in two main categories of situation. Firstly, in the circumstances of a threat arising that provided Australia with a very long defence preparation time, the Australian security structure would not possess an independent capacity to proliferate large high-technology systems. In the second situation, of a very prolonged high-intensity conflict, battlefield losses could not be replaced by similar large high-technology systems.

However, in compensation for the lack of production capacities for major sophisticated items, very significant resources of all types would be freed to concentrate on Australia's small-system high-technology and medium- and low-technology requirements. In these fields, Australia already possesses most of the industrial capacities required to design and produce small arms, light and heavy wheeled vehicles, small ships, light and medium missiles, remotely piloted vehicles, many types of communication equipments, etc.[60] Potentially, there exists great scope for the imaginative exploitation of these already acquired technologies to satisfy many of the new emerging high-priority national security equipment requirements.

This is not intended to be an argument for the peacetime production of all low- and medium-technology systems, all high-usage parts for high-technology systems and a carefully selected number of small high-technology systems within Australia. It would certainly be desirable for a large number of them to be produced domestically. However, in peacetime conditions, the small quantities of equipment required may make such production extremely expensive and unacceptable politically. Perhaps even more important than full-time small-scale domestic production would be the possession of a capability to transfer rapidly large portions of civil industrial capacity to meet those national security requirements not normally supplied by domestic industries. Because of the scope of local civil production capabilities, the potential currently exists to produce a wide range of low- and medium-technology and some specialized high-technology systems in a fully mobilized domestic economy. However, in practice, for this potential capacity to be exploited at short notice, elaborate peacetime preparations would be required. For instance, firm decisions would need to be made concerning those types of equipment that would be required in the circumstances of particular national security crises. Comprehensive equipment designs would need to be finalized in peacetime and prototypes tested thoroughly. Production dies and jigs could then be made so that volume manufacture could commence at short notice. The processes of converting civil industrial facilities to produce national security requirements might even be tested in key areas. The potential benefits from this type of close and detailed civil/military interface can be expected to be very significant. According to Ford Australia's Manager of Truck Operations, J. A. Tweeddale, the normal lead time for a new vehicle production-line exceeds three years from the decision to commence. However, he has assessed that this time could be reduced to well under twelve months, if preliminary planning for the transfer of productive capacity is comprehensive.[61] The time that might be saved in other production processes — in the electronics and ship-building industries, for example — might be far greater.

The development of a high degree of self-reliance in national security capacity will necessitate a greatly improved working relationship between political leaders, their national security advisers and large components of civil industry. A much greater degree of co-operation and consultation will be required over a wide range of matters, but most particularly concerning procurement policy.[62] The design of the national security structure will need to be determined, at least partly, by the capacities of domestic industry to produce and support important equipment. Significant trade-offs would be involved in this process. For example, an imported heavy armoured vehicle X may be considered to provide the most appropriate technical means of performing an important offensive ground-force function. However, X may be extremely expensive to support with purely domestic resources and impossible to produce locally. This may make the option of an alternative domestically produced lighter armoured vehicle Y, which is one-third the unit cost and one-quarter the life-cycle cost of X, much more appropriate. Larger numbers of a lighter domestically produced and supported vehicle may optimize overall national security capacity in the face of a wide range of potential threats for a given resource input. Many of the trends arising from recent military technological developments may add further support to options involving larger numbers of smaller, medium-technology dispersible equipmens, not only on the ground but also in the sea and air environments.[63]

If Australia requires a high level of self-sufficiency in crisis situations, it will be necessary to develop a capacity to produce a large proportion of the country's defence equipment at short notice. With many types of equipment, arrangements might be made for foreign designs to be produced under licence in Australia. In some areas, there may be scope to undertake joint research and development programmes with foreign countries with which Australia shares important technical requirements. However, because of Australia's changed strategic situation, there are likely to be an increasing number of technical requirements and specifications that are peculiarly Australian. There are also likely to be some technical concepts that may not warrant foreign development, but which, because of Australia's unique national security environment, may be particularly suitable for local employment. It would be primarily to these latter areas that Australia's research and development capacity would need to be directed. The development of successful prototypes would make domestic peacetime production of some equipments feasible. Other systems might be readied for rapid production by mobilized civil industries in crisis situations.

Most of the desirable trends in national security industrial policy discussed above are far removed from current experience. At present, many areas of Australian secondary industry are declining and this in turn is impacting directly upon Australia's future national security industrial support capacity.[64] In those industries that are heavily dependent upon defence contracts in periods of peace, there is an urgent requirement for defence equipment procurement to be phased in a long-term planning structure. This would exert a stabilizing influence upon workloads and permit production processes to be integrated and made more efficient. In addition, active measures are required to ensure the continued viability of those civil industries whose supporting role would be critical in a range of pressure and threat situations.

6. The Largely Unrecognized Need to Prepare for the Involvement of Civil Society in National Security Crises

The introduction of new weapons and weapon platforms following the Industrial Revolution had the effect of making armed forces far more dependent upon the comprehensive support of the civil sections of society. During periods of war, it became necessary to divert the greater part of total national resources to supply the requirements of the armed forces. In this sense, Australia did experience the draining effect of modern conflict during the two world wars. However, a related consequence of modern developments in warfare did not have an immediate impact upon Australia. During the nineteenth and twentieth centuries, larger sections of civil societies became important military targets in their own right. Cities, towns, industrial concentrations and transport nodes all became the subject of direct attacks in major wars. However, in contrast to the experience of most of the modern world, Australia's civil infrastructure and population remained relatively immune from direct experience of the pressures of international crisis and war. Primarily because of their remote location, Australia's major centres of population have never been the subject of serious pressure or attack. Thus apart from a brief period during the Second World War, Australians have not been motivated to take measures to ensure their personal survival should such a major crisis eventuate.

However, the transformation in Australia's security environment increases greatly the importance of preparing the population mass for the types of threats that may arise. With the Australian armed forces orienting their capacities more towards operations on and from the continent itself, the potential for the public to be affected directly by national security crises is rising considerably. The major implication is that the direct involvement of the total population and society in future crises must be recognized and appropriate strategies and contingency plans formulated in advance.

It is clear from this discussion that Australia's national security establishment is confronted by a series of critical challenges. Because of the changed nature of its strategic environment, Australia now needs to develop an independent capability to deter, defer and if necessary meet a very wide range of pressures and threats. But Australia's current strategy formulation, force expansion, intelligence, communications, command and control, industrial and total civil support capacities have been evolved during a long history of foreign commitments in support of major power allies. They were never designed to be appropriate for, nor are they suited to, the type of national security environment likely to confront Australia in the 1980s and 1990s.

What is required in this radically altered strategic situation is the evolution of a new Australian national security strategy from first principles. It is necessary to question what should be the functions and priorities of the national security structure in the new environment. What types of contingencies should it be designed to meet? What are the most efficient and economic technical means of providing the capabilities desired? And how might the existing structure best be transformed to satisfy the new demands? Nothing less than a fundamental re-examination is required if Australia's national security strategy is to be viable in the years ahead.

Notes and References

1. For those readers who are unfamiliar with the character of the Australian Defence Force, Appendix A summarizes briefly its shape, size and operational capacity.
2. Programmes and Budget Division, Department of Defence, *Making Defence Decisions* (Canberra, August 1975), p. 6; quoted in T.P. Muggleton, "An Evaluation of the Analytical Infrastructure for Force Structure Decision-making in the Australian Defence Department" (unpublished B.A. (Hons) thesis, Department of Economics, Faculty of Military Studies, University of New South Wales, Royal Military College, Duntroon, 1976), p. 32.
3. W.L. Morrison, "The Role of the Minister in the Making of Australian Defence Policy since the Re-organization of the Department of Defence", in *The Defence of Australia: Fundamental New Aspects*, ed. Robert O'Neill (Canberra, Strategic and Defence Studies Centre, Australian National University, 1977), p. 74.
4. Rear-Admiral A. M. Synnot, "The Changing Challenge for Our Defence Force", in *Australia's Defence*, ed. J. Birman (Perth: Extension Service, University of Western Australia, 1976), p. 11.
5. Morrison, "Role of the Minister in the Making of Australian Defence Policy since the Re-organization of the Department of Defence", in *Defence of Australia*, ed. O'Neill, p. 79.
6. Ibid., p. 78.
7. It is difficult, if not impossible, to write comprehensively and with complete clarity concerning the problems and difficulties of the current security planning system because official information concerning anything but its formal structure is unavailable on the public record. As a consequence, it has been necessary to rely heavily in the following analysis upon the accounts of those who have been involved personally in the current system, those who have studied its operations in detail and those who have observed its performance from an external vantage-point over a long period.
8. F. A. Mediansky, "The Danger of Mixing Defence and Politics", *Sydney Morning Herald*, 10 May 1976, p. 7.
9. Robert O'Neill, "The Development of Operational Doctrines for the Australian Defence Force", in *Defence of Australia*, ed. O'Neill, p. 138.
10. Robert O'Neill, "How Effectively will that $12,000 Million Be Spent?" *Australian Financial Review*, 10 June 1976, p. 4.
11. Desmond J. Ball, "Equipment Policy for the Defence of Australia", in *Defence of Australia*, ed. O'Neill, pp. 101-2.
12. Muggleton, "Evaluation of the Analytical Infrastructure for Force Structure Decision-making in the Australian Defence Department", pp. 52-53.
13. This passage appears in ibid., pp. 25-26. It is composed almost entirely of phrases and short sentences taken from Department of Defence, *The FYRP System New Major Equipment Component* (Canberra, June 1975), p. 2; and also Programmes and Budgets Division, Department of Defence, *Making Defence Decisions* (Canberra, August 1975), p. 6.
14. Ibid., pp. 35-36.
15. K. J. Foley, "Planning for Australia's Defence: Exercises in Non-rationality", in *Australia's Defence*, ed. Birman, p. 19.

16. Muggleton, "Evaluation of the Analytical Infrastructure for Force Structure Decision-making in the Australian Defence Department", pp. 32, 36.
17. Ibid., p. 38.
18. K.J. Foley, "A Study of the Feasibility of Introducing Program Budgeting into the Shire of Eltham" (report commissioned by the Shire of Eltham, June 1976), p. 2; quoted in ibid., p. 54.
19. Ball, "Equipment Policy for the Defence of Australia", in *Defence of Australia*, ed. O'Neill, p. 117.
20. Morrison, "Role of the Minister in the Making of Australian Defence Policy since the Re-organization of the Department of Defence", in ibid., pp. 84-85.
21. Ibid., p. 71.
22. The bureaucratic forces brought to bear in national security decision-making are discussed in detail in Chapter 6.
23. Kevin J. Foley, "Selecting an Australian Tactical Fighter Force: Marginal Strategies, Rationality and the Australian Aircraft Industry", in *The Future of Tactical Airpower in the Defence of Australia*, ed. Desmond Ball (Canberra: Strategic and Defence Studies Centre, Australian National University, 1977), pp. 125-26. This matter is also discussed by F. A. Mediansky, "The Defence White Paper", *Pacific Defence Reporter* 3, no. 6/7 (January 1976): 11-13.
24. Muggleton, "Evaluation of the Analytical Infrastructure for Force Structure Decision-making in the Australian Defence Department", pp. 7, 56.
25. Derek Woolner was Research Adviser to both Mr L. H. Barnard and Mr W. L. Morrison during their terms as Minister for Defence.
26. Muggleton, "Evaluation of the Analytical Infrastructure for Force Structure Decision-making in the Australian Defence Department", p. 56.
27. Sir Arthur Tange, *Australian Defence, Report on the Reorganization of the Defence Group of Departments*, presented to the Minister for Defence, November 1973, p. 44. This aspect of the Tange Report is also noted by Morrison, "Role of the Minister in the Making of Australian Defence Policy since the Re-organization of the Department of Defence", in *Defence of Australia*, ed. O'Neill, p. 78.
28. Ideally, it should be the government's task to determine clearly what are to be the supreme goals of the national security structure. Is the system to be designed so as to prevent threats arising, to avoid conflict, to deter or defer an opponent, to defeat an enemy, to compel a disproportionate response, to extract a favourable exchange ratio or to achieve some other objective? It is conceivable that a government may wish to apply all of the above criteria in various situations; but if this is the case, in what types of situations and in what order of priority?

    It is also important to note here that it would be highly desirable, if not essential, for a large degree of political agreement to be reached between the major parties concerning the general strategic objectives to be adopted. Changes of basic national security objectives with changes of government would present major difficulties of a fundamental nature for the total system.
29. It is a very complex matter to derive appropriate background assumptions for the determination of the capacities required for deterrence to be successful. For example, should it be assumed that an opposing state could devote its total mobilizable resources against Australia (i.e. the absolutist approach)? If not, what assumptions is it appropriate to make concerning the resources that an attacker may be able to make available? It can be argued, for instance, that Australia's national security structure should have the capacity to deter only those forces that an opponent could "reasonably" be expected to spare from other tasks (i.e. the marginalist approach). Hence it can be reasoned that, if the costs to an opponent of mounting this type of marginal action can be raised above the marginal benefits that are imputed, the opponent would be

theoretically deterred. These matters are discussed by Foley, "Selecting an Australian Tactical Fighter Force: Marginal Strategies, Rationality, and the Australian Aircraft Industry", in *Future of Tactical Airpower in the Defence of Australia*, ed. Ball, pp. 129 ff.

The major problem with this type of theory is simply that it is too far divorced from reality. Statesmen rarely make careful cost-benefit analyses when deciding on a course of action. As Adam Roberts points out:
> In some cases where states are concerned as much with face, reputation or high principles as with more mundane and measurable values, and where they pursue their interests by threatening or using force, cost-benefit analysis quickly becomes irrelevant. It is well to remember that most wars result from a process of commitment and counter-commitment, threat and counter-threat, claim and counter-claim, perception and mis-perception: not from a single calculation by one side that a war or military occupation would be worthwhile.

Cited from Adam Roberts, *Nations in Arms: The Theory and Practice of Territorial Defence* (London: Chatto & Windus, for International Institute for Strategic Studies, 1976), p. 93.

30. These tentative doctrinal objectives for the Australian national security structure have been deen developed from a series of roles outlined for the Australian Defence Force by O'Neill, "Development of Operational Doctrines for the Australian Defence Force", in *Defence of Australia*, ed. O'Neill, pp. 129-30. This list of objectives has intentionally been limited to those related specifically to the defence of Australia. Other less essential functions also could be mentioned, such as the provision of disaster relief, the capacity to contribute to United Nations peace-keeping forces and the training of allied forces, etc.
31. A possible means of undertaking this process of experimentation to meet Australia's requirements is discussed by Robert O'Neill, "The Influence of Recent Developments in Conventional Weapons Technology on Strategic and Tactical Doctrine: Consequences for Australia" (paper presented to United Service Institution of Australian Capital Territory, Canberra, 5 May 1976), pp. 1-6.
32. Ibid., p. 4.
33. The "core force" concept is very difficult to explain satisfactorily in a few words. However, in its most elementary sense, it refers to the forces maintained during periods of peace that would form the "core" or basis for expansion at mobilization. This, and other related concepts, are elaborated and discussed in greater detail in Chapter 7.
34. It has been calculated for this discussion that between 2½ to 5 years' active preparation time would be required in order to expand the present 33 000-man regular army with its 22 000-man poorly trained reserve to a well-trained 150 000-man army, and between 4 to 8 years defence preparation time for it to be expanded to a well-trained 250 000-man army. For the time to approximate the lower figures, it needs to be assumed that there are no problems experienced in rapidly expanding the training facilities, that there are no problems in providing the equipment requirements of the expanded force, that the peacetime forces have an over-preponderance of long lead time middle-ranking officers and specialists already in their ranks, that nearly every newly trained soldier can be immediately used to train others and that during the expansion process army units are not required for operational or active security duties. If it is assumed, however, that during the expansion process significant forces would be required for active security duties, that not all newly trained personnel could be used to train others, that the normal levels of middle-rank officers and specialists were apparent in the core force, as at present, and also that

difficulties are experienced in establishing the expanded training facilities and in equipping and housing the greatly expanded forces, the time requirements tend to lengthen towards the upper estimates.

It should be also noted here that the times required to expand the present Air Force and Navy by a similar percentage increase would almost certainly exceed those for the Army by far. This is primarily because of the long lead time character of the many highly skilled officers and technicians who play central roles in air force and naval activities and operations. Major items of air force and naval equipment are also likely to be more difficult to acquire at short notice.

35. The problems experienced by the Israelis are noteworthy in this context. See *Agranat Commission of Inquiry into Yom Kippur War, Partial Report*, Israel Government Press Office, 2 April 1974; and A Shlaim, "Failures in National Intelligence Estimates: The Case of the Yom Kippur War", *World Politics* 28, no. 3 (April 1976): 348. This question is discussed further in a later part of this chapter.

36. This would depend heavily upon assumptions that are made concerning the numbers of men required to secure vital installations, the numbers required in supporting roles, logistics, etc., the numbers required in the training structure to provide a capacity to expand further if needed and the numbers of men required to be held in reserve to guard against a possible escalation by the enemy. In raid-type scenarios, the overall manpower requirements also would depend heavily upon the effectiveness of the air, ground, sea and undersea surveillance systems that Australia possessed to monitor enemy activities across the vast expanses of its continental space, offshore maritime zones and the enemy's home waters. If these systems were highly effective, the requirements for army personnel on the ground could be reduced significantly.

37. It should be noted that the addition of very meagre resources to those that would be required for raids would permit an enemy to exacerbate greatly the problems for Australia. Thus in some situations, a raid-bombardment or raid-mining scenario may be more likely than a simple raiding campaign. While these more complex campaigns would require very little additional effort from the attacker, the impact upon the manpower requirements of the defence could be very significant.

38. During the period of mobilization, it is most likely that the enemy also would be expanding its forces, possibly at a rate faster than that of which Australia is capable. Thus even in the event that a decision were made to mobilize very early during a period of heightening tension, there of course could be no guarantee that the final force ratios would be favourable to Australia.

39. The exception is in Australia's active defence preparation prior to the onset of hostilities with Japan in 1941. The defence preparation time in that instance was approximately two years and six weeks. The details of other individual cases, of course, are open to dispute. However, the major point to be made by this discussion is more difficult to question seriously, i.e. the order of magnitude of defence preparation time available in recent historical experience. There appears to be no evidence to suggest that defence preparation time in a future conflict situation involving Australia is likely to be an order of magnitude several times greater than that available to other countries in recent history.

40. It should be noted that assumptions of this nature are not uncommon in the Australian defence establishment. For instance, in the Interim Report of the Joint (Parliamentary) Committee on Foreign Affairs and Defence, *Industrial Support for Defence Needs and Allied Matters* (Canberra: Parliament of Australia, June 1977, Para 2.10), it is stated without any supporting argument or attempted justification that:

It has been assessed by the Committee that it would take him [a potential enemy] three years to build up the capability to mount a major raid on Australia and five years to mount an invasion.

It is upon these highly contestable assumptions that the primary objectives for Australia's industrial support capacity are determined for this important study: Recognizing that a high-level threat to Australia could arise in a situation of world chaos and that there would then be a strong likelihood that overseas supplies would not be available during either the build-up or the combat period, the Committee has concluded that:

    (a) Australia's defence industrial base, in R & D, design, production, overhaul and repair, should be maintained in peacetime at a level of capability and capacity from which, given five years warning, expansion to self reliance in the provision of equipment of moderate complexity could be achieved. Such achievement could require stockpiling now in those areas where current deficiencies could not be overcome within the five year time frame;

    (b) The planned rate of expansion should be such that, within three years from go-ahead, industry would be capable of providing the Services with the level of support needed to resist a major raid. [para. 2.12]

The weakness of the background assumptions of this important report undermines seriously the value of its conclusions.

41. See, for example, L. H. Barnard, Ministerial Statement on Australian Defence, Australia. House of Representatives, *Debates*, Twenty-eighth Parliament, 22 August 1973, p. 239.
42. It needs to be emphasized that the process of identifying the general nature of an opponent's intentions may in itself be very difficult. However, even when this is determined in fairly unambiguous terms, there may be great doubt and uncertainty concerning the nature of the intended attack, its objectives, its timing, its location, the technologies and tactics to be employed, etc. Australian uncertainties concerning these matters, in many circumstances, might affect the nature and vigour of the government's response.
43. This type of situation would represent a classic illustration of the strategic principle of disproportionate response. The opponent's great advantage could be gained because in normal circumstances the attacking forces would possess the initiative for attack. They would be free to choose the time, place, mode, method and duration of operations. In most respects, the demands of these circumstances are analogous to the widely held requirement for a 10 to 1 force ratio to defeat guerrilla insurgencies. See this discussed in John S. Pustay, *Counterinsurgency Warfare* (London: Collier-Macmillan, 1965), pp. 86-87.
44. The most potent and readily available means of conflict escalation would be the threat, and possibly the use, of Australia's long-range air and naval bombardment and interdiction capacity against the opponent's homeland and surrounding waters. At least in theory, these units could be employed for the performance of two types of offensive function: to attempt to destroy the opponent's offensive forces in their home-bases or to attack a much broader range of infrastructure targets, ports, support shipping, railways, roads, centres of industry and possibly major cities. The first option may be militarily difficult if the opponent's strike forces take the form of medium- and low-technology surface vessels and aircraft. These can be readily dispersed and are difficult to detect in many types of coastal environment. The second type of retaliatory option would have a limited utility in this type of situation because of its very great diplomatic ramifications. In addition, it is possible that, in the future, regional states will be able to deter this type of deep infrastructure retaliatory strike through their acquisition of highly survivable long-range counter-bombard-

ment capabilities in the form of air-, ground- or sea- launched cruise missile forces.
45. Alternative means of developing surge capacity are discussed in some detail in Chapter 9.
46. See *Third Report of the Royal Commission on Intelligence and Security: Abridged Findings and Recommendations* (April 1977, tabled in the House of Representatives by the Prime Minister, Mr Fraser, on 5 May 1977), p. 17.
47. For detailed descriptions of super-power technical intelligence-gathering capabilities, see P. J. Klass, *Secret Sentries in Space* (New York: Random House, 1971); and also Ted Greenwood, "Reconnaissance and Arms Control", *Scientific American* 228, no. 2 (February 1973): 14.
48. Over-the-horizon radar and long-range passive sonar sensors could be expected to have significant potential in this field. See the discussion in Chapter 2 and Appendix B.
49. See this discussed in A. Shlaim, "Failure in National Intelligence Estimates: The Case of the Yom Kippur War", *World Politics* 28, no. 3 (April 1976): 348.
50. These matters are discussed at length in a series of unpublished papers delivered to a Conference on Strategic Issues, held at the Leonard Davis Institute for International Relations, Hebrew Univerity of Jerusalem, 7-9 April 1975. In particular, see A. Ben-Zvi, "Surprise Attacks: Theoretical Aspects"; A. L. George, "Warning and Response: Theory and Practice"; and B. Whaley, "The Causes of Surprise in War".
51. The types of variables that would need to be monitored are discussed in the papers cited above; ibid. In addition, see M. I. Handel, "Perception, Deception and Surprise: The Outbreak of the Yom Kippur War", a paper delivered at the same conference.
52. The term "general intelligence" is defined by Normal Gelb in the following terms:
> General intelligence deals with such matters as a country's topography, the character of its shores, beaches and tides (if it borders the sea) and of its rivers and other inland waters; details of its economy and of its transportation and communications systems; the character of its people and a wide range of other general areas of information.

Gelb distinguishes "general intelligence" from "political intelligence", "strategic intelligence" and "tactical intelligence". See Norman Gelb, *Enemy in the Shadows: The World of Spies and Spying* (London: William Luscombe, 1976), pp. 18 ff.
53. The entire Australian continent has now been mapped in 1:250,000 scale, but only approximately 40 per cent of these maps are contoured and many are over fifteen years old. In 1965, a programme was commenced to provide a complete coverage of the continent in the more detailed 1:100,000 scale within ten years. However, because of budgetary cut-backs and rigidly imposed staff ceilings, the programme was only approximately 50 per cent complete at the end of 1977.

The lack of up-to-date knowledge and detailed charts on much of Australia's coastline and adjacent waters is also a serious problem. Some areas of Australia's northern coastline remain essentially uncharted and for others, the most recent material was produced in the nineteenth century. The difficulties of navigation in such conditions are highlighted in *Sailing Instructions for the North and West Coasts of Australia* (Washington, DC.: United States Defense Mapping Agency, Hydrographic Centre, rev. edn, 1976).
54. In some coastal areas, this type of assistance is already provided by the Voluntary Coastal Patrol, the Voluntary Coastguard and on an *ad hoc* basis by Australian commercial fishing and other vessels operating in coastal waters. There is, in addition, the remnants of the wartime coast-watcher organization. However,

because of its classified nature, it is difficult to evaluate the strength and/or operational capacity of this structure. There would appear to be considerable scope for rationalizing and integrating the intelligence-gathering capacities of these disparate groups and individuals.
55. R. J. O'Neill, "Structural Changes for a More Self-reliant National Defence", *Dyason House Papers* 2, no. 3 (January 1976): 2.
56. Ibid.
57. The Swedes have employed these principles in the development of their national command and control structure and claim considerable benefits from the co-ordination of civil and military areas of authority.
58. The major areas of domestic production deficiency are outlined in Chapter 3 and possible means of instituting compensatory measures are discussed in Chapter 10.
59. This point is elaborated in the Interim Report of the Joint (Parliamentary) Committee on Foreign Affairs and Defence, *Industrial Support for Defence Needs and Allied Matters*. In particular, see the discussion in paras 5.63 and 5.64.
60. Australia's capacity in these fields is discussed in ibid.
61. This matter was raised in the discussion following J.A. Tweeddale's address to the United Service Institution of the Australian Capital Territory on 1 June 1977. For the text of his address, see J. A. Tweeddale, "The Defence Capability of the Australian Vehicle Manufacturing Industry", in *The Defence Capability of Australian Industry* (Canberra: United Service Institution of the Australian Capital Territory, 1977), pp. 8-31.
62. The Parliamentary Joint Committee on Foreign Affairs and Defence is critical of some aspects of the current situation in this area. See Interim Report of the Joint (Parliamentary) Committee on Foreign Affairs and Defence, *Industrial Support for Defence Needs and Allied Matters*. In particular, see the discussion in paras 3.27-3.29.
63. See this matter discussed in Chapter 2. The impact of volume upon the relative cost disadvantage of Australian versus foreign production is elaborated by Desmond J. Ball in "Australia's Tactical Air Requirements and the Criteria for Evaluating Tactical Aircraft for Australian Procurement", in *Future of Tactical Airpower in the Defence of Australia*, ed. Ball, pp. 88 ff.
64. The nature of the decline in Australia's secondary industrial capacity is discussed at length in the report to the Prime Minister by the Committee to Advise on Policies for Manufacturing Industry, *Policies for Development of Manufacturing Industry* (Jackson Committee Report), Green Paper (Canberra: Australian Government Publishing Service, October 1975), vol. 1.

Part 3

CONSTRAINTS ON CHANGE

5
Practical Constraints on Change

Notwithstanding the obvious weaknesses in Australia's current national security system, the scope for major alterations is, in practice, rather limited. Because of the nature of Australian society and its position within the international environment, there is a large number of physical, economic, social, diplomatic and political factors that effectively constrain the potential for change. For instance, the size of the national economic "cake" restricts the dimensions of the budgetary "slice" that can be allocated for national security expenditure. In the total world environment, Australia's economy is comparatively limited in size, its gross domestic product being $A90 220 million in 1977-78, less than half of that of Canada, less than a third of that of the United Kingdom and approximately a twenty-fifth of that of the United States.

The Limits of Domestic Industry

Australian national security policy is constrained not only by the scale of the domestic economy but also by its character. For instance, the capacity of Australia's secondary industry to produce the quantity and quality of goods required by the national security force within acceptable time and cost parameters is limited. Writing in 1974, Brigadier P. J. Greville summarized these capabilities in a rather optimistic fashion in the following terms:
A perusal of our present capacity indicated:

   a. that we could manufacture all the vehicles (A, B and C)[1] needed by the Services. To do this, however, we must develop or get a licence to build one or more diesel or multi-fuel engine and transmission sets for the vehicles;
   b. we have the capacity to produce our own communications systems, and some at least of our electronically controlled weapons systems;
   c. we have the capacity to produce our own transport aircraft and some of our needs for first and second line aircraft;
   d. we can produce our own ships;

e. we can produce most small arms, conventional weapons and munitions;
   f. we can produce special foods, shelter, clothing.[2]

In fact it is doubtful whether Australia possessed all of these capacities even in 1974. It certainly does not possess them in 1980.[3] In order for Australia to acquire the capacity to produce all of the components required for the construction of A vehicles, transport aircraft and warships, a major and highly specialized expansion of the country's industrial capacity would be essential. In the current economic and national political environment, this type of development appears highly unlikely. In fact, in recent years, it has been made clear by a variety of sources that the national security support capacity of Australia's secondary industry has suffered a relative decline.[4] This appears to be primarily because the rapid growth in Australia's mining sector has raised the domestic costs of labour and capital to new heights and, as a consequence, weakened the competitive position of the manufacturing sector.[5] These problems have been exacerbated by the processes of rapid industrialization in South-East Asia. The developing countries of this region have been very successful in producing low-technology, high labour-intensity manufactures, which have commanded a widening price advantage as Australia's labour costs have continued to rise. Consequently, many manufacturing processes that were formerly undertaken within Australia have been transferred offshore or replaced by those overseas.

The current developments in Australian mining and Asian manufacturing both appear to be of a long-term nature. As a consequence, in the future there is likely to be a further decline in Australia's manufacturing industry and hence in the country's independent defence support capacity. The trend is already firmly established. Between 1962-63 and 1972-73, the proportion of gross domestic product derived from the manufacturing sector fell from 27.6 per cent to 24.2 per cent and by 1977-78 it had declined still further, to 18.6 per cent.[6] Perhaps an even more significant indicator is that in the 1962-63 to 1972-73 period, the proportion of private fixed capital expenditure directed to the manufacturing sector fell from 25.7 per cent to 19.7 per cent.[7] As the Jackson Committee Report points out, it appears that Australia's manufacturing industries have attempted to maintain their earnings and profitability by running down capital stock.[8] The overall implication of these trends has been described by Sir Ian McLennan in the following terms:

> I think it can be said that Australian industry is now at a lower stage of relative technology, that is relative to overseas countries, than it was in

1939 and, similarly, I think it can be said that the development of new equipment requires much more sophistication than it did then.[9]

These considerations constrain heavily the levels of domestic industrial support that can be assumed in emergency situations.

Manpower Limits

Australia's manpower strength is also limited in both quantity and quality. The Borrie Report emphasized that Australia's post-war population growth rate is declining to a very low level.[10] During the 1980s and early 1990s, there is expected to be an almost constant 130 000-140 000 males reaching the age of eighteen each year.[11] Moreover, the limited scale of this potential civil and military workforce has been eroded further by a significant change in the occupational patterns of young people. Most notably, during the late 1960s and early 1970s there was a significant growth in the proportion of young adults attending tertiary educational institutions fulltime and a tendency for them to remain there for longer periods.[12] While these trends have now largely stabilized, their effect has been to reduce significantly the size of the 17 to 25-year-old male workforce available for recruitment by both domestic industry and the armed services.[13]

These developments may effectively limit the range of strategic options open to Australia. The demanding nature of the minimum aptitude selection criteria for military service already means that substantially more applicants are required than the number of vacant recruit positions. Yet with the pool of young potential recruits being restricted to an almost static level and civilian incomes rising continuously, it may prove to be much more difficult and expensive than in the past to retain and expand current regular service manpower strengths.

The relative ease with which current service ceilings are being met appears to be primarily a consequence of the high rate of domestic unemployment. As Glenn Withers has pointed out:

> At present unemployment is permitting some gradual build-up of force strength without increasing relative pay. The crunch will come if the unemployment problem is successfully resolved . . . [14]

The means available to overcome this problem of restricted regular manpower supply in the long term are very limited. The most controllable variable determining enlistment rates is that of service pay.[15] However, the price elasticity of supply for military manpower in Australia appears to be low, particularly in comparison to that in the United States.[16] Withers has calculated that, in Australia, a 10 per cent increase in service pay would only invoke a very moderate 10 per cent rise in enlistment applications.[17] This limited supply response, together with the reduced scale of the available manpower pool, constrains heavily the levels of regular professional service manpower that can be maintained in Australia within the currently accepted budgetary parameters. Any proposals for greatly expanded full-time military manpower would need to depend on either a vastly increased budgetary allocation or some form of national manpower mobilization or conscription. The limited availability of manpower for part-time military service further restricts Australia's future security options. However, it is important to note that the apparent reluctance of Australians to perform part-time military service is a product not only of their failure to enlist but also of their high rate of withdrawal and resignation. The very low retention rate, and hence the modest strength of part-time military forces, would appear to be due more to the unfavourable conditions of part-time service than to any deep-seated social or political attitudinal constraint.[18]

The Limits of Public Support

The potential for change in Australia's national security system is also restrained heavily by the values and attitudes of the domestic population and its political representatives. As we have seen in Chapter 3, Australians are generally apprehensive about the potential for future national security crises and many fear Australian involvement in a major war. However, expressions of strong opinion and concern by the Australian public concerning national security issues have been by no means continuous or consistent. As Dr W. H. Smith points out:

> ... it is all too evident that interest in defence is largely spasmodic. True there is a continuing concern over vaguely defined perils which are seen to originate in the Asian hordes, world communism, global population pressures and the like; and it may be that some of these fears have basis in fact, particularly if the West is considered to be a spent force in world politics. When in the past direct threats to Australia have been identified — Russia in the nineteenth century, Japan after the raid on Darwin, the communist thrust in Southeast Asia — public opinion has usually greatly exaggerated the degree of danger. But currently, at least, there is widespread scepticism about potential specific threats to Australia.[19]

The propensity of Australians to overreact to both menacing and peaceful international developments is no doubt due to a large number of factors. Certainly one important influence is the gross inadequacy of foreign news coverage and interpretation in the Australian media. As Henry Albinski has pointed out: "Historically the Australian press has, by common consent, been disgracefully deficient in this area."[20] It is a reflection of the importance placed upon national and, indeed, international security issues by the Australian media and public that there is only one journalist acting as an essentially full-time defence correspondent in the domestic mass radio, television and newspaper media.[21]

Dr Smith has identified a second major reason for the tendency of Australians to overreact in response to national security issues:

> On the one hand, Australian society does seem largely uninterested in defence except in extreme situations and tends to leave matters to the experts and the military professionals. On the other hand, governments have encouraged the idea they are the repository of wisdom in such matters and have been pre-disposed to keep defence questions out of the arena of public debate.[22]

In this type of environment, the public is rarely informed in a well-balanced routine manner of developments in the national security sphere. When the passage of unusual, newsworthy and possibly potentially threatening events captures widespread attention, the reporting is frequently sensationalized and the poor state of the public's background knowledge tends to facilitate an attitudinal overreaction. In the current situation, a high level of expertise in national security affairs is attained by only a small and select group of bureaucrats, military officers, diplomats, politicians and academics.[23]

Despite fluctuations of interest, especially government interest, concerning the seriousness and probability of external threats, Australian attitudes towards military service have been remarkably consistent over the past thirty-five years. The most precise records in this area concern public opinion poll results to questions regarding compulsory military service. For instance, as can be seen in Table 4, from 1943 to 1973 an average of more than 73 per cent of the Australian population has consistently expressed its approval of compulsory military service for young men.[24] However, it is notable, in Table 5, that public approval is moderated somewhat when poll questions concern selective or non-universal enlistment and the possibility of conscript service overseas.

The poll figures also display a difference of opinion on conscription between those in an age group liable for call-up and those who are older. In Table 5, the figures for both 1964-65 and 1971 show a divergence of opinion according to age, although in both cases a majority of potential conscripts still supported the call-up even though it was selective and entailed possible overseas service. It appears that while a very large proportion of the population per-

Table 4. Australian attitudes to compulsory military training, 1943-73 (% response).

Date	June 1943	June 1945	Dec. 1945	May 1946	Dec. 1946	July 1948	Mar. 1949	June 1949	Feb. 1950	June 1956	June 1961	Mar. 1973
Question	(a)	(b)	(c)	(c)	(d)	(e)	(c)	(f)	(f)	(g)	(h)	(i)
Yes	79	74	78	76	73	75	76	74	74	83	73	78
No	14	24	19	19	20	20	17	19	20	11	21	18
Undecided	7	2	3	5	7	5	7	7	6	6	6	4

Questions:
(a) Should compulsory military training for young men continue after the war?
(b) After the war, would you favour compulsory military training for young men of 18?
(c) Do you favour or oppose compulsory military training for young men of about 18?
(d) Do you favour or oppose compulsory military training?
(e) Do you favour or oppose compulsory military training for young men?
(f) If a referendum were held, would you vote for or against compulsory training?
(g) In your opinion, should compulsory military training continue or stop?
(h) Would you favour or oppose again having compulsory military training?
(i) Would you favour or oppose all young men going to military camp for several months?

Source: See Note 24.

ceives a general need for national security forces and is even prepared to support universal conscription, they are significantly less keen to be involved individually as participants. No doubt there are many reasons for this, such as the perception by individuals that full-time military service is a potentially disruptive influence to civil careers and normal patterns of social behaviour. However, an important influence also may be an apparent divergence between publicly perceived military attitudes, practices and social mores and the changing nature of those values held in the wider community.[25] The broad nature of the attitudinal changes taking place in civilian society are summarized in the Jackson Committee Report in the following terms:

> The long standing ethic of delayed gratification has far less weight than before; individuals in today's affluent society want opportunities for pleasure and relaxation now ... Since governments now assume more responsibility for caring for aged and sick people, there is less incentive to accumulate funds to maintain a standard of living in retirement ...
> Current attitudes include the belief that a complete person should show independence of mind and make his own personal choices.
> It is widely accepted, at the same time, that individuals have the right to be well informed about decisions affecting them, to be involved in mak-

Table 5. Australian attitudes to two years' full-time military service, with possible overseas deployment, for a randomly chosen minority of men aged twenty, 1964-71 (% response)

Date	Dec. 1964	Apr. 1965	Sept. 1965	Jul. 1966	Mar. 1967	Mar. 1967	Dec. 1968	Aug. 1969	Oct. 1969	Oct. 1970	June 1971	Sept. 1971	Sept. 1971	Sept. 1971	Sept. 1971	Sept. 1971
Question	(a)	(a)	(b)	(c)	(c)	(c)	(c)	(d)	(d)	(d)	(e)	(f)	(f)	(f)	(f)	(f)
Age group (if specified)	"Adult"	"Youth"				"Youth"						16-20	21-25	30-49	50-69	≥70
Yes	71	68	69	68	70	57	68	63	58	58	53	53	66	70	74	76
No	25	29	23	26	25	40	29	32	32	34	37	39	27	22	17	17
Undecided	4	3	8	6	5	3	6	5	10	8	10	8	7	8	9	7

Questions:

(a) The government plans to register all young men of 20 and to call up about 7000 a year for two years' full-time service, overseas if necessary. Do you favour or oppose that?

(b) Each year about 8400 20-year-old men are called up for two years' military training, with possible overseas service. Are you for or against that call-up?

(c) Each year about 8000 20-year-olds are called up for two years' military training, with possible overseas service. Are you for or against that call-up?

(d) Election issue: End conscription for national service [i.e. say no] or continue two years' national service, with possible overseas service [i.e. say yes].

(e) Of all young men aged 20, 1 in 12, selected by ballot, is called up each year for two years' military training, with possible overseas service. In your opinion, should that call-up be continued [i.e. say yes] or ended [i.e. say no].

(f) In your opinion, should compulsory military training continue or be ended?

Sources: See Note 24.

ing the decision if they choose, and to accept or reject the outcome. Open education is reinforcing such attitudes.
Some emerging values question the rationale of the exercise of authority and power in any form. At one time older people derived authority from accumulated experience and wealth. But the pace of change within one generation has made experience look less relevant, property and wealth less authoritative...
The decline of the work ethic is now an accepted thrust of change in the affluent society... Affluent, better-educated workers are asking for work to have meaning in itself, and to have purpose to which they can subscribe. But there is no clearcut evidence that people do not want to work at all. Rising educational standards and the demands discussed above are simply incompatible with a large pool of people willing to do dirty, unpleasant, monotonous work.[26]

It may be that the values and culture of the Australian military establishment and, most particularly, the public's perception of them may not be completely compatible with the changing values of the total society. The essentially hierarchial and authoritarian nature of the armed forces and the high level of discipline implicit in service membership may lose much of its appeal as young people seek more independence of mind, more control over their work environments and more participation in decisions affecting their employment. If the perceptions of military life held by young Australians clash with their developing aspirations, their propensity to accept the current type of regular military service, either voluntarily or compulsorily, is likely to decline.

Budgetary Limits

In the face of an expanded range of potential difficulties in recruiting regular service manpower, it is possible that the public may be prepared to ameliorate the problem by sanctioning substantially higher levels of funding. Certainly public opinion poll results show that Australians are in favour of larger armed forces.[27] They also show that the public sees at least the current levels of defence expenditure as desirable, with nearly half favouring a definite budgetary increase.[28] However, the views of the public appear to be less clear when the specific financial consequences and alternative (or "opportunity") costs are displayed in poll questions.[29]

It is notable that, should there be a broadly perceived serious threat to Australia, there is scope for a significant increase in defence expenditure. During the Second World War, national security spending reached 40 per cent of the national product.[30] However, during the past thirty years, the balance of social, political, military and bureaucratic forces in Australia has meant that the country has devoted a relatively stable proportion of its resources to national security. As can be seen from Figure 1, in recent years Australia has consistently spent approximately 3-4 per cent, or slightly less, of gross domestic product on defence. Since the height of the Vietnam War, this has implied a steadily decreasing percentage of total government outlays. At a time when serious pressures and threats are perceived to be notably absent from Australia's strategic environment, it is not difficult to justify continuing expenditure at this low level. In fact, in the current circumstances, it can and has been argued that increased expenditure upon the defence forces is detrimental to Australia's long-range security interests.[31] The case can be made that if finance that would otherwise be expended on defence were to be allocated in the short and medium term into industry, education and the development of national infrastructure, in the long term this investment might serve to expand the capacity of the country's mobilization base. When forcefully put, this argument cannot be dismissed readily. Certainly it places little emphasis upon the requirements of maintaining both continuous deterrence and the capacity to expand deferment and defensive potential rapidly, but on the other hand, it does serve to highlight the fact that decisions to determine the allocation of total government resources inevitably involve political compromises that, in nearly every circumstance, will act to constrain the level of resources available for national security purposes. However, it is by no means clear that present allocative decisions are made by any systematic process of rational decision-making. Desmond Ball paraphrases Bernard Schaffer to explain his perception of the processes of budgetary allocation:

> Do we really have here a policy that has to be met by an expenditure of 3% of GNP, or do we have a compromise between a series of impulsive or instinctive decisions on the one hand (eg. that Australia must have some sort of defence forces) and a purely extrinsic decision that the expenditure will be fixed at no more and no less than 3% of GNP? It is possible that we have the worst sort of compromise: a defence system that has stabilized at a particular level of expenditure, high enough to be a burden on the economy but not high enough to provide a worthwhile defence at all.[32]

In the simple terms of social and political realities, it would appear that in the absence of an obvious and generally perceived national security threat, there are limits to the levels of defence expenditure that governments will sanction. However, as far as the public itself is concerned, opinion poll results indicate that, in the current environment, it may be prepared to support defence expenditure levels higher than those of recent years.

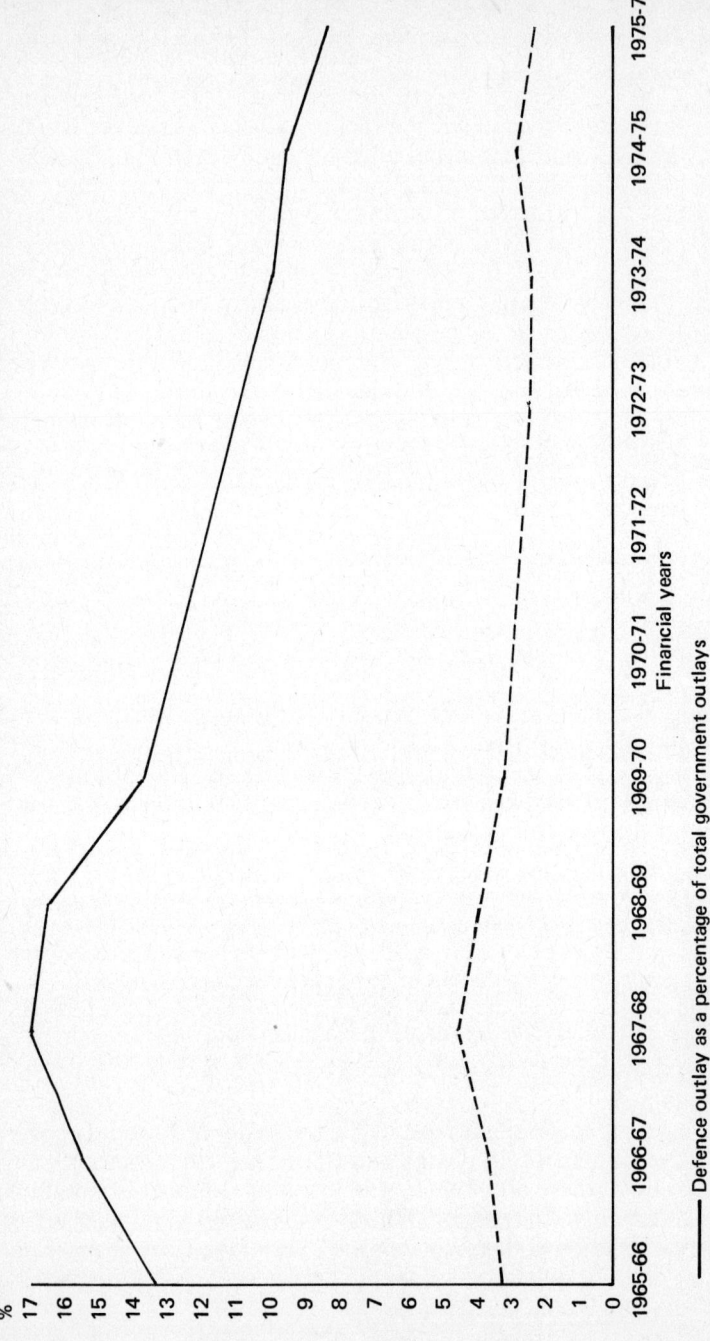

Fig. 1. Defence outlay as a percentage of total government outlays and gross domestic product, 1965-66 to 1975-76.

——— Defence outlay as a percentage of total government outlays
- - - - Defence outlay as a percentage of gross domestic product

Source: J. Tie, J. O. Langtry and R. J. O'Neill, *Australia's Defence Resources: A Compendium of Data* (Canberra: Strategic and Defence Studies Centre, Australian National University, 1978), p. 5.

External Constraints

There are, in addition, three major external influences that may act to constrain the scope for changing Australia's security strategy and structure.

First, it should be noted that those countries that supply high-technology equipments to Australia can also determine, to a degree, the nature of the technologies that are to be made available. President Carter's arms-sales policy is largely illustrative of this potential.[33] In practice, the transfer of arms to those countries that do not have major defence treaties with the United States has been restrained significantly by the President's initiative. While this particular set of restrictions does not currently apply to Australia, it should be noted that the transfer of many advanced technologies is already heavily constrained.[34] It is not inconceivable that, in some circumstances, the United States may decide that it is in its own interests to restrict the flow of technologies and equipments further. Alternative suppliers might be available for most types of low- and medium- and some types of high-technology equipment. However, if Australia required access to the most sophisticated and advanced technologies, particularly those that could be employed in long-range strategic roles, it is extremely doubtful whether these would be made available, either in normal times of peace or in crisis situations.

The second major external constraining influence may arise in the form of greatly extended international disarmament agreements and regulations. The St Petersburg Declaration, the Hague Convention and the Geneva Protocol formally limit the acquisition and use of weaponry that has indiscriminate effects, that causes unnecessary suffering or superfluous injury and that can kill or wound individuals in a treacherous manner. In recent years, the International Committee of the Red Cross and the General Assembly of the United Nations have sponsored major international conferences in an attempt to reach agreement on the prohibition of a wider range of weaponry. Those systems that have been under the most intense discussion include incendiary, time-delay, blast-fragmentation and small-calibre projectile weapons, as well as new potential weapons developments (such as high-powered lasers). In the field of conventional weaponry, it is very difficult to foresee the type of agreement that eventually might be reached, the time scale likely to prevail and the potential impact upon Australia's security options. However, in a broader sense, it is notable that Australia's signature and ratification of the Hague Convention, the Nuclear Non-proliferation Treaty and the Biological Weapons Convention already limit the scope for considering a wide range of security concepts involving nuclear, biological and chemical weaponry. Future arms-control agreements may serve to restrict Australia's strategic options to an even greater degree.

The final major area of external constraint upon change in Australia's national security strategy involves consideration of the reactive response of neighbours, allies and potential enemies. It is possible that Australia's adoption of certain types of security options may lack credibility in the view of several important external actors. For instance, if Australia's capacity to operate jointly with the United States declined significantly and was not replaced or compensated for by an increased self-defence capability, the United States might view its own interests in the regional environment to be more vulnerable as a result. Diplomatic and possibly other forms of pressure might be applied in an effort to achieve a reversal of policy. Because of the historically close alliance relationship with the United States, any major alteration of Australian security policy is likely to necessitate a judicious and sensitive process of detailed explanation.

Australia's adoption of other types of security concepts might stimulate reactions of a different kind. Some external actors might view particular options as being offensive or aggressive. It is conceivable that, in some circumstances, important global and regional actors may be alienated and hence may respond in a hostile fashion. Unfavourable diplomatic reactions might even serve to offset any purely military advantages that particular strategic concepts might promise. Regional and global reactions could effectively undermine Australia's primary strategic goals of preventing conflict and deterring and deferring its occurrence. Sensitivity to these constraining external influences needs to be regarded as an essential element of any process of national security strategy formulation.

Overall, this array of constraints on change plays a major role in determining the boundary between proposals that are practical and those that are impractical. Some of those factors that heavily influence the position of these bounds of practicality may be very similar in the 1980s and 1990s to those of the 1960s and 1970s. For instance, it can be stated with some confidence that, in the absence of a serious international crisis, the level of national security expenditure is likely to be in the same general order of magnitude (in real terms) as at present.

On the other hand, there are some dynamic factors that are likely to force substantial alterations to the bounds of practicality in the future. For example, in the 1980s, the support capacity of domestic secondary industry is likely to decline and there may be increasing restrictions on external equipment supply. These factors may serve to constrain heavily Australia's future technology options. In the area of regular service manpower, it is clear that the maintenance of current numerical ceilings will become increasingly expensive and the potential for regular manpower expansion will be limited severely. In another sphere, changing civilian values and attitudes may have the effect of undermining, to some degree, the attractiveness of traditional military life-styles. This is likely to impact not only upon the propensity for young people to enlist for the conventional type of military training but also upon the status of civil-military relations in general. Thus while some constraints on Australia's processes of national security formulation are likely to remain relatively unaltered in the 1980s, there are others that will magnify existing policy limitations.

The primary conclusion to be drawn from this discussion is that future processes of strategic and structural adaptation will need to be very selective. While it is possible that the altered nature of Australia's strategic circumstances may stimulate the requirement for a radical change in defence posture, any such proposal will need to be considered carefully in the light of the limited scale and flexibility of the nation's security resources.

Notes and References

1. "A", "B" and "C" vehicles can be defined as follows: "A" vehicles are fighting vehicles that are armed and/or designed to carry weapons, e.g. tanks, armoured personnel carriers, mechanized infantry combat vehicles, certain recovery vehicles, etc.
   "B" vehicles are non-fighting vehicles of all types that are not specifically designed to carry offensive weapons and do not fall within the "C" vehicle category.
   "C" vehicles comprise equipment designed for construction, excavation, highway maintenance and other types of plant and equipment of predominantly engineer usage.
2. Brigadier P. J. Greville, "Infrastructure Requirements for a Self-reliant Defence Policy", *United Service* 28, no. 2 (October 1974): 84.
3. The defence support capacity of the munitions, aircraft, ship-building and related industries is discussed at length in the Interim Report of the Joint (Parliamentary) Committee on Foreign Affairs and Defence, *Industrial Support for Defence Needs and Allied Matters* (Canberra: Parliament of Australia, June 1977).
4. In particular, see the discussion in the report to the Prime Minister by the Committee to Advise on Policies for Manufacturing Industry, *Policies for Development of Manufacturing Industry* (Jackson Committee Report), Green Paper (Canberra: Australian Government Publishing Service, October 1975), vol. 1, p. 59.
5. This relationship between the mining and manufacturing sectors has been termed the "Gregory thesis". For details, see Glenn Withers, "Economic

Futures and Australian Defence Policy", *Australian Journal of Defence Studies* 1, no. 2 (October 1977): 122-23.
6. Committee to Advise on Policies for Manufacturing Industry, *Policies for Development of Manufacturing Industry* (Jackson Committee Report), p. 62; an Organization for Economic Co-operation and Development, *OECD Economic Surveys: Australia* (Paris: OECD Economic Co-operation and Development Review Committee, 1979), p. 56. The figures and discussion in the OECD Survey suggest that during the mid- and late- 1970s, the contraction of Australia's manufacturing industry proceeded at a more rapid pace than during the previous decade and far exceeded the decline that reasonably could be attributed to the international trend apparent in many advanced economies of a resource shift from secondary to tertiary sectors.
7. *Policies for Development of Manufacturing Industry*, p. 62.
8. Ibid., p. 61.
9. Sir Ian McLennan, then Chairman of the Broken Hill Proprietary Co. Limited and Chairman of the Defence Industrial Committee, "The Defence Capability of Australian Industry", an address to the United Service Institution of the Australian Capital Territory, 3 May 1977; published in *The Defence Capability of Australian Industry* (Canberra: United Service Institution of the Australian Capital Territory, 1977), p. 8.
10. *Population and Australia: A Demographic Analysis and Projection* (Borrie Report) (Canberra: Australian Government Publishing Service, 1975), vol. 1, p. 7.
11. Ibid., loc. cit.
12. See the table of actual and projected rates of enrolment in tertiary institutions, ibid., p. 396.
13. Actual and projected male work participation rates for the age groups 15-19 years and 20-24 years are presented in diagrammatic form, ibid., p. 334. A similar point is made with earlier statistics by Darcy McGaurr, *Conscription and Australian Military Capability* (Canberra: Strategic and Defence Studies Centre, Australian National University, 1971), p. 2.
14. Withers, "Economic Futures and Australian Defence Policy", p. 127.
15. In the long term there are, of course, other variables that are amenable to manipulation. For example, alterations to the minimum selection criteria might be expected to increase manpower supply and changes to conditions of service and to social relationships within military structures may serve to reduce the rate of manpower wastage.
16. This point is discussed by McGaurr, *Conscription and Australian Military Capability*, pp. 14-16.
17. This was discussed by Darcy McGaurr in a lecture on manpower policy to the Australian Army Staff College, Queenscliff, Victoria, May 1977.
18. Several factors contributing to the unsatisfactory strength of part-time military forces in Australia are discussed in *Committee of Inquiry into the Citizen Military Forces Report* (Millar Report) (Canberra: Australian Government Publishing Service, 1974), pp. 49-50. The opinions of those individuals who were serving or had served in the Citizen Military Forces in the early 1970s are recorded in Appendices C and D of the report. Several specific areas of dissatisfaction are identified in these analyses.
19. W. H. Smith, "The Determinants of Defence Policy" (paper delivered to Conference on Armed Forces and Australian Society, Royal Military College, Duntroon, Canberra, 20-22 May 1977), pp. 9-10.
20. Henry S. Albinski, *Politics and Foreign Policy in Australia: The Impact of Vietnam and Conscription* (Durham, N.C.: Duke University Press, 1970), p. 11.
21. Frank Cranston is Defence and Aviation Correspondent for the *Canberra Times*.

22. Smith, "Determinants of Defence Policy", p. 11.
23. The high degree of concentration of specialized human capacities in security and strategic affairs is perpetuated by the long-term neglect of these subjects in Australia's military colleges, universities and colleges of advanced education. Australia's situation contrasts markedly in this respect with nearly every other advanced Western state. For instance, in the United States, there are numerous military, academic and corporate organizations that teach and conduct research in the field. Most of these are listed as Corporate Members in *List of Members* (London: International Institute for Strategic Studies (IISS), 1974), pp. 86-89. In the United Kingdom, there are several military colleges and university departments dealing explicitly with strategic studies. For details, see the IISS Corporate Membership list. In Canada, apart from the National Defence College, there is a very strong Canadian Institute of International Affairs and Strategic Studies, as well as ten universities with military professorships. For details, see Richard A. Preston, "The Study of War and Its Causes", *Canadian Defence Quarterly* 7, no. 1 (Summer 1977): 46-50.

    By contrast, in Australia, there is no Department of Strategic Studies at the Royal Military College at Duntroon (the subject was first offered as an undergraduate option only in 1977), nor is a Department of Strategic Studies planned for the new Australian Defence Force Academy (ADFA). For details, see Paul Mench, "Education and Officers: Changing Concepts of Officer Education" (paper delivered to Conference on Armed Forces and Australian Society, Royal Military College, Duntroon, Canberra, 20-22 May 1977), pp. 28-33. In the universities, the situation is little better. There is a small number of isolated academics holding teaching positions in various universities who occasionally contribute to debates on global, regional and national strategic issues. The only academic structure in Australia that is specifically tasked with the full-time study of strategic matters is the Strategic and Defence Studies Centre at the Australian National University. Despite the energetic efforts of all who have been associated with this body since its inception in 1967, its size remains miniscule. It is still without a single tenured academic position and its Head is on loan from the Department of International Relations. This long-term neglect of defence and strategic studies in Australia accounts in no small way for the quality and quantity of the expertise in strategic affairs that is apparent in the parliament, the public service, the military structure, academia, the media and the general community.
24. The information contained in Tables 4 and 5 was obtained directly from the card-index files of the Roy Morgan Research Centre Pty Ltd, 77 Pacific Highway, North Sydney. A detailed analysis of the 1971 poll results, displayed in Table 5, was published in the *Sun-Herald*, 3 October 1971, p. 27.
25. This question is discussed briefly by Smith, "Determinants of Defence Policy", pp. 13 ff.
26. Committee to Advise on Policies for Manufacturing Industry, *Policies for Development of Manufacturing Industry* (Jackson Committee Report), pp. 125-26.
27. In 1971, ANOP asked the question, "Should the size of Australia's armed forces be increased or reduced?" 59 per cent replied that they favoured an increase, 19 per cent favoured a reduction and 22 per cent were unsure. *Australian Public Opinion Newsletter* 1, no. 1 (September 1971): 29. It is difficult to evaluate this type of result because opportunity cost factors are not introduced into the question. If, alternatively, it was asked whether the size of the armed forces should be increased even though it would require an increase of taxes or a cut in education or social security expenditures, a more accurate gauge of public opinion could be derived.

28. In 1971, ANOP asked the question, "Should Australia increase, decrease or leave as it is its defence spending?" 46 per cent replied that they favoured an increase, 40 per cent that it should be left as it is, 10 per cent favoured a decrease and 4 per cent were unsure. *Australian Public Opinion Newsletter* 1, no. 1 (September 1971): 31. As with the case cited in Note 27, it is difficult to interpret this result in the absence of opportunity cost factors.
29. The only clear example of this that is available is the response to a question asked by the Roy Morgan Research Centre in October 1952: "Compulsory military training now puts 34 000 youths into camp each year. Soon, 60 000 youths will become 18 each year, and to train them all would cost another £10 million a year. Do you favour training them all, or exempting some?" 66 per cent responded that they favoured training them all, 29 per cent favoured exempting some and 5 per cent were unsure. This result displays a significant softening of attitude from the responses given to questions concerning the desirability of *compulsory* (i.e. universal) military training. (See Table 4).
30. Details are given by Brigadier Greville, "Infrastructure Requirements for a Self-reliant Defence Policy", p. 81.
31. This case was argued in some detail by Mr Bill Hayden, MHR (then Opposition Spokesman on Defence) in an address to the Joint Services Staff College, Canberra, 10 May 1977, pp. 3-5.
32. Desmond J. Ball, "The Politics of Australian Defence Decision-making", unpublished paper (Canberra: Strategic and Defence Studies Centre, Australian National University, 1977), pp. 9-10.
33. President Carter's arms-sales policy is described in detail by Bernard Weinraub, "Carter Moves to Cut Back Sales of U.S. Arms Abroad", *New York Times*, 20 May 1977, p. 1.
34. The United States holds the details and results of most advanced research and development programmes and many production programmes very closely, for both national security and commercial reasons. Australia and other close allies of the United States gain access to some of this information through a number of international agreements and exchange programmes. Many of those in which Australia participates are listed in Department of Defence, Australian Defence Scientific Service, *Weapons Research Establishment Annual Report 1975-76* (Canberra: Australian Government Publishing Service, 1976), p. 55.

6
Bureaucratic[1] Resistance

How the System Works

In Australia, national security policy is formulated through the interaction of a large number of autonomous or semi-autonomous actors. Many of the actors are organizations or cohesive groups, but some are individual persons. At the very top of the structure are the Minister for Defence, the Chief of Defence Force Staff (CDFS), the Secretary of the Department of Defence and a handful of senior military and civilian officers. The influence and power-base of each of these major actors varies in both formal and informal senses. In terms of legal power and responsibility, it is clear, under the Defence Act, that the minister is pre-eminent.[2] However, in practice, his power is constrained by a variety of factors: for example, the tenure of a minister is frequently short and of an uncertain duration, his expertise in defence matters is often very limited and the demands of the Cabinet, parliament, public appearances and electoral duties serve to reduce effectively the time he can devote to departmental matters.

The formal powers, authority and responsibility of the CDFS, as principal military adviser to the minister, appear in the Defence Act and in the ministerial directives. In practice, the CDFS and his staff are the undisputed providers of military judgement and a major source of military information for civilian actors in the system. As a consequence of the Tange reforms, the CDFS has been given the right of direct access to the minister. However, in practice, the powers of the position have been degraded by a relatively high turnover of personnel.

The legal powers of the Secretary of the Department, as principal civilian adviser to the minister, are outlined in the Public Service Act, the Defence Act, the Audit Act, the Finance Regulations and also in the Ministerial Directives. In practice, the secretary not only has direct access to the minister but all of the advantages of a potentially long tenure. The secretary can devote himself full-time to the most important tasks at hand; he can gain extensive experience, accumulate knowledge and co-ordinate the generation of centralized policies.

The differing nature of the formal and informal power held by each of the three major actors serves to prevent a complete dominance of the system by any one of them. However, it also means that all three possess independent capacities to resist change by mobilizing their own individual and organizational sources of influence and authority.

Depending upon the nature of the matter at hand, a number of other actors can play important roles in the processes of national security policy formulation. Most notable are the Prime Minister, the ministers and Departments of Finance, Treasury and Foreign Affairs, Cabinet itself, parliamentary committees and pressure groups such as industry bodies and the Returned Services League. Possessing a much lower level of influence are individual parliamentarians, medium-level bureaucrats and military officers, ministerial advisers, journalists, academics, etc. All of these actors manoeuvre, pressure and bargain in an effort to influence the shape of the national security policy that is adopted and implemented. Their motivation in most instances is a genuine concern for the country's national security. However, as Morton Halperin points out from American experience, this concern can be manifested in a variety of forms:

> Their problem is to determine what is in fact in the national security interest. Officials seek clues and guidelines from a variety of sources. Some hold to a set of beliefs about the world which provide strong clues, eg. the Soviet Union is expansionist and must be stopped by American military power. Others look to authorities within the government or beyond it for guidance. Many bureaucrats define what is necessary for the nation's security by a set of more specific immediate interests. For some these may be personal: "Since, in general, I know how to protect the nation's security interests, whatever increases my influence is in the national interest". For others the immediate interests relate to domestic political interests: "Since a sound economy is a prerequisite to national security I must oppose policies which threaten the economy"; or "since only my party knows how to defend the security interests of the United States I must support policies which keep my party in power".
>
> For many participants the immediate objectives which provide strong clues for what is in the nation's security interest are the interests of the organization to which they belong. Career officials come naturally to believe that the health of their organization is vital to the nation's security. So also do individuals who are appointed by the President to senior posts in Washington foreign policy bureaucracies. This tendency varies depending on the individual, the strength of his prior conviction, his image of his role, and the nature of the organization he heads.[3]

Hence although there may be agreement, in the most general sense, concerning overall long-term national security objectives, the variety of attitudes possessed by the multiplicity of actors within the government policy-making system means that short-range, immediate objectives differ greatly.

It is perhaps not surprising that those with an overwhelming experience in economic matters tend to see solutions primarily in economic terms, that those with diplomatic backgrounds frequently place undue emphasis upon the techniques of diplomacy and that those with experience in advanced tactical aircraft, ships or armoured vehicles tend to concentrate upon military solutions and usually in the context of those systems with which they are most familiar. As Darcy McGaurr points out, individual bureaucratic actors or coalitions of actors working within their own value systems seek to optimize functions that they subjectively view to be of primary importance:

> Anti-submarine and maritime surveillance capabilities are each contributed to by both the RAAF and the RAN. Each can be expected to propose expenditures which promote a more effective operation of the forces which it contributes, i.e. each can be expected to attempt to sub-optimize. It is unlikely that the result would be the best combination of forces from the two services considered together.[4]

The divergent views of the participating actors are subjected to a complex process of evaluation, bargaining and compromise. Some actors are likely to concentrate upon setting the scene and the parameters of debate, others may make firm proposals and others again may have the power to react, modify, delay, determine the method of implementation, veto, etc. The eventual outcome will depend heavily upon the relative power of those involved and their individual capacity to influence the matters at stake.

In this type of environment, it is frequently in the interests of individual actors to attempt to form coalitions or alliances to enhance the prospects of successful action on matters they consider to be important.[5] Some of these coalitions tend to be of an almost continuous nature, as, for example, that between the former Department of Supply and the local defence industries.[6] Others may be short-term alliances, sometimes between policy-making actors who normally share a strong adversarial relationship. For example, Desmond Ball cites the case, in July 1973, of the RAAF supporting a Cabinet decision to postpone the replacement of the Mirage III fighters.[7] The apparent motive was to increase the prospects of an eventual decision being made in favour of the McDonnell Douglas F-15.

It seems clear that, as Graham T. Allison points out, the final product of the national security decision-making process should not be viewed as a completely rational and consistent response to objectively determined requirements.

> The decisions and actions of governments are intranational political resultants: resultants in the sense that what happens is not chosen as a solution to a problem but rather results from compromise, conflict and confusion of officials with diverse interests and unequal influence; political in the sense that the activity from which decisions and actions emerge is best characterized as bargaining along regularized channels among individual members of the government. Following Wittenstein's employment of the concept of a "game", national behaviour in international affairs can be conceived of as something that emerges from intricate and subtle, simultaneous, overlapping games among players located in positions in a government. The hierarchical arrangement of these players constitutes the government. Games proceed neither at random nor at leisure. Regular channels structure the game; deadlines force issues to the attention of incredibly busy players. The moves, sequences of moves, and games of chess are thus to be explained in terms of the bargaining among players with separate and unequal power over particular pieces, and with separate objectives in distinguishable subgames.[8]

The policies that emerge from this type of system are frequently difficult to predict with certainty. As Allison explains it, "internal politics is messy".[9] Because of the very nature of the system, policy outcomes and reactions cannot be expected to be internally consistent or in any sense rational from an external objective point of view.

The workings of national security bureaucracies are made even more confusing by many of the methods employed by actors in the system to further their interests. For instance, the policies advocated by many parties may not necessarily represent their view of the ideal outcome so much as a calculated bargaining stance that they perceive to maximize the probability of an ideal outcome being derived. As Desmond Ball notes:

> This may mean that the initial proposals presented to the bureaucracy could bear little resemblance to the desired policy; but it is only the outcome of the decisional process which is important.[10]

In practice, this activity can effectively warp the basis for judgement in several key areas of the decision-making process. It is frequently difficult to distinguish between objective scientific, military and analytic information provided to support the decision-making process and bureaucratic political viewpoints shrouded in the same language and format.

While distinctions between bureaucratic political statements and real opinions and objectives are frequently difficult to make, the problem can be eased to some degree by the fact that bureaucratic interests tend to follow recognizable patterns. Halperin argues that bureaucratic actors strive primarily to maintain or improve their autonomy, organizational morale, functional "essence", roles and missions, and their budgets.[11]

Autonomy is most commonly sought because individual actors and organizations tend to believe that their specialist skills and/or experience qualify them ideally for determining the optimum method of task performance and the scale of resources required.

A high level of personnel motivation and morale is sought not only because it generates work efficiency but also because it tends to raise the status of the organization's leadership. Hence bureaucrats are frequently prepared to resist changes and efficiencies if they suspect that the morale of the organization will be affected detrimentally.

Career officials are usually keenly aware of what the essence of an organization is and should be in terms of its characteristics and tasks. Although in large organizations, there are inevitably differences of view, in national security structures these seem to be somewhat limited. For instance, in the RAAF the almost universally regarded essence or core of the structure is its high-performance combat aircraft and their functions. In the Army, it is the "sharp end" armoured units and infantry battalions. In the RAN the essence is represented primarily by the frigates and destroyers and the Navy's carrier and strike aircraft. Support aircraft, support shipping and minority specialist forces in all services tend to be accorded a lower priority and are frequently regarded as being of more marginal significance.

The intensity with which organizations will act to safeguard those roles, structures and equipments they regard to be central components of their essence can be highly dysfunctional if altered external circumstances produce a requirement for significant organizational adaptation. As Roger A. Beaumont points out, this form of institutional conservatism is readily apparent in many military structures:

> Weapons systems have a social function for the professional, and those new ideas which suggest turmoil, or too much emphasis on youth or on new bodies of expertise, are naturally suppressed in the same way that pioneer physicians like Jenner, Semmelweiss and Freud were opposed in various fields. The professional system has more involved than merely performing a mission. It is a community with social needs. Professional soldiers and sailors, starved for budgets and rank in peacetime through most of Anglo-American history, have been steadily on guard

against upstarts. Until the nuclear era, only wartime instability brought on growth, sudden rich resources and anxiety produced dramatic change, and victory tended to lull the successful.[2]

Thus in the absence of substantial wars or other traumatic disturbances, there is a very great tendency for national security systems to retain the general form, structures, equipments and practices that were derived from the previous major conflict. Despite a changing external environment and altered operational tasks, large military bureaucracies tend to continue heavy commitments to traditional systems and functions.[13] Darcy McGaurr illustrates this point from his experience of the Australian national security structure:

> Since each service consists largely of groups whose careers involve the operation of particular items of equipment, it is not surprising that a motive for many equipment proposals is simply the replacement of existing equipment at the end of its operational life. If HMAS Melbourne is not replaced by another platform for fixed wing aircraft, a way of life which has been a source of satisfaction and pride to present senior RAN officers and which is the aspiration of many young servicemen may vanish. To the extent that a service can be expected to seek replacement for aging equipment rather than promote new capabilities which have no existing interest group to support them, the system is conservative.[14]

The follow-on imperative or replacement complex is thus a natural product of large national security bureaucracies.[15] It is a mechanism that effectively secures key elements of the perceived essence of military structures.

The fourth major goal for bureaucratic actors concerns the acquisition, possession and maintenance of roles and missions. Functional divisions between competing bureaucracies are rarely clear and incontestable. Hence the development of new or varied roles and missions frequently provides a basis for bureaucratic conflict.[16] An organizational actor is most likely to seek new roles and functions if it perceives that it would be placed in a disadvantageous position by new areas of responsibility being conceded to a bureaucratic rival. This was the general nature of the bureaucratic squabble between the RAN and the Army over control of the new heavy landing-craft in the early 1970s.[17]

In other instances, an organization may judge a new function to be peripheral to its essence and to represent a potential source of resource diversion from areas of higher priority. This has been the attitude of both the RAAF and the Army to airfield surface-to-air missile (SAM) defence systems since the early 1960s.[18] It is perhaps not surprising that the obsolescence of the Bloodhound airfield defence SAMs has not been heralded by the clamour for a replacement system.

The fifth and final area of competing bureaucratic interest relates to budgetary stimuli. Bureaucrats naturally prefer budgets of large dimensions because the factor of size impacts directly upon relative power and bargaining strength. Hence proposed changes in policy or patterns of action are usually scrutinized laboriously for their potential effects upon budgetary allocations. Halperin cites one American example where an armed service was prepared to subordinate concerns of organizational essence to those of potential budgetary gain:

> ... the Army was interested in acquiring responsibility for the deployment of MRBM [medium-range ballistic missiles] in the 1950s, in part because this would give the Army a strategic nuclear role. The Army hoped that this would justify its getting an increased share of the over-all defense budget, since the existing allocation was based on the Army having no strategic function.[19]

In other situations, when bureaucrats perceive that additional functions under consideration are unlikely to be accompanied by supplementary funding, their adoption is almost certain to be opposed, regardless of the function's objective significance for overall national security capacity.

The Problems of Bureaucratic Adaptation

The partially non-rational nature of the decision-making processes in large national security bureaucracies impacts directly upon the prospects for appropriate and systematic change when this is required because of variations in external circumstances. Bureaucratic structures designed specifically to perform a particular type of function and that become well-practised in it are constrained very little by institutional behaviour patterns. However, when requirements change, organizations normally find it extemely difficult to restructure their form, operating procedures and equipments to meet the new situation. R. W. Komer noted this institutional inflexibility in the application of United States policy in Vietnam:

> Each organization inevitably tended to make policy to conform in practice to that with which it was most familiar — to play out its standard organizational repertoire. Each reflected that fact of institutional life cited by an anonymous White House aide who wrote that "bureaucracy as a form of organization tends to contort policy to existing structures rather than adjusting structures to reflect change in policy".[20]

National security bureaucracies appear to have particularly strong vested interests in the status quo.[21] In some respects, this is not very surprising, since there are strong motivations for this type of decision-making to be undertaken in a conservative manner. Most notably, it must be recognized that an alteration of national security policy can have momentous consequences for the outcome of future international events. Clearly national security bureaucracies bear a very heavy responsibility for decisions that are, or are not, made in their area of authority. To some degree, at least, individuals, groups and organizations can be held accountable for any judgements that prove to be seriously in error. Thus in many environments, the stimuli to entertain radical new ideas, to experiment or to rapidly adapt are very weak. A major consequence is that in many national security structures, institutional conservatism itself becomes a way of life. Well-established social mores, patterns of behaviour, types of equipment, work locations and levels of activity frequently become relatively easy to perpetuate indefinitely. In this type of environment, little imagination, skill and effort is required for individual bureaucrats to avoid making the sort of mistakes that might damage their career progression. Komer discusses his perception of the problem under the heading "institutional inertia":

> Bureaucrats prefer to deal with the familiar. It is more comfortable and convenient to continue following tested routines, whereas to change may be to admit prior error — a cardinal bureaucratic sin. So, whether private or public, civilian or military, organizations typically like to keep operating the way they are operating, and to shift only slowly in response to changing situations. And the more hierarchical and disciplined they are — military organizations are almost archetypes — the greater the built-in institutional obstacles to change except slowly and incrementally. Even a cursory review of the fate of many military innovations and innovators would be sufficient to illustrate the point. Dr Vannevar Bush, World War II head of the Office of Scientific Research and Development, has described some of the obstacles to technological innovation in the military services even during wartime. To him, military organization "suffers from a disease that permeates all governmental... organizations — the daft belief that if one does nothing one will not make mistakes, and the drab system of seniority and promotions will proceed on its way".[22]

As a consequence of these factors, when large national security structures are required to change, they tend to react in highly conventional ways and usually according to precedent. The balance of well-established competing interests almost always means that decisions are made and actions implemented that will not disturb institutionalized practices and structures. Policy agreements tend to follow the line of least bureaucratic resistance.

When national security structures are confronted by an altered external environment and a clear requirement for change is evident, it cannot be anticipated that the processes of adaptation will be simple or easy. Some bureaucrats prefer to ignore the requirements for change and concentrate on meeting the pressures of ongoing activities. Other bureaucrats prefer to support existing systems on the basis of their capacity to perform in previous environments. As Beaumont points out, bureaucratic defence by reference to historical precedent is not a new theme in military affairs:

> There were peacetime battles over the introduction of rifles, ironclads, breech-loaders, battleships, airplanes, tanks, aircraft carriers and on and on. One reason the old guard fought hard against novelty was that the old systems worked in war — even if the war may have been fifty years earlier.[23]

Other bureaucrats tend to feel a high level of institutional loyalty to an organizational structure with which they have been associated over an extended period. These individuals frequently brand proposals for significant change as unworkable. Senior bureaucrats also often perceive the challenge of new ideas, concepts, technologies and structures to represent a threat to their well-established personal positions. Beaumont describes this type of reaction following the First World War:

> The swiftness with which the "old guard" returned to pre-1914 military systems and traditions of soldiering in America, France, Britain, Italy and Germany has been described by those who saw the rejection of armour, aviation and shock troops as blindness to military necessity. But the guardians of the old way knew the new weapons were a young man's game, and that more than tactical advantage was implicit in their use. Real reform, they sensed, would put too much power in the hands of junior officers, as it had in Turkey and Italy. And so from 1918 until the middle of World War II, the battleship dominated naval tactical thought in all major fleets. Young George Patton and Dwight Eisenhower were warned that their enthusiasm for armour would hurt their careers.[24]

Even when the requirement for change is accepted in strategic policy, military bureaucratic structures are adept at warding off the disturbance that would be implicit in meaningful adaptation. A wide array of bureaucratic "games" can be played to defer and modify policy proposals and even firm government directions to change. For example, one tactic is to institute studies of the new requirements. If it is considered that their conclusions are likely to be disturbing, those conducting the work can be given poor direction, inadequate resources and insufficient time. The preliminary reports that result then can either be rejected as unsatisfactory or alternatively accepted in a qualified manner for subsequent analysis. Working groups then can be established to examine particular aspects in greater detail over an extended period of time. The results of widely dispersed semi-autonomous working groups can be expected to become available progressively. This permits piecemeal shelving of individual specialized proposals on various grounds or, alternatively, the qualified acceptance of those proposals that are more broadly supported by bureaucratic actors. Actual implementation requires the passage of an even more complex bureaucratic mill.[25] The final result is usually a verbal acceptance of the changing nature of the external environment and the mouthing of a generalized requirement for change, but the substance of what is actually done concerning operating concepts, procedures, doctrines, equipments, etc. is frequently of marginal consequence, if indeed it can be distinguished at all. As Halperin points out, large bureaucracies are ideally equipped to absorb pressures for change with a minimum of disturbance.

> In many cases . . . officials reach consensus by designing an ambiguous policy which avoids substantial costs to the different interests of the participants, including the interests of the organizations involved. The compromise avoids making choices on priorities and leaves organizations free to continue operating as they have in the past and to control their own operations. Once a decision is made, the organizations themselves shape the way in which it is implemented.[26]

In national security structures, these processes of comfortable accommodation normally provide adequate scope for individual actors and organizations to pursue their own entrenched interests. For highly institutionalized special interest groups, such as the armed services, this has particular significance. As James Thompson remarked, "the military mind develops its own momentum in the absence of clear guidelines from the civilians".[27]

Factors Acting to Perpetuate Bureaucratic Inertia

There are at least five major factors that serve to perpetuate institutional inertia in Australia's national security bureaucracy. The first concerns the inadequacy of political direction and oversight; the second, the misdirection of personal and organizational incentive patterns; the third, the absence of meaningful analyses of structural performance; the fourth, the relative rigidity of the Australian Public Service system; and the fifth, the intensity of bureaucratic secrecy.

The entire Australian government bureaucracy suffers from ministerial control that is highly variable and frequently incoherent.[28]

Limited ministerial involvement and direction of departmental activities makes it possible for large sections of the bureaucracy either to lose a sense of policy direction or to develop their own. The Report of the Royal Commission on Australian Government Administration (the Coombs Report) emphasizes the vital role of clearly stated government objectives in determining the efficiency of administrative bureaucracies:

> Of primary importance to efficiency in the bureaucracy, then, is clarity in the objectives of the government and in the priority which is to be attached to them. Clear and effective processes will be required by which the government establishes and reviews its objectives and their priorities. To provide an adequate base for administrative performance, such objectives must be more than general directions for a department or agency as a whole. They must be capable of expression in sufficient detail to provide a program of work not only for the department or agency but also for sections and units, functional and geographical, within it. Only if this is possible will departments and agencies receive adequate political direction on which to base their administrative processes, or will individual officers receive an adequate stimulus to effort and an ability to relate their individual performances to group objectives.[29]

However, the derivation and expression of such clear policy objectives is not always easy. As Dr H. C. Coombs has pointed out:

> Of course, ministers do not always have clear objectives and frequently lack the capacity to formulate them. Ministers are chosen from a limited field by processes which give little weight to administrative and executive competence.[30]

In this respect, the absence of provisions for the appointment of non-parliamentary members as Cabinet ministers can be seen as an inherent weakness of the Westminster system of government. Means must be found to increase the capacity of ministers to direct bureaucratic activity effectively.

The second major influence supporting bureaucratic inertia arises from the fact that personal career incentive patterns in large public service bureaucracies are dominated by the pressures for conformity. Adaptive response on an individual or a subgroup organizational level tends to rouse peer group resistance as well as to clash with the institutional norms embodied by senior bureaucrats. The penalties for questioning the system may include transfers to areas of mechanical routine work and restricted promotion. Progression is gained by working within the system and accepting its procedures, values and operational limitations.

The third major factor is the reluctance of public service structures to attempt to obtain a meaningful index of their operational efficiency.[31] As Komer points out, "organizations are usually neither long on self criticism nor very receptive to outside analysis of their performance".[32] In the specific case of Australia's security structure, the task is made doubly difficult by the absence of a clear political statement or uniform perception of national security goals. It is no doubt true that the uncertain nature of Australia's strategic environment does not make this task easy. However, as is argued in Chapter 7, this does not make its performance impossible. In its absence, there can be no means of conducting even the most simple test of functional efficiency and many pressures for significant structural change are effectively constrained.

The relative rigidity of the Australian Public Service system represents a fourth contributing factor in the perpetuation of institutional inertia. Restrictions on lateral recruitment, personnel exchanges and postgraduate study and research effectively limit the potential to develop expertise to optimal levels in important functional areas.[33] In those sections of the Australian bureaucracy that deal with national security issues, contact with domestic and international research bodies and organizations is particularly restricted. This contrasts markedly with the policy and practice in nearly every other Western democracy.

The very limited nature of bureaucratic incentives to be highly efficient and adaptive is discussed at length in the Coombs Report. Great emphasis is placed in these findings upon the limited accountability and scope for initiative in the system, particularly for senior public servants.[34] The stultifying impact of the system upon personnel is described most graphically by Dr Coombs:

> I found the younger members of the bureaucracy impressive. Those recruited to what might broadly be called policy work generally are intelligent, educated and socially involved ... The raw material with which the system has to work is of good quality.
>
> But what does it do with it? Corresponding discussions with older officials who have experienced twenty or so years of its impact left me with a profoundly different impression. Years of involvement in routine and ritualistic processes, an inability to see the outcome of work done, a sense of isolation from those with whose affairs government administration is concerned and a prevailing flatness in the quality of life, official and unofficial, generally has destroyed much of the vitality and concern which no doubt were as evident twenty years ago among them as it now is among their successors ...
>
> It is of course from those who have gone through these experiences that, predominantly, the top echelons of the bureaucracy are chosen. Fortunately there are some of exceptional capacity and resilience who have come through relatively undamaged and some who by good plan-

ning, good management or good luck have evaded the routine and the ritual. Nevertheless, many of those at the top reflect the flatness and unimaginativeness which years without stimulus have imposed upon them. For them the cardinal sin is "to rock the boat". It was of them that John Osborne wrote in *Look Back in Anger* saying, "They spent their time mostly looking forward to the past" ... There is I believe something seriously wrong with a system which so stultifies worthwhile human beings.[35]

National security structures are endowed with a fifth and extremely powerful means of perpetuating their institutional inertia, in their capacity to restrict the flow of bureaucratically sensitive information. In the national security field, there are naturally a large number of matters that are properly held under a high level of security classification. While Australia's governmental bureaucracies in general have a reputation for over-secrecy,[36] it is therefore not surprising that the Department of Defence is most noted in this regard. General operating philosophies, concepts, doctrines and a wide range of bureaucratic actions and inactions are consistently and effectively shrouded from public view. One obvious and most important consequence is to limit inquiry and investigation by the media, academics, members of the public and even members of Parliament.[37]

Means of Encouraging Adaptation

Because of the natural bureaucratic characteristics of Australia's security structure, its capacity to adapt to meet the requirements of the country's changing strategic environment is limited. As a consequence, a sustained effort is required to encourage and, if necessary, compel bureaucratic adaptation. This must be done in a realistic manner. For instance, it is not possible to prohibit the processes of bureaucratic politics, bargaining and compromise. As James Forrestal, the first United States Secretary of Defence, pointed out, bureaucratic politics is an integral part of any government decision-making process:

> I have always been amused by those who say they are quite willing to go into government but they are not willing to go into politics. My answer ... is that you can no more divorce government from politics than you can separate sex from creation.[38]

Rather than to seek their abolition, the processes of bureaucratic politics require redirection, with active measures being taken to counteract the institutional disincentives for flexible change. Let us now examine six tentative proposals that might be expected to stimulate the changes required.

1. More Effective Ministers

Firstly, there is an urgent requirement to strengthen ministerial capacities to direct the bureaucracy with clarity and, where necessary, precision. An array of possible measures conceivably could contribute to this process. For instance, in theory at least, political parties intentionally could select parliamentary candidates who possess high levels of expertise in vital areas of government responsibility and seek to groom such individuals for ministerial duties. Ministers themselves could make more active efforts to educate themselves concerning the vital issues in their portfolios. To some degree, ministers could also seek much broader assistance from external advisers and sources of information. Yet, in practice, the scope for all of these possibilities is constrained severely by a number of conflicting pressures, which characterize the real world. For example, a wide range of occupational, social and political forces effectively prevents all but a few experts entering parliament and gaining ministerial control in their area of specific interest. As was mentioned earlier in this chapter, the demands of parliament, the constituency, public speaking and other commitments absorb a very large proportion of the time available to ministers and reduce effectively their capacity to direct departments and authorities that come under their control. Furthermore, the tenure of individual ministers in particular portfolios is also frequently relatively short and hence much of their time tends to be taken up by basic familiarization and learning functions. Ministerial advisers of an appropriate calibre can be very useful, but they are frequently difficult to recruit and their relationship to the government bureaucracy as a whole has been the source of many difficulties and disputes in the past.[39]

In these circumstances, it may be desirable to redefine the responsibilities of ministers and senior bureaucrats so as to retain the authority of ministers undiminished, but to concentrate their attention on the determination of a series of centrally important and readily definable policy issues. This would be an effective means of increasing the level of bureaucratic accountability for the performance of clear ministerial directions. This was a major recommendation of the Coombs Report.[40]

2. Bureaucratic Incentives to Adapt

Civil and military training and incentive systems need to be restructured so as to place a much higher premium upon flexibility and adaptiveness. The simple regurgitation of conventionally accepted solutions and responses needs to be questioned at all levels. Organizational conformity and submission needs to be replaced as a criterion of career progression by a preparedness to question, to innovate actively and to experiment. When discussing the requirement to exploit fully the potential of the new military technologies, Dr Malcolm Currie, the former United States Director of Defence Research and Engineering, argued for a review of personal incentive patterns in the following terms:

> ... we must remove barriers to innovation which often exist. Innovation that might alter a service's role or mission is often resisted as are concepts that might "threaten" support to a program that has already been "sold". Stronger incentives for innovation and risk must be supported ... We must more clearly recognize the right and the need to fail. Too often those in DoD feel that they cannot afford a "failure" with Congress and the news media ready to second guess everything. Too often to-day's bureaucrats substitute research for insight, management for leadership and experience for guts — because it's the safe thing to do. We must move together to strengthen the innovation which has been our nation's hallmark.[41]

The same problems were recognized in the Coombs Report and a large number of its recommendations are directed towards their solution:

> A persistent theme of this Report, underlying many of its recommendations, is the need for adaptability, for those in the administration to be aware of and responsive to the facts of social change. We have made it clear that an effective response must be preceded by analysis of the nature of the changes occurring, examination of the alternative responses in the light of the government's ojectives, and further analysis of the means available to make the response. We have also emphasised that adaptability implies a readiness to take risks, to experiment, in the interests of finding the right means to achieve greater efficiency. If the spirit of these recommendations infuses the attitudes of officials, adaptation is more likely to become a continuous, self-generating process. It would not, however, be wise to rely wholly on such internal sources of self criticism and adaptability. External stimulus is from time to time necessary, as is the "lateral thinking" of persons with wide but different experience.[42]

The commissioners then proceed to recommend the more frequent institution of studies and inquiries into the functional performance of sectors of the public service.[43] These might be expected to have a very important role to play. However, in practice, they could be supplemented by a much broader range of initiatives, some of which are outlined on the following pages.

3. Flexible Bureaucratic Task Forces

When the requirement arises for a new programme that does not readily fit the practised organizational repertoire of existing bureaucratic structures, it may be best to establish an autonomous *ad hoc* task force for its development, implementation and management. This would not involve an expansion of the bureaucracy, but rather the introduction of a larger amount of structural fluidity. Under this concept, personnel, funding and resources would be made available for reallocation from existing structures to perform specific functions within task force programmes. For each new programme, there normally would be an initial requirement for a small central task force staff to be established, around which specialists could operate at particular stages of each project. This would mean, for example, that once the detailed planning for a particular programme was completed, individual planners frequently could be reallocated directly to new task forces. If the autonomy of individual actors from their parent organizations could be increased, a higher level of objectivity in decision-making might be achieved.

4. A Total Programme Role for Task Forces

If a primary objective of bureaucratic restructuring is to achieve a high level of objective rationality in policy adoption and implementation, it would be necessary to reduce the current gap between stated policy intentions and actual achievement. General Maxwell Taylor has stated the nature of the problem as he experienced it in Vietnam:

> One of the facts of life about Vietnam was that it was never difficult to decide what should be done but it was almost impossible to get it done, at least in an acceptable period of time.[44]

The problems of implementation have been studied in considerable depth by J. L. Pressman and A. B. Wildavsky.[45] They concluded that one of the major reasons why programmes are rarely carried out in the manner their designers intend is the number of decision-points structured into the processes of implementation. Desmond Ball summarizes the particular case that they studied in the following terms:

> An oversimplified schematization of the programme shows that there were 15 principal participants, with differing perspectives and objectives and senses of urgency, some 30 decision-points, and about 70 separate "agreements" necessary. Even if the probability of agreement was 99% at each clearance point, the overall probability of programme success could be less than half after 70 clearances. As Pressman and Wildavsky remark, "the remarkable thing is that new programmes work at all".[46]

The general integrating processes of the recent reorganization in

Australia's Department of Defence have had the effect of reducing significantly the number of organizational actors and, to some extent, the number of decision-points for the implementation of many types of policies. However, through the application of the integrated task force concept, there would be scope for even greater advances. Task forces that are created to develop a programme concept and determine an optimum solution ideally also would be provided with the authority and resources required to manage the programme's detailed implementation. This would serve to reduce drastically the number of decision-points that would confront individual programmes and might be expected to encourage better decision-making because of the extended period of time that would be available for the consideration of each issue.

5. Flexible and Imaginative Bureaucratic Managers

The personnel characteristics required for highly original conceptual development and analytical programme management differ markedly from those required for routine line management or for the satisfactory peacetime command of operational service units.[47] In a situation where major changes in the country's environment demand flexible adaption at all levels, there is a greatly enhanced need for both civil and military personnel to be selected, trained and retrained with these requirements in mind.

An array of measures could be instituted to facilitate this process. For instance, much greater emphasis could be placed upon the qualifications and training of both civil and service personnnel prior to and in the years immediately following their recruitment. In order to increase the general awareness, knowledge, flexibility and adaptability of young officers, much greater use could be made of staff colleges, universities and professional associations such as the United Service Institutions. During their periods of service, civilian and military officers could be encouraged to further broaden their thinking and experience through the provision of greater freedom to participate in, and contribute to, internal and external journals, conferences and other avenues of debate. Another possibility, which was recommended in the Coombs Report, would be to draw more extensively upon the great benefits that can be gained through exchanges of personnel with other government agencies, large firms in industry and commerce, academic institutions and some types of voluntary agencies.[48] This would encourage not only a broadening of experience of those officials who temporarily vacate their normal positions but also an injection of new knowledge and expertise through those individuals temporarily transferred into the national security structure. In many areas requiring very high levels of conceptual adaptability, these characteristics could be fostered further through an expansion of short-term appointments and an increased emphasis upon lateral recruitment. Only through such a wide range of complementary measures could the imaginative and adaptive capacity of the bureaucratic managers in Australia's national security structure be increased substantially.

6. Public Debate on Important National Security Issues

At present in Australia, the closed nature of the debate on many national security issues appears to be a consequence more of bureaucratic convenience than security necessity. The contrast between Australia and nearly every comparable Western country is most marked in this respect. The national security structures of most Western states make an active effort to disseminate information, to argue their case in detail and, in some instances, even to fund independently organized public conferences, seminars and discussions.[49] The closed nature of the government institutions involved in national security affairs in Australia is undoubtedly a major factor contributing to the mediocre standard of press reporting, parliamentary debate and public understanding. However, it must also be a significant influence in determining the nature of the decision-making processes and the quality of the decisions made within the structure. As Desmond Ball commented:

> What is needed is more open argument. Positions of participants will still be reached subjectively, and the resultant decisions "irrationally" but at least the positions would have to be justified, and the decisions would be subject to expert and professional criticism.[50]

One of the more obvious consequences of the Australian national security structure being so closed is that it is extremely difficult for an external researcher to gain a comprehensive view of its functional efficiency. However, the commentaries of experienced external observers and of those formerly involved in the system support the general contention that it shares many, if not all, of the bureaucratic weaknesses that are evident in foreign systems and, in some instances, has these weaknesses in a higher degree than do other systems.[51] The implications of this for the prospects of future change are very important. In particular, it means that the potential for adapting Australia's national security system is limited not only by a wide range of physical, economic, social, diplomatic and political factors but also by major bureaucratic constraints. As a consequence, if proposals for change are to have any prospect of adoption and implementation, they not only must be structured to fit within the parameters of the non-bureaucratic constraints but also must be formulated in such a manner as to manage or accommodate bureaucratic influences.

Certainly the processes of meaningful change are demanding and difficult. It is almost always easier for individuals and bureaucratic structures to repeat well-established operational repertoires. However, it is now clear that if Australia's national security structure is to be adapted in the type of fundamental manner that is required, it will be necessary to take active steps to encourage a much higher level of bureaucratic flexibility than has been apparent in the past.

Notes and References

1. The labelling of institutions as "bureaucracies", their personnel as "bureaucrats" and their processes as "bureaucratic" has often carried pejorative connotations. This is not intended here. In this book, these terms are used to describe governmental institutions that are organized hierarchically, the personnel in their employ and the behaviour that is typical of them.
2. The absolute and relative powers of the Defence Minister, the Chief of Defence Force Staff and the Secretary of the Department of Defence are discussed at greater length by W. L. Morrison, "The Role of the Minister in the Making of Australian Defence Policy since the Re-organization of the Department of Defence", in *The Defence of Australia: Fundamental New Aspects*, ed. Robert O'Neill (Canberra: Strategic and Defence Studies Centre, Australian National University, 1977), pp. 71 ff.
3. Morton H. Halperin, *National Security Policy-making* (Lexington, Mass.: Lexington Books, 1975), p. 5. This type of explanation led Don K. Price to make the much-heralded statement that "Where you stand depends on where you sit." See this cited and discussed in Graham T. Allison, *Essence of Decision: Explaining the Nuclear Missile Crisis* (Boston: Little, Brown & Co. 1971), p. 176.
4. A. D. McGaurr, "Defence Procurement — In Search of Optimality" (paper delivered to Conference on Armed Forces and Australian Society, Royal Military College, Duntroon, Canberra, 20-22 May 1977), p. 12.
5. For a detailed discussion of the role of bureaucratic alliances and coalitions, see Morris Janowitz, *The Professional Soldier: A Social and Political Portrait* (Glencoe, Ill.: Free Press of Glencoe, 1960). pp. 283 ff.
6. This relationship is described in Desmond J. Ball, "The Politics of Defence Decision-making in Australia — The Mirage Replacement", unpublished paper (Canberra: Strategic and Defence Studies Centre, Australian National University, 1975), p. 43.
7. Ibid., p. 42.
8. Allison, *Essence of Decision*, pp. 162-63.
9. Ibid., p. 146.
10. Desmond J. Ball, "The Politics of Australian Defence Decision-making", unpublished paper (Canberra: Strategic and Defence Studies Centre, Australian National University, 1977), p. 37.
11. See this case outlined in detail in Halperin, *National Security Policy-making*, pp. 7 ff.

12. Roger A. Beaumont, *Military Elites* (London: Robert Hale, 1976), pp. 79-80.
13. In this respect, the goal of maintaining a national security organization's perceived "essence" is closely related to the concept of militarism as defined by Alfred Vagts:
    > Every war is fought, every army is maintained in a military way and in a militaristic way. The distinction is fundamental and fateful. The military way is marked by a primary concentration of men and materials on winning specific objectives of power with the utmost efficiency, that is, with the least expenditure of blood and treasure. It is limited in scope, confined to one function, and scientific in its essential qualities. Militarism, on the other hand, presents a vast array of customs, interests, prestige, actions and thought associated with armies and wars and yet transcending true military purposes. Indeed, militarism is so constituted that it may hamper and defeat the purposes of the military way. Its influence is unlimited in scope. It may permeate all society and become dominant over all industry and arts. Rejecting the scientific character of the military way, militarism displays the qualities of caste and cult, authority and belief.

    See Alfred Vagts, *A History of Militarism* (London: Hollis & Carter, 1959), p. 13.
14. McGaurr, "Defence Procurement — In Search of Optimality", pp. 14-15.
15. See the discussion of this concept in J. R. Kurth, "The Political Economy of Weapons Procurement: The Follow-on Imperative", *American Economic Review* (Papers and Proceedings 62, no. 2 (May 1972): 304-18.
16. In national security policy, as well as in a number of other important areas of government responsibility (education, health, social welfare, etc.), Australia faces major political and bureaucratic problems because of the division of powers under the Australian Constitution. In theory, the centralization of defence powers should provide the Commonwealth with unquestioned authority in national security affairs. However, in practice, even in times of national emergency, the federal structure of Australian government can, and has, constrained national action. See this detailed in S. J. Butlin, *War Economy 1939-42* (Canberra: Australian War Memorial, 1955), p. 353.

    Peacetime consultation and co-operation on a wide range of national security policies that affect state and local authorities is likely to be necessary if the influence of the Constitution as a constraint on action is to be minimized.
17. For an account of how the Navy won this struggle, see "Navy to Run the Army's Landing Craft", *Sydney Morning Herald*, 4 January 1973, p. 9.
18. See the discussion of this issue by E. P. Esmonde, "Air Defence Artillery", *Army Journal*, no. 324 (May 1976): 45 ff.
19. Halperin, *National Security Policy-making*, p. 14.
20. R. W. Komer, *Bureaucracy Does Its Thing: Institutional Constraints on US-GVN Performance in Vietnam* (Santa Monica: Rand Corporation, 1973), R-967-ARPA, pp. 15-16.
21. Morris Janowitz elaborated this point in the following terms:
    > The dependence of the military on the status quo — whether that status quo is industrial capitalism or communism — reinforces traditionalism. Traditional attitudes are institutionalized by the requirements of military organization and planning. When war-making becomes more technical, the military establishment requires years of preparation and advance thinking. Sudden developments are resisted as disruptive, for it takes years to translate ideas into weapons systems.

    See Janowitz, *Professional Soldier*, pp. 22-23.
22. Komer, *Bureaucracy Does Its Thing*, pp. 65-66.
23. Beaumont, *Military Elites*, p. 115.
24. Ibid., p. 26.
25. Some of the specialized problems of implementation are discussed later in this chapter.

26. Halperin, *National Security Policy-making*, p. 5.
27. Quoted in Komer, *Bureaucracy Does Its Thing*, p. 66.
28. The problem of ineffective ministerial control is elaborated in *Royal Commission on Australian Government Administration Report* (Coombs Report) (Canberra: Australian Government Publishing Service, 1976), pp. 33-34, 54.
29. Ibid., pp. 33-34.
30. H. C. Coombs, "The Commission Report" (text of an address to the National Press Club, Canberra, 11 August 1976); published in Cameron Hazlehurst and J. R. Nethercote, eds, *Reforming Australian Government: The Coombs Report and Beyond* (Canberra: Royal Institute of Public Administration (ACT), in association with Australian National University Press, 1977), p. 55.
31. This point is emphasized in *Royal Commission on Australian Government Administration Report*, pp. 54-55.
32. Komer, *Bureaucracy Does Its Thing*, p. 73.
33. The nature of these restrictions and their impact upon the efficiency of the Australian Public Service is discussed at length in *Royal Commission on Australian Government Administration Report*, pp. 145-46, 165-81.
34. Ibid., pp. 36-55.
35. Coombs, "Commission Report", in *Reforming Australian Government*, eds Hazlehurst and Nethercote, pp. 50-51.
36. This case is made in H. V. Emy, *Public Policy: Problems and Paradoxes* (Melbourne: Macmillan, 1976), p. 51. It also has been the source of frequent comment by defence correspondents in the Australian media. For example, see "An Obsession with Secrecy", *Pacific Defence Reporter* 3, no. 8 (February 1977): 2; and "Defence Must Move to Improve Their Public Image If They Are to Retain the Present Levels of Government and Financial Commitment", *Pacific Defence Reporter* 3, no. 9 (March 1977): 2. This issue is discussed in a very formal and limited manner in the Coombs Report. See *Royal Commission on Australian Government Administration Report*, pp. 345-53. As P. N. Troy has remarked: "the report glosses over the secrecy of decision-making and the monopolization and manipulation of information at senior levels of bureaucracy." See P. N. Troy, "And Now the Bad News", in *Reforming Australian Government*, eds Hazlehurst and Nethercote, p. 88.
37. This matter was the subject of discussion following the presentation of a paper by T. B. Millar, "Some Indicators and Conclusions", at a seminar of the United Service Institution of the Australian Capital Territory in September 1974. See *United Service* 28, no. 2 (October 1974): 94.
38. Forrestal is quoted by Allison, *Essence of Decision*, p. 147.
39. The potential and problems of employing external ministerial advisers are discussed in considerable detail by Morrison, "Role of the Minister in the Making of Australian Defence Policy since the Re-organization of the Department of Defence", in *Defence of Australia*, ed. O'Neill, pp. 79-83. There is also a useful discussion of the matter in *Royal Commission on Australian Government Administration Report*, pp. 78-81.
40. For details, see *Royal Commission on Australian Government Administration Report*, pp. 95-98.
41. Quoted in "Currie Cautions on Soviet Missile Gains", *Aviation Week and Space Technology* 104, no. 21 (24 May 1976): 57.
42. *Royal Commission on Australian Government Administration Report*, p. 407.
43. Ibid., pp. 407-9.
44. Quoted by Komer, *Bureaucracy Does Its Thing*, p. 8.
45. J. L. Pressman and A. B. Wildavsky, *Implementation: How Great Expectations in Washington Are Dashed in Oakland; or, Why It's Amazing that Federal Programs*

Work at All, This Being a Saga of the Economic Development Administration as Told by Two Sympathetic Observers Who Seek to Build Morals on a Foundation of Ruined Hopes (Berkeley, Calif.: University of California Press, 1973).

46. Desmond J. Ball, Review of *Implementation* by J. L. Pressman and A. B. Wildavsky, *Politics* 9, no. 1 (May 1974): 108-9.
47. The existence of a problem in this area has been recognized by Admiral Sir Victor Smith, a former Chairman of the Chiefs of Staff Committee:
    The problem here is that the more time that an officer spends on courses or in field postings the less time there is for him to develop the special skills required in policy formulation. One solution that comes to mind is that a Service officer should be selected relatively early in his career and his future postings in the main, but by no means exclusively, would be at Russell [i.e. the Department of Defence offices].

    See Admiral Sir Victor Smith, "Military and Civilian Inputs into Defence Policy" (paper delivered to Conference on Armed Forces and Australian Society, Royal Military College, Duntroon, Canberra, 20-22 May 1977), p. 6.
48. See this detailed in *Royal Commission on Australian Government Administration Report*, pp. 145-46.
49. Perhaps most notable in this regard is the Swedish Ministry of Defence. It allocates a small proportion of its budget each year to encourage public debate on national security issues through the subsidy of a wide range of conferences, seminars, etc., and by funding the publishing of major discussion papers and reports written by prominent members of the national security structure.
50. Desmond J. Ball, "Some Notes on the Decision-making Process in the Australian Defence Establishment", unpublished paper (Canberra: Strategic and Defence Studies Centre, Australian National University, 1975), p. 27.
51. See, for instance, *Royal Commission on Australian Government Administration Report*, and the works of Desmond J. Ball and A. D. McGaurr cited in this chapter; also Morrison, "Role of the Minister in the Making of Australian Defence Policy since the Reorganization of the Department of Defence", in *Defence of Australia*, ed. O'Neill, pp. 71 ff: and K. J. Foley, "Labor's Strategy of Continental Defence: Substance or Shadow?", in *The First Thousand Days of Labor*, eds R. Scott and J. L. Richardson (Canberra: Canberra College of Advanced Education, APSA Conference, 1975), vol. 1.

Part 4

DERIVING FUTURE POLICY

7
Gaining a Sense of Direction

The Planning Problem

One of the major themes of this book is that the future quality of Australia's security will be much more dependent upon the scale and character of its independent efforts. Probably the most vital element of this greatly expanded requirement for self-sufficiency is the need to develop an indigenous capacity to plan coherently the allocation of the nation's scarce security resources. However, Australia's current security planning system has been largely inherited from the forward defence era. It has not been designed for, nor does it appear to be suited to the demanding functions it is now required to perform. As was discussed in Chapter 4, the Strategic Basis documents have highlighted effectively the notable trends in the strategic environment. However, they have not provided an appropriate basis for the derivation of clear strategic concepts, planning objectives or expenditure priorities. As a consequence of this systemic failure, it appears that in recent years individual sections of the Defence Department and the armed services have been forced to develop their own structures, operational concepts, priorities and philosophies.

The fundamental problems and difficulties that confront Australia's security planners are recognized within the Department of Defence, but the conceptual manner in which they are currently managed is of limited effectiveness. In simple terms, the official rationale can be explained as follows.

It is generally accepted that Australia's security forces must be capable not only of responding satisfactorily to immediate pressures but also of expanding rapidly to meet the requirements of more demanding contingencies. In order to meet the immediate response requirement, it is argued that the existing force structure (the force-in-being) is constructed so as to provide a basic capability to react quickly to a number of low-level pressures and threats. But, in addition, in order to provide the key elements of a capacity to meet more demanding pressures and threats, the force-in-being is modified gradually as Australian perceptions of the strategic environment (expressed in the Strategic Basis documents) indicate the changed nature of the country's long-term security needs. Thus, at least in theory, the structure of the force that would exist at mobilization (the core force) gradually changes character over time to more closely satisfy those requirements that are identified in the Strategic Basis documents.[1]

One of the major problems with this concept is that, because of the uncertain nature of the strategic environment and hence of future contingencies, it is impossible, in the Department's view, to determine the optimal shape of the fully mobilized force structure (the terminal force). In fact, because there is an almost infinite range of conceivable pressures and threats, the core force is designed in such a manner that it is capable of expanding relatively quickly into the size and shape of a large number of terminal forces.[2] In order to maximize the potential speed of this multi-directional force expansion capacity for a given resource input, the core force is designed to include a very large number of high-technology, high-complexity, long lead-time capabilities. It is in this context that a wide range of very advanced equipments and technologies can be justified in terms of the maintenance of the "state of the art". It is argued that if a particular type of capacity is important in meeting an array of potential contingencies, the development and maintenance of high levels of expertise in the field serves to reduce significantly the minimum time required to expand that capacity, should it be necessary to do so.

The primary difficulty with this is that, because of the lack of clarity concerning the contingencies that are to be accepted for planning purposes, the system fails to perform any of its major objectives satisfactorily. Certainly the present security system does possess a token capacity to meet a large number of contingencies, but it is important to realize that the price of this nominal multiple-contingency flexibility and adaptability is very high. In effect, it necessitates the procurement of small numbers of practically every conceivable unit and equipment type. This dilution of the limited resources that Australia can devote to national security functions over a wide variety of unit and equipment types limits heavily economies of scale in procurement, maintenance, training and practically every other area of national security activity. Moreover, because the combat personnel who can be mobilized readily are so widely dispersed, in a functional sense, the total structure's immediate response capacity is constrained severely. But perhaps the most important weakness of all is that this wide diffusion of expertise limits heavily the current security concept's surge capacity. As was discussed in Chapter 4, in order to meet the demands even of some relatively minor harassment and raid scenarios, the current force-in-being requires periods of defence preparation time that are unrealistically long.

Thus, in summary, the utility of Australia's present security planning concept should be the cause of considerable concern. The limited immediate operational response and surge capacity of the current structure is justified primarily by the perceived requirement in an uncertain strategic environment of retaining a capacity to expand in almost any direction, however slowly, should the need arise. The practical effect of this planning concept upon the structure of the armed forces is particularly significant. Despite major changes to Australia's strategic environment and the nature of its security requirements, the current force structure and that officially postulated for the 1980s is almost identical in shape and form to that of the mid-1960s at the height of the forward defence era.[3] Is it to be concluded that the force structure that was designed for and presumably was suited ideally to the demands of committing single service formations overseas to complement the foreign deployments of major power allies is also, by some extraordinary coincidence and good fortune, the structure that is ideally suited to the demands of securing Australia's immediate environment with a high degree of independence? It is difficult to avoid the judgement, from the information available on the public record, that despite official recognition of the changes in Australia's strategic circumstances, their full implications and ramifications have not been appreciated and, as a consequence, the security system has not been adapted to meet the new requirements. This represents a major systemic failure, but it is difficult to foresee any substantial progress being made in the absence of a comprehensive reformation of the country's security planning system.

Because the task of independently planning Australia's security in the future is of a quite different character to that of the forward defence era, it demands a completely fresh approach. We need to design a process of rigorous security planning within which a wide range of conceptual and structural options can be tested thoroughly for their capacity to satisfy Australia's new national security requirements. Only through such a system would it be possible to approach optimality in the determination of priorities and the allocation of resources.

But what standards could Australia's security planners use to evaluate such a broad range of strategic options? It is argued in the following pages that the most appropriate criteria for Australia's future security planning are fourfold: contingencies, doctrinal objectives, constraining influences and the additional requirements of national policy. Let us examine briefly the manner in which they might be employed.

1. Contingencies

In a very real sense, the major underlying cause of Australia's current security planning problem is the high level of strategic uncertainty with which the country is confronted. Thus the nature of possible future pressures and threats is a logical starting-point for the processes of coherent security planning. This major area of uncertainty is not easily clarified. As Darcy McGaurr points out, the almost imponderable nature of Australia's future security environment presents a much more severe planning problem than that faced by a wide range of advanced Western states:

> The lack of a foreseeable threat means Australia has no pressing defence problem. However, the same phenomenon is at the root of our defence planning problem. Paradoxically, a country like Israel with a far greater defence problem has a less complex defence planning problem. The threat is there. It can be measured and observed and planned against. All the NATO nations develop their force structure to counter those of the Soviet bloc. Australian governments realize that lack of threat in the short term does not eliminate the need for defence preparedness in the long term. The problem is one of allocating limited resources between a very large array of possible defence projects.[4]

The minister for Defence, D.J. Killen, has also emphasized the constraining influence of the uncertain strategic environment and hinted at a conceptual solution:

> If there was a perceived threat it would make defence planning ever so much easier because you know precisely where you want to spend your money, how you want to spend your money and when you want to spend your money. But there is no perceived threat, and so as a consequence of that one must take into account contingencies, and the contingencies again must be tinged with reality.[5]

But the questions arise as to which contingencies should be considered and how they should be derived and expressed. It is argued in Appendix C that it is possible to reduce the wide array of conceivable pressures and threats into a form that is manageable for planning purposes without oversimplifying greatly its potential diversity. This is achieved by carefully selecting a set of scenarios that, in terms of national security response requirements, is representative of the full range of future possibilities. The contingencies elaborated in these scenarios would provide an ideal initial foundation for the processes of detailed security planning. Their potential utility in this role brought Desmond Ball to conclude:

> In strategic planning, there is no substitute for a contingency/options approach, i.e. making conscious decisions concerning the contingencies to be prepared against and those to be ignored, and then selecting options to fulfil the required capabilities. This, however, requires both more positive strategic guidance and stronger decisions than are seen today.[6]

In other words, a primary means of overcoming the current difficulties of planning in Australia's uncertain strategic environment would be to design and test in concept a wide range of strategic and structural options for their capacity to meet the demands of a representative and agreed set of scenarios.

2. Doctrinal Objectives

However, it would be extremely difficult to determine those security concepts and structures that would most adequately meet the requirements of the agreed scenarios in the absence of any clear measures of efficiency. Strategic and structural options could be tested in the circumstances of the representative scenarios, but what would be the basis for their evaluation? Would the most efficient options be those with the greatest capacity to deter an enemy, to defer the onset of hostilities, to defeat an opponent, to cause an opponent to institute a disproportionate response, to prevent wholesale defeat, or perhaps a combination of all the above? A clear statement of national security doctrinal goals would be central to any process of coherent security planning. As was discussed in Chapter 4, it would be most appropriate for this second planning criterion to be determined by the government of the day, although preferably in the context of a bipartisan political consensus.

3. Constraining Influences

With the derivation of the first two categories of planning criteria, it would be possible to design and evaluate conceptually a wide range of alternative security strategies and structures for their capacity to meet the demands of the doctrinal objectives in the circumstances of the representative scenarios. Yet this form of evaluation would be largely removed from reality. There would be no explicit limits on finance, manpower, technology, social and diplomatic factors or many other restraining influences that are present in the real world. These multi-dimensional constraints would need to be integrated into any process of coherent planning. Many of those factors that constrain Australian security options — finance, manpower, public attitudes, industrial capacity, technical skills, etc. — have been discussed in Chapter 5. However, for a comprehensive process of national security planning, they would need to be elaborated in much greater detail. In practice, this integration might best be done by the Department of Defence, for approval by the government.

4. Additional Requirements of National Policy

On the basis of the first three categories of planning criteria, alternative concepts and structures could be tested for their capacity to optimize doctrinal objectives in the context of the representative scenarios, while not transgressing the bounds set by the elaborated constraints. However, the processes of planning on these bases alone still would be deficient. It would be possible to design alternative strategies and structures with a comparable capacity to satisfy the established criteria, but which would differ markedly in their impact upon the nation at large. Great variations could be expected to be evident in the strength of domestic industrial support, research and development, intelligence, repair and maintenance capacities required by each proposal. Alternative security options also may differ markedly in the levels of their structural flexibility, adaptability and endurance. The nature of all of these characteristics would be of significance to any government because they impact in a major fashion not only upon the basic form of national security policy but also upon a broad range of domestic and international political, economic and social concerns. As a consequence, it would be important for the government of the day to be given scope to select and define basic objectives for those categories of additional planning requirements that it regards as being important — for example, the levels of Australian industry participation, procurement offsets, domestic research and development, dependence upon foreign sources of intelligence and upon foreign sources of equipment supply, etc.

The General Character of a Coherent Planning System

The provision of all four categories of planning criteria would provide a comprehensive conceptual basis for the construction and detailed evaluation of a wide range of alternative strategic concepts and structures in realistic circumstances. Alternative options could be tested for their capacity to maximize doctrinal goals in the circumstances of the selected scenarios while satisfying the additional requirements of national policy and not transgressing the bounds set by the elaborated constraints. Through this process, it should be possible to make optimizing decisions concerning the most efficient strategic concepts, structures and even details of the most efficient organization and equipment types for a given financial input. The progression of this analysis is illustrated in a simplified form in Figure 2 and elaborated in full in Appendix D.

This pattern of testing in concept a wide range of security options offers great scope for overcoming many of the serious weaknesses of the present security planning system. Most obviously, it would encourage greatly increased creativity in security structure design, but perhaps more importantly, the clarity of national security objectives and goals would make it possible for the planning processes to be more directly end-product or functionally oriented. A total-systems view could be adopted, in the sense that all security resources theoretically could be available for inter-system trade-offs and interactions, in order to maximize the achievement of the stated goals within given total resource constraints. In an economic sense, it should be possible to determine the optimal distribution of marginal resource inputs and also to undertake full input-output analysis.

Judgements on most of the matters in this process could be expected to be both complex and difficult to reach. Thus in all decision-making in the planning system, and particularly in the derivation of representative scenarios and the evaluation of alternative security concepts and structures, it would be highly advantageous to limit, as far as possible, the scope for purely intuitive judgements. The role of analytical studies and research could be increased greatly. However, where intuitive decisions are unavoidable, it would be desirable for the questions involved to be structured carefully, to ensure a high level of decision-making precision and to facilitate the application of the most advanced expertise available.

Ideally, the processes of generating and testing alternative security concepts described above would produce a conceptual strategy and structure that approaches an optimization of national security objectives for the level of resources available. However, because of heavy existing investments in equipment, personnel training, facilities, etc., it might prove impossible for the Australian security system to adopt any new security solution in the short term. As a consequence, it would be necessary to transfer the optimizing strategy and structure to a long-term planning framework so that clear and unambiguous guidance could be made available for the gradual adaptation of the existing security system. Detailed decision paths could be elaborated for system transformation and key decision-points could be identified and phased so that the broadest

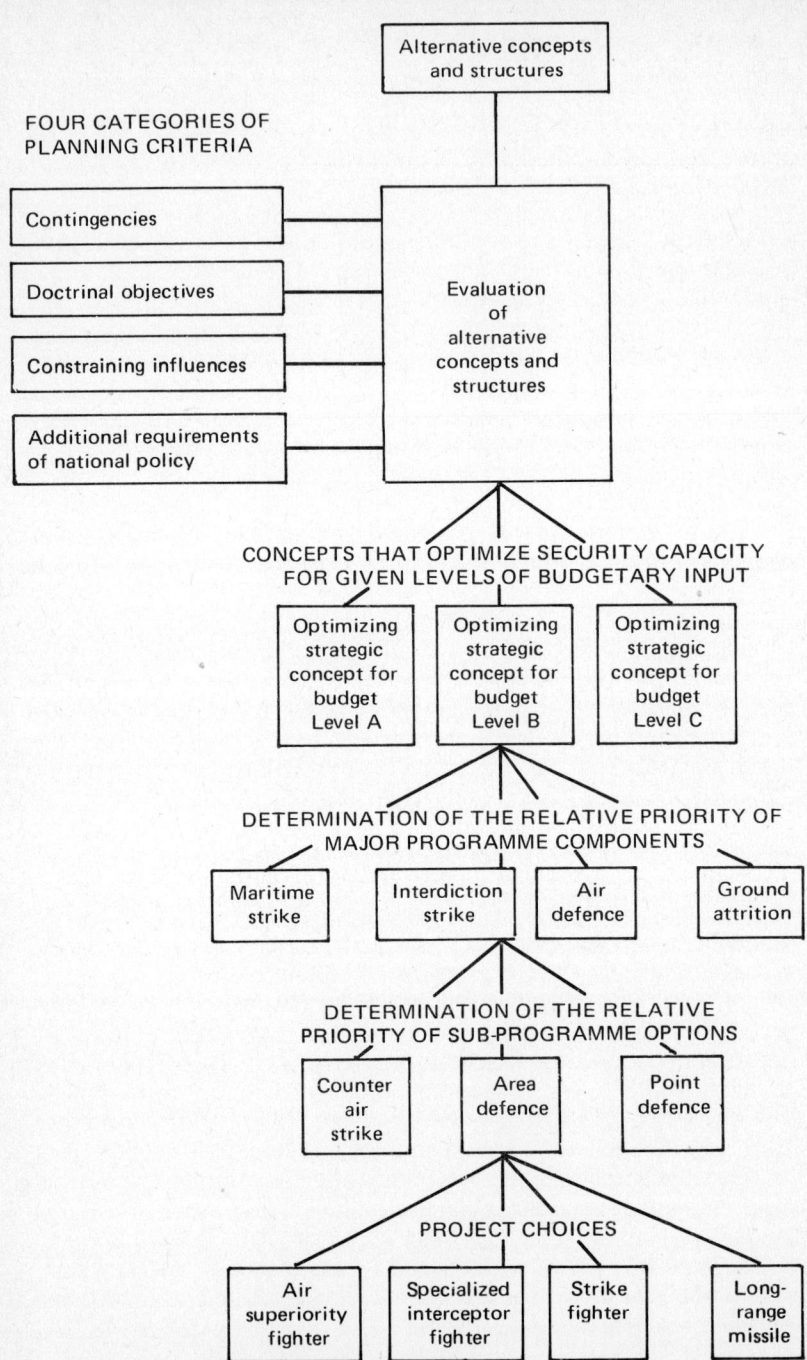

Fig. 2. Simplified representation of a potential security planning process

possible array of options is kept open until the last possible moment. In practice, this approach would serve to increase the importance of long-term perspectives, improve freedom of action in decision-making and optimize the system's capability to adapt rapidly to meet unforeseen developments. As a consequence, the need for *ad hoc* decision-making should be reduced to a minimum.

In summary, a well-integrated, security planning system should improve decision-makers' understanding and control of those factors that are capable of rapid change. It should be possible for risks and uncertainties to be identified, clarified and described at an early stage and for unambiguous policy direction to be made available to all sections of the security structure on a continuous basis. In total, these developments could be expected to increase substantially effective governmental influence on the essential elements of security planning and improve greatly the responsiveness of the system to changes in the nation's strategic environment.

Notes and References

1. The conceptual relationship between the force-in-being, the core force and the terminal force was the subject of a notable debate on the morning of 28 October 1976 at the "Defence of Australia: Fundamental New Aspects" Conference, held by the Strategic and Defence Studies Centre at the Australian National University. The description of the current planning system appearing in the text is derived primarily from the explanations made by senior Department of Defence officers on that occasion.
2. This process of multi-path force expansion planning is described by Desmond J. Ball, "Equipment Policy for the Defence of Australia", in *The Defence of Australia: Fundamental New Aspects*, ed. Robert O'Neill (Canberra: Strategic and Defence Studies Centre, Australian National University, 1977), p. 119.
3. Although the shape of the force structure appears to be relatively static, significant measures are being taken to develop and adopt concepts, doctrines and procedures more appropriate to Australia's new strategic circumstances. This is discussed in detail by Robert O'Neill, "The Development of Operational Doctrines for the Australian Defence Force", in ibid., pp. 138-43.
4. Darcy McGaurr, "The Case for a Balanced Defence Policy", *National Times*, 3-8 March 1975, pp. 50-51.
5. Address by the Minister for Defence, the Hon. D. J. Killen, to the 62nd Annual Congress of the Returned Services League, Canberra, 7 September 1977, p. 8.
6. Ball, "Equipment Policy for the Defence of Australia", in *Defence of Australia*, ed. O'Neill, p. 119.

8
Wider Strategic Options

It has been argued at some length in this book that the task of securing the Australian continent in the last quarter of the twentieth century differs substantially from the historical requirements of forward defence. Australia now requires a capacity to deter, defer and, if necessary, meet a much broader range of military, diplomatic, economic, political, social and psychological pressures, and it needs the capacity to perform many of these tasks independently. However, it is by no means clear that the concepts and structures that have been inherited from the previous era will provide the most cost-effective means of performing these more demanding functions in the future. Indeed, in earlier chapters it was argued that in the context of the new strategic environment, the current security concepts and structures suffer from a series of major weaknesses. Thus when discussing Australia's future planning requirements in the previous chapter, it was suggested that an extensive series of strategic and structural options should be constructed conceptually and tested for their functional effectiveness in satisfying the nation's new security requirements.

But what are the characteristics of Australia's future security options? The primary purpose of this chapter is to introduce and briefly discuss a series of strategy themes that might be viewed as potential components or "building-blocks" in constructing alternative conceptual options. The individual strategy themes do not all offer the prospect of a coherent and complete solution to Australia's national security requirements. They have different objectives, employ different types of resources, hold the potential to secure different aspects of Australian society and are designed primarily to meet different types of pressure and threat. Each has the capacity to combine with other themes to produce a variety of alternative conceptual options for evaluation in the processes of long-range planning.

Strategy Theme 1   A Nuclear Weapons Capability

Australia might conceivably develop nuclear weapons for a wide range of reasons. One of the most obvious motivations might be to provide a completely new dimension to Australia's deterrence capacity. While nuclear weapons would have a capability to perform this function, it is important to realize that their credibility in this role would be limited. They could only be expected to provide effective deterrence against a relatively small category of pressures and threats. For instance, they would not constitute a credible deterrent, nor an effective response or defensive capacity, against a wide range of pressures of peace, international crises and some of the less-demanding pressures of international aggression. Even in the context of the more demanding pressures of international aggression, the value of such a deterrence capacity would be limited severely if Australia's potential opponents already possessed a similar force with a retaliatory capability.

A second potential reason for Australia acquiring nuclear weapons might be to gain international prestige and bargaining power. Certainly Australia's diplomatic actions are likely to be given more attention if the country possesses nuclear weapons, yet the international value of this attention could not be expected to be very pronounced, for even the major powers have found it difficult to translate their nuclear capabilities into concrete political gains. Moreover, if Australia's acquisition of a nuclear weapons capability spurs a regional power to follow suit, the net result might be a reduction in the country's overall security because of Australia's high level of population concentration and its consequential vulnerability to nuclear attack.

A third possible motive for developing nuclear weapons would be to acquire greatly increased tactical battlefield firepower. Certainly the area blast effects of most nuclear explosives are of an order of magnitude greater than any conventional munition. However, there are limits to the utility of firepower *per se*. For instance, even if it were politically feasible to do so, it would not be appropriate or cost-effective in military terms to employ nuclear weapons against terrorist groups or small-scale raiding parties. Furthermore, as is discussed later in this chapter, their military utility in even the more conventional large-scale battlefield situations is limited.

All nuclear weapons options are also constrained heavily by a broad range of cost factors. Because of their technical complexity, nuclear weapons and their associated delivery systems are not procured readily. Their development in Australia not only would be expensive financially but it also would impose a heavy drain upon skilled manpower.[1] In addition, because of their highly controversial nature, the diversion of scarce national resources to their procurement, in most circumstances, would be a highly sensitive and potentially divisive political issue.

In practice, there are three distinct categories of nuclear weapons options available to Australia. The first is to attempt to develop a global strategic deterrence capacity. This would be designed, as was De Gaulle's *force de frappe*, "to tear a limb off" or cause unacceptable damage to even a super-power aggressor.[2] The acquisition of this type of system would entail the development of an extremely sophisticated launch-on-warning or survivable second strike capacity.[3] Even if it is assumed that this would only require the development of comparatively simple plutonium warheads, these would have to be miniaturized and fitted to a highly survivable and reliable delivery system.[4] There are several alternative modes of delivery potentially available. An intercontinental ballistic missile (ICBM) or sea-launched ballistic missile (SLBM) system, even of a comparitively crude nature, would cost billions of dollars and take many years to develop.[5] The range of Australia's strike aircraft, even with multiple refuelling from aerial tankers based in Australia, would be insufficient to provide a credible deterrent against a super-power opponent. By far the most attractive option would appear to be a submarine- and/or air-launched cruise missile system. The most advanced cruise missiles currently under development have a range of approximately 3200 km.[6] In order for multiple, high-value targets to be reached by such a system, either the range capability would need to be extended or the launching platforms would need to release the missiles from vulnerable positions close to the opponent's borders. In addition, the type of highly accurate cruise-missile guidance system needed would be difficult to develop domestically, even if it were only required to be sufficiently precise for counter-city strikes. It would probably need to be assumed that the global positioning satellite (GPS) system would not be always available in crisis situations.[7] TERCOM, MAGCOM and MICRAD systems and operational data might also be difficult to obtain.[8] However, if all of the above options are foreclosed, it is possible that the new types of laser gyros currently becoming available may be sufficiently accurate to perform cruise-missile guidance for counter-city attacks.[9]

In short, it is conceivable that Australia could develop a marginal global strategic nuclear deterrent, but only after the investment of vast national resources over an extended period and at the expense of a considerable disturbance to international, and possibly also internal, political relationships.

A second and more frequently discussed nuclear option would be the development of a regional strategic deterrent.[10] For this type of system, a plutonium warhead mounted on a sea- or air-launched cruise missile would again appear to provide the most cost-effective solution. However, because the requirements for range, survivability, early warning and quantity would be relaxed considerably from those required for the global deterrent option, the overall expense and drain on resources could be expected to be of a lower order of magnitude. These considerations, in most circumstances, could not be expected to moderate significantly the strength of the international and domestic political reaction.

The final nuclear option for Australia would be the development of a weapons system for purely tactical battlefield firepower purposes. The most likely delivery candidates for this task would be air-, sea- or ground-launched short- or medium-range cruise missiles. However, it is important to note that the battlefield utility of tactical nuclear weapons would be limited. Despite their enormous firepower potential, nuclear weapons do not reduce greatly the requirements for precise target acquisition and delivery accuracy in most tactical situations. For instance, in the maritime environment, a 20-kiloton warhead must be delivered to within $1^3/_8$ kilometres of a ship if it is to be destroyed, and a 200-kiloton bomb within 4 kilometres.[11] In land warefare, in most types of terrain, nuclear attacks against armoured formations require an even greater degree of accuracy to be effective.[12] Thus for tactical battlefield purposes, nuclear explosives really substitute for the new forms of highly accurate terminal guidance. The destruction of multiple targets with one warhead is likely to occur only if the targets are highly concentrated, yet even in this type of situation, cheaper and less politically sensitive conventional weapon options are already available. In the ground environment, terminally guided submunition dispenser weapons can destroy or disable large vehicle formations. At sea, relatively inexpensive terminally guided anti-ship missiles have proved to be extremely effective. In fact, as was discussed in Chapter 2, a range of other developments in weapons technologies is already encouraging a high level of force dispersal and hence reducing the prospects of destroying multiple targets with a single nuclear strike.

There is a final major difficulty should Australia acquire nuclear weapons for tactical purposes. If an opposing country also possesses nuclear weapons, it may be tempted to respond to their use by retaliating against Australia's small number of highly concentrated and very vulnerable population centres. The realization of this danger may effectively deter Australian governments from exercising the tactical nuclear option.

Strategy Theme 2   Adapted Conventional Military Systems

For Australia, this is essentially a status quo option. In the absence of an international or domestic political crisis, which might reveal its fundamental inadequacies, the present conventional military concept represents a very attractive political and bureaucratic option. It basically permits a continuance of Australia's inherited force structure, with slight modifications to accommodate the more obvious requirements of continental defence.[13] In general terms, the Army would probably retain its conventional division structure and the Navy would still be dominated by destroyers, frigates, a few submarines and an appropriate number of support ships. The Air Force would be equipped with basically the same kinds of strike, fighter, transport, maritime and trainer aircraft as at present, although there may be scope for reducing the number of aircraft types operated.

The greatest advantage of an adapted conventional military structure is that in most respects it already exists. Many of the equipments and doctrines are familiar to the Australian armed forces and most of the skills and personnel are already held. Thus in terms of political and bureaucratic realities, its relatively undemanding nature makes it realistically achievable. This is important, because while the civilian and military personnel in Australia's national security structure have learned to accept change over the years, this has been limited primarily to that designed to improve their performance of traditional functions. Thus, for instance, there has been a general acceptance of a degree of integrated defence management and the level of change associated with the introduction of new types of equipment. The scale and type of change required for the adapted conventional force option would be of a comparable nature to that required in the past and hence would be unlikely to cause excessive disturbance to entrenched vested interests and life-styles.

Conventional military structures are also relatively easy for the public to understand and accept. During the course of this century, a large proportion of the Australian population has served actively in these types of military units. This basic familiarity is reinforced by the readiness with which the public can comprehend the relatively simple concepts by which conventional operations can be explained. Units are frequently deployed in concentrations and, on the ground, the progress of linear fronts is easy to plot and understand.

Another factor that reinforces public acceptance of conventional military forces is the fact that they are possessed by most advanced Western states with whom Australia normally compares itself. In reality, this is a practical advantage of some significance because it means that conventional force options automatically possess a high degree of equipment and operational compatibility with Australia's major allies.

The adapted conventional military force option possesses yet other significant advantages. For instance, the major equipment components of the concept — large surface ships, tactical aircraft and conventional army formations — are, by their very nature, highly visible. If these equipments possess a credible operational capacity in crisis situations, they are likely to be well-suited to perform the deterrence function.[14]

Another great advantage of conventional military forces is their operational flexibility. They are generally adaptable to nearly any type of terrain, climate and vegetation and they are capable of effectively performing both offensive and defensive tasks against a wide range of enemy forces.

However, for Australia's continental defence requirement, it is doubtful whether an adapted conventional military structure can provide an appropriate solution on its own, since it suffers from a series of important practical and conceptual difficulties.

Firstly, for a large number of reasons, it is a very expensive option. It requires high levels of technical and conceptual skill to be effective both on the micro (platoon, squadron and vessel) level as well as at the macro (operational command) level. High levels of skill imply not only high-performance manpower, mostly operating full-time, but also extensive training time and complex training facilities.

Conventional military options also require complex and expensive capital equipment items at or close to the "state of the art". Bearing in mind Australia's limited budgetary resources, this factor causes major problems. As was discussed in Chapter 2, large surface ships, conventional tactical aircraft and main battle tanks now require a host of supporting units and equipments if they are to survive and be effective on the modern battlefield. However, for a country with Australia's resources, the procurement of all of these mutually supporting battlefield elements means that only very small quantities of each type of equipment can be bought. This may provide a capacity for small numbers of people to maintain contact with the current "state of the art", but it limits heavily effective operational capacity. For this to be developed to a level that would be appropriate to meet any serious pressure of national aggression, an elaborate process of rapid force expansion would be required. Yet, as was discussed in Chapter 4, while manpower may be difficult to raise and train rapidly, the types of complex conventional equipments required — ships, tactical aircraft and armoured vehicles —

may be even more difficult, if not impossible, to obtain at short notice. Thus in Australia, the adapted conventional military concept raises a very serious dilemma. For conventional units to be effective on the modern battlefield, a large number of mutually supporting equipments and technologies is required. However, in order to maintain expertise in them all, the total structure's capacity to meet meaningful pressures and threats independently is very limited.

There are several other major difficulties with adapted conventional forces. For instance, because such forces are composed of relatively small numbers of high-technology units, which are frequently employed in concentrations, they are particularly vulnerable to technological obsolescence in the face of an innovative opponent. As was discussed in Chapter 2, most of the important equipments held by conventional military forces — tactical aircraft, surface ships, armoured vehicles, etc. — are all becoming increasingly vulnerable to new generations of relatively inexpensive but highly effective counter-systems. Thus it is conceivable that, in some environments at least, conventional unit equipments, in the future, may be rendered completely obsolete by the introduction of new weapons technologies. But even further than this, these high-technology concentrations of defence capital are also vulnerable to an opponent's imaginative employment or exploitation of the new technologies through the introduction of new strategic concepts, tactical doctrines or operational procedures.[15] Conventional military forces are thus particularly vulnerable to rapid obsolescence and decisive defeat at the hands of a technically advanced, innovative opponent.

A further practical difficulty arises from the fact that the possession of small numbers of highly capable conventional units effectively limits deployment options when enemy intentions are unclear. For example, in the circumstances of major raids by a regional power or a multiple battalion attack by a major power on Australia's northern coasts, it may be very difficult to commit immediately the bulk of Australia's conventional defence force to that area for fear of a secondary, more serious attack in the populous and strategically important south-east or south-west of the continent. The possession of small numbers of high-technology conventional forces tends to seriously complicate deployment options.

The commitment of only token conventional forces to resist these types of remote attacks would be of restricted utility because of another major limitation on conventional force capability — their relatively high vulnerability to adverse force ratios. Certainly a very large number of factors determine success on the conventional military battlefield — terrain, vegetation, weather, equipment, morale and leadership, to name just a few. Yet conventional military units, because of their relatively concentrated battlefield formations and large and obvious support structures and facilities, are frequently susceptible to rapid defeat by conventional forces of comparable expertise but larger dimensions. For Australia, the most important implication is that, while conventional forces may be appropriate to meet lower and medium pressures of national aggression, if confronted by numerically superior conventional forces, they may be susceptible to rapid defeat.

Strategy Theme 3   Territorial Defence

Territorial defence structures are designed specifically to provide nations with an independent means of defending in depth their own territory. The primary aim is to raise an opponent's costs and risks not only of entering but also of residing in the host country. This is done by refusing to fight a superior enemy on his own terms, depriving him of rapid victory and forcing him to conduct a protracted and expensive campaign. As a group of Rand Corporation analysts described it:

> The intent is not to hold territory in the initial stages of an invasion but ultimately to bog down an invader by making continued occupation of the country too costly to be worth while.[16]

Territorial defence is not simply another term for guerrilla warfare. Although territorial defence in some environments may involve a substantial element of reliance upon guerrilla techniques and variants of these, it may also involve some reliance upon heavy weapons (e.g. tactical aircraft, small offensive surface ships, submarines, armoured vehicles, etc.), which are not normally regarded as being part of the guerrilla's armoury. In essence, territorial systems usually possess a guerrilla-type capacity to survive and to strike almost continuously from multiple directions and in multiple dimensions. Territorial units have a capacity to disperse and operate for long periods in small "packets" in such a way that for the enemy they represent an intangible target very difficult to acquire and destroy. However, territorial defence forces also may have a capacity to perform "frontal" defensive operations for short periods. This normally involves activities more akin to those of conventional forces at state frontiers or along clearly defined military fronts, whether they be static or mobile, thin or deep. The coexistence of the more irregular aspects of territorial defence doctrine with those of frontal defence can be seen most clearly in the military structures of Sweden, Finland and Yugoslavia.[17]

The most important component of territorial defence forces is the large numbers of well-trained, dispersed but co-ordinated small units. As was discussed in Chapter 2, the operational capacity of this type of unit is being enhanced greatly by developments in conventional military technology, but there are other important advantages that can be derived from this type of structure. The nature of the manpower required means that the vast majority can be supplied in the form of locally based part-time forces. This tends to be not only a very economic means of providing large military forces but it also means that units can be mobilized rapidly to operate in familiar terrain and hence are not readily susceptible to either regional or nation-wide surprise attacks.[18]

Because of the nature of the Australian land mass, its status as an island, its size, its variations of terrain, vegetation and climate, and its small but generally nationalistic population and its relatively limited financial resources, it can be argued that the territorial defence option is particularly well-suited to Australia's national security requirements.[19] It would appear to provide the basis for developing a very formidable deterrence capacity that was both regionally and globally inoffensive. However, for Australia in the 1980s, there are a series of factors that serve to undermine heavily the concept's political, military and social acceptability.

The most serious difficulty in employing the territorial defence concept is that it would require the mass involvement of civil society. If the public commitment required was limited simply to an acceptance of conscription for service within Australia, or even increased financial expenditure, it can be deduced from the poll results displayed in Chapter 5 that these measures conceivably might be accepted by the community. But adoption of territorial defence would necessitate public acceptance of a concept that requires active mass preparations for war fighting within the nation's borders.[20] The implications for mass public involvement and probably great suffering in wartime situations tends to deter governments from the ready adoption of territorial defence strategies. The human and social costs of such a struggle would be far more bearable if a firm prospect of achieving early victory could be promised, but it is implicit in the nature of a territorial defence struggle that the issue is not decided in a single battle, or even by a single criterion. In fact, the true complexity of such a defence posture is difficult for many mass publics to comprehend fully. It is perhaps not surprising then that the territorial defence concept appears to be most readily accepted and entrenched in those countries that have suffered the ravages of invasion and have a history of mounting protracted partisan resistance. Certainly the prerequisites for the successful adoption of a territorial defence concept include a high level of social cohesion and a very deep and almost universal national commitment to the country's defence. It is possible that these conditions might be satisfied in Australia if the country were confronted by a serious threat that was readily apparent to the entire community. In these circumstances, domestic political constraints conceivably might be overridden by the cohesive forces of nationalism and ideology.

There are, however, several further problems with the territorial defence concept. One major difficulty is that large urban populations appear to be particularly vulnerable because of their ready accessibility and susceptibility to terror campaigns and reprisals. As Adam Roberts points out:

> Despite all such possibilities the urbanization of societies undeniably adds to the problems of territorial defence, and inevitably modifies its character. This is particularly true in countries such as Switzerland and Sweden [and Australia], whose cities are near land or sea frontiers and hence immediately vulnerable. The Swiss in the Second World War, when they envisaged the possibility of abandoning their towns and villages to the enemy and continuing the struggle from mountain strongholds, knew they would be running the risk of vicious and extensive retaliation. The situation in Finland in the Second World War was different and much more favourable to protracted struggle. As an eyewitness observer of the war in Finland wrote at the time: "A nation which is concentrated in towns is most vulnerable from the air; 83 per cent of Finland's population was rural . . ." There is an obvious significance in the fact that the three European countries which proved most adept at conducting defence in depth in the Second World War — Yugoslavia, Albania and Finland — were relatively underdeveloped, not heavily urbanized, and covered with large expanses of forest.[21]

Although Australia has a strong rural tradition, the reality of the situation is that nearly 86 per cent of the population is now concentrated in urban areas.[22] The country's vulnerability to an opponent's counter-measures may serve to weaken seriously the utility of territorial defence strategy in Australia.

Another potential difficulty for the territorial defence concept is that its flexibility in the face of a wide range of scenarios is limited. Certainly it can provide a formidable deterrent and defensive capacity against the threat of a major assault. It can also provide a localized ready reaction capacity to meet a large number of minor pressures and threats. However, because of its inherently defensive character, territorial defence structures are not normally well-equipped to rapidly mount conventional ground-force counter-offensives against limited assaults or lodgements, particularly at remote locations. The air and naval components of such a structure might be able to respond quickly with a concentration of defensive firepower, but in a country the size of Australia, territorial defence forces are unlikely to possess the ground-force mobility required to confront an opponent quickly with major forces in areas remote from the primary centres of population. This relative absence of strategic mobility and concentration also means that territorial defence forces are not readily adaptable to contingencies requiring their deployment overseas.

The final major conceptual difficulty of territorial defence strategy is the requirement to rationalize the need for tactical ground-force mobility with the necessity of maintaining and protecting aircraft and ship support and maintenance facilities that are inherently fixed in character. Air and naval facilities, to some degree, can be duplicated, dispersed, camouflaged and protected, but in the final analysis, if continued air and naval activity is to be regarded as central to the struggle, the defences surrounding air and naval bases and support facilities must necessarily become somewhat more frontal and conventional in character.[23]

In summary, the territorial defence concept represents a specialized means of independently maximizing a country's deterrence capacity when confronted by the threat of a major conventional assault. However, primarily because of its limited capacity to provide an effective response to the full range of potential pressures and threats, it is unlikely to satisfy Australia's security requirements on its own.

Strategy Theme 4   Civilian Resistance

The civilian resistance concept is a non-violent means of undermining an opponent's willpower. It is not a camouflaged form of defeatism. On the contrary, civilian resistance strategists argue that the invasion and occupation of a country represent merely the beginning of an extended struggle.[24] Far from signifying defeat, they point out that the presence of large numbers of occupation forces provides an ideal environment within which the opponent's willpower can be undermined. By employing a wide variety of means, civil resistors aim to demonstrate to an opponent that its view of the issue at stake is unrealistic and that the forces of repression brought to bear are not only ineffective but also counter-productive.

Civilian resistance strategy can be viewed as having two distinct dimensions. On the one hand, it involves non-cooperation and active non-violent resistance to the opponent's activities. In practice, this may mean a refusal to obey directions and laws, a refusal to pay taxes, a refusal to accept changed work directions and perhaps, at least for short periods, a refusal to work at all. Civilian resistance can also involve a wide range of disruptive activities that go beyond simple non-cooperation. Attempts may be made actively to interfere with the opponent's activities by occupying administrative centres, staging sit-downs to prevent vehicular movements, disrupting transportation centres, etc. In perhaps its most extreme form, civilian resistance can involve the organized demolition of major infrastructure items — bridges, factories, mines, tunnels, etc. — before they can be brought under an invader's control.

The second dimension of civilian resistance activity involves a deep and probing moral and intellectual appeal to the opponent's representatives in the country, the members of its armed forces, administrative services, etc. Through mass public involvement, continuous attempts can be made to persuade individuals to defect from the opponent's regime, either overtly or passively. Over time, the many components of this strategy can produce an environment of defiant resistance and subversion that, in many circumstances, can effectively deny an opponent many of the fruits that otherwise would be available to a military victor.

The concept of civilian resistance should not be confused with the principle of pacifism. Attachment to pacifist principles is only one of the many possible reasons for rejecting violent means of applying pressure to an opponent. Legal considerations, attachment to particular beliefs or an objective and practical assessment of the crisis situation at hand can all be appropriate and reasonable motivations for adopting non-violent methods in a given environment. However, it should not be implied that the adoption of a non-violent stance needs necessarily to be absolute. In many situations, civilian resistance techniques can and have been combined effectively with more violent activities carried out either in other regions or, alternatively, undertaken within the same region but by different sectors of the community.[25]

During the course of this century, there have been many civilian resistance campaigns that have reduced significantly the control an invading state has managed to establish over a subject country. Perhaps the most notable instances emerged from the French occupation of the Ruhr in 1923 and the many forms of civil resistance that were organized in countries occupied by the Axis powers in the Second World War.[26] The well-executed evacuation of most of Denmark's Jews and non-cooperation the Norwegian teachers displayed to prevent the introduction of Nazi ideology into Norwegian schools are perhaps the best-known examples of the latter struggle.[27] However, one must be realistic in evaluating the effectiveness of civil resistance techniques in pressuring invading powers to withdraw. While in several instances such activities have undoubtedly contributed in a significant way to the invader's problems, in no historical case have they alone been responsible for the expulsion of an invading force. This can be explained, at least partially, by the fact that in the past, civilian resistance techniques have been grasped in desperate situations as a final "last ditch" means of continuing organized opposition. It might be expected that with the development of proper planning, organization and training prior to the onset of hostilities, the effectiveness of civilian resistance techniques could be enhanced greatly.

However, the concept of civilian resistance also suffers from several other fundamental problems. Firstly, by its very nature, it is most effective where and when the enemy requires extensive local contact and co-operation to achieve its objectives. While these conditions would apply if an opponent wished to occupy and exploit Australia's extensive urban environments, they most certainly would not apply in the strategically valuable but remote and sparsely occupied regions adjacent to Australia's northern and north-western coasts. In these areas, civil non-cooperation, even if it took the extreme form of destroying local facilities before an enemy could arrive, would be effective for only a limited period. Thus if it were an opponent's intention not to invade the whole country but merely to occupy a valuable but sparsely inhabited portion, civilian resistance techniques, on their own, could not be expected to provide a credible deterrent or response capacity.

In reality, civilian resistance techniques can be effectively applied only in the most defensive situation, when a nation's major population centres are occupied by enemy forces. In these circumstances, an enemy can be inconvenienced seriously and possibly, over time, even threatened by this activity. Thus it follows that, if it is possible to demonstrate an effective civil resistance capability before hostilities begin, the deterrence potential of such a stance could be considerable. Adam Roberts has expressed this view in the following terms:

> An important element in military deterrence is making it clear to an enemy not simply that he cannot gain by aggression, but also that he will positively lose. Civilian defence might involve such a threat — that the enemy will, if he attacks the civilian defence country, run the risk of losing control over his own troops and officials, or over his allies or dependent nations, or possibly even have to face an organized revolt in his own country.[28]

In practice, there can be expected to be major difficulties in developing and exercising, during a period of peace, the type of highly efficient civilian resistance structure than conceivably could hold some deterrence value. To do this, a government would need to admit publicly that more conventional security options might be inadequate on their own to prevent occupation of large parts of the country. The expression of this type of governmental realism is rarely viewed as being politically palatable, even in the most threatening of international environments.

Strategy Theme 5   Economic Defence

Increasing global economic interdependence implies increasing national vulnerability to interruptions in world trade. As a consequence of this realization, the United States, Britain, France, Japan, Sweden, Switzerland, South Africa and a number of other states have instituted a variety of economic defence measures to safeguard national economic capacity, both in periods of international crisis and in the face of pressures of national aggression.[29]

Comprehensive economic defence strategies have three major components: a reduction of import dependence, detailed planning to facilitate the transformation of the national economy to meet the demands of international crises and the contribution of economic defence considerations to the processes of planning and evaluating new industry and infrastructure developments.

As was discussed briefly in Chapter 3, Australia's dependence on imports is limited to relatively few commodity areas. Australia produces more than its own requirements in foods and basic metallic minerals. However, in the fields of liquid fuels, an array of chemical materials and several high-technology manufactured goods, Australia is currently dependent to a large degree upon foreign sources of supply. In some of these instances, external dependence may not be permanent. For example, it is quite possible that new import-substituting natural resource deposits will be discovered. In the case of some raw materials that are currently imported, Australia does possess significant deposits, but at present these are uneconomic to exploit.[30] It is conceivable that in the case of some of these materials, fluctuations in world prices could make their exploitation economically feasible during the coming decade.

Economic defence planners can encourage a higher degree of material self-reliance through a number of policy initiatives. Firstly, in those instances where Australia possesses limited but fast diminishing supplies of readily accessible materials of strategic importance, active measures can be instituted to conserve remaining stocks.[31] Secondly, in many industries it is feasible to encourage the substitution of readily available domestic resources for some imported materials. The scope here is particularly notable in the substitution of natural gas, coal, solar and wind energy for imported oil in many industrial and domestic heating and some transport applications. A third category of economic defence policy initiatives is the development and exploitation of new domestic resources to expand even further the processes of import substitution. Oil from coal processes, methanol from natural gas and coal, ethanol from plants, the reprocessing of industrial wastes to derive hitherto imported chemicals and the development of marginally economic import-substituting mining and chemical processes might all play an integral part in such a programme.[32]

Despite extensive processes of import substitution, there are still likely to be some resources of strategic importance that Australia lacks — fuel oil, some chemical raw materials (sulphur, mercury, esters, amino compounds, etc.) and some specialized high-technology manufactured goods.[33] With little prospect of domestic supplies becoming available in quantities sufficient to satisfy national demands in crisis situations, there may be little choice but to stockpile. With many of the commodities involved, the quantities used are very small. In these instances, stockpiling using conventional facilities is unlikely to cause serious difficulties. However, in the case of some chemical raw materials and fuel oil, specialized storage programmes would be necessary. Most solid chemical materials can be stored safely in above-ground stockpiles. Where large quantities are required for long periods, abandoned open-cut mines or quarries might be filled, with the final surface being revegetated or sealed. By far the largest storage problem likely to confront Australia would be that of fuel oil. Fortunately, many other countries have an even more extreme problem in this regard and the technology of bulk storage is now highly developed.[34] Although above-ground metal and rubber tanks can be employed, by far the most economic and environmentally safe technique is bulk storage in underground excavations or abandoned mines.[35] As Australia is well supplied with the latter, it would appear that the prime physical means of undertaking such a programme is already available.[36]

The second major component of economic defence strategy involves detailed planning for the transformation of the national economy to meet the demands of particular types of international crises. Basically, this involves the development of a range of highly detailed contingency plans so that in an emergency all components of the national economy can be mobilized quickly and efficiently. Means of rapidly transforming industrial production were discussed in Chapter 4. In addition, the details of national resource reallocation for both military and civil purposes would need to be determined in advance. Manpower, transport, fuel and power, communications, construction, food and water would all need to be incorporated into the economic defence planning system. These processes of detailed planning not only would identify potential problem areas and permit their solution in advance but also would provide a basis for informing the general public of economic defence priorities.

There is a third element in comprehensive economic defence planning. This involves the evolution and expression of economic defence considerations and constraints in the processes of industry and governmental economic and infrastructure planning. It would be desirable for economic defence considerations to be evaluated seriously in the planning, design, siting and construction of new facilities, plants and projects of all kinds. Economic defence considerations might not be overriding in many instances, but deliberations on their significance could be expected to impact in a major way upon the form of the national economic infrastructure in the long term.

Economic defence programmes are not without their costs. By their very nature, they represent an additional constraint upon the free flow of market forces in the international economy. Developing a capacity to satisfy a higher proportion of national demands from domestic resources involves additional economic expense because of its contravention of the economic laws of comparative advantage. Meaningful economic defence measures also incur a diplomatic cost because of the unfavourable reception that such a policy is likely to receive from those countries that have traditionally exported strategic materials and goods to Australia.

In addition, economic defence programmes require a significant budgetary allocation from the national security vote to cover the costs of administration and detailed planning, the development and management of resource stockpiles and the subsidy of conservation and other measures in private industry. In Australia's current situation, the structural and bureaucratic constraints upon the development of an economic defence structure are unlikely to be surmounted in the absence of any strong political lobby perceiving such a programme to be in its interests.

Strategy Theme 6   Civil Defence

There are three major developments in Australia's national security environment that serve to heighten the requirement for an effective civil defence structure. Firstly, in the absence of a comprehensive programme for international nuclear disarmament, it is difficult to dismiss the long-term potential for either a regional or global nuclear war. In the history of warfare, very few weapons, once they have been developed, deployed and actually used in combat, then have been reserved permanently from further use in international conflicts.

A second and related development is that the conventional destructive potential and long-range delivery capacities that are becoming available to both the super-powers and to regional states are of an order of magnitude greater than those of the past.[37] These first two factors impact directly upon the third. As was discussed in Chapter 4, Australia's strategic reorientation towards meeting the pressures of international crises and international aggression independently requires that the Australian Defence Force direct its resources primarily towards operations on and from the Australian continent. One major consequence of this development is that service installations and centres of population and production capacity within Australia are likely to be involved far more directly in future national security crises. The significance of this factor is further compounded by the fact that Australia's population is extremely vulnerable because of its very high levels of geographic concentration. In other words, international capacities to direct destructive firepower over long ranges are increasing markedly. In this environment, if Australia participates in future conflicts, it is not only likely to be more intimately involved but it will also be more vulnerable to enemy counteraction. Active population protection and damage limitation measures would appear to be of increasing importance to Australia's overall national security.

The civil defence concept is not new to Australia. During the 1950s and 1960s, a small group of civil defence and state emergency service specialists formulated operational procedures and doctrines specifically to fulfil Australia's requirements.[38] Moreover, active state emergency service organizations were developed in each state and territory, but despite the initiative of the experts and the dedication of a large number of volunteers,[39] these organizations have experienced extreme difficulties in developing any more than the most basic of frameworks.

The most significant problems have arisen directly as a result of a notable absence of political and bureaucratic interest. This has been manifested most obviously in the levels of federal, state and local government funding.[40] The overall neglect is reflected clearly in nearly every aspect of Australian civil defence activity: full-time and part-time personnel strengths, training activities, local facilities, equipment holdings, civil defence research, etc. The levels of current equipment holdings have been discussed in detail by the former Director-General of the Natural Disasters Organization, Major-General A.B. Stretton. He pointed out that "it is estimated that of the 618 local units . . . over half have only 10% or less of their equipment requirements".[41] In regard to urban area evacuation programmes, very little applied work and detailed planning has been done, although some conceptual studies have been undertaken.[42] The blast and fallout shelter programme has been limited almost completely to studies, the dissemination of information to interested parties and planning the emergency conversion of selected city sites for shelter purposes.[43] The current state of Australia's civil defence system compares most unfavourably with the majority of advanced and many underdeveloped states.[44] In these circumstances, it is worth considering the potential of a comprehensive civil defence programme in Australia.

In well-integrated civil defence systems overseas, there are usually four categories of mutually supporting activity: evacuation, shelter, rescue and relief, and warning.

One of the simplest, most effective and least expensive civil defence measures is to provide facilities for the controlled dispersal of concentrated urban populations across the expanses of sparsely occupied, but readily accessible, rural and underdeveloped regions. Evacuation systems are normally structured so that in the circumstances of a worsening international situation, the precautionary evacuation of non-working people — children, the elderly, the incapacitated, etc. — can be undertaken first. Facilities for satisfying the physical needs of the dispersed civilian population — food, shelter materials, clothing and other supplies — need to be stockpiled in advance in the dispersal regions. Although all of the available mass media are used to inform the public of these preparations, it is common in Europe for precise plans, maps and personal instructions to be published in telephone directories.

The second element of most integrated civil defence systems is a shelter programme. Frequently two separate categories of shelter are constructed: those that are adjacent to or under residential buildings and larger structures constructed within cities or closer to places of work. In Sweden, for instance, residential shelter construction is compulsory for every building that houses two or more families and is positioned either in a vulnerable area or in a town with more than five thousand inhabitants.[45] That programme is estimated to add approximately 2 per cent to new residential building costs.[46] The public is encouraged to utilize the space provided by the shelters for a variety of peacetime activities. The smaller residential shelters are frequently used as storage areas, libraries, activity or local community centres. The large shelters in cities or at workplaces are used as parking stations, theatres, recreation areas and gymnasiums and, over time, largely pay for their own construction.

The third element of most integrated civil defence structures is a trained relief or rescue force. The actual methods of force formation employed overseas vary widely, but in most countries large numbers of people are trained in a part-time manner to perform rescue, fire-fighting and basic medical tasks. For operations within large towns and cities, specialized equipment and advanced training are required for effective function performance. While civil fire, rescue and medical facilities can be integrated into this relief system, the scale of the requirement that must be anticipated in wartime situations is of a magnitude that makes the training and equipping of large part-time forces essential.

The fourth and final civil defence element is a warning mechanism to detect the approach of potential threats and to initiate appropriate local, regional and nation-wide response measures. Because of its geographic isolation, Australia is confronted by peculiar difficulties in this regard. In many circumstances, it seems probable that a heightening of regional or global tensions would provide sufficient notice to trigger precautionary civil defence measures. However, if Australia is to be assured of preliminary warning of a bomber, intercontinental ballistic missile (ICBM), submarine-launched ballistic missile (SLBM) or long-range cruise missile attack, a much more advanced detection system would be required. The over-the-horizon backscatter radar Australia is developing for long-range surveillance purposes should be capable of detecting and tracking the approach of long-range bombers and large cruise missiles.[47] However, the detection of ICBMs, SLBMs and probably long-range cruise missiles of small dimensions may require the purchase of a surveillance satellite capability.[48] As Australia already possesses numerous ground stations with a capacity to monitor such a system, the major expenses involved would be those of the satellite itself and its positioning. This might cost between $50 million and $200 million.[49] However, as one satellite could be expected to operate effectively for at least ten years, and it might also perform secondary military and/or civil functions, an annual cost of between $7 million and $25 million might be acceptable.[50] A satellite surveillance system could be expected to provide an effective 30-minute warning of incoming ICBMs and a 5-minute-plus warning of SLBMs and sea-launched cruise missiles fired from platforms close offshore.[51] Under most circumstances, this would be sufficient to permit at least partial shelter occupation.

Australia already possesses the basic organizational framework and much of the manpower and technical expertise required for an integrated and highly effective civil defence network. However, a great deal remains to be done if the conceptual potential of civil defence is to be approached in Australia. As a bureaucratic problem, such an effort would involve the diversion of resources away from already established programmes and priorities. As a political issue, the apparent remoteness of the scenarios for which it is designed makes it easy to neglect in the absence of a widespread public demand for protection.

Strategy Theme 7 Psychological Defence

The primary objectives of psychological defence structures are to inform the public, in periods of peace, what it is expected to do in crisis situations and to ensure an adequate flow of accurate news and information during the actual course of a crisis or conflict. In those countries employing this concept, the existing civil media are employed extensively in the performance of both of these functions.[52] In preparing for their special tasks in crisis situations, the peacetime facilities of the media are usually analysed carefully, to determine their survivability and effectiveness in a range of hostile environments. Decisions then can be made to restructure or back up existing arrangements by duplicating or protecting facilities. In a crisis situation, a properly structured psychological defence system can provide a capability to largely eliminate rumours, defeat enemy propaganda and strengthen national resolve.

Many of the issues raised in this chapter have yet to be considered seriously by Australia's security planners. Primarily because the nation's security function has been tied intimately to the activities of major power allies for so long, the consideration of alternative force structures in Australia has been limited almost completely to relatively minor variations of the conventional, major power-derived order of battle. Force structure debates have tended to centre almost entirely on numbers and types of aircraft, destroyers, aircraft carriers, infantry battalions, armoured vehicles, etc., but now, with the changes in Australia's environment stimulating a requirements to independently deter, defer and, if necessary, defend against a much wider range of potential pressures and threats, the scope of the force structure debate needs to be broadened considerably.

All of the strategy themes that have been discussed in this chapter suffer from major weaknesses and problems when viewed in isolation. However, by drawing selectively upon the positive elements of a number of themes, it is possible to construct strategy and structure conglomerates that possess an efficient capacity to meet a wide range of pressures and threats. For instance, the following strategy themes could be combined in various ways to produce several alternate conceptual solutions. Adapted conventional units might be used for peacetime surveillance and policing duties, as well as to provide an immediate counter-attack capacity in more serious scenarios. Territorial defence forces might be employed to provide a highly survivable attrition capacity in the circumstances of major assaults, as well as a local rapid-reaction force in the context of a wide range of less-demanding contingencies. Civilian resistance forces might be available to organize resistance should major population centres fall into enemy hands. In addition, economic, civil and psychological defence measures might be employed, to provide the total community with a degree of protection from the broad array of economic pressures and direct physical and propaganda assaults.

Combinations of these strategy themes could serve to optimize Australia's response capacities to particular types of threat or pressure. The precise character of the individual strategy themes and the emphasis given to particular elements would not be a simple matter to determine. Consequently, as was discussed in Chapter 7 and is elaborated in greater detail in Appendix D, it would be necessary to generate and test, in concept, alternative mixes of strategy themes for their effectiveness in meeting a wide range of contingencies. Only through such a detailed evaluative process could a combination of themes be chosen that would optimize, in a demonstrable fashion, deterrence, deferment and defensive capacity for a given financial outlay.

Notes and References

1. A detailed analysis of the costs to the Australian community of a series of nuclear weapon/delivery system options appears in *An Australian Nuclear Weapons Capability*, the published reports of syndicate deliberations on this subject (Canberra: United Service Institution of the Australian Capital Territory, 1975), pp. 3-11. (The author participated as a syndicate member in the preparation of the first of these reports.)
2. Exactly what level of damage might be viewed as unacceptable by a superpower is discussed at length by Geoffrey Kemp, *Nuclear Forces for Medium Powers* (London: International Institute for Strategic Studies, 1974), Adelphi Papers 106 and 107, pts 1-3.
3. A launch-on-warning capacity is one that would be triggered by the receipt of intelligence indicating that an enemy had either launched, or was about to launch, a major attack upon Australia's nuclear forces. A second strike capacity is one that is designed to survive an initial enemy assault, thus providing, in all circumstances, the option of a retaliatory counter-attack.

4. The problems of warhead miniaturization for the purposes of satisfying the space and weight constraints of military delivery systems are highly complex and not amenable to ready solution without extensive testing. See this discussed by Ted Greenwood, George W. Rathjens and Jack Ruina, *Nuclear Power and Weapons Proliferation* (London: International Institute for Strategic Studies, 1976), Adelphi Paper 130, p. 4.
5. The costs of these options and the relative potential of an array of similar options is discussed in United Service Institution of the Australian Capital Territory, *Australian Nuclear Weapons Capability*, p. 8.
6. For details of recent developments in cruise missile systems, see Appendix B.
7. In a crisis situation, the United States would have the option of closing down the non-secure navigation signals of the GPS system. It is also possible that, in a world crisis, the Soviet Union might attack and effectively destroy many of the United States satellite systems that have global strategic functions. For details of their developing capability in this field, see Clarence A. Robinson, "Soviets Push for Beam Weapon", *Aviation Week and Space Technology* 106, no. 18 (2 May 1977): 16-23; and also "Soviets Launch Another Killer Satellite Test", *Aviation Week and Space Technology* 106, no. 26 (27 June 1977): 18.
8. Terrain contour-matching (TERCOM), magnetic contour-matching (MAGCOM) and microwave radiometric (MICRAD) navigation systems may all be options if Australia were to develop a long-range cruise missile. For details of their operation, see Appendix B.
9. For details of these cruise missile navigation and guidance systems, see Appendix B.
10. This option is discussed at length in the report of the first syndicate in United Service Institution of the Australian Capital Territory, *Australian Nuclear Weapons Capability*, pp. 1-12.
11. These figures are given by Ian Bellany, *Australia in the Nuclear Age: National Defence and National Development* (Sydney: Sydney University Press, 1972), p. 96.
12. This is partly because of the masking effect of undulating terrain and vegetation cover and also because of the relatively good protection provided by armoured vehicles themselves.
13. Australia's current force structure is elaborated and discussed in Appendix A.
14. A major consequence of the discussion in Chapter 2 is that the credibility of the major equipment components of the adapted conventional option is falling, especially when they are confronted by a sophisticated, well-equipped and well-trained opposing force. In the future this is likely to impact in an adverse manner upon the deterrence capacity of this type of force.
15. This theme was raised in his congressional testimony by the former U.S. Director of Defence Research and Engineering, Dr Malcolm Currie:
    I note that the acceleration of technological change has increased the danger of technological surprise. I am less concerned about the appearance of new weapons, *per se*, than with innovative uses of technology based on a superior understanding of technology's ultimate significance to future warfare.
    See "Currie Urges Vigorous R and D Program", *Aviation Week and Space Technology* 104, no. 7 (16 February 1976): 38-39.
16. G. J. Pauker, Steven Canby, A. Ross Johnson and W. B. Quandt, *In Search of Self-reliance: US Security Assistance to the Third World under the Nixon Doctrine* (Santa Monica: Rand Corporation, 1973), R-1092 p. v.
17. The co-existence of regular and irregular defence concepts is discussed in Adam Roberts, *Nations in Arms: The Theory and Practice of Territorial Defence* (London: Chatto & Windus, for the International Institute for Strategic Studies, 1976), pp. 115-16. See also Lieutenant-General Otto Yliriskü, "The

Frontier Guards", in *The Defence Forces of Finland* (supplement produced by the *Army Quarterly and Defence Journal* in 1974), p. 37. The Yugoslav defence forces have developed a concept of force transformation from regular to irregular operations and vice versa. See Colonel-General Pavle Jaksic (ret.), "On Mutual Transformations between Frontal and Partisan Warfare", in *The Yugoslav Concept of General People's Defence*, ed. Olga Mladenovic (Belgrade: Review of International Affairs, 1970), pp. 220 ff: and also Colonel-General Stane Potocar, "On the Strategy of Armed Struggle", in *Total National Defense in Theory and Practice*, ed. Blagoje Svorcan (Belgrade: Norodna Armija, 1975), pp. 170 ff.

18. The relative costs of territorial defence forces are discussed by Horst Mendershausen, *Territorial Defense in NATO and Non-NATO Europe* (Santa Monica: Rand Corporation, 1973), R-1184, p. vii.
19. See this case made in a tentative fashion in R. Babbage, "Strategic Options for the Defence of Australia", *United Service* 28, no. 2 (October 1974): 15-27.
20. The political difficulties of accepting the prospect of combat on a country's own territory are discussed at length in the West German context by Mendershausen, *Territorial Defense in NATO and Non-NATO Europe*, pp. 12 ff.
21. Roberts, *Nations in Arms*, p. 237.
22. This is detailed in *Population and Australia: A Demographic Analysis and Projection* (Borrie Report) (Canberra: Australia Government Publishing Service, 1975), vol. 1, p. 6.
23. This problem is discussed by Adam Roberts, *Total Defense and Civil Resistance: Problems of Sweden's Security Policy* (Stockholm: Research Institute of Swedish National Defence, 1972), p. 75.
24. See this case made by Adam Roberts, "Civilian Defence Strategy", in *Civilian Resistance as a National Defence*, ed. Roberts (Harmondsworth: Penguin, 1969), pp. 278 ff: and also by Anders Boserup and Andrew Mack, *War Without Weapons: Non-violence in National Defence* (London: Frances Pinter, 1974), pp. 37 ff.
25. Magne Skodvin, an authority on Norwegian resistance during the German occupation, has emphasized the interaction of violent and non-violent activities in that struggle:

    My own view, based mainly on the experience of the German occupation of Norway, is that violent and non-violent resistance need to co-exist and supplement each other.

    See Magne Skodvin, "Norwegian Non-violent Resistance during the German Occupation", in *Civilian Resistance as a National Defence*, ed. Roberts, p. 181.

    Jeremy Bennett illustrates the same point when discussing the effectiveness of the Danish resistance movements:

    Sabotage precipitated the crisis and caused the fall of the Government. It provided encouragement to the civilian population which was already seething with unrest but needed a spark to set it off. The fact that the resistance groups were in touch with the strike leaders meant that the disturbaces were to a certain extent controlled and the Germans were faced with a united front employing both violent and non-violent means of resistance simultaneously. A member of the staff of General von Hanneken, the German Commander in Chief, wrote at this time that, with the outbreak of strikes and sabotage, "the reputation of the German Army sank and, in a menacing way reached rock bottom".

    See Jeremy Bennett, "The Resistance against the German Occupation of Denmark 1940-45", in ibid., p. 193.
26. For details, see Wolfgang Sternstein, "The Ruhrkampf of 1923: Economic Problems of Civilian Defence", in ibid., p. 128; and other papers in the same volume.

27. For details of these non-violent actions, see Bennett, "Resistance against the German Occupation of Denmark 1940-45"; and Skodvin, "Norwegian Non-violent Resistance during the German Occupation", in ibid., pp. 162-203.
28. Roberts, "Civilian Defence Strategy", in ibid., p. 253.
29. For details of foreign developments in this field, see Peter Cross, "US Wants Our Minerals: Stockpile Idea to Foil Third World Bans", *Australian*, 31 December 1976, p. 3; Warren Beeby, "US Looking to Coal for Energy", *Australian*, 10 October 1974, p. 9; and Malcolm Colless, "Japan May Join in Study on Oil from Coal", *Australian*, 15 October 1974, p. 11. For details of the Swiss economic defence programme, see Jerry Wilson Ralston, *The Defense of Small States in the Nuclear Age* (thesis published by the Department of Political Science, University of Geneva, Geneva, 1969), pp. 160 ff. For details of South African, French and British developments, see a report in *New Scientist* 57, no. 835 (1 March 1973): 485. For a brief summary of the Swedish Economic Defence System, see Sven Hellman, "The Concept of Total Defence", in *The Defence of Australia: Fundamental New Aspects*, ed. Robert O'Neill (Canberra: Strategic and Defence Studies Centre, Australian National University, 1977), pp. 28, 36. For a more detailed account and discussion, see Ruth Link, "The Best Defence is a Good Defence", *Sweden Now* 11, no. 2 (1977): 18-22.
30. For example, there are large quantities of low-grade phosphate at Duchess in northern Queensland, which are currently marginally economic. For details, see A. J. Driessen, "Fertilizer Materials", in Bureau of Mineral Resources, Geology and Geophysics, *Australian Mineral Industry 1973 Review* (Canberra: Australian Government Publishing Service, 1975), p. 141. (This review includes information to June 1974.)
31. By far the simplest and least expensive means of ensuring a future supply of scarce strategic materials is to leave a proportion of those resources, which are currently exploited, in convenient locations in the ground. The conservation of a proportion of the remaining Bass Strait oil stocks might be justified on these grounds.
32. The prospects of supplying Australia's domestic requirements for fuels and energy in national security crises are discussed at length in a series of papers appearing in *Proceedings of the Institute of Defence Science*, no. 53 (August 1974). See also Lieutenant-Colonel M. J. Ball, "Oil Supply and National Security", *Army Journal*, no. 328 (September 1976): 5-26.
33. These materials are itemized in an unpublished appendix to Brigadier P. J. Greville, "Infrastructure Requirements for a Self-reliant Defence Policy", *United Service* 28, no. 2 (October 1974): 69 ff. For more detailed accounts of currently known mineral deposits, see Bureau of Mineral Resources, Geology and Geophysics, *Australian Mineral Industry 1973 Review*.
34. The relative costs and utility of various oil storage techniques in Australia is discussed by Alex Hunter, "Oil and Defence", in *Problems of Australian Defence*, ed. H. G. Gelber (Melbourne: Oxford University Press, 1970), pp. 178-80.
35. See this technology described and discussed at length by John G. Trotter and Michel Pachet, "Underground Storage", *Petroleum Review* (November 1974): 727 ff. See also an article entitled "21 Million Barrel Underground Storage Capacity Planned for Sullom Voe", *Petroleum Times* (1 November 1974): 9-10. For details of the U.S. strategic oil reserve programme, which involves the underground storage of 500 million barrels of crude oil by 1980, see S. Terry Atlas and William J. Cook, "Energy: Salt Domes", *Newsweek* 90, no. 5 (1 August 1977): 55.
36. One fringe benefit provided by stockpiling programmes is a capacity to hedge against fluctuations in the international prices of strategically important com-

modities. This factor could be expected to facilitate long-range industry development planning.
37. This matter is discussed at length in Chapter 2.
38. The civil defence planning undertaken in this period is summarized by Air Vice-Marshal W. E. Townsend, Director of State Emergency Services in New South Wales, "Overseas Developments in Civil Defence" (unpublished paper presented to National Emergency Services College, Mount Macedon, Vic., 24 May 1977), pp. 30-31.
39. There are currently over 30 000 active members of state and territory emergency service units. For details of the current membership, see a paper prepared by the former Director-General of the Natural Disasters Organization (unpublished paper delivered to 1977 Industrial Mobilization Course, Mount Macedon, Vic., 24 May 1977), p. 10.
40. Major-General Stretton has also discussed the financial status of civil defence programmes in Australia, ibid., pp. 10-25.
41. Ibid., p. 14.
42. The inadequate condition of Australia's evacuation planning is detailed in "Summary of Discussions and Conclusions" (unpublished paper produced following a Seminar on Civil Defence held at National Emergency Services College, Mount Macedon, Vic., 3-6 August 1975), pp. 2, 3, 6.
43. The limited scope of Australia's shelter programme is cited in ibid., p. 1; but see also a paper written by a member of the Natural Disasters Organization's National Fallout Survey Team, L. W. Wynn, "Fallout Shelters" (unpublished paper delivered to 1977 Industrial Mobilization Course), esp. pp. 14-20.
44. Australia's relatively poor state of development in civil defence programmes is illustrated most clearly in Townsend, "Overseas Developments in Civil Defence"; but also by reference to Kurt Ek, *Civil Defence to Protect and Save Lives* (Stockholm: Swedish Civil Defence Administration, 1970); and also "Civil Emergency Planning in Norway" (unpublished paper prepared by Directorate of Civil Defence and Emergency Planning, Oslo, 1975).
45. For details, see Ek, *Civil Defence to Protect and Save Lives*, pp. 29 ff.
46. This point was made in "Special Survey on Sweden", *Australian*, June 1972, p. 2.
47. The capabilities of this system are discussed in Appendix B.
48. For a satellite to be capable of performing cruise missile detection, as well as ICBM and SLBM detection tasks, it would probably need to incorporate advanced high-altitude large optics (HALO) technology. For details, see Barry Miller, "Advances in Missile Surveillance Pushed", *Aviation Week and Space Technology* 105, no. 2 (12 July 1976): 17-18.
49. These cost figures should be viewed only as generalized approximations. They are derived from more detaileed calculations undertaken in 1973, based on the costs of the U.S. 949 and 647 satellite programmes. See Ross E. Babbage, "A Strategy for the Continental Defence of Australia" (unpublished M.Ec. thesis, University of Sydney, 1974), p. 127. Costs obviously would vary according to the type of satellite actually procured. However, it should be noted that with the Space Shuttle becoming operational in the early 1980s, the costs of orbital placement are likely to be reduced significantly. A total system cost of $150 million has been quoted by the vice-president of Hughes Corporation for a combined communications and regional surveillance capability. For details, see Ken McGregor, "Australia May Again Look at a Domestic Satellite System", *Australian Financial Review*, 19 August 1977, p. 17.
50. These figures are calculated to include annual operating costs.
51. ICBM and SLBM warning times of these magnitudes are cited in "Satellites

Provide Early Warning of ICBMs", *Aviation Week and Space Technology* 95, no. 17 (25 October 1971): 14.
52. For details of Swedish psychological defence preparations, see Ralston, *Defense of Small States in the Nuclear Age*, pp. 90-91.

9

New Manpower Concepts

The Problems of the Status Quo

As with most aspects of its national security structure, Australia's military manpower system is a function of past requirements. Since the Second World War, Australia has relied primarily upon small, highly trained, professional forces in all three services. This has made it possible to maintain a conventional armed forces structure that has been highly compatible with those of Australia's major power allies. Standing professional forces readily absorb high-technology systems and their inherent flexibility makes them very well suited to overseas commitments at relatively short notice.[1]

However, Australia's changed strategic environment effectively generates force structure requirements that are quite different to those of the past. In this new situation, Australia's small standing military forces suffer from several important deficiencies.

Firstly, as was discussed in Chapter 4, Australia now requires a much greater force expansion or surge capacity. In the first thirty days following an order to mobilize (M+30),[2] Australia requires fully equipped and trained armed forces of a magnitude substantially greater than can currently be produced.

Australia does possess small supplementary reserve forces in all three services, but in total these number only 24 500 and the efficiency and overall military utility of these units leaves a great deal to be desired.[3] As the (Millar) Committee of Inquiry into the Citizen Military Forces reported:

> We have seen a progressive deterioration in ... [the] reserve component to its present state, which, despite the best efforts of its members, must be regarded as unsatisfactory and in urgent need of reorganization and rehabilitation.[4]

The length and nature of the Army Reserve training cycle (normally a 14-day annual camp and 12 days of weekend or evening training) effectively restricts its peacetime efficiency, as well as its potential for wartime service.[5] It has been estimated officially that in a crisis situation, the current reserves could not be ready for combat duty before M+180 to M+300.[6] This is too slow to be of significant assistance in meeting a wide range of scenarios that are characterized by short defence preparation times. But even if the existing reserve forces could be deployed in time to meet the contingency at hand, their very limited numbers would severely restrict their battlefield potential.

Because of these obvious weaknesses, a possible alternative function for the current reserves in crisis situations might be to serve as a basis for further force expansion. However, even in this cadre role, a study commissioned by the Millar Inquiry concluded that, from a level of 20 000 enlisted personnel, it would take three years to expand to 55 000, and even that would be possible only if a considerable imbalance in the rank structure were accepted.[7]

Australia's armed forces as they currently stand have not been designed to optimize surge capacity, but in the new strategic environment, many pressures and threats may arise quickly and Australia requires a capacity to meet them with a much greater degree of independence than has been necessary in the past. As a consequence, there is now a clear and urgent need for alternative manpower systems to be examined for their capability to provide the higher level of force expansion capacity that is required.

The second major weakness of Australia's current small professional military forces is that, as was discussed in Chapter 5, the costs of servicing and maintaining forces of this type are rising dramatically. The trends in Australia's defence budgetary allocation from 1965-66 to 1975-76 can be seen in Figure 3. As the costs of full-time manpower and its maintenance have risen, the proportion of the budget remaining for new capital equipment, the construction of new defence facilities, the maintenance and development of defence industrial support and other important national security functions has fallen dramatically.[8] This type of standing manpower cost-squeeze phenomenon is not confined to the Australian military structure. It has been the subject of extensive inquiry in a number of advanced Western countries during the past decade. In West Germany, for example, the capital expenditure share of the defence budget fell from 41.1 per cent in 1968 to 30.6 per cent in 1972.[9] The German government realized that if this trend were allowed to continue unchecked and if the manpower structure as it then existed were retained unaltered, the proportion of the defence budget that would be available for capital expenditure in 1981 would be reduced to an unacceptable 7.3 per cent. As a consequence, a Force Structure Commission was established in July 1970, to examine alternative military structures. One of its prime directives was to derive force

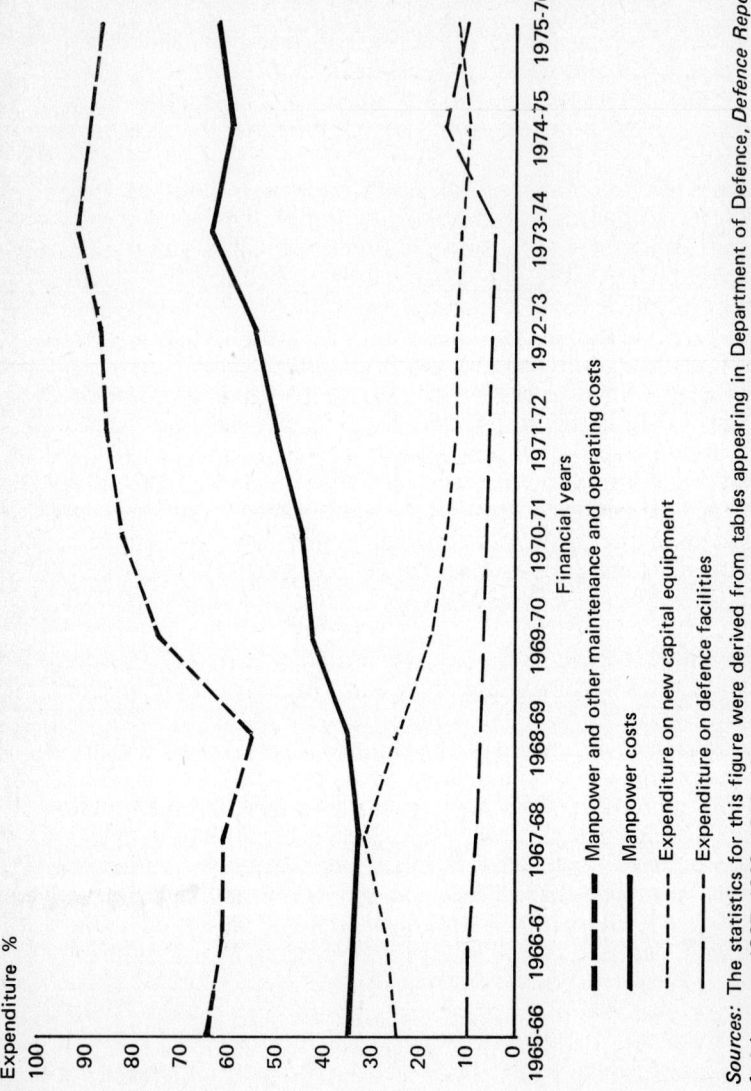

Sources: The statistics for this figure were derived from tables appearing in Department of Defence, *Defence Reports* for the years 1967, 1968, 1970, 1975 and 1976 (Canberra: Australian Government Publishing Service).

Fig. 3. Categories of expenditure as a percentage of the total defence budgetary vote, 1965-66 to 1975-76.

structure alternatives so that within the postulated budgetary allocations for the late 1970s and 1980s, the proportion of the defence vote allocated to capital expenditure would not fall below the minimum acceptable level of 30 per cent.[10]

A number of similar investigations and measures have been undertaken in other countries, to ensure that capital expenditure as a proportion of defence budgets has remained in the 25-35 per cent category.[11] This high level of concern and remedial activity contrasts markedly with Australia's recent experience. Even allowing for international differences in the methods of calculating manpower and capital expenditures, it seems clear that the proportion of Australia's defence budget now allocated to capital expenditure is much lower than that of comparable countries and insufficient for the long-term sustenance of "state of the art" conventional forces. As Desmond Ball has remarked, "most developed defence establishments seem to have a ratio of equipment spending to the total defence vote which is 2-3 times better than Australia's."[12] The major implications of permitting manpower and maintenance expenditures to continue to dominate Australia's defence budgets will be to restrain heavily the processes of structural adaption to the new strategic requirements and to limit severely the operational capacity, flexibility and endurance of the total defence system. A thorough examination of alternative means of overcoming the standing force cost-squeeze problem is overdue in Australia.

The third and final major weakness of the present professional force structure is that its dimensions are restrained by the number of recruits who can be attracted as volunteers. As was discussed in Chapter 5, the absolute size of the manpower pool available in Australia during the 1980s will be limited and relatively stable in size. When this is combined with the inelastic supply function for military manpower,[13] it becomes clear that in normal economic circumstances, it will be very difficult and expensive to significantly expand the professional standing forces beyond their current levels. This imposes a very severe constraint upon the nation's capacity to react to changes in the strategic environment. As was discussed in Chapter 4, a resort to conscription in crisis situations does not provide a satisfactory means of supplementing existing force levels within the time constraints of a wide range of scenarios.

It can be concluded from this discussion that there are three important new criteria to be considered when evaluating alternative types of manpower systems for Australia's future national security requirements.

1. It is of central importance to boost the dimensions of the

defence force that can be mobilized within a short period, such as four to six weeks.

2. Because, in the past, defence budgets have not been compensated fully for the rising costs of professional personnel, and it appears unlikely that this will be done in the future, it is imperative that the proportion of the total defence budget allocated to personnel be expended in such a manner that it can produce a larger and more effective mobilized force. In practice, this implies a requirement to reduce significantly the total force's costs per mobilized man.

3. It is important to recognize the inelastic supply constraints on Australia's voluntary full-time manpower pool and develop alternative ways of raising forces.

The Potential of Latent Manpower Options in Australia

The three new criteria for Australia's national security manpower system create a requirement for part-time, mobilization-dependent or latent forces. The former United States Secretary of Defence, Melvin Laird, explained clearly the rationale for such forces in his congressional statement on the 1972 defence budget:

> Lower sustaining costs of non-active duty forces, as compared to the cost of maintaining larger active duty forces . . . allows more force units to be provided for the same cost as an all-active force structure, or the same number of force units to be maintain at a lower cost.[14]

The costs of latent or non-active forces are lower than those of comparable standing forces primarily for three reasons. Firstly, as latent personnel perform national security duties for only a relatively small proportion of the year, they are only paid for that time. Secondly, the rates of equipment usage (rounds fired, miles travelled, hours steamed or flowen, etc.), tend to be somewhat less per year than for standing units and thus lower operations and maintenance costs are incurred. In addition, the capital equipment holdings of latent forces normally have a lower rate of natual attrition. The third reason why latent forces tend to be less expensive than standing forces is that, in most countries, latent force personnel are not entitled to most of the fringe benefits enjoyed by full-time personnel, except when they are on active duty. The peacetime requirements for full-time medical, dental, travel, recreational and other support services is thus usually much reduced. As a consequence of these factors, Martin Binkin asserts that the average *per capita* personnel costs of reserve forces in all four U.S. armed services are approximately one-fith of those for otherwise comparable active standing units.¹⁵ In some European military structures, the contrast is even more marked.¹⁶

However, in order to compare the total annual costs of latent with standing force units, a financial allowance for operations and maintenance (fuel, repairs, etc.), for the construction of facilities and for the procurement of capital equipment must be added to the personnel costs of each type of force. It is here that an important difference between various types of latent military units emerges. Obviously the capital equipment, facilities and operations and maintenance costs of a fighter-bomber or destroyer unit are much greater per man than those of a light infantry unit, regardless of whether it is manned by full-time or part-time personnel. Thus in highly capital intensive units, especially those operating complex ships and combat aircraft, the large size of capital equipment, facilities and operations and maintenance costs tends to reduce the overall significance of the savings that can be made by operating such units with part-time personnel. Herman Boland illustrates the point by referring to U.S. Navy reserve ships. In their case, initial acquisition accounts for more than 60 per cent of the costs of operating these vessels over a ten-year life cycle.¹⁷ Thus the potential savings that can be made by substituting part-time forces for full-time professionals are much lower in specialized high-technology and skill areas than in units employing low and medium technologies and relatively unsophisticated skills. In fact, in the case of the United States, the total annual costs of a reserve destroyer unit have been cited in congressional hearings as 60 per cent of an active destroyer unit, those of a reserve air defence squadron between 40-46 per cent of an active squadron and those of an infantry battalion 21 per cent of those of an active unit.¹⁸ The higher the proportion of total unit costs taken up by personnel and maintenance expenditure, the greater the potential for gain by latent force substitution. In practice, there are a variety of factors that effectively limit the scope for adopting latent force options in Australia. Firstly, latent forces of most types tend to be generally less capable on the battlefield than similarly equipped standing units. However, this weakness of latent forces should not be overemphasized. As might be expected, the capacity of part-time units varies greatly according to a large number of factors, but particularly in the amount of effective training they receive. As Horst Mendershausen points out:

> A latent force can, of course, be a thing of many different hues and colors. The fact that it is not standing, i.e. not made up of men living permanently in barracks next to their equipment, may mean that it is no force at all. Its members may be reservists with some previous but

largely forgotten military training, spread out over civilian society, unassigned to specific units or functions, practically unrecallable and, if recalled, not immediately (if ever) usable. Its units may be paper organizations; its equipment primitive, in bad condition, or nonexistent; its leaders, superannuated. "Forces" exist which have several if not all of these characteristics. Yet to assert that these are the necessary characteristics of a latent force, as some partisans of standing forces sometimes do, merely invites a similar caricature of standing forces as barracks full of time-serving, crime-prone, soldier-playing, and in time of real challenge, hapless ruffians. Latent forces can also be well-trained and retrained soldiers, familiar with their tasks and equipment, quickly recallable and smoothly assignable, capably officered, and well-equipped. They can, moreover, be intertwined with standing elements, permanent cadres or specialists in many, including highly efficient, ways.[19]

There certainly have been a large number of instances where part-time forces have acquitted themselves very well in combat. For example, the performance of the Israeli tank crews in recent wars has been acclaimed almost universally as being first class.[20] In some respects, an even more notable case is cited by Adam Roberts:

> During the battle of France in 1940, groups of Me 109 fighter aircraft frequently flew over Swiss territory. They were regularly intercepted by Swiss citizen pilots flying exactly the same aircraft — Me 109s. The rate of scoring was 7 to 1 in favour of the Swiss; not figures to be shrugged off as quite insignificant.[21]

The proven combat capacity of well-trained, well-equipped and well-led latent force units has encouraged a large number of countries to attempt to exploit their full potential. A notable example is the United States. In the U.S. Army, for instance, 43 per cent of total manpower, 38 per cent of division increments, 66 per cent of support increments and 56 per cent of air defence batteries are provided by reserve forces. In the U.S. Navy, 34 per cent of anti-submarine warfare squadrons are operated by reserves and 25 per cent of the U.S. Marine Corps divisions and air wings are provided by reserve forces.[22] For the U.S. Air Force, 50 per cent of airlift crews, 50 per cent of fighter air defence strength and 50 per cent of tactical reconnaissance capacity is now provided by Air Force Reserve and Air National Guard units. Reserve units are also providing 33 per cent of U.S. tactical fighter strength and 20 per cent of the Air Force's strategic air refuelling capability.[23] The important role played by latent forces in the military structures of the United States and most European NATO and neutral countries is difficult to dispute seriously. Although on a direct unit comparison basis, most European and U.S. latent force units are marginally less capable than their comparable full-time equivalents, their lower overall costs and the natural process of post-mobilization capability equalization reinforce their cost-effectiveness in most environments.

The second major constraint on the widespread adoption of latent force options is that because of their part-time nature, they tend to be slower to mobilize than standing full-time forces. In practice, well-trained and well-organized latent units are limited in their mobilization only by the simple administrative task of gathering personnel from their normal civilian activities. In fact, in some countries, latent force mobilization times rival those for standing forces.[24] The biggest constraint on latent force mobilization occurs only when part-time units are insufficiently prepared for immediate commitment to combat.[25] Post-mobilization training can effectively delay the processes of total force deployment for very long periods.[26]

A further constraint on the employment of latent force units is that there are some military functions that are not well suited to part-time personnel operation because they require round-the-clock duty, even in periods of peace. Regional surveillance, reconnaissance, intelligence and basic command functions all fall into this category. It is notable in this context that those components of the Australian Defence Force that may require full-time operational status in the new strategic environment may not be the same as those judged to require it in the past.

Another constraint upon the development of latent forces is that many of the people who might normally volunteer for part-time service in periods of peace occupy full-time posts in the civil community of a "reserved" nature, from which they could not easily be removed in a time of crisis. This factor tends to reduce the size of the manpower pool eligible for latent force recruitment and if personnel in organizations of a marginally "reserved" character are permitted to join the forces, it may also serve to complicate the actual processes of mobilization.

A fifth major constraint on the substitution of part-time for full-time personnel is that a large proportion of defence manpower in Australia, as in all Western states, consists of civilians who perform administrative and support functions. Because of the continuous nature of their work requirement, there is no financial incentive to replace these individuals by larger numbers of part-time personnel operating in rotation.

As can be seen from Table 6, despite the problems of international comparisons, the size of Australia's civilian "tail" does not appear to be out of proportion to those of comparable Western countries. Moreover, a detailed breakdown of the distribution of civilian manpower within the Australian defence structure reveals

Table 6. Comparative tabulation of civilian personnel strengths in defence establishments

Country	Numbers of civilians ('000s)	Civilians as a percentage of all full-time defence personnel
Britain	330	91
Canada	39	43
Australia	39	36
West Germany	168	35
United States	1122	34
Denmark	14	32
France	131	27
Italy	82	20
Austria	8	17
Sweden	30	37 (5)
Switzerland	21	43 (3)

Sources: The figures for all countries except Australia are drawn from Erwin Häckel, *Military Manpower and Political Purpose*, p. 17. Häckel emphasizes that his figures are approximations only and they relate to 1969-70. Those for Australia are drawn from Department of Defence, *Defence Report 1976*, p. 59; and from D. J. O'Connor, "The Contribution by the Defence Factories to Australia's Defence Capability", in *The Defence Capability of Australian Industry* (Canberra: United Service Institution of the Australian Capital Territory, 1977), p. 3. Note that the figures for Australia relate to 1976-77. The figures for Sweden and Switzerland are the percentages of average peacetime armed force strength. The percentage figures in parantheses are calculated on the basis of full mobilization strengths.

It is difficult to draw detailed conclusions from this table. Some countries employ civilians for a much wider range of tasks than others. A large civilian "tail" may not necessarily be a symptom of civilian bureaucratic inefficiency but rather an indication of high levels of military specialization and efficiency. In fact, there appears to be a close correlation between the size of the volunteer element in the armed forces and the size of the civilian defence administration.

that this sector performs many functions that are of central importance to the overall capacity of the national security system. For instance, civilian personnel provide direct support to combat and training units, and in so doing, free military personnel from many purely administrative tasks. Civilians also provide much of the repair, maintenance, production and supply vital to the defence structure's operational capacity and endurance.[27] This is not to suggest that

Table 7. Australia: Functional distribution of full-time defence manpower, 1976

Categories of employment	Service	Civilian	Total
Combat forces	23 600	–	23 600
Direct logistic support to combat forces	6400	900	7300
Specialist support (e.g. medical services, communications)	5300	1000	6300
Stores and supply	3200	5000	8200
Workshops and repair facilities	2900	900	3800
Quality assurance, inspection	100	1300	1400
Naval dockyards: Construction and refit programme	100	5300	5400
Training staff, direct support and servicemen in training	17 700	1800	19 500
Support to reserves and cadets	1600	100	1700
Research and development	400	5700	6100
Central and departmental functions and specialist administrative services	2300	3700	6000
Defence regional offices: provide financial, audit, civil personnel and management support to the Services and the Department	–	1900	1900
Service command and district HQs and administrative units: provide administrative support to service units and establishments	5200	2900	8100
Defence factories	–	7961	7961
Total	68 800	38 461	107 261

Sources: Department of Defence, *Defence Report 1976*, p. 19. The figures relating to defence factories were gained during a conversation with a spokesman for the Department of Productivity and were correct as at September 1977. (The Department of Productivity controls the defence factories.)

economies could not be made in Australia's civilian support structure. If, for instance, Australia follows the general trends dictated by modern technological developments and reduces the number of large surface naval ships in the fleet, it may be possible to reduce gradually the size of the civil workforce engaged in naval dockyards. In the defence factories, where surplus capacity and underemployment are perennial problems in times of peace, the central national security objective should be the preservation of skills and capacities rather than simple employment.[28] In this type of situation, it may be preferable to reallocate funding so that highly efficient capital equipment and plant can be installed, but only operated in periods of peace by fully-trained personnel operating on a part-time basis. The wage and salary savings derived might be invested in expanded emergency production capacities or, alternatively, reallocated to other more pressing national security priorities. There may be additional potential for savings by reducing the level of civilian support provided to a large number of components of the national security structure.

Overall, it must be concluded that the scope for substituting latent for full-time service and civilian manpower in the Australian national security structure is limited. The large number of civilians and the substantial proportion of servicemen whose functional tasks do not render them easily replaced by part-time personnel effectively provides a relatively large and stable (in real terms) fixed manpower cost factor in the national security system. Those functions that remain most amenable to latent forces do not require round-the-clock peacetime duty, can be performed by exploiting skills already held in the civil community and/or involve skills that are mastered readily by significant sections of the civilian population. However, in addition, the potential scope for employing part-time forces in the Australian national security structure also varies greatly according to the type of latent force systems considered.

Alternative Latent Force Systems

There are three broad categories of latent manpower systems: those involving universal conscription, selective conscription and voluntary service. Let us now examine the possibilities and problems of each of these options as they might be applied in the Australian environment.

1. Universal Conscription

A large number of Western countries employ universal conscription systems to train young men for a period of between nine and thirty-six months.[29] As well as being very common in an international sense, universal conscription also appears to be by far the most popular type of military manpower system with the Australian population. During a series of public opinion polls, more than 60 per cent of the respondents have consistently expressed their preference for a programme of compulsory military service of between three and twelve months. However, despite its apparent popularity, a system of universal conscription would be extremely difficult to implement satisfactorily in practice and would not necessarily provide a basis for meeting Australia's national security requirements.

During the 1980s and 1990s, a reasonably constant 130 000-140 000 young men will reach the age of eighteen each year and under a system of universal conscription, they would all be liable for call-up. Even if 40 or 50 per cent of these were rejected on medical, educational, conscientious objection or some other grounds, universal conscription would still provide 70 000-85 000 young men to be trained and equipped annually.[30] The cost of equipping the numbers involved with even the most basic infantry weaponry, in itself, would impose a significant strain on the defence budget. In addition to equipment costs, the expense of feeding, training and paying a force of this size would have to be met. Moreover, the capacity of the regular forces to train effectively the large number of conscripts who would be involved in such a scheme must be the subject of considerable doubt. It is notable that the Army experienced extreme difficulty in providing even the most basic training to the 28 000 youths who were enlisted annually under the National Service Training Scheme between 1951 and 1957.[31] It is thus reasonable to anticipate that, in the absence of a very major restructuring of the regular forces, the conscription of even larger numbers of young people in the 1980s or 1990s would encounter similar difficulties.

The running costs of such a scheme would vary according to the length of conscript training. It is here that one of the major dilemmas of the universal conscription option becomes apparent. The popularly favoured conscription period of 3-6 months might be sufficient to train recruits in the absolute basics of territorial defence, civil defence or civilian resistance, if these alternative strategies were to be adopted, but it would be extremely difficult to teach the skills required for the effective performance of conventional military operations in this period.[32] Hence in order to train conscripts to perform efficiently the military functions required of them, at least six months is likely to be necessary for those trained in territorial defence, civil defence and civilian resistance units and a minimum of nine to twelve months for those destined for conventional units. Because of the numbers involved, this type of training effort would occupy fully almost the entire regular forces and the budgetary costs would undoubtedly be high.

Moreover, the national security utility of such a training system would be heavily dependent upon a range of supporting measures. It is important to realize that a simple system of conscripting young men for several months' military service, on its own, would be very wasteful of civil manpower and military resources. The majority of conscripts returning to civil employment would rapidly lose their acquired military skills. In order to avoid the natural wastage of training and equipping large numbers of personnel and then permitting a natural attrition of their operational capacity, it would be important to retain conscripts in formed units and to institute a system of compulsory supplementary training periods. Without the reinforcement of acquired skills and knowledge, and the subsequent development of additional expertise that such a system would permit, the national security value of a universally conscripted force would be very limited unless the period of initial full-time training was of extended duration.

There are many other complications and problems that have been experienced by countries employing systems of universal conscription. For instance, although it is rarely described as such, conscription is a tax in kind, and as a consequence, many of the real costs are hidden. Regardless of an individual's personal preferences or productivity in another occupation, universal conscription provides no legal option but to undertake training for the period required. In this sense, universal conscription represents an inefficient and unreasoned use of labour resources. Many of the frictional costs, expressed in terms of disrupted production and education systems, although hidden and difficult to quantify in a simple budgetary sense, are no less real.

A related problem arises as a result of the significant proportion of each age group that is inevitably excluded from the call-up on medical, educational, conscientious objection or other grounds. In most countries employing universal conscription, it is a continuing political and social question whether such individuals should be required to pay a compensation tax or suffer some other type of penalty in lieu of their labour tax in kind.[33] This same question could be expected to be the source of debate and potentially of political disagreement if such a system were to be introduced in Australia. The final major difficulty of a system of universal conscription is that in a period of peace, with no clear and obvious external threat to the nation, it is doubtful whether Australians as a whole would consider national security preparations of such a socially disruptive nature to be warranted. Despite the fact that well over 60 per cent of the population has consistently expressed its support for universal conscription for at least three months service, approximately 25 per cent of the sample has also expressed consistent opposition to any form of compulsory military training. If only a small proportion of the young men conscripted proved to be unwilling or recalcitrant recruits, the costs in terms of political and military turbulence and social discord may be sufficient, over a period, to outweigh any possible benefits.

2. Selective Conscription

Under a system of selective conscription, it is possible to limit the intake of recruits specifically to match national security requirements. This also means that those recruits who are called up can be trained for much longer periods of time without imposing severe strains on the national economy. Full-time training for a period of between nine and eighteen months is sufficient to impart a high level of skill in either conventional, territorial, civil defence or civilian resistance techniques and thus selective conscription potentially provides much greater scope for the application of the full range of alternative strategic concepts.

As with universal conscription, if a selective system's cost-effectiveness is to be maximized, it is necessary to retain trained people in mobilizable units for several years following their initial call-up. This requires the institution of a system of supplementary training at regular intervals.

Another feature shared by universal and selective conscription systems is that much of the total cost to the economy and society is expressed in terms of overridden preferences, disrupted careers, interrupted courses of education, etc. and as such is largely concealed from quantifiable assessment or easy public scrutiny. However, in addition, the budgetary costs of such an option could be expected to be substantial, particularly if compensatory taxes are not levied on those who avoid the call-up. In this situation, the requirements of Australian political and social equity would require, in normal peacetime circumstances, that those who are conscripted be well paid and provided with a wide range of post-conscription support services. The level of financial generosity that such a policy would imply could amount to a substantial budgetary burden.[34]

It is clear from the opinion poll results displayed in this chapter and in Chapter 5 that the Australian public favours either a form of universal conscription or a totally voluntary military structure. These preferences most probably have been reinforced by the experiences of the Vietnam era and by the changing nature of the social values held by the Australian public. As a consequence, despite its relative attractiveness in purely military terms, the political problems of the selective conscription option are likely to thwart any serious attempt to seek its reintroduction in peacetime.

3. Voluntary Latent Forces

The primary emphasis in voluntary latent force systems is the selective employment of civilians who possess skills that can be further developed for national security purposes. Because recruitment is voluntary, there is little political or social difficulty in acquiring appropriate numbers of each type of recruit required, as long as the market price for part-time skilled labour can be met or exceeded.

The most efficient type of voluntary system is one where the length of full-time service and the frequency and duration of supplementary training periods are varied according to the technical skills, the rank and responsibility of individual recruits.[35] For instance, a high school graduate who desires to be trained as a sergeant in a territorial defence unit may require nine months' full-time training with four weeks' full-time supplementary activity every second year. A similar high school graduate who desires to become the driver of an armoured personnel carrier in a conventional armoured cavalry unit may require twelve months' full-time training and three weeks' supplementary duty annually. A fully qualified civil truck driver may require only three months' full-time duty to be trained as a truck driver in an army logistics unit. Supplementary training periods in his case might be limited to three weeks' full-time duty every second year. A fully qualified pilot of a civil jet airliner might require six months' full-time training to reach the standards required of air force fighter-bomber pilots or two months to reach those required of a military transport pilot. Supplementary training for these individuals might average three days per month for a part-time fighter-bomber pilot and one day per month for the pilot of a military transport aircraft.[36]

Voluntary latent manpower systems provide the potential to draw heavily upon a wide range of skills already existing in the civil community. For the individuals employed in such a system, the skills learnt in both the civil and military spheres would tend to be mutually reinforcing. Both civil and military employers, as well as the individuals concerned, would stand to gain. In addition, the system effectively would provide strategic planners with a great deal of flexibility. Over time, force structures could be tailored precisely by controlling closely the numbers of particular types of skilled individuals recruited.

The overall costs of such a system would be expressed in quite different terms to those of the conscript options. The training and manpower costs per hour most probably would be higher than those for comparable standing units. This particularly would be the case if it were decided to pay the full market price for the services of the individuals concerned. In these circumstances, it would be necessary to award what would be, in effect, overtime rates and because many of those involved would possess high levels of skill in their civilian employment, their part-time service would command high rates of pay.[37] An additional factor would be that the periods of training for these individuals, although relatively short, could be expected to be very intensive and thus incur high maintenance, support and capital attrition costs. However, despite these relatively high hourly costs, the price per fully trained and equipped mobilized man could be expected to be substantially lower than that for comparable full-time standing personnel.

In summary, this type of voluntary latent force system is adaptable to a wide range of strategic concepts. Although it may involve higher budgetary costs per mobilized man than either type of conscription system, voluntary latent forces do appear to be much less politically sensitive and socially and economically disruptive. As a consequence, this option, or some variant of it, would appear to provide the most desirable form of latent military manpower in the absence of a serious and obvious national security threat.

The Interaction of Strategy and Manpower Options

The potential for employing latent force options in Australia varies greatly according to the types of strategy options considered. If Australia continues to rely heavily upon conventional military strategies and structures, the potential for latent force substitution is limited to the selected introduction of "hybrid" and "cadre" units of the same general mobilized nature as present standing units. Hybrid units contain a mix of full-time and part-time elements within a full-time professional command and control structure. Cadre units, on the other hand, maintain only a skeleton of full-time personnel (normally under 35 per cent), to assist in peacetime organization, administration and the maintenance of equipment and facilities. The vast majority of cadre unit positions are filled by part-time individuals on mobilization.[38] The potential savings a mix of standing and latent conventional units can provide are evidenced by the increasing popularity of such options, particularly in Western Europe. As Kenneth Hunt points out, this is the type of system the West German Force Structure Commission concluded would best suit its needs:

> ... the German Force Structure Commission ... has proposed that the existing 33 brigades (which are substantially under-strength) be reduced to 24 at full-strength and 12 in cadre, to be brought up to full size by the mobilization of reservists within three days. (It will be noted that the recommendation produces three extra brigades, thus involving more equipment.) Costing is, of course, difficult to estimate, since it will vary ... depending on how much reservists are paid when they are called up for training or in crisis. It will vary, too, with the size of the regular cadres, the length of training that reservists get each year and the arrangements for looking after their equipment. All that can be said here is that manpower costs, which are forming an increasing part of defence budgets, should be markedly lower.[39]

Steven Canby, a senior United States defence analyst, has argued the case for an even more extensive substitution of West Germany's standing divisions for hybrid and cadre units:

> German ground forces total 340,000 in peacetime, of which 35,000 are in the territorial forces and 28,000 in the various defence agencies. Assuming wartime division slices of 20,000, the German field army of 277,000 could produce a 25 division structure, say 7 Category I division slices at near full strength; 8 Category II at 50 per cent strength; and 10 Category III at 25 per cent strength. With a similar cadre ratio and assigned strength in the defence agencies, France could support 23 divisions, the Netherlands 64 and Belgium 54. Another combination to increase immediate front-line readiness and overall structure, while reducing German visibility, would be to lower the German contribution to 17 higher readiness divisions (10 Category I and 7 Category II), and lower the French and Benelux cadre ratio, increasing their division structure from the 35 above to 51 divisions, to correspond with their more rearward geographical position in peacetime. Personnel in the defence agencies can also be used to enrich the active force content of the cadre units upon mobilization as is done in Israel.[40]

It is difficult to translate these concepts into the Australian environment with any precision without a much more thorough examination of the proportion of the total defence force that is required full-time and the means that might be available to raise and train latent personnel. However, it might be concluded from the thrust of this discussion and also from the nature of Australia's military traditions that standing latent force mixes could provide a basis for resolving at least partially two of the three fundamental difficulties now confronting Australia's military manpower planners. For instance, it would be possible to ease significantly the constraints on Australia's force expansion capacity, caused by the limited absolute numbers of available full-time personnel, by adopting latent manpower options. This same action also holds potential for reducing the percentage of the budget allocated to manpower and its maintenance. If the financial savings made as a result of the processes of latent force substitution were to be expended on capital equipment, facilities, defence industries, etc., the current funding constrainst in these areas could be greatly relieved.

The surge capacity problem is much more complex and its solution is heavily dependent upon the degree of flexibility that is acceptable in selecting operational strategic concepts. As can be seen from the hypothetical substitution function FL, shown in Figure 4, a partial replacement of full-time conventional forces by latent conventional units would expand the total mobilized capacity available at $M+30$ quite significantly.[41] From position F in this illustration, if ten full-time units were phased out in favour of comparably equipped and trained latent units (at X), the total mobilized force could be increased by 100 per cent.[42] However, when the limited overall scope for latent force substitution in the existing Australian national security structure is considered, it is doubtful, within the current budgetary parameters, whether this type of action would be sufficient to satisfy the surge capacity requirements of a wide range of potential pressures and threats.

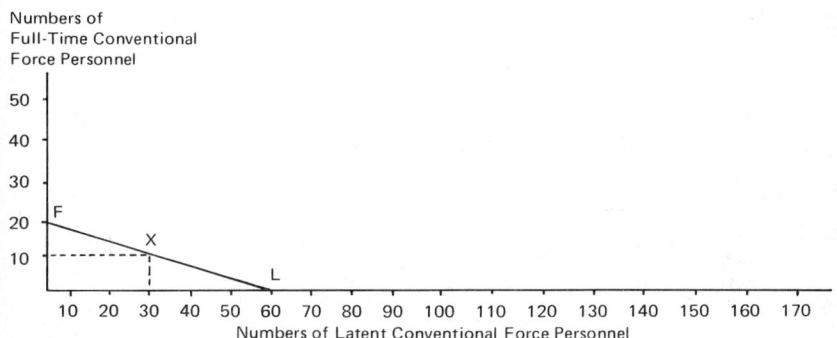

Fig. 4. An approximate cost substitution function between full-time conventional force personnel and latent conventional force personnel

One means of producing an even greater surge capacity would be to substitute not only latent conventional forces but also latent territorial defence, civil defence and civilian resistance units. Because of their relatively simple training, equipments and to some extent, operating procedures, even larger numbers of these units could be procured for the price of a standing conventional unit. However, for Australia's national security purposes, the simple production of large numbers of trained personnel is not the only criterion of importance. Those units that are trained must be capable of substituting for conventional forces in the types of contingencies in which maximum surge capacity is likely to be required. Both civil defence and civilian resistance personnel would be incapable of performing this function. The primary role of civil defence forces is to prevent damage to the total community and to mitigate the effects of conflict and natural disasters. Civilian resistance is designed to raise an enemy's costs of residence, particularly in areas of high population concentration. Clearly the deterrence, deferment and defensive role of expanded civil defence and civilian resistance forces could not effectively substitute for reduced numbers of conventional units in primary military conflicts. In this context, the only conceptual strategic alternative to full-time and latent conventional units is territorial defence forces.[43]

As can be seen from Figure 5, a much larger increase in surge capacity can be procured by substituting full-time personnel with individuals trained and equipped in latent territorial units rather than the latent conventional force alternative.[44] In the hypothetical

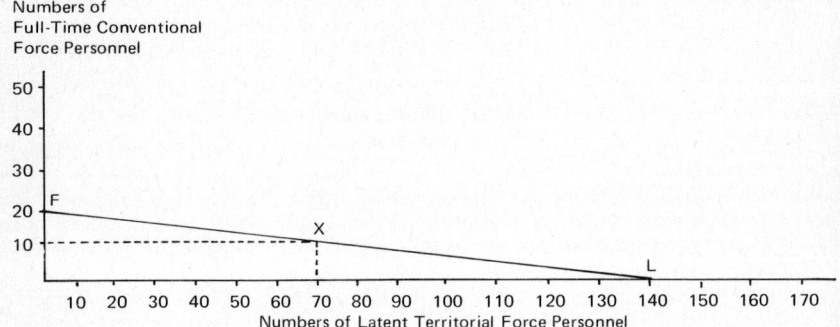

Fig. 5. An approximate cost substitution function between full-time conventional force personnel and latent territorial force personnel

instance displayed in the figure, the phasing out of 10 units of full-time personnel would permit a 400 per cent increase in total $M+30$ strength. This is not to suggest that a mix of 70 latent territorial defence units and 10 full-time conventional units (or alternatively a mix of 5 full-time conventional, 15 latent conventional and 70 latent territorial units) would possess four times the deterrence, deferment and defensive capacity of 20 full-time conventional units on their own. In Australia's continental defence environment, latent territorial defence units rarely would provide an absolute substitute for the high mobility, flexibility and firepower of conventional units on a one-on-one basis. However, in a large number of contingencies, when the strength of surge capacity would be critical to the outcome of the conflict, the utility of territorial defence units is likely to be much higher than their marginal rate of cost substitution. In other words, it may be possible to procure 7 latent territorial units for the price of every full-time conventional unit, but in many continental defence scenarios, conventional units are not likely to be 7 times as effective as those trained and equipped for territorial defence. In force-on-force, rather than unit-on-unit comparisons, standing/latent-conventional/territorial force mixes are likely to provide a more effective capacity to meet a wide range of scenarios than simple and traditional standing conventional force options.[45] This represents a marked contrast to the situation that applied in the forward defence era, when latent force options, and particularly non-conventional latent force options, were of far lower utility.[46]

There is, in addition, a secondary category of factors that further supports the potential significance of territorial defence forces in meeting Australia's surge capacity requirements. In a time of international crisis and severe threat, it should be possible to mobilize rapidly those standing and latent conventional forces, as well as any latent territorial forces, as then exist. However, if the government injects a large increase in funding in an attempt to further expand mobilizable capacity, it is clear from the discussion in this chapter that a much stronger manpower and effective battlefield response could be gained from a territorial defence-heavy expansion than from a primary expansion of conventional forces. This is partly a consequence of the moderate level of technological and operational complexity of territorial defence forces and the resultant relative simplicity of their training.

A second and possibly more important factor may apply if external sources of supply, particularly of heavy capital equipment, are restricted severely. In this type of situation, Australia's force expansion capacity may be limited effectively not so much by manpower shortages as by the military equipment production capacity of Australia's domestic industry. To a large extent, this was the case during the Second World War, and there is little reason to believe that Australia's industrial support capacity is currently any stronger, in a relative sense, than in the years preceding that conflict.[47] As a consequence, the character of any future mobilization should be planned within the context of the limitations of domestic support industry. This is of particular significance, because as was discussed in Chapter 5, it is unlikely that Australia will, in the future, possess an indigenous capacity to produce the major hardware requirements of conventional units. However, by contrast, it is quite possible that

Australian industry will possess a capability to provide most, if not all, of the equipment and supply requirements of territorial units. Hence in a crisis situation, it would appear that territorial units could be raised and trained faster, less expensively and in larger numbers than conventional units. They may provide a very valuable security option in situations where the requirements of self-sufficiency are at a premium.

Thus it would appear, in conclusion, that Australia's defence manpower policies are in need of thorough review. The current standing conventional force structure has been derived to meet the requirements of successive foreign commitments, primarily in support of those made by major power allies. In retrospect, it has proved capable of performing most of the functions related to that task, but now that Australia's security environment demands that a much greater priority be given to independent operations on the continent itself and in its immediate surroundings, the country's historically derived military structure appears to be much less appropriate.

Over time, attempts to maintain the current national security manpower system can be expected to become increasingly expensive, difficult and even dangerous. However, Australia does appear to have several attractive options. The time is now ripe for them to be examined thoroughly, specifically with a view to satisfying the requirements of Australia's new strategic situation.

Notes and References

1. The strengths and weaknesses of standing professional forces are discussed at length by Erwin Häckel, *Military Manpower and Political Purpose* (London: International Institute for Strategic Studies, 1970), Adelphi Paper 72, pp. 3 ff.
2. The choice of this period as a target for force structure design, of course, is open to debate. Its selection is intended merely to provide clearer perspective to the discussion in Chapter 4 concerning the lengths of active defence preparation time likely to be received prior to the onset of a wide range of threats.
3. For details of Australia's reserve force strengths, see Department of Defence, *Defence Report 1978* (Canberra: Australian Government Publishing Service, 1978), p. 57.
4. *Committee of Inquiry into the Citizen Military Forces Report* (Millar Report), (Canberra: Australian Government Publishing Service, 1974), p. 43.
5. The time obligations for some special units, such as the "Bushmen's Rifles" and commando units, do differ from those given in the text. Full details are provided in the chapter entitled "Conditions of Service, Pay and Administration" in the Millar Report, ibid., pp. 101-16.
6. Ibid., p. 51.
7. Ibid., p. 50.
8. The full impact of these developments on the overall force structure is not fully conveyed by this diagram, for not only have manpower and maintenance costs risen dramatically during this period but so have equipment costs. See this dis-

cussed by Desmond J. Ball, "Australia's Tactical Air Requirements and the Criteria for Evaluating Tactical Aircraft for Australian Procurement", in *The Future of Tactical Airpower in the Defence of Australia*, ed. Ball (Canberra: Strategic and Defence Studies Centre, Australian National University, 1977), pp. 61-65. The end result has been that not only has a smaller proportion of the total defence budget been allocated to capital equipment but, in addition, the equipment-buying capacity of a given number of fixed-year dollars has also fallen.
9. These German figures and the nature of the problem throughout Europe are discussed by Kenneth Hunt, *The Alliance and Europe, Part II: Defence with Fewer Men* (London: International Institute for Strategic Studies, 1973), Adelphi Paper 98, p. 9.
10. The full rationale for the West German Force Structure Commission is given in a section entitled "The Task" in Force Structure Commission of the Government of the Federal Republic of Germany, *The Force Structure in the Federal Republic of Germany: Analysis and Options* (Bonn: Force Structure Commission, in concurrence with the Federal Government, 1972-73), pp. 3-6.
11. See, for example, Committee on Defence, *Summary of the First Part of Report of Government Committee on Defence Presenting General Outlines of the Future Development of Sweden's Total Defence and Security Policy* (Stockholm, 1976), pp. 10 ff.; Major-General Nils Sköld, *Defence Policy for the 1970's and 80's* (Stockholm: Secretariat for National Security Policy and Long-range Defence Planning, Ministry of Defence, 1974), pp. 75 ff.; and Charles Grossenbacher, "Procurement and Deployment of Armaments", in *The Defence Forces of Switzerland* (supplementary booklet published by the *Army Quarterly and Defence Journal*, 1974), p. 35. The efforts of the Belgians, Dutch and Danes in this field are discussed in Horst Mendershausen, *Territorial Defense in NATO and Non-NATO Europe* (Santa Monica: Rand Corporation, 1973), R-1184, p. 7.
12. Desmond J. Ball, "Equipment Policy in the Defence of Australia", in *The Defence of Australia: Fundamental New Aspects*, ed. Robert O'Neill (Canberra: Strategic and Defence Studies Centre, Australian National University, 1977), p. 104.
13. An inelastic supply function for manpower implies that a disproportionately low number of people will volunteer for military service even when large increases in pay and allowances are offered.
14. Cited in Martin Binkin, *US Reserve Forces: The Problem of the Weekend Warrior* (Washington, DC: Brookings Institution, 1974), p. 1.
15. Ibid., p. 14.
16. The relative costs of a number of latent manpower systems are discussed in Häckel, *Military Manpower and Political Purpose*, pp. 18-22; and also in Mendershausen, *Territorial Defense in NATO and Non-NATO Europe*, p. vi.
17. See this discussed in Herman Boland, "Reserve Forces", in *Studies Prepared for the President's Commission on an All-volunteer Armed Force* (Gates Commission, November 1970), vol. 2, pp. iv—3—32.
18. See the Statement of the Deputy Assistant Secretary of Defence for Reserve Affairs, *Reserve Authorization Hearings Before Subcommittee Two, House Armed Services Committee* (U.S. House of Representatives), 14 July 1973, p. 10.
19. Mendershausen, *Territorial Defense in NATO and Non-NATO Europe*, p. 20.
20. For details of the combat performance of Israeli latent force units, see Captain Roy A. Werner, "The Other Military: Are US Reserve Forces Viable?", *Military Review* 57, no. 4 (April 1977): 20.
21. H. Guisan, *Bericht an die Bundesversammlung uber den Aktivdienst 1939-1945*, vol. 3, p. 47; cited by Adam Roberts, *Nations in Arms: The Theory and Practice of*

Territorial Defence (London: Chatto & Windus, for International Institute for Strategic Studies, 1976), p. 107.
22. For details, see Binkin, *US Reserve Forces*, p. 10.
23. These figures are drawn from the testimony of General D. C. Jones, Chief of Staff, United States Air Force, before a Subcommittee of the Committee on Appropriations, U.S. House of Representatives, *Department of Defense Appropriations 1977*, Part 1, 2 February 1976, p. 68.
24. Martin Binkin states that some U.S. Air Force Reserve tactical units have met deployment standards surpassing those set for active units; see Binkin, *U.S. Reserve Forces*, p. 9. The Swedes claim to be able to mobilize their complete structure within seventy-two hours; see Roberts, *Nations in Arms*, p. 98. The Swiss claim a capability to be fully mobilized within forty-eight hours; see "A Look at the Swiss Army" (official translated digest of D. Borel, "Aperçu de l'armée suisse"), *Revue Militaire Suisse* (September 1972): 1. The Israelis claim a mobilization time of thirty-six hours, but during an exercise in August 1974, 90 per cent of Israeli combat units were mobilized in a record twenty-two hours. For details, see "Israeli Military Manpower Raised to 400,000", *International Defence Review* 10, no. 2 (April 1977): 205.
25. It is notable that in the absence of large, well-equipped and easily mobilized latent army units at the commencement of the Second World War, the first Australian division to be deployed (the 6th Division, Second AIF) was ready for combat only after eight months' intensive training. For details, see Gavin Long, *To Benghazi* (Canberra: Australian War Memorial, 1952), pp. 68, 126.
26. Where post-mobilization training is necessary, the smaller the unit to be deployed, the shorter the period of post-mobilization training that is generally required. In other words, it is normally much simpler and quicker to deploy post-mobilization trained latent forces as army companies, aircraft squadrons or individual ships than as divisions, wings or ship squadrons.
27. A case can be made, on economic grounds, for the replacement of military personnel by civilians in an even wider range of defence tasks. See this case made briefly by R. E. Babbage, D. J. Ball, J. O. Langtry and R. J. O'Neill, *The Future Operational Requirement and Officer Development* (Canberra: Strategic and Defence Studies Centre, Australian National University, 1977), pp. 3-4.
28. The problems of operating the defence factories in periods of peace are discussed at length in the Interim Report of the Joint (Parliamentary) Committee on Foreign Affairs and Defence, *Industrial Support for Defence Needs and Allied Matters* (Canberra: Parliament of Australia, June 1977).
29. Those Western countries operating universal conscription systems include France, Belgium, the Netherlands, Norway, Denmark, Austria, Finland, Italy, Sweden, Switzerland and Israel.

   The general preferences of Australians in this regard were displayed in the poll results reproduced in Chapter 5. However, in addition, Australian Gallup Polls sampled the opinion of the public with greater precision on two occasions in 1972. On the first occasion, people were asked which proposal "came closest to their ideas about compulsory military training". (Note that this question is highly ambiguous.) The results were as follows:

All young men to camp for 6 months	42%
All young men to camp for 3 months	21%
Total of those in favour of training "all young men"	63%
1 in 12 for 18 months, as now	11%
Only full-time volunteers	19%
No military training	4%

No opinion 3%
On the second occasion, the question remained the same and despite a different set of alternatives, the results were comparable:

All young men should go to camp for about 12 months	38%
All young men should go to camp for about 3 months	28%
1 in 12 should be called up for 18 months, as now	7%
We should have only full-time volunteers	20%
There should be no military training in Australia	4%
No opinion	3%

See *Australian Gallup Polls*, April/June 1972, Release no. 2338; and *Australian Gallup Polls*, November 1972, Release nos. 2362-2365.
30. It is conceivable that the rejection rate for conscripts might be even greater than this. In the selective conscription system, which operated in Australia between 1964 and 1972, approximately 70 per cent of those balloted into the scheme did not actually serve. A large proportion were rejected on educational, medical or conscientious objection grounds, but in addition, those who were married and those undertaking religious training to become ministers of religion or priests were also excluded. A further number had their service obligation deferred because of their involvement in trade or professional courses of education. For details, see Roy Forward, "Conscription 1964-1968", in *Conscription in Australia*, eds Roy Forward and Bob Reece (St Lucia: University of Queensland Press, 1968), pp. 120-22. It is notable that in foreign countries employing systems of universal conscription, the proportion of each age group that actually serves is, in several instances, over 85 per cent. See Häckel, *Military Manpower and Political Purpose*, pp. 4-9.
31. For details of the National Service Training Scheme, which in a modified form continued until 1959, see Neville T. Shields, "National Service Training, 1950-1959", in *Conscription in Australia*, eds Forward and Reece, pp. 66-78.
32. The length of the initial training period in the Swiss Army is only four months. The Swiss freely admit that this restricts severely the efficiency of their personnel in conventional units until they have successfully completed a series of supplementary training periods. See Häckel, *Military Manpower and Political Purpose*, p. 11.
33. The Swiss, for example, levy a special military tax or Militärpflichtersatz on all Swiss males who for medical or other reasons do not serve in the army. For details, see ibid., p. 21. A wide range of equalization methods is also discussed in Force Structure Commission of the Federal Republic of Germany, *Force Structure in the Federal Republic of Germany*, pp. 158-67.
34. For details of the support measures provided to Australian conscripts in the scheme initiated in 1964, see Forward, "Conscription 1964-1968", in *Conscription in Australia*, eds Forward and Reece, pp. 123-26.
35. A similar categorized system is used to train Swedish conscripts. For details, see *The Swedish Army* (official booklet produced by the Press Department of the Swedish Army Staff, n.d.) pp. 7-11.
36. The training times cited in this section, although intended to be merely illustrative, are comparable with those employed in other countries.
37. The high hourly rates of pay awarded to voluntary latent forces might be resisted strenuously by full-time military personnel. This objection might be overcome, at least partially, if the latent force rates of pay were reduced below civilian overtime levels, but were made non-taxable. This could be expected to provide a strong incentive to a wide range of skilled civilians whose normal incomes are subject to high rates of progressive income tax.
38. Cadre and hybrid units are discussed at length in Force Structure Commission of the Government of the Federal Republic of Germany, *Force Structure in the*

Federal Republic of Germany, pp. 100-91; and also by Hunt, *Alliance and Europe*, pp. 29-34.
39. Hunt, *Alliance and Europe*, p. 31.
40. Steven L. Canby, *The Alliance and Europe, Part IV: Military Doctrine and Technology* (London: International Institute for Strategic Studies, 1975), Adelphi Paper 109, pp. 20-21.
41. Figures 4 and 5 have been drawn on the assumption that the latent/full-time personnel substitution functions are linear in character. It is doubtful that this would be the case in practice. They may be convex, concave or a combination of both. However, as is pointed out in Notes 42 and 44, the general nature of the rates of substitution is soundly based.
42. The central assumption of Figure 4 is that a mix of well-trained and well-equipped latent air, sea and ground conventional forces can be procured for one-third of the cost of a comparable mix of full-time conventional forces. This is consistent with the evidence provided earlier in the chapter.
43. In order for territorial defence forces to substitute substantially for conventional units, action would need to be taken to compensate for these forces' limited strategic mobility. In Australia's case, the most effective means of overcoming this problem would be to raise a disproportionate number of territorial defence units in the more vulnerable, exposed and isolated parts of the country. This would effectively provide these regions with a readily mobilized local defensive capacity and free the conventional force components for more direct counter-offensive activities.
44. The major assumption underlying Figure 5 is that seven well-trained and equipped latent territorial units can be procured for the price of one full-time conventional unit. In reality, this may be an over-conservative estimate. Using 1971 statistics, Horst Mendershausen has argued that West Germany's mixed conscript and standing professional forces were seven times more expensive per mobilized man than Switzerland's latent *conventional* units. See Mendershausen, *Territorial Defense in NATO and Non-NATO Europe*, p. 23. It is reasonable to anticipate that Swiss territorial defence units, if they existed, would be even less expensive.
45. The utility of large numbers of latent territorial units would be at a premium in those scenarios where the requirements for surge capacity are most pressing. See the discussion of these contingencies in Chapter 4.
46. Erwin Häckel described those situations for which latent medium-technology forces are most suited in the following terms:
    > ... all-militia forces provide an economically and psychologically attractive method of mobilizing a nation to the defence of its own territory by relatively primitive military means, at the cost of strictly limited mobility and flexibility within the national territory and none whatever outside it. They are thus more appropriate to nations whose military commitment is exclusively limited to their own defence than they are to those with any wider involvement.

    See Häckel, *Military Manpower and Political Purpose*, p. 30.
    The nature of Australia's strategic reorientation renders this type of force far more appropriate than it was in the forward defence era. However, because of the size of Australia's continental expanses, such forces are likely to require a greater level of mobility than that mentioned by Häckel.
47. The constraining influence of Australia's industrial support structure during the Second World War was demonstrated most clearly in October 1943, when the War Cabinet ordered the Army to release 20 000 men to strengthen industrial production. For details, see Gavin Long, *The Six Years War: A Concise History of Australia in the 1939-45 War* (Canberra: Australian War Memorial and Australian Government Publishing Service, 1973), p. 317.

10

The Challenge of Appropriate Response

This book's central argument is based on the proposition that Australia's strategic environment has altered substantially during the past decade. The general nature of this change has been recognized publicly by the government, the opposition and by significant elements of both the military and civilian bureaucratic structures. However, the full implications and consequences of the changing environment do not appear to have been delineated in any comprehensive or integrated form. Thus although individual elements of the defence structure have perceived the general need for change, their perceptions of the detailed nature of the new requirements based on their particular interests, values and experiences have varied greatly. As a consequence, the processes of adaptation have tended to be piecemeal and fragmented.

The discussion in this volume represents only a limited initial approach to the problems of adapting to the changed strategic environment. No attempt has been made to derive the precise form of an optimal Australian security response structure, nor has a definitive means of determining such a structure been prescribed. Rather, attention has been focused primarily on the nature of the new requirements and the introduction of some broader conceptual options.

During the course of this analysis, two major themes have emerged that are deserving of brief comment in conclusion.

1. The Increased Scale of Australia's Security Requirements

The first theme is that the task of securing the Australian continent and its immediate interests in the 1980s will be much more demanding than preparing to make single-service commitments overseas to support the foreign deployments of major power allies. This is partly because of the greatly increased requirements for independence in national security capacity. The traditional and highly institutionalized limited liability approach, involving a presumption that the resources of allies would be available in crisis situations, is no longer valid. However, the increase in the scale of the new requirements is also due to the fact that the strategic environment of the 1980s and 1990s will be characterized by a much more expansive range of pressures and threats, some of which could develop at very short notice.

In combination, these factors are the cause of a major problem. The resources required to develop an indigenous capacity sufficient to deter or, if necessary, defer and defend against the new range of potential pressures and threats are of a magnitude substantially greater than those currently allocated to the task. Moreover, it is unlikely that the proportion of total national resources devoted to the security function on a full-time basis will be increased substantially in the absence of a serious and obvious threat. As a consequence, Australia's security planners are confronted by a wide gap between the ends desired and the means available.

In these circumstances, the only way of satisfying indigenously the demanding requirements of the new strategic environment is to draw more extensively upon the latent capacities already existing in the civil community. This is not to advocate the mass militarization of the total society. In practice, this proposal would involve a relatively inconspicuous process of planning and low-level preparation to facilitate the transfer of a wide range of civil capacities to perform national security functions at short notice.[1] The potential for employing latent manpower and manufacturing capacities has been discussed in earlier chapters. However, preparations could be made to exploit fully a much wider range of civil resources: primary industry; air, road, rail and sea transport; communications; fuels and power; food and water; medical facilities and services; police forces; etc.

Planning national security responses on the assumption that a significant proportion of civil resources would be available in emergency situations could be expected to impact upon the priorities of the total community and most particularly upon those of the established security system. In an overall sense, it would encourage the concept of the nation at large generating and maintaining its own security. To some extent, it would also facilitate the design and development of civil resources with long-term national security requirements as a significant, although not necessarily dominant, consideration. But perhaps most importantly, the acceptance of this type of concept would make it possible for full-time national security resources to be allocated primarily to supplement and enhance the much greater latent potential of the civil community.[2] This type of approach would prevent duplication of service and civilian capacities and would encourage the integration and rationalization of the total society's national security resources.

The full ramifications of this concept are far-reaching. It essentially provides a means by which Australia's security capacity can be extended far beyond that which the country can afford to devote to the task on a full-time basis. It possesses the potential to multiply Australia's independent response capacity very substantially.

2. The Changed Character of Australia's Security Requirements

If means may be found to eliminate, or at least alleviate, the national security resources gap, there remains the challenge represented by the second major theme of this book: that of adapting the character of the established security system. The nature of the national security task now confronting Australia is fundamentally different to that of the 1960s and early 1970s in several important respects. First, it is clear that the environment of future operations will be characterized by quite different technology, terrain, climate, ground-cover, population and infrastructure features to those of the past. The unique nature of the Australian continent and its immediate surrounds increases greatly the desirability of developing original solutions to satisfy the local requirements.

The second major alteration in Australia's security task is that the threat environment is of a substantially different nature to that of the past. In the future, many potential threats may be primarily economic, political, social and psychological in character. As a consequence, a response capacity that is limited to diplomatic and military means will be inappropriate and, in many circumstances, ineffective. In the face of such a variety of potential pressures and threats, it will be necessary to be able to draw upon a wide range of diplomatic, economic, civil, psychological and military defence resources at short notice. Thus in the new strategic environment, Australia needs a multiple-component national security policy and system rather than simply separate, but co-ordinated, foreign and defence policies.

The fundamentally altered nature of these requirements also imposes new demands and pressures upon the processes of Australian security policy formulation. It is now necessary to develop indigenously a strategy and structure that optimizes Australia's independent national security capacity. This cannot be expected to be a simple task, for there are no comprehensive solutions to the new security requirements that are immediately obvious. As a consequence, a major effort is required to develop an efficient evaluation system within which a wide range of strategy options can be conceptually tested for their capacity to contribute to an optimal solution. The model derived from such a process could be structured into a long-range planning system, to provide coherent and consistent direction for the security structure's development.

However, before any fundamental changes can be planned, it is essential that the need for change be acknowledged. Because of the wide range of bureaucratic influences that constrain meaningful adaptation, such acknowledgement will be difficult to achieve. Even if it is achieved, effective changes will only be instituted if complementary measures are taken to moderate significantly the highly institutionalized pressures for conformity with out-dated ideas, the unquestioning adherence to precedent and the processes of protecting established vested interests. The functional performance of existing structures will need to be reviewed, the knowledge and experience held by civilian and service policy-makers broadened, many of the processes of security policy formulation opened to public scrutiny and personnel incentive patterns restructured to encourage a much higher level of experimentation and innovation.

Certainly these processes of fundamental reassessment and adaptation would be demanding and difficult to implement successfully. They would require a major and concerted effort by a large number of people over an extended period of time. Strong and coherent leadership would be required of both the government and its senior advisers. Largely because of these factors, the prospects for substantial progress in the immediate future are not favourable. In the absence of any generally perceived serious and immediate threat to Australia's security, it has been possible for the stimulus for major change largely to be ignored. In recent years, it has almost always been easier for individuals and political and bureaucratic structures to concentrate on repeating well-established routines and to postpone meaningful investigation of the basic issues at stake. As Dr T. B. Millar described the situation:

> Australians...are groping self-consciously for their own identity while blandly deferring the problem of security — not because of economic restraints but because of a habit of hedonism, procrastination and dependence.[3]

Although it may not be universally appreciated in the present environment, the perils of constantly deferring a thorough investigation of these problems are very real. Australia is in danger of perpetuating many strategic concepts that were derived during the forward defence era into a new strategic environment in which they are patently inappropriate. Although the penalties of this type of intransigence may be barely apparent in the short term, in the long term they may be extremely severe. As J. K. Galbraith has emphasized, the influence of a dynamic external environment cannot be resisted indefinitely:

> The enemy of conventional wisdom is not ideas but the march of events... the conventional wisdom accommodates itself not to the world that it is meant to interpret but to the audience's view of the world. Since the latter remains with the comfortable and familiar, while the world moves on, the conventional wisdom is always in danger of obsolescence. This is not immediately fatal. The fatal blow comes when the conventional ideas fail signally to deal with some contingency to which obsolescence has made them palpably inapplicable. This, sooner or later, must be the fate of ideas which have lost their relation to the world.[4]

Thus the most fundamental and urgent challenge to Australia's security system in the 1980s is that of appropriate adaption to the requirements of the changing strategic environment. Australia can no longer afford to refrain from acknowledging the importance of the problem and from instituting a comprehensive process of policy review.

Notes and References

1. The concept of security planning in normal periods of peace, on the assumption that in serious crisis situations large sections of civil society can be redirected to perform national security functions, is by no means new. It is employed by a number of small and medium-sized states that are confronted by large and potentially overwhelming security problems and require a means of managing them independently. It has variously been termed Total Defence, All Nation Defence or General People's Defence.

   For details of the concepts employed in Sweden and Yugoslavia, see Adam Roberts, *Nations in Arms: The Theory and Practice of Territorial Defence* (London: Chatto & Windus, for International Institute for Strategic Studies, 1976), pp. 84-123, 172-217. For further details on Sweden's Total Defence concept, together with a detailed discussion of its Swiss equivalent, see Jerry Wilson Ralston, *The Defense of Small States in the Nuclear Age* (Geneva: Department of Political Science, University of Geneva, 1969).

2. For instance, if it were appreciated that several thousand heavy road transports could be made available at short notice in crisis situations, the armed services most probably would refrain from purchasing such equipment. Moreover, they could plan in advance and in detail to employ this enormous resource in the most efficient manner possible. There might even be a case for managing the civil road transport fleet, perhaps by limiting alternative brands of equipment, so as to rationalize peacetime and crisis support, maintenance and servicing requirements.

   Similar potential exists in the air transport industry. If it were taken for granted that in a crisis situation most of the resources of Qantas and the

domestic airlines would be available for national security tasks, the efficient utilization of this very extensive resource could be prepared in detail in advance. Acceptance of this concept might also encourage a rationalization of equipment types not only among the commercial airlines themselves but also between the airlines and the three armed services. Preparations for the employment of civil air resources in security crises have been undertaken in many countries. For example, see details of the United States Civil Reserve Air Fleet Program in General William G. Moore, jun., U.S.A.F., "Airlifts Contribution to Mobility Planning"; and Robley L. Mangold, "Airlines Contributions to the Nation's Strategic Mobility", in *Proceedings of the 1977 Worldwide Strategic Mobility Conference* (conference sponsored by the Organization of the US Joint Chiefs of Staff Logistics Directorate, Los Angeles, 2-4 May 1977), pp. II-B-8, II-B-9 and II-I-1 ff.
3. T. B. Millar, "From Whitlam to Fraser", *Foreign Affairs* 53, no. 4 (July 1977): 871.
4. J. K. Galbraith, *The Affluent Society* (New York: Hamish Hamilton, 1958), p. 10.

APPENDIXES

Appendix A

The Shape, Size and Capacity of Australia's Current Defence Force: A Brief Summary

This appendix has been written to provide a short briefing on Australia's current defence structure for those readers who are unfamiliar with the subject.

In 1977, out of a total population of 14 200 000, 70 057 people were employed as full-time members of the Australian Defence Force. Military service for all personnel was voluntary. In that same year, Australia spent $A2.43 billion on defence out of an estimated gross national product of $83.5 billion (i.e. approximately 2.9 per cent).

The main features of the Australian Defence Force are as follows:

AUSTRALIAN ARMY

Regular manpower strength: 32 084
Reserves with training obligations: 22 300

Major Units

6 infantry battalions
1 armoured regiment
1 reconnaissance regiment
1 armoured personnel carrier regiment
1 special air service regiment
1 medium artillery regiment (140 mm guns)
2 field artillery regiments (105 mm howitzers)
1 light anti-aircraft regiment (40 mm Bofors guns and Rapier surface-to-air missile systems)
1 aviation regiment (Pilatus Porter and Nomad fixed-wing light aircraft and Bell 206B-1 light helicopters)
3 field engineer regiments
1 field survey regiment
2 signals regiments

Major Equipments

- 87 Leopard medium tanks
- 778 M-113 armoured personnel carriers
- 34 140 mm guns (World War II vintage)
- 254 105 mm howitzers
- 72 M-40 106 mm recoilless rifles
- Redeye light surface-to-air missiles
- 17 Pilatus Porter light aircraft
- 9 Nomad light aircraft
- 50 Bell 206B-1 light helicopters
- 32 watercraft

Major Equipments on Order

- 16 Leopard medium tanks
- 35 fire-support vehicles (M-113 armoured personnel carriers with Scorpion turrets and 76 mm guns)
- 20 Rapier surface-to-air missile launchers
- 10 Blindfire air defence radars (to provide a night and bad weather capability for Rapier fire units)
- 2 Nomad aircraft

Discussion

The regular army is organized so as to provide the basic framework of a single infantry division. Its primary features are its six understrength infantry battalions and its numerous specialized supporting regiments.

The current army structure possesses a very limited immediate response capacity. If given three to four weeks' notice of an emerging crisis, it might, at best, be capable of deploying a two-battalion task force, with appropriate supporting units (i.e. approximately 2000-2500 men), to a remote part of the Australian continent. The maintenance of this type of force in a distant location on a permanent basis would stretch current army resources to their limits.

The regular/reserve army forces also possess a very weak rapid expansion (surge) capacity. The mobilization potential of the current army structure is discussed in considerable length in Chapters 3 and 4.

Royal Australian Navy

Permanent force personnel strength: 16 342
Reserves with training obligations: 917

Major Units

- 1 aircraft carrier (can carry 8 A4 Skyhawks, 4 S2 Tracker aircraft and 5 Sea King/Wessex helicopters, or similar combinations)
- 6 Oberon-class submarines
- 3 Perth-class destroyers (armed with Tartar surface-to-air missiles, Ikara anti-submarine missiles and 127 mm guns)
- 1 modified Daring-class destroyer (armed with 6 115 mm guns and a 3-barrelled Limbo anti-submarine mortar)
- 6 River-class destroyer escorts (armed with Seacat surface-to-air/ surface-to-surface missiles, Ikara anti-submarine missiles and 2 115 mm guns)
- 1 coastal minesweeper (modified Ton-class)
- 2 coastal minehunters (modified Ton-class)
- 12 Attack-class patrol boats
- 1 fleet oiler
- 1 training ship
- 1 destroyer tender
- 6 landing craft
- 4 Survey and research ships
- 2 reserve training ships

Fleet Air Arm

20 combat aircraft
- 1 fighter-bomber squadron with 7 A-4G Skyhawk aircraft
- 2 anti-submarine warfare squadrons with 3 S-2E and 11 S-2G Tracker aircraft (5 more Trackers in reserve)
- 1 anti-submarine warfare/search-and-rescue helicopter squadron with 7 Sea King and 2 Wessex 31B helicopters
- 1 training/fleet support/search-and-rescue and survey helicopter squadron with 5 Bell UH-1H, 2 Bell 206B and 4 Wessex 31B helicopters
- 1 fixed-wing training and trials squadron with 8 MB-326H Macchi, 3 TA-4G and 2A-4G Skyhawk and 2 HS-748 electronic warfare training aircraft

On Order

- 4 FFG-7 patrol frigates (armed with Standard surface-to-air missiles, Harpoon anti-ship missiles, a 76 mm automatic gun and 6 torpedo tubes. Each will be capable of carrying 2 light anti-submarine helicopters.
- 1 fleet replenishment ship
- 1 amphibious heavy-lift ship
- 15 Fremantle-class patrol boats

Discussion

Despite an active refit programme, many of the major units of the Royal Australian Navy (RAN) will become obsolete in the 1980s. The aircraft carrier (HMAS *Melbourne*), the last of the Daring-class destroyers, the fleet oiler, the single remaining coastal minesweeper, the two coastal minehunters, two of the survey and research ships and the two reserve training ships will all reach the end of their useful lives either before or during the mid-1980s. By the late 1980s, the first of the River-class destroyers will also be approaching obsolescence, together with the destroyer tender and the 12 Attack-class patrol boats. Because of the lengthy design, construction, fitting-out and working-up periods associated with naval shipping, decisions concerning the operational capacity of the RAN in the late 1980s and the 1990s will need to be made soon.

In its current form, the RAN possesses a capacity to project (through HMAS *Melbourne*) a light air-strike and limited anti-submarine warfare force to remote locations in the region. In recent years, Fleet Air Arm Tracker aircraft have also been operated from airfields in northern Australia during the "dry" season, in a coastal-patrol/fishing-surveillance role.

The primary contribution of the RAN's submarine fleet is its very effective long-range surveillance, anti-submarine and surface-ship attack capacity. This force can operate without protective air cover for long periods in areas dominated by hostile forces.

In the circumstances of a substantial threat, the anti-submarine capacity of the Navy as a whole would be limited to the effective control of one, or at most two, focal points around the Australian coast. (The choice here would probably be between protecting the immediate Sydney area; the Melbourne, Bass Strait, Cape Otway triangle; or the environs of Cape Leeuwin — the south-western corner of Australia.)

If the entire fleet were to be dedicated to the convoying task, it might be able to provide a degree of protection to two or perhaps three medium-size (10-20 vessels) groups of ships over voyages of 2500-3000 nautical miles. But in a realistic crisis situation, when other demands would be pressing, the current forces could probably only escort one convoy at a time. Presumably this is one area where Australian defence planners have been inclined to place heavy reliance upon United States supportive capacities, but in the light of recent statements by a succession of American admirals, any such assumptions would appear to be poorly founded.[2]

The RAN possesses a very weak counter-mine capacity — perhaps barely sufficient to maintain access to one of Australia's major ports. There is no specialized mine-laying capacity in the current fleet.

The heavy landing ship on order and the six existing landing craft will provide a capacity to transport and land a battalion group with specialist support on to a remote shoreline. However, unless such a fleet is protected heavily by additional naval units, it will be very vulnerable to nearly every form of attack.

The Attack-class patrol boats were designed primarily for peacetime surveillance duties, but because of their limited endurance and numbers, provide only a modest presence in those areas immediately adjacent to the Australian coast most frequented by foreign fishing and other miscellaneous craft.

While the two hydrographic survey ships are relatively modern, the enormous scale of the task before them implies that it will be many decades before large sections of Australia's coastline are charted in any more than a cursory manner. (This matter is discussed in Chapter 4.)

Finally, it should be noted that the support structure of the Navy is vulnerable because of its very high level of concentration. Major units of the fleet are normally based in and rely upon the facilities provided within Sydney Harbour. A much lower level of capacity is provided at Melbourne (Williamstown), Fremantle (HMAS *Stirling*), Jervis Bay (HMAS *Creswell*), Brisbane (HMAS *Moreton*), Cairns (HMAS *Cairns*) and Darwin (HMAS *Coonawarra*).

Royal Australian Air Force

115 combat aircraft
Permanent force personnel strength: 21 631
Reserves with training obligations: 490

Major Units

2 strike/reconnaissance squadrons with 20 F-111C aircraft
3 interceptor/ground-attack fighter squadrons with 48 Mirage IIIO aircraft. (Two squadrons are currently deployed to Butterworth in Malaysia.)
1 reconnaissance squadron with 13 Canberra B20 aircraft.
2 maritime reconnaissance squadrons:
1 with 10 P-3B Orion and
1 with 10 P-3C Orion aircraft
5 transport squadrons:
1 with 12 C-130E Hercules,

1 with 12 C-130H Hercules,
2 with 22 DHC-4 Caribou and
1 with 2 Boeing 707, 2 BAC-111, 2 HS-748 and 3 Mystere 20 aircraft
1 forward air-control flight with 6 CA-25 Winjeel aircraft
1 operational conversion unit with 14 Mirage III O/D aircraft
1 helicopter transport squadron with 6 CH-47 Chinook helicopters (6 more in reserve)
3 utility helicopter squadrons with 47 UH-1H Iriquois helicopters
Training squadrons and schools with 80 MB-326 Macchi, 8 HS-748T2, 37 CT-4 Airtrainer aircraft.

Discussion

Large portions of the RAAF aircraft fleet will also become obsolete during the next decade. By the mid to late 1980s, the Mirage III O/Ds, the Canberra B20s, the P-3B Orions, the C-130E Hercules, the DHC-4 Caribou, the UH-1H Iriquois helicopters and the CA-25 Winjeels will all be reaching the end of their useful lives. This will necessitate a series of re-equipment decisions in the early 1980s which will largely determine the shape, structure, and operational capacity of the RAAF until at least the turn of the century.

As it currently exists, the RAAF contains the mix of elements developed during the forward defence era. The small F-111C fleet provides the country's long-range air-strike capacity and soon will also perform the long-range reconnaissance task. With the Canberra aircraft approaching retirement, four of the remaining F-111Cs are being fitted with reconnaissance pallets, to provide a specialized capability in that role. The capacity of the 16 remaining F-111Cs in both the air-to-ground and anti-ship role will remain limited because of their lack of effective stand-off weaponry.

The air-defence capacity of the RAAF is restricted not only by the very limited number of fighter aircraft available but also by their restricted range, the approaching obsolescence of their weaponry and their inflexible and highly concentrated basing system. In addition, the force as a whole is not structured, co-ordinated or controlled within any sort of continental air-defence command. Indeed, two of the three Mirage interceptor/ground-attack squadrons remain overseas in Malaysia. If the entire fighter force were returned to Australia and integrated into the existing service and civilian radar network, it might be capable of providing a basic twenty-four-hour air-defence coverage for two major operating areas (any two of the following: Darwin-Katherine, Cairns-Townsville, Brisbane-Amberley, Perth, Sydney-Newcastle, Melbourne-Geelong, etc.).

The two maritime reconnaissance squadrons provide an effective long-range area surface surveillance and a more local anti-submarine search and attack capability. With the addition of appropriate stand-off weaponry, these aircraft could also provide a useful long-range maritime strike capacity to supplement that provided by the F-111s.

The RAAF's rotary and fixed-wing transport fleet is sufficient to provide all three services with the level of support required for routine activities and for exercises. Presumably, in a crisis situation, the RAAF's current air-transport capacity could be supplemented by aircraft and crews drawn from the domestic airlines and Qantas.

Summary

The force structures and operational capacities of all three of Australia's armed services remain largely a product of past requirements. Although forward defence was formally discarded as a viable strategic policy in the early 1970s, the fundamental reorientation to Australia's more immediate security concerns has yet to be reflected in any substantial and co-ordinated manner in the design and capabilities of the Defence Force.

The Army currently lacks the capacity to meet any but the most minor threat at short notice. If a demanding contingency were to arise in the period ahead, the Army only would be capable of a suitable response if it were to be fortuitously provided with a very extended period in which to prepare.

The Navy is confronted by the spectre of block obsolescence, with a very large proportion of the fleet due to be decommissioned by 1990. In the event of a serious security crisis arising in the next decade, the RAN's capacity to perform many of the tasks likely to be expected of it will be marginal in some and neglible in others.

The operational capacity of the RAAF is also oriented more to the requirements of the forward defence era than to those of the defence of Australia. Australia does not currently possess a system of continental radar coverage, an integrated air-defence command structure, a carefully designed system of bases or the numbers and types of aircraft required to provide an efficient capacity to control Australia's air space in a crisis situation.

Even from these very brief summary notes, it is clear that Australia's force structure is seriously deficient in a number of important areas. When viewed in the light of the nation's greatly altered and much more demanding security requirements, it would appear that a thorough reassessment is overdue.

Notes and References

1. Except where otherwise stated, the statistics used in this Appendix have been drawn from *The Military Balance, 1978-1979*, (London: International Institute for Strategic Studies, 1978); and Department of Defence, *Defence Report 1978*, (Canberra: Australian Government Publishing Service, 1978).
2. Numerous statements could be cited to illustrate this point. For example, Vice-Admiral J. H. Doyle, Deputy Chief of Naval Operations (Surface Warfare), during the course of his congressional testimony, stated:
   > I was thinking about, if we get in a NATO conflict, keeping the sealanes open in the Atlantic. I think we could do that. I think it would be tough, and we would take heavy losses in the beginning, but we would eventually do that. So that gives it a slim margin.
   >
   > In the Pacific, on the other hand, I think that all we could be sure of doing would be to keep the sealane of communications open between the United States and Hawaii, and Alaska. As far as keeping them open in the Western Pacific and Japan and Hawaii, and so forth, I think that would be very uncertain.

   Testimony of Vice-Admiral J. H. Doyle, Deputy Chief of Naval Operations (Surface Warfare), before the Committee on Armed Services, U.S. Senate, *Fiscal Year 1977 Authorization for Military Procurement, Research and Development and Active Duty, Selected Reserve and Civilian Personnel Strengths*, Part 5, 22 February 1976, p. 2639.

   Admiral E. R. Zumwalt, a former U.S. Navy Chief of Operations, made a similar point to a *Canberra Times* reporter during his visit to Australia in early 1979:
   > In the event of a conventional confrontation with the USSR he believed that despite such agreements as ANZUS and its defence guarantees to the Philippines, Taiwan, the Republic of Korea and even Japan, the US Navy would have to withdraw from west of Hawaii in order to be able to transfer as much capability as possible to the Atlantic to maintain links with NATO in Europe.
   >
   > "We would still be faced with a two-ocean conflict with what is virtually a one-ocean navy," he said. ... "For a long time you have relied on the ANZUS alliance. At the time we signed it we meant every bit of it and we had the power to back it up. We still mean it but we just don't have that sort of power any more. We would be fully engaged trying to look after our own interests."

   Frank Cranston, "Do Not Rely on US: Zumwalt", *Canberra Times*, 2 February 1979, p.1.

Appendix B

The New Conventional Military Technologies: What They Are and What They Do

For many readers, Chapter 2 will have provided the first indication of the very great advances that are currently underway in conventional military technology. Perhaps this is not very surprising. Many of the most important developments are very recent. In addition, the inherent complexity of the subject and its heavy permutation with jargon has effectively prevented the lay person with an interest in the subject gaining a basic understanding of the important issues at stake.

This appendix has been designed to overcome these problems. It represents a concise briefing on the current state of conventional military technology. In form, it elaborates in turn, and in much greater detail, the eight major areas of advance that were summarized early in Chapter 2.

The New Technologies

1. Greatly Enhanced Precision-guidance Capacities

By using various terminal homing techniques, it is now possible to direct rockets, bombs, artillery rounds, mortar rounds and other types of ordnance to impact accurately upon targets of small dimensions, whether they are stationary or mobile. There are two broad categories of terminal-guidance technique. Systems in the first category rely for homing upon those characteristics of the target that distinguish it from its surrounding environment. Those systems in the second category of terminal guidance rely upon highly accurate navigation to impact upon fixed targets with known locations or upon mobile targets passing known locations.

The vast majority of precision-guidance techniques fall into the first category and rely upon the target's distinguishing characteristics. The simplest and earliest examples of precision guidance employed visual target tracking and the radio control of a missile to close and impact upon a target. Slightly more sophisticated systems were developed, particularly for anti-tank usage, which again relied upon unaided optical target tracking, but utilized a very fine wire connection unravelled from the missile through which guidance commands could be passed.[1] The latest generation of wire-guided missiles still rely upon visual target tracking, but as long as this is achieved through the optics on the launcher, accurate weapon guidance is automatic.[2]

Electro-optical or television-guided weapons carry a visual sensor on board that beams pictures of the scene ahead back to the weapon controller.[3] Hence in theory at least, these weapons can be launched into a target area without a specific target first having been identified. Target acquisition and detailed guidance can be performed through the weapon's sensor once it arrives in the general target area. Thus some electro-optical glide-bombs, for instance, possess a true "launch, leave, then aim" capability.

A very advanced development of existing optical terminal-guidance techniques may provide a highly reliable "fire and forget" capacity for a range of tactical weaponry. Current developments in focal-point array technology are directed towards the development of an integral optical target "lock-on" system. This will involve the acquisition of a target through a weapon's on-board sensor, either before launch or during flight, and the automatic homing of that weapon upon the locked target image without command processing or assistance through electronics on the launching platform.[4]

There are, in addition, other types of precision guidance that require initial optical or optically assisted target tracking. For instance, laser beam-riding systems require the direction of a low-power laser beam so that co-located weaponry can fly down the "pencil" beam of laser light to impact upon the target.[5] Laser designation systems also involve the direction of a low-powered laser beam at the target. However, in this case, the ordnance can be launched from locations remote from the designator and need only be fired into the general "basket" area of the target. Laser designator homing ordnance is designed to guide itself automatically to targets that are "illuminated" by "friendly" laser designators.[6]

All of the precision-guidance techniques so far described require optical target sighting and, if the targets are mobile, optical tracking. Thus in their "pure" form, these systems are inherently limited because darkness, rain, fog, snow, smoke, smog and dust can effectively reduce non-assisted optical visibility to very low levels. Many of these difficulties can be overcome by the fitting of alternative imaging systems for target tracking. For example, image intensification systems such as low-light television, can artificially enhance, in a passive manner, the light that is available for night viewing. Passive infra-red sensors provide an even more valuable capacity to see through not only darkness but also dust, smoke, smog and limited amounts of fog, snow and light camouflage. These systems develop images from the thermal, rather than the optical, signature of targets against their background environments.

Infra-red technology is also being used in a non-imaging precision-guidance technique. In those environments where a target's heat signature provides an obvious differential to its surrounding environment, infra-red "heat-seeking" missiles provide a valuable terminal guidance option. For example, the thermal contrast provided by jet aircraft engines against the relatively cool and uniform expanse of the sky has meant that infra-red homing has been employed as the dominant means of terminal guidance for light air-to-air missiles since the 1950s. In recent years, infra-red homing heads have also been fitted to an array of ordnance designed for shipping and surface targets. Infra-red seekers can now be "tuned" to discriminate in favour of particular types of temperature and spacial signature. Most recently, this has meant that artillery pieces, armoured vehicles and other ground targets, which are frequently warm and of moderate size (but not intensely hot or very large), can be attacked with discriminating infra-red homing techniques.

The metallic composition of many battlefield targets provides the basis for distinguishing them from their background environments through the use of radar sensors. Some missiles carry small active radar sets aboard, which can acquire targets and generate homing commands.[7] Others, in the semi-active homing category, can home in on the radar signals beamed by the launching platform and reflected by the target.[8]

There are other features distinguishing particular types of targets from their surroundings that can be used for precision guidance. For instance, the United States is developing homing sensors that identify and home on the vibrations of agitated metal components. Others distinguish some types of targets (e.g. artillery) by acoustic techniques.

The final class of targets that are relatively easily distinguished for precision-guidance purposes from their background environments are those that emit electronic signals. Radar-emitting targets not only can be acquired relatively easily but weaponry can be equipped with a guidance system to home on to the signal's source.[9] This type of anti-radiation precision guidance has been developed to the point where it can home on the very faint emissions forthcoming from the back lobe or rear of an antenna and from the weak transient signals that remain for a short time after the radar is shut down but not isolated from its power source.

The second major category of precision guidance involves extremely accurate navigation to known fixed points at which targets are located or through which mobile targets are passing. Inertial navigation systems have been available for many years. However, new ring-laser and nuclear magnetic resonance gyro technology appears likely to provide greatly improved accuracy within constrained weight, size and cost parameters.[10] Because of their inherent lack of complete precision, it seems probable that most inertially guided conventional weapons systems will be supplemented by a specialized form of terminal homing.

The terrain contour-matching navigation technique (TERCOM) provides a very precise method of long-range navigation via a series of over-land way points. An essential prerequisite of this system is that the detailed characteristics of the terrain at each way point and at the target's location must be obtained in advance, either by satellite reconnaissance or by some other method. By using the ground elevation characteristics as inputs, digital terrain maps of each way point must be constructed and inserted into the missile computer memory for instant on-site recognition. Upon launch, the missile is directed towards the first way point and, as it is approached, the guidance system rapidly scans the terrain profile. Divergence or drift from the optimal course can be detected instantaneously by comparing the stored digital contour map with that being sensed by the missile's altimeters. Corrective command steering can then take place before the missile changes course for the next way point. Upon approaching the target itself, the missile again compares the stored digital map with its sensor's image of the terrain below and then automatically directs its impact on to the allocated portion of the ground.

In the United States' strategic cruise missile programme, an alternative form of terminal guidance may be employed in conjunction with TERCOM, for terminal target recognition. On-board scene-matching area correlation (SMEAC) equipment can store a black-and-white negative film of the target site instead of a digital map. When the missile reaches the target area, a positive image of the external scene is superimposed upon the stored film. The missile flight-path can then be adjusted until the images match. Obviously, unless image intensification or passive infra-red techniques are used in this process, its application would be limited to daylight and fair weather conditions that are smoke-, smog-, rain-, fog- and snow-free. In operational form, the total system is expected to demonstrate a guidance accuracy comparable to that of short-range electro-optical missiles.

In addition, there are long-range ordnance navigation techniques that determine position during flight by extremely precise sensing of the earth's natural magnetic field.[11] Others use passive microwave radiometric technology (MICRAD) to sense the natural radiation of the earth's surface and calculate precision position fixes.

Yet other forms of long-range navigation such as Tacan, Vor, Loran and Omega use active ground-based radio beacons. The receipt of continuous emissions from these radio networks makes it possible for positions to be determined continually through a series of rapid trigonometric calculations.

There is a related ordnance navigation system of some significance that uses an opponent's fixed radar and jamming emitters and where necessary, supplementary specialized emitter beacons to provide the basis for a complex emitter reference grid across the battlefield. When established, this grid can be used as a source of reference, when non-emitting objects are acquired and targeted on the battlefield. Targets acquired within this system can then be attacked by ordnance fitted with distance-measuring equipment (DME) guidance heads. Such systems can navigate precisely to given fixed points by referring continuously to their sensed position within the adopted emitter grid. The great advantage of DME guidance is that it can be used in all weather and visibility conditions and the disposable ordnance guidance units can be produced relatively inexpensively.

Perhaps the ultimate form of beacon positioning will be available from the U.S. Navstar global positioning satellite (GPS) system, which was partially deployed for experimental purposes during 1978. GPS terminals initially weigh 13.6 kg and may eventually cost less than US$10 000 each. For this price, they should provide a wide range of weapons platforms and ordnance systems with highly jam-proof position-fixing, with accuracies within 9 metres 90 per cent of the time and 5 metres 50 per cent of the time.

Many of these precision guidance techniques can be countered effectively by an opponent who is well prepared. For instance, a range of passive measures can be employed to foil optical tracking. Special camouflage materials and a range of operational techniques, such as terrain-masking, can be employed to maximize the difficulties of optical tracking. Heat suppression measures and materials can be employed to reduce infra-red signatures. Several systems exist to provide warning of active infra-red energy and laser illumination. Screens of smoke, dust and fog can be generated rapidly in some tactical environments not only to inhibit and prevent optical tracking but also to dissipate laser beams employed for munition guidance and target-ranging.[12] Most types of active navigation beacons and radio-command links can be jammed or degraded. Infra-red homing and anti-radiation missiles can be decoyed and magnetic and radiometric navigation systems spoofed. In addition, there are automatic counter-measure systems available for many applications. One notable example, which the United States currently has in advanced development, is an aircraft optical counter-measures pod, which is designed to sense weapon flashes and automatically direct a high-power laser beam to destroy or seriously damage the eyes of the weapon controller.

There are also precision-guidance counter-counter-measures. The security of radio-command links can be improved; operating procedures can reduce the opportunities for an opponent to detect the use of laser designators; laser designator homing ordnance can be coded to match the frequency of the designator to which it is assigned; and infra-red homing weapons can be tuned to match the signature of the target sought.

In addition to these many refinements of precision-guidance technology, there is a significant trend in weapon design that is likely to complicate further the task of countering the new precision-guidance technologies. This concerns the development of multi-sensor terminal guidance. In the case of some light weapons systems, this can be expected to be manifested in the development of a modular character. Light SAM systems, for instance, may be designed for the alternative fitting of infra-red homing, passive radar-seeking and laser beam-riding guidance heads. Man-portable anti-tank missiles may be fitted with alternate laser beam-riding or tuned infra-red homing guidance heads. For weapons of greater size, significant advances in a series of antenna designs are making it possible for a wide range of alternative guidance or homing systems to be accommodated aboard individual weapons. There are a large number of programmes currently under development that fall into this category. For instance, the U.S. Army has initiated a programme to provide the laser designated cannon-launched guided projectile (Copperhead) with a secondary infra-red homing capability. Several anti-radiation weapons that are already deployed possess a home-on-jam capability.[13] The future prospects of a target that is under attack being able to counter effectively all potential types of missile guidance at once seems highly improbable.

In summary, it can be seen that the new technologies are proliferating the means available to hit acquired targets and exact locations with precise accuracy. The overall consequence is that, if a mobile target can be acquired or the location of a fixed target can be determined, it is becoming much more likely that it will be hit by the first round of ordnance that is fired.

2. More Efficient Propulsion Systems

The propulsion systems of most types of weapons platforms and weapons themselves are being improved significantly. Most particularly, there are several current research and development efforts that appear to promise very much improved fuel, weight and space efficiencies.

For nuclear submarines, there is great potential for increased efficiency and decreased weight and noise through the employment of superconducting and segmented magnetic motors. For conventional submarines and torpedoes, the closed-cycle Brayton gas turbine, the Stirling engine and a combination of the Stirling and Walter engines show promise. New types of batteries are also becoming available.

In small and medium-sized surface shipping, the trend towards gas turbines, either on their own or in a CODOG or CODAG arrangement with diesels, may be further strengthened by the proliferation of new types of naval platforms, surface-effect ships, hydrofoils, semi-submerged hull systems, etc.[14]

In the field of aircraft engines, there has been a great amount of research into the use of ceramic components. Their introduction may make it possible for the production costs of some types of engine to fall dramatically. In addition, the employment of ceramic components should enable the normal operating temperature of many engines to be increased significantly. This, in turn, will have a favourable impact upon fuel economy.

In weapons themselves, new forms of high-density propellants will give much increased speed and range to man-portable systems. For applications where rockets of larger dimensions with longer sustained power and high speeds are required, integrated rocket/ramjet designs will greatly enhance the accepted norms of performance. In the field of cruise missiles, where speed is normally compromised heavily by the requirements of fuel efficiency, range and compact dimensions, small turbo-jet and turbo-fan engines can be expected to be improved further and to become far more common.

In total, these developments in propulsion systems are providing both weapon systems and platforms with greater range, speed and fuel efficiency, while at the same time contributing to the reduction of their sound, heat, radar and other media signatures. On the tactical operational level, the new propulsion systems and terminal-guidance technologies, when combined, provide an unprecedented capacity to hit accurately targets that can be acquired and identified, even at very long range. On the strategic level, much of the traditional tyranny of distance, in the sense of isolation, is being replaced by a new tyranny of military accessibility.

3. More Effective Conventional Warheads

The destruction potential of conventional warheads has increased greatly in recent years. A variety of new technology warheads have been developed to meet specific battlefield requirements. For instance, for the purpose of disabling, delaying and channelling concentrated movements of enemy forces, minelets and bomblets of "fist" size have been developed. Because of their relative cheapness, these weapons can be laid over large battlefield areas by aircraft, artillery and ground-based dispenser systems.[15]

For the neutralization of airfield runways, hardened aircraft shelters and other similar structures, terminally accelerated penetrator bombs have been developed not only with a capacity to pierce thick concrete but also to cause extensive heaving and disturbance beneath large areas of the surface.[16]

A third major development in conventional warhead technology has been that of fuel-air explosives. These are designed to spray rapidly and then ignite an aerosol cloud of highly volatile fuel. The effect is to exert very high overpressures over the immediate area of the explosion. In the case of a large third-generation weapon, the overpressures generated by a strike in the immediate target area are comparable to those that would be produced by the detonation of a 20 kiloton nuclear explosion at a distance of less than two hundred metres. The blast-wave effect is between 2.7 and 5 times that produced by an equivalent quantity of TNT. Immediate applications are for mine clearance, for the destruction of hard targets, bunkers, aircraft shelters, armoured vehicles, ships, etc., and as an anti-personnel weapon against units in the open and in entrenchments.[17] In the longer term, it also may be possible to mount fuel-air explosive canisters on or above the sea-bed as anti-shipping mines. Once triggered, fuel and buoyant detonating mechanisms could be released to the surface, where the vaporizing cloud could be ignited in a similar manner to that of a surface-delivered warhead.

There are two other warhead developments of note. One involves the use of navel-shaped-charge concepts. The other involves the use of complex multi-stage warheads. The most notable example of this advance is the hard structure munition (HSM) warhead being developed by the U.S. Air Force for the destruction of bunkers, aircraft shelters, bridge piers and other hardened targets. It is believed to take the form of a shaped-charge munition with a secondary follow-through warhead.

The main consequence arising from these new warhead technologies is that, if a target can be hit, the resulting destruction is likely to be far greater for a given warhead volume and weight than has been the case in the past. So when the new conventional warheads are combined with the new precision-guidance and propulsion technologies, it becomes clear that if a target can be acquired and identified, there is now an order of magnitude increase in the probability that it can be destroyed quickly even if it is positioned at a distant location. As a consequence of these developments, it seems likely that target acquisition and identification, even at extended ranges, will become an increasingly important function on the conventional battlefield.

4. Greatly Improved Long-range Surveillance and Target Acquisition Technologies

The efficiency with which long-range detection, identification and tracking systems can operate depends heavily upon the strength of the signature contrast between the target and its background environment. The high level of contrast between a fast-moving, warm or hot metallic aircraft against the cool and almost uniform expanse of the sky makes the long-range detection of aircraft possible. Large, noisy, warm, metallic ships on the surface of the sea present a similar contrast signature, which renders them also susceptible to long-range detection. On the other hand, submarines operating within the very dense sea environment represent quite a different type of long-range detection problem. Despite the fact that sound and other emissions from sub-surface craft pass in uneven patterns, there are now clear indications that in many environments long-range detection and identification of submarines is possible. Small or moderately sized targets on the earth's surface that do not radiate active electronic emissions are even more difficult to detect and identify at long range. The ground itself is an extremely dense and uneven environment, which can provide effective masking for a wide range of targets from long-range detection by nearly every type of sensor.

Satellites currently carry an array of optical photographic, infrared, radar and electronic intelligence sensors for the detection, location, identification and tracking of objects of military significance on the ground and on the surface of the sea. The specific capabilities of each type of sensor are highly classified, but one expert in the field has calculated that the resolution of current U.S. optical photographic sensors is at least 35 centimetres and may be significantly lower.[18] It is also known that a new type of sensor system is under development that will permit flying aircraft and large cruise missiles to be detected and tracked from space.[19]

However, satellite surveillance sensors do suffer from a number of significant weaknesses. If the ground support facilities are highly concentrated and positioned in obvious locations, in some types of conflict they may be vulnerable to early destruction. In addition, it should be noted that satellites themselves can be intercepted and destroyed by some missile systems deployed by the super-powers. Hence unless a state has the capacity to incorporate a series of extremely expensive counter-measures, a satellite's survival cannot be assured under all circumstances. Another difficulty arises from the fact that in order to be effective, many satellite sensor systems have to be launched into low altitude orbits. This reduces satellite life-span, necessitating system replacement at frequent intervals. As a consequence, it appears that some types of satellite-borne military sensors are likely to remain exclusively in the hands of a small number of major powers. The technology involved is extremely complex and the costs of developing, procuring and actually positioning sensor packages in space are likely to deter the active involvement of most states.

A most promising method of detecting aircraft, large cruise missiles and some types of surface shipping at long range is over-the-horizon backscatter (OTH-B) radar. The development of the Jindalee OTH radar system was discussed briefly in Chapter 1. Essentially, these systems consist of an advanced active phased-array radar transmitter that emits high-frequency, high-powered signals, which are frequently adjusted to minimize the degrading effects of natural or man-made ionospheric disturbances. This type of signal harmony is important because the objective is to bounce the signals off the ionosphere, to detect targets at ranges between 800 and 3200 km, or even further, around the curvature of the earth.[20] The efficiency with which this can be done varies greatly according to the matching of frequencies to the current state of the ionosphere. Signals beaming off the ionosphere impact upon targets and return again via the ionospheric "mirror" to a separately located receiver station. The filtering of targets from the enormous amount of "noise" and clutter created by the signal's reflection off the earth's surface and by the ambient electro-magnetic activity deriving from the earth and extra-terrestrial sources is an extremely difficult process and can be done only by using the Doppler principle. This involves the detection of objects that move against a relatively stable background environment.[21] Hence in the detection of aircraft, large cruise missiles[22] and large metallic fast-moving shipping,[23] this type of system can be effective in most environments.[24]

As a long-range detection system, OTH radar displays obvious potential. There are strong indications that refinements to this type of system may provide accuracies that would make direct vectoring of intercept aircraft possible.[25] However, when difficult ionospheric conditions are experienced or when an opponent attempts to jam the system, it may be necessary to dispatch an airborne warning and control system (AWACS) aircraft to the target's vicinity, to vector intercept aircraft more precisely.[26]

An integral and obvious part of all OTH radar systems is their extremely elaborate high-frequency receivers. In this connection, it is notable that a very large proportion of civil and military communication is also undertaken within this frequency spectrum. Thus in the words of Philip J. Klass, the avionics editor of *Aviation Week and Space Technology*:

> ... any type of OTH radar is also potentially a means for eavesdropping on high frequency radio communications that might otherwise be too weak for ordinary radio communication receivers.[27]

General Gordon T. Gould of the United States Air Force has supported this view by stating in his congressional testimony that: "It is clear from what we know that this system will have intelligence value."[28] It is by no means clear whether use of an OTH system for these purposes would require the shut-down of the radar transmitter. It may well be possible to modulate the receiver at microsecond intervals, to permit both functions to be performed simultaneously.[29]

Further development of the OTH backscatter radar principle may provide additional capabilities of great value. Most importantly, it may be possible to employ Bistatic or Sanctuary concepts to OTH radar.[30] This would involve the construction of multiple OTH radar receivers at forward sites, most probably several hundred or even thousands of kilometres distant from the centrally located transmitter. These forward receivers would not necessarily need to be as large or complex as the current base sites and certainly would not be expected to be prohibitively expensive. Some might be mobile, perhaps mounted aboard heavy trucks, ships or even large aircraft.[31] The development of Sanctuary OTH radar concepts would offer two major advances in system capability. Firstly, the reception of the transmitter signals that return from targets to receivers at multiple locations would make target tracking far more accurate through the use of multiple triangulation techniques. Secondly, and perhaps even more importantly, the forward receivers would be able to detect and track aircraft, large cruise missiles and metallic fast-moving ships in their vicinity in a completely passive manner. This capacity would facilitate command and control, and perhaps even ordnance targeting, without a requirement to emit active signals from forward positions or to conduct active airborne reconnaissance. The tactical and strategic significance of this type of capability might be of crucial importance in many environments.

The potential exists for an even more refined capacity if more than one OTH radar transmitter is deployed. By using variable frequency techniques, the United States has apparently demonstrated a capacity not only to detect and track aircraft targets but to identify them positively as well. According to *Flight International*:

> Tests have showed that — provided the frequencies used are such that the wavelength is longer than the largest dimension of the target, and that two or three different frequencies are used — examination of the amplitude, phase and polarization of the reflected signal gives each target a recognizable signature. During trials with models it has proved possible to differentiate the Mig-19, Mig-21, F-104 and F-4.[32]

The further development and deployment of OTH radar systems would appear to be not excessively expensive and hence their acquisition by a number of large and medium powers can be anticipated during the 1980s and 1990s.[33]

Of complementary significance in this field is the newest generation of AWACS aircraft. Aircraft of this type are equipped with powerful radar and carry very advanced computer processing and communications systems. Their overall tasks are many and their capabilities extend beyond that of long-range surveillance. However, in the context of this discussion, it should be noted that by utilizing the altitude at which they patrol for long periods, these systems can detect air, naval and some ground movements far beyond the horizon-imposed constraints of conventional radar installations on the earth's surface. Aircraft or cruise missiles flying at altitudes from ground level to 30 000 metres can be detected and tracked readily from AWACS aircraft, if they fly within a radius of approximately 600 kilometres. If necessary, the electronic systems on board can be used to vector friendly aircraft for interception.[34]

The problems and difficulties of acquiring comprehensive long-range underwater surveillance, until recently, have appeared intractable. However, a number of important technological developments is altering dramatically the potential for reliable submarine and surface ship detection, identification and tracking. As Dr G.H. Heilmeier explained to Congress:

> Through DARPA sponsored experiments, the ocean has been found to

be a far more tractable underwater sound environment than we had previously thought. Improved detection ranges appear to be achievable. These techniques were previously thought to be impossible with acoustic undersea arrays. We are now attempting to demonstrate a revolutionary capability for detecting submarines.[35]

Much of the progress to which Dr Heilmeier refers is attributable to the multi-sensor integration programme called Seaguard (which is the subject of discussion later in this appendix), but individual sensor techniques have also advanced significantly as a result of a number of very important developments. Most notable in this regard is the new generation of long-range passive sonar sensors, which possess a capacity to detect and track both surface and submarine movements in large parts of the world's oceans. Since the early 1950s, the United States and its NATO allies have deployed hydrophone sensors on or just above the sea-bed of the Atlantic. The original SOSUS (sonar surveillance system — for area use) and Caesar (for barrier use) systems have been enhanced since that time through five distinct development phases.[36] The latest generation upgrades these systems and supplements them with three new types of passive surveillance sensor.

Currently, the United States is deploying a greatly improved towed array surveillance system (TASS). This is a linear sensor that is towed for several miles behind naval shipping so that it can detect the "noise" of submarines and ships through the multiple salinity and temperature layers of the surrounding ocean. This system is to be partially replaced in the early 1980s by an even longer and more sensitive surveillance towed array sensor system called SURTASS. This system will require a specialized ocean-going tug, called T-AGOS, and it may employ very advanced sonar array techniques with an aperture in two dimensions.

The third new type of long-range passive sonar system is called the moored surveillance system (MSS). This is a self-mooring sonobuoy system, which can be dropped by aircraft, ships or submarines and which is designed to act as a semi-permanent listening barrier. MSS systems are capable of being monitored by aircraft, ships or coastal installations in the vicinity.

The sounds that are detected by these passive sonar systems are processed in large computer banks either on shore or aboard ships. This permits the detection, generalized locating and tracking of particular ships and submarines with a high degree of reliability. In addition, particular classes of ship and even, in some cases, individual ships of a class can be identified by their sound signatures. The inherent sophistication of the discriminatory capacity of these systems makes decoying or spoofing with specialized noise-making torpedoes and other false targets extremely difficult.[37] However, to some extent, it is possible to jam actively a proportion of their capacity by overwhelming them with generated noise. As with the jamming of OTH radar and other long-range surveillance sensors, this action, by its very nature, would serve to prevent surprise and to alert opposing forces.

It is clear that new technologies for long-range target detection and identification are providing greatly enhanced capacities. In the air, satellite sensors and OTH radar alone may be sufficient to direct intercept aircraft at long range in some environments. However, in many situations, supporting AWACS aircraft and conventional ground-based radar systems may also be required. In the maritime environment, satellite sensors as well as OTH and advanced AWACS radar systems are likely to provide a supplementary capacity to long-range passive sonar sensors in the detection and tracking of surface shipping. In the more difficult undersea environment, it now appears that passive sonar arrays can provide a detection and identification capability and a more generalized locating and tracking capacity. In the land environment, no comparable long-range surveillance capacity appears to be available for the detection of targets that do not radiate significant quantities of electro-magnetic energy.[38]

5. A Proliferation of Battlefield Target-Acquisition and Identification Systems

For objects on the battlefield to be targetable, they must be identified and located precisely. As has been discussed above, in the air environment, these functions can be performed by satellite sensors or OTH radars alone in many situations. However, in some circumstances, AWACS aircraft and ground-control intercept radars are likely to be required in addition.

The precise location of surface shipping can also be performed by OTH radars, AWACS and conventional ground-based radars. Satellite-borne optical, radar, infra-red and electronic sensors are available to the super-powers and also may be procured by other major powers. For undersea and also some surface locating applications, active and passive sonar systems have been employed extensively since the Second World War. Great advances have been made in all types of sonar systems during the past thirty years, particularly in signal processing and computer techniques. In specific applications, air-delivered sonobuoys have acquired a directional and multi-level detection capability.[39] Wide-aperture submarine hull-mounted sonar arrays are being deployed to provide a long-range surface-ship targeting capacity, thus facilitating cruise missile attacks from submerged locations.[40] In addition, a new specialized type of sonar is being developed to detect water disturbances as they are produced by submerged vessels rather than the noise generated within submarines themselves.[41] There are also indications that a new extremely sensitive type of sonar is under development that will provide warning to submerged submarines of overflying aircraft.[42]

In surface ships, hull-mounted sonar systems are being encased in rubber domes, in an effort to reduce ambient noise. However, this and other advances in surface-ship hull-mounted sonars do not overcome the basic difficulties of penetrating oceanic temperature and salinity layers. Thus, although hull-mounted sonars are now extremely powerful and highly refined, the newest systems have been described as being the "ultimate ox-cart".[43] Towed passive array sonar systems overcome most of the difficulties of hull-mounted systems because they can be trailed in such a manner that they penetrate and operate within the layers of the ocean between which submarines normally operate.[44] In addition to the towed array systems that have been designed primarily for large area strategic purposes, there are others that have been designed primarily for precise targeting within more limited areas. For instance, the United States has developed a tactical towed array sensor (TACTAS), which is intended to provide frigate-, destroyer- and cruiser-size ships with a capacity to detect, classify and target a submarine for attack before it itself can be detected by the submarine. A similar but specialized towed array is being fitted to Poseidon ballistic missile-firing nuclear (SSBN) submarines in refit, as part of the integrated Unique system. This will probably be towed by deep-diving submarines in such a manner that it floats up through the salinity and temperature layers towards the sea's surface, providing a capacity to detect the approach of hostile submarines and surface ships from long ranges.

Experiments are also under way with an airborne towed array system, primarily for helicopter usage. This type of sensor may find much expanded application as the U.S. Navy moves towards multipurpose V/STOL aircraft and considers lighter-than-air vehicles for some categories of anti-submarine warfare (ASW) duty.[45]

Because of the inherently dense and complex nature of the land environment, battlefield acquisition, identification and targeting in this sphere is a much more complicated process. Natural undulations in terrain and variations in natural vegetation, geology, fauna and many other factors greatly complicate the efficient operation of nearly every type of sensor system. As a consequence, there is a very wide range of complementary target-acquisition systems being developed, each of which will have a capacity to perform only part of the total function.

Perhaps the simplest type of target-acquisition sensor used in the ground environment extends the capabilities of the human eye and normal optical and electro-optical systems. The most important objective in this field has been to provide an effective vision capacity at night, in periods of bad weather, fog, sleet, rain, snow and through smog, dust and smoke. Inexpensive active (spot-light) infra-red systems were first introduced in the 1950s, but these had a limited range capacity and were readily detectable.[46] In the mid-1960s, passive image intensification systems were developed. However, these possessed a very limited capacity in poor weather and became temporarily ineffective if subjected to bright light sources, tracer rounds, flares, shell-bursts or spot-lights.[47] Passive or far infra-red devices were then developed with a capacity to permit target acquisition at night, through smoke, smog and moderate amounts of fog, rain, sleet, snow and dust.[48] This technology has now been applied to a very large number of specific applications — for instance, night-vision goggles have been developed weighing less than one kilogram and possessing a night-vision range of 100 metres.[49] One particular night-sight for crew-served weapons weighs 4 kilograms and possesses a range of at least 1200 metres, but more probably 3700 metres.[50] A long-range observation and target-acquisition device weighing approximately 30 kilograms has been produced with an even greater capacity.[51] Several airborne forward-looking infra-red (FLIR) sensor systems have been developed for reconnaissance, target acquisition and designation. Some FLIR systems are carried under aircraft in specially designed pods. In one of these, called Pave Tack, the FLIR surveillance and target acquisition sensor is permanently aligned to a low-powered laser designator, which is capable of guiding laser homing weaponry. Others, such as the extremely powerful TRAM system, have been integrated into aircraft structures to perform similar functions.

An important and relatively new application of passive imaging infra-red technology has been in the partial replacement of radar and other sensors for ground- and sea-based aerial surveillance and target acquisition. Most notably, the Swedish IRS-700 system has been designed primarily for passive aircraft and missile detection and tracking. The United States has a similar infra-red scanning system under development that is designed to stare at the horizon, to detect the rise of warm mortar or rocket projectiles. When employed in conjunction with a laser radar, mortar and artillery projectiles can be accurately tracked and enemy firing points targeted promptly and accurately. These infra-red scanning systems possess a very great advantage over comparable radar systems because their non-emitting passive nature greatly complicates enemy attempts to acquire them as targets.[52]

Many types of radar systems are employed for ground target acquisition. For instance, there are man-pack systems that can detect ground troops at 5000 metres and vehicles at 10 000 metres. There are small and inexpensive phased-array radars, laser infra-red radars and millimetre radar systems that are suitable for fitting to small remotely piloted vehicles (RPVs) and which, in many applications, are virtually unjammable.[53] There are also medium-range moving-target indicator systems, such as the stand-off target-acquisition system (SOTAS), which can be stationed between 1000 and 2000 metres altitude, 15-20 kilometres behind the forward edge of the battle area (FEBA), to locate moving targets beyond the enemy's FEBA. The targeting information acquired by this system can be relayed to firing points or strike aircraft in real time, to permit timely and efficient attacks.

There are, in addition, longer-range side-looking airborne radar systems that can be orbited further behind the FEBA. For instance, the United States Army in-flight data transmission system (AIDATS) can acquire ground targets more than 330 kilometres away and also beam the information in real time to ground and air locations for both command and control and targeting purposes. In addition, there is potential for a new generation of synthetic aperture radar, which may provide some types of tactical strike aircraft with an autonomous medium-range ground target acquisition capacity or large stand-off aircraft with a ground target vectoring capacity.

There is a host of other ground target acquisition sensor technologies under development to locate radars, radio emitters, jamming systems, gun flashes and the sounds of artillery. Some of these technologies are being developed for ground-based, aircraft and RPV applications, but many are also being developed for sensor "packages" that can be fired, dropped or launched to operate autonomously in areas occupied by the enemy. The main U.S. unattended ground sensor effort is directed through the remotely emplaced battlefield sensor system (REMBASS) programme, which involves the use of seismic, magnetic, optical, infra-red and acoustic sensors of various types that are designed not only to detect targets autonomously but also to classify them and provide bearings for accurate target location. These systems will then possess the capacity to communicate targeting information either directly or through a data-link on a high-flying aeroplane, to strike aircraft and ground-based fire units.

Certainly many of these battlefield target-acquisition systems can be spoofed, decoyed and jammed. In the ground environment, remotely emplaced sensors can be spoofed with misleading contacts, some types of imaging infra-red sensors can be decoyed with spurious heat sources and many types of radar can be jammed or destroyed with radar-homing weapons. At sea, some types of passve sonar systems can also be decoyed and in some circumstances jammed. Active OTH radars, AWACS or ground-based surveillance and intercept radars can also be jammed, decoyed and spoofed through the employment of a variety of expendable and re-usable electronic warfare equipments.

However, there is a second major counter-measure trend that is confronting the expanding array of battlefield target-acquisition technologies. This concerns the widespread development and application of stealth technologies to reduce weapons system and weapons platform signatures. The heightened demand for these has developed not only from the realization that area surveillance and battlefield target acquisition technologies have made very great advances but also from the fact that the new precision-guidance, propulsion and warhead technologies increase greatly the probability of rapid destruction once a target is acquired. Thus in the air, there is a move towards relatively inexpensive unmanned aircraft (drones and RPVs) to perform some of the more dangerous tasks. In addition, new materials and design technologies are being applied in an effort to reduce the optical, radar, acoustic and infra-red signatures of aircraft.

At sea, there have been extensive and continuing efforts to reduce the noise, heat and magnetic signatures of both submarines and surface craft. The naturally non-magnetic characteristics of plastic hulls have stimulated their introduction for counter-mine vessels. In addition, because of their capacity to absorb more sound than they reflect, advanced reinforced plastics are also likely to be introduced for a range of submarine applications.

In the ground environment, many new camouflage techniques are being employed that extend far beyond conventional counter-optical systems. Infra-red absorbing and reflecting paints, netting and clothing have been produced. Anti-radar netting is widely deployed and many new types of optical, radar and infra-red decoys are available. There are also programmes to develop new types of dust-, smoke- and aerosol-generation equipments.

6. Increasingly Sophisticated Communications, Command and Control (C^3) Systems

One of the major consequences of new technology developments has been the proliferation of nearly every category of military system. Area surveillance, target-acquisition, classification and locating systems, as well as weapons systems themselves, have all multiplied in different forms. However, while in most cases there are more systems of different types and the capabilities of individual systems have risen greatly, the overall effectiveness of military structures as a whole in performing their prime functions has not been enhanced automatically by a comparable increase in efficiency. Total structural effectiveness is dependent heavily upon the manner in which the numerous individual systems are co-ordinated and directed. If this co-ordination, command and control function is performed with maximum efficiency, in many environments the potential for overall task performance will exceed the sum of maximum individual system capacities. It is this "force multiplier" capacity of C^3 that stimulated Dr Malcolm Currie, the former United States Director of Defence Research and Engineering, to emphasize its importance in his congressional testimony:

> I believe that development of integrated intelligence and target engagement systems represents the great challenge and opportunity of the next decade for DoD. These systems will integrate high-altitude sensors, stand-off airborne radars and other sensors, secure communications, computers capable of real-time processing and fusing of sensor data, and surgically accurate weapons. We are approaching this capability.[54]

The most basic requirement in this type of development is reliable, secure and speedy communication links for both weapon control and military unit command and control. In both areas, reliability, speed and security must be traded off against the costs involved in providing the most technically advanced communications for each particular task. For instance, the costs of obtaining high security for line-of-sight data links for air-to-ground weapons systems are very great indeed. Thus the highly secure link for the Condor weapon is extremely expensive, whereas that for the modular guided glide-bombs, while being far less secure, is also relatively inexpensive. Quality/quantity trade-offs between these two extremes are necessarily a central element of communications decision-making.

However, there have been several breakthroughs in communications technologies that promise high security and high data rates at a much reduced cost. Of relevance to precision-guided weapon and RPV links are developments in optical fibres, permitting multichannel, high-quality transmission through fibres that have the appearance of light fishing-line, and several techniques for rapidly changing the radio frequencies of guidance commands and directing them precisely towards the receiver so as to enhance the security of transmissions and limit the scope for enemy interference.

General purpose communication links are also being transformed through the application of high data rate, jam-resistant and highly secure time-synchronized frequency-agile techniques. This technology will be applied very broadly with the deployment of the United States' joint tactical information distribution system (JTIDS). For the United States, this system will provide the communications linkages by which a wide range of command, control and weapons systems will be tied together.

One notable addition to command and control capacity is being provided by the deployment of AWACS aircraft. These possess the co-ordination capacity to expand greatly the battlefield potential of a wide range of other systems. For example, the Boeing E-3A system not only can detect naval and air movements and control interceptions and counter-measures, but also can track and take messages in a passive manner from friendly ground units that are equipped with simple transponders. The E-3A can guide friendly attack aircraft along corridors it "sees" are free of the enemy's radar-emitting anti-aircraft installations. It can also give friendly anti-aircraft units details of approaching enemy aircraft, thus forestalling a need to identify themselves electronically by turning on their own radar sets. However, perhaps most importantly, AWACS aircraft can provide a reasonably comprehensive real-time overview of the air, sea and ground battlefield for the command structure.

At sea, a comparable effort to multiply overall capacity by multiple-system integration is under way under the United States code name Seaguard. Much of this effort is designed to exploit fully the technology advances in long-range passive sonar arrays. Dr Currie indicated the direction of the programme in his congressional testimony:

> It is interesting — even astounding — that one can hear for thousands of miles under water and this phenomenon offers several advantages for detecting and locating submarines. Signals from a distant source are necessarily faint and suffer by confusion with the noise created by many intervening sound sources. If the same signals can be detected at several different times and places, however, these separate representations can be combined mathematically in ways that remove the unwanted sounds and leave the desired information in a usable form.[55]

Dr Heilmeier, the former Director of DARPA, elaborated on this multiple detection localization capacity by referring to some experiments conducted in 1972:

> The experiments demonstrated, among other things, that, while underwater sound conditions are constantly changing, they do remain relatively fixed or coherent for brief periods. Thus, if the whole problem can be worked in a series of shorter time slices, the ocean appears to be a much more benign acoustic medium than was previously thought.[56]

In order to acquire, collate and process incoming multi-sensor material within these shorter "time slices", one of the largest computer systems in the world, the Illiac IV system, has been mobilized on a full-time basis.[57] The potential returns from this effort have been identified and quantified in a series of U.S. Joint Chiefs of Staff studies, code named Narac-G, Seamix I, Caploc and Capstone.[58] Vice-Admiral Daniel Murphy, the U.S. Director of Anti-Submarine Warfare and Ocean Surveillance Programs, alluded to the results of these studies in his congressional testimony:

> All I can say with certainty is that ASW operational personnel feel strongly that coordinated operations enhance the effectiveness of each platform. In the case of undersea surveillance, the probability of detection of a [deleted] SSN in the mid-North Atlantic by a single P-3C aircraft is:
>
> [deleted] when unaided by other sensors or platforms about [deleted] as great when assisted by [deleted] in a vectored-type search about [deleted] as great when assisted by a [deleted] about [deleted] as great when assisted by a [deleted].
>
> It is obvious that, when patrol aircraft are provided positional information from a surveillance system, their effectiveness becomes multiplied significantly. This force mutliplier effect of undersea surveillance is also applicable to other tactical platforms such as our SSNs [nuclear-attack submarines].[59]

Larry Booda, editor of the magazine, *Sea Technology*, described the force multiplier impact of these developments in very clear terms:

> Here is a hypothetical case. In a fleet anti-submarine warfare (ASW) exercise, that fleet has x number of sensors available to it for submarine detection and tracking. With them it can make y number of contacts and process them through its command and control network.
>
> In this exercise all of the fleet's data is relayed ashore via satellite. There a command and control centre which integrates it with all other detection data from a variety of sources including: Air Force aircraft and satellites, and Navy aircraft equipped with photographic infra-red and electronic sensors; Navy land-based aircraft similarly equipped; and Navy and allied fixed bottom listening sensors.
>
> There the information would be digested and analysed in near real

time by already operational computers and the results sent back to the fleet.

Such an exercise has already been conducted. With the meld of detection elements described above, the number of contacts was 3y! — three times the number made by the fleet alone, depending on its ship and aircraft capabilities.[60]

In the light of these developments, it was perhaps not surprising that Dr Currie could report to Congress that: "We are on the threshold of vastly improved ASW capability to counter the growing number of Soviet nuclear attack and fleet ballistic missile submarines."[6]

The requirement for advanced C^3 capabilities is probably most pronounced in the ground environment because it is here that system and unit proliferation has been most pronounced. In addition, there is a need for a large number of ground units and ground-based systems to be linked and co-ordinated with a variety of air and maritime forces. In response to this extensive requirement, a mix of specialized small-unit, large-unit and total battlefield systems is being developed. For example, the United States is developing an artillery battery computer system (BCS), which will enhance gun survivability by permitting widespread gun displacement and, in addition, provide a much more rapid response capacity to forward observer fire requests.[62] One level above BCS, the Tacfire system co-ordinates the fire of several batteries and keeps a real-time record of ammunition stores for all batteries. The French Army have gone a step further by matching the Rita tactical communications system to the Atila artillery fire control system so as to produce a capacity to record battlefield positions, evaluate targets acquired and select the optimum choice of weapons, type of ammunition and the time to fire. This system is designed to provide a high level of surprise by permitting a flexible and rapid concentration of fire from dispersed emplacements.

There are also other types of specialized command and control systems such as the Tipi and Magis systems. These are designed to collect and collate communications intelligence (COMINT), electronic intelligence (ELINT), remotely emplaced sensor information and data from side-looking radars, mapping radars, infra-red mapping and target-acquisition systems, verbal reports and photo reconnaissance. The output of these systems is precise up-to-date information, to permit timely command and control decision-making. To back up this type of operation, there is an array of general purpose support systems such as the tactical operations system (TOS). This provides general purpose computer capacity to receive, process, store, retrieve, display and disseminate selected information.

At the very highest level of ground battlefield command and control, the United States is attempting to integrate the five major functions of land combat — mobility, firepower, intelligence, support and command and control — into a semi-automated co-ordinated system called the integrated battlefield control system (IBCS). According to U.S. Army Brigadier Wilson Reed, the IBCS:

> ... will electronically tie the sensors to the reactive means — the "beep" to the "boom" as it were — and have the soldiers free to do what they do best — think, co-ordinate and control. The potential seems limitless.[63]

Thus it appears that new military technologies are not only improving greatly the capacity of individual military systems but also providing new and highly sophisticated means of integrating multiple battlefield systems. The overall effect is to produce a greatly enhanced structural capacity in mission performance.

7. New Weapons Concepts

Rapid advances in a large number of military technologies are expanding greatly the technical capacities of many traditional types of weapons systems. For example, modern precision-guidance, propulsion and warhead technologies have revolutionized long-range bombardment capacities by making it possible to produce compact cruise missile systems that can be launched from standard torpedo tubes, aircraft pylons, shipboard canisters and ground vehicles, to hit fixed targets up to 3200 kilometres distant with accuracies of a few metres. Shorter-range systems, especially those designed for the anti-ship function, are limited more by the problems of precise target acquisition than those of range and accuracy.

Developments of comparable significance are under way in the field of tank gun systems. New types of propellant, cartridge, projectile, gun barrel and automatic-loading mechanism have been applied to produce both liquid and solid propellant automatic tank guns of the future. It has been found that because of the greatly increased muzzle velocities and firing rate of these weapons, an armour-piercing fin-stabilized discarding-sabot (APFSDS) tank gun round of only 75 mm calibre is sufficient to penetrate all types of conventional and spaced armour currently deployed. An additional bonus is that the same guns also can be equipped with infra-red homing rounds, to perform a supplementary anti-aircraft function. This type of rapid-fire, high-penetration capacity should increase greatly the combat effectiveness of armoured forces in the first few seconds of combat. Historical analysis suggests that action in this period is frequently decisive in determining battlefield outcomes.

Technological advances in other fields are having the effect of reducing greatly the costs of lightweight weaponry. The United States' improved light anti-tank weapon (ILAW-Viper) programme, for instance, has produced a weapon with a capacity considerably superior to that of the current M-72, for less than US$100 per unit. Cost-effectiveness is being raised in other fields by the design of weapons with a multi-purpose capacity. For example, there are strong indications that the missile that will eventually replace Dragon and Tow in the United States' inventories (tentatively named the advanced heavy anti-tank missile (AHAMS)) will have a very high flight speed, be laser beam-riding and be effective not only against armoured vehicles but also aircraft.

The new technologies also have expanded greatly the scope for decreasing costs with the adoption of modular concepts. Perhaps the best example of this development is the GBU-15 family of guided glide-bombs. Initially, this system is to have three interchangeable warhead types — a conventional high explosive, a minelet and bomblet cluster, and a hard structure munition. A fuel-air explosive warhead is likely to be added in the mid-1980s. All of these warheads will be designed so that they can be fitted with either a cruciform medium-range wing guidance kit or a planar long-range wing guidance kit. Any combination of the above also will be compatible with television, laser designator homing, imaging infra-red or distance-measuring equipment guidance heads. All possible combinations will be fitted with the same aerodynamic control and data-link modules. In other words, it is now becoming possible to construct inexpensively from these alternative components an aircraft weapons load to suit the lighting, weather, terminal defence and target characteristics of a specific mission. A modular guided glide-bomb has even been equipped with rocket boosters to demonstrate the potential for short-range ground- and ship-launched applications.

Rapid advances in technology are also making completely new weapons concepts feasible. One of the more important developments is that of sensor weapons. These are being developed in many forms, for many different operational environments. In the air, miniature unmanned drone aircraft have been produced that can be programmed to fly into enemy air space and loiter there for up to six hours, waiting to acquire the emission of an enemy radar. When this is done, the aircraft can fly into the target automatically and, with its integrated warhead, cause severe damage. In the future, advanced, discriminating, non-imaging infra-red and other sensors may be employed aboard these aerial loitering mines for the attack of armoured vehicles and other targets.

A similar ground-based development, called the self-initiated attack missile (SIAM), can be left or dropped unattended in enemy territory. When the missile detects a pre-programmed enemy aircraft "signature", it is capable of automatic launch and target homing.

At sea, the United States has developed a new family of mines, to largely replace the aging stock that was compromised during operations in Vietnam. The CAPTOR (encapsulated torpedo) mine is essentially a Mk46 homing torpedo, coupled with a complex anti-submarine detection system. It is designed for operation in a variety of water depths and in practice would be air-, surface- or submarine-dropped outside harbours, or in straits and narrows, to await the specific sensor signature of its assigned categories of target, whence it can launch automatically. For shallower and intermediate depths and for generalized anti-submarine and anti-ship purposes, the CAPTOR mine is to be complemented by the propelled rocket-assisted mine (PRAM) and the Quickstrike mine. All of these sensor-weapon mines possess an area coverage several orders of magnitude greater than that of conventional mine systems.

One of the most notable and potentially significant new types of weapons system may be high-powered lasers. There are many different types of laser, each of which possesses particular attributes. However, the technical complexities are immense and the barriers to practical employment for military purposes very great. The most notable problems arise in precision pointing and tracking, the development of durable high-power optics, high-energy propagation through the earth's disturbed atmosphere, thermal blooming (overheating of the air in transit causing laser refraction) and penetration of the vaporized cloud that often forms when a beam initially strikes a target. For many applications, there are additional environmental problems such as laser attenuation in fog, rain, sleet, snow, smog and in the high levels of humidity, which are common in coastal and sea environments. These limitations can also be exploited in counter-measure systems such as smoke screens and aerosol sprays.

Recent research and development efforts, however, have overcome some of the more serious technical difficulties. For instance, the thermal blooming problem can be overcome by careful laser focusing and pulsing the beam to prevent the air through which the laser transits from overheating. The very large adaptive optics programme that has been undertaken in the United States has demonstrated a capacity to overcome most of the problems caused by atmospheric disturbances and aircraft slip-streams.[64]

Thus despite a number of continuing difficulties, there remain several potentially promising military applications for high-power lasers. Lasers as a bomber-defence system are attractive because they work particularly well in the clear atmosphere of high altitudes. However, despite the relatively large carrying capacity of these aircraft, the power sources that are available with current technology remain too bulky and heavy to be practical.[65] In the ground-based air defence role, the United States already has a test unit fitted aboard an amphibious armoured assault vehicle.[66] This system has destroyed unmanned aircraft in flight, but also has been plagued by reliability problems in simulated operational conditions.[67] In shipboard air defence applications, many of the power problems can be overcome, but in this environment, laser transmission attenuation problems caused by atmospheric humidity are accentuated.

Much of the current high-powered laser research and development effort is centred upon space-based applications, which fall beyond the purview of this discussion. However, in addition, a variety of tactical applications are being pursued actively. In contrast to a decade ago, there is now no question that very high-powered lasers can be built. The major uncertainty remaining is whether they can be developed successfully into reliable and effective military weapons that can compete in cost-effectiveness terms with more conventional weapons systems.

8. New Weapons Platforms

Developments in a wide range of technologies are providing a very much broader array of transport and weapons platform options. For example, in the area of heavy-lift air transport, there are several proposals for very large transport aircraft with between three and four times the load-carrying capacity and twice the range of the large aircraft now operational. Flying-wing concepts carrying lightweight cargo containers, very large conventional transport aircraft and new types of hybrid heavy-lift airships have all been proposed for this function.

A second and possibly related type of aircraft development, which could appear in approximately the same time-frame, is a very long-endurance ocean surveillance and patrol aircraft. This concept may be fulfilled by the deployment of a combination of existing technologies — an already deployed civil airframe, an AWACS radar system, a long-range FLIR, other surface surveillance and advanced ASW sensors and an array of stand-off precision-guided weapons systems. This type of aircraft would possess a capacity to perform many of the tasks that are currently undertaken by carrier-borne aircraft.

The United States is considering a new generation of medium-weight V/STOL aircraft for naval aircraft carrier and general purpose shipboard applications, as well as to overcome some of the airfield vulnerability problems of land-based aircraft. The first of these systems will probably be subsonic or transonic, with a multi-role capacity to perform ASW search and attack, surveillance, surface ship attack, ground strike, troop transport, resupply and general logistic support and utility functions. The second aircraft will be a supersonic strike fighter, possibly a development of Rockwell's XF-12A prototype design or the McDonnell Douglas AV-8B.

A range of advanced fighter programmes is also under way, with the emphasis on improvements in agility, speed and survivability. Some new fighter concepts, such as those employed in the U.S. high manoeuverability aircraft technology (HIMAT) programme, are being tested in small-scale remotely piloted vehicles. Others, such as Boeing's micro-fighter concept, have been the subject of very extensive paper and wind-tunnel study. This particular experimental aircraft programme, which has received extensive encouragement from the United States Air Force and Navy, employs very advanced "supercruiser" wing technology in a small aircraft, several of which could be carried aloft, launched and retrieved by a host airborne aircraft carrier. All of the new fighter aircraft concepts involve the extensive use of stealth technologies. Composite materials, special design techniques and paints are being employed extensively, in an effort to reduce optical, radar, acoustic and other signatures to a minimum.

There are, in addition, several more radical aircraft proposals under active study. For example, the United States is actively experimenting with an X-wing concept aircraft, the wings of which can rotate in the manner of a helicopter at slow speeds, but at high speeds can lock and perform the lift function of conventional wing surfaces. Much attention has also been directed towards advanced research on a possible aerodynamic successor to currently deployed swing-wing aircraft. Instead of altering the angle of both wings so that they move symmetrically in relation to the aircraft fuselage, oblique-wing aircraft simply pivot a single rigid wing so that one end swings forward and the other rearwards. This highly-simplified technique already has been proven aerodynamically feasible and displays great potential in a number of aircraft applications.

The final major area of development in airborne technologies is that concerning remotely piloted vehicles (RPVs). There appear to be three distinct categories emerging. Mini-RPVs weigh under 100 kg and can be readily carried by two people. Medium-sized RPVs weigh up to 2000 kg, are frequently air-launched and normally possess a relatively long-range multi-mission capacity. The largest

RPVs are of conventional aircraft size and normally require full-sized aircraft ground facilities. The most notable example of this last category was the now cancelled Compass Cope system, which had a 30-metre wingspan and was designed to cruise at an altitude of well over twenty thousand metres for up to thirty hours, primarily for electronic and communication intelligence, data link and ground and sea reconnaissance missions.

Mini-RPVs derive the greatest proportional benefit from the absence of an on-board pilot. They are normally of model aeroplane size, although not necessarily of model aeroplane configuration, can be made of fibreglass and plastic for low radar reflection (comparable to a bird), have a very low infra-red signature, can be made very quiet and very hard to see, and even if sighted, are very difficult to hit with small-arms fire. Even if hit, small calibre rounds can harmlessly pass through large portions of their structure. The proximity fuses of medium and large calibre rounds, 30 mm and above, are normally insensitive to targets with such a small signature. With a capacity for launch and recovery from the back of a truck, with radii of action approaching 160 kilometres, the capacity to perform reconnaissance, kamikaze hard target killing, radiation homing, defence suppression, data relay, electronic jamming and laser designation tasks, and with a price tag under US$20 000, the future widespread employment of mini-RPVs appears assured.

Seaborne platforms may be transformed dramatically during the next quarter-century by the extensive employment not only of small but also medium and perhaps even large sea-going hydrofoils, hovercraft and other unconventional hull concepts. The United States ocean-going patrol hydrofoil (PHM) programme has been a technical and operational success, but the costs of the very short production run currently envisaged appear excessive. In Britain, similarly sized and armed hovercraft systems, which have a 1600 kilometre range capability, are being studied. In a separate development, the United States is actively pursuing the utility of large sea-going hovercraft, with plans for the construction of a 3000-tonne rigid side-wall surface effect ship. These types of systems have already proven to be technically reliable and economic in many environments. They promise surface speeds of between 40 and 100 knots in all but the worst weather, reduced vulnerability to mine, torpedo and missile attacks, greatly improved standards of platform stability and a quantum jump in overall mission flexibility.

A third type of unconventional hull configuration is under development, primarily for small and medium-sized, long endurance deep ocean missions. Called the semi-submerged hull concept, it consists of two torpedo-shaped underwater propulsion systems arranged in a catamaran configuration and attached to an above-surface hull platform by aerofoil-shaped pylons. The advantages of this concept are its naturally high propulsion efficiency, the very high levels of stability it provides to small platforms and the minimal degradation of speed it suffers in heavy seas.[68]

The new technologies are also enhancing greatly the capacities of both nuclear and conventional submarines. As was discussed earlier, new propulsion systems show promise of enhancing range, endurance and speed capabilities while at the same time reducing platform signatures. In addition, laminar-flow technology is reducing greatly the underwater drag of submarines and torpedoes, and hence also contributing significantly to advances in range and speed. The increasingly frequent employment of plastics and other non-metallic materials is reducing submarine acoustic and magnetic signatures, while in some instances, providing deeper diving capacities at low cost.

Transport and weapons platforms in the ground environment are generally being developed by a process of evolution rather than revolution. However, there are two new technology developments that may have a very great impact upon a range of ground battlefield platforms. The first of these is a new type of composite armour-plating called Chobham armour. Believed to be composed of layers of plastic, ceramic and metal armour-plating, Chobham armour can be bolted on to some existing heavy armoured vehicles, to provide a capacity to survive attack from all currently deployed ground-fired anti-armour munitions.[69] As this armour is only expected to add approximately 1-2 per cent to the cost of new armoured vehicles, in time, it can be expected to be deployed widely on the ground battlefield.[70] This, in turn, will necessitate the development of a new range of anti-tank weaponry and probably a considerable modification of anti-armour techniques and tactics.[71]

The second major technology advance in ground battlefield weapons platforms is somewhat related to the first. The development of rapid-firing, very high-velocity tank guns of 75 mm calibre, which was discussed earlier in this appendix, means that new generation tanks may not need to be constructed to withstand the very great weight and recoil forces of current 105 mm and 120 mm tank guns. As a consequence, the United States is actively pursuing, through the high mobility and agility (HIMAG) programme, the possibility that new generation tanks may be relatively light (i.e. between 20 and 40 tonnes), have low profiles, be very agile and relatively inexpensive. Current indicators are that this type of tank concept may be deployed in the late 1980s.

For an elaboration of the overall impact and ramifications of these developments in military technology, reference should be made to the discussion in Chapter 2.

Notes and References

1. Examples of this type of system include Entac, Malkara, Mosquito, Swingfire, Saggar, etc.
2. Examples of these more advanced anti-tank missile systems include Tow, Dragon, Milan, Hot, etc.
3. Examples of this type of system include the various electro-optical glide-bombs, Walleye, Hobo and the electro-optical GBU-15, as well as the powered Maverick, Martel, Condor and LUZ-I, etc.
4. This should not be confused with optical lock-on and weapon guidance through the electronic systems aboard launching platforms. This has been deployed for several years in a number of systems; for example, see a diagramatic explanation of Walleye 2 guidance in *Aviation Week and Space Technology* 99, no. 24 (10 December 1973): 15. There is also a detailed explanation of this second technique, as it operates in the Maverick system, by John S. Phillip, "Precision-guided Weapons", *Aerospace International* 13, no. 2 (March/April 1977): 23-24.
5. Laser beam-riding weapons include the RBS-70 light surface-to-air missile system and the AHAMS prototype anti-tank systems.
6. An example of this type of system is the cannon-launched guided projectile (CLGP) Copperhead. For a relatively simple account of laser-designated artillery systems, see B. E. Blunt, "Surface to Surface Artillery: Developments in Fire Support in the 1980s", *Royal United Services Institute Journal* 119, no. 4 (December 1974): 15.
7. Examples of this type of system include Harpoon, Exocet, Kormoran, etc.
8. Semi-active radar-homing missiles include Sparrow, Matra R530, Skyflash, etc.
9. Examples of this type of weapons system include Shrike, Harm, Brazo, etc. There are also several other anti-radiation weapons under consideration. One proposal is to fit a radiation homing head to the Copperhead cannon-launched guided projectile. Another is to fit an anti-radiation and a new generation infra-red seeker sensor together on the Maverick missile. See *Aviation Week and Space Technology* 106, no. 19 (9 May 1977): 59; and *Flight International* 110, no. 3537 (25 December 1976): 1834.
10. Much of the applied work done on ring-laser gyros has been undertaken within the U.S. Simplified Inertial Guidance-Demonstration (SIG-D) and the Advanced Tactical Inertial Guiding System (ATIGS) programmes. ATIGS and microwave area correlation technology have now been combined by the U.S. Navy to provide a new and inexpensive guidance system for long-range air-to-ground missiles. See *Flight International* 110, no. 3537 (25 December 1976): 1834.
11. One example of this type of system is MAGCOM, which operates in a manner similar to TERCOM, except that its position-fixing sensors are purely magnetic.
12. In the United States, the Mobility Equipment Research and Development Centre (MERDC) has developed devices to produce almost instant smoke, fog and aerosol screens. See report on MERDC in the Defense Marketing Services, *Market Intelligence Report* (October 1975): 5.
13. For details of the operation of Shrike, Standard ARM and HARM anti-radiation missiles, see R. T. Pretty, ed., *Janes Weapon Systems 1977* (London: Jane's Yearbooks, 1976), pp. 150, 158, 159.
14. CODOG is an acronym for combination of diesel *or* gas (turbine). Under this

system, the vessel can be propelled at any one time by either propulsion plant on its own. CODAG stands for combination of diesel *and* gas (turbine), implying that both propulsion systems can be used simultaneously, if required.

15. The West Germans have produced the Pandora, Medusa and Dragon Seed dispenser systems. They are also developing a new air-delivered dispenser system called Strebo (MW1), which permits a degree of control over the bomblet or minelet delivery pattern. For details, see Stefan Geisenheyner, "Pandora, Medusa, Dragon Seed — A Defensive Weapons Mix for Europe", *Aerospace International* (May-June 1971): 56-58.

    The United States has a similar system, called Gator. See the statement of Captain G. R. Bowling, Head of the Tactical Air Launched Weapons Section, U. S. Navy, before the Subcommittee on Tactical Airpower of the Committee on Armed Services, U. S. Senate, *Fiscal Year 1977 Authorization for Military Procurement, Research and Development, and Active Duty, Selected Reserve and Civilian Personnel Strengths*, Part 10, 15 March 1976, pp. 5308 ff.

16. For example, see the detailed description of the Durandal penetration bomb in R. T. Pretty, ed., *Jane's Weapon Systems 1976* (London: Jane's Yearbooks, 1975), p. 502. This report states that concrete slabs of up to 40 cm (approx. 16") thick can be penetrated with this weapon. See also the description of Thomson-Brandt's 100 mm tactical support bomb in *NATOs Fifteen Nations* 21, no. 2 (April-May 1976): 97. It is reported that Britain is developing a completely new type of anti-airfield weapon, designated JP233. For details, see *Flight International* 111, no. 3551 (2 April 1977): 832; and also Group-Captain Tony Mason (RAF), "Technology and Airpower", *Flight International* 112, no. 3578 (8 October 1977): 1002.

17. For details of fuel-air explosive (FAE) developments, see Desmond J. Ball and Steven J. Rosen, "Fuel Air Explosives for Medium Powers", *Pacific Defence Reporter* 3, no. 10 (April 1977): 17 ff.; G. Johannsohn, "Fuel Air Explosives Revolutionise Warfare", *International Defense Review* 9, no. 6 (December 1976): 992 ff.; and also C. A. Robinson, jun., "Special Report: Fuel Air Explosives — Services Ready Joint Development Plan", *Aviation Week and Space Technology* 98, no. 8 (19 February 1973): 42 ff.

    Despite their obvious potential it should be noted that the performance of FAEs can be degraded significantly by rain, fog, snow, sleet and to a lesser extent by naturally high humidity environments.

18. These calculations are made by Ted Greenwood in "Reconnaissance and Arms Control", *Scientific American* 228, no. 2 (February 1973): 14-15.

19. See the reports on the high-altitude large optics (HALO) and the Teal Ruby programmes in *Aviation Week and Space Technology* 106, no. 9 (28 February 1977): 13; and *Aviation Week and Space Technology* 106, no. 13 (28 March 1977): 11. For more substantial articles on this subject, see Barry Miller, "Advances in Missile Surveillance Pushed", *Aviation Week and Space Technology* 105, no. 2 (12 July 1976): 17 ff.; and Barry Miller, "Aircraft Detection System Advances", *Aviation Week and Space Technology* 106, no. 25 (20 June 1977): 22-23.

20. These range figures are cited in *Air Force Magazine* 59, no. 7 (July 1976): 56. They are slightly in excess of those that have been released officially in Australia. See, for instance, "Schematic of Operation of Over the Horizon Radar", *Triad*, no. 2 (1977): 7.

21. The technical operation of OTH-B radar is described fully by Desmond J. Ball, "Jindalee — Over-the-Horizon Radar in the Defence of Australia", *Pacific Defence Reporter* 3, no. 8 (February 1977): 17 ff.

22. The question of whether OTH-B radar systems are capable of detecting the

very small radar signatures of modern long-range cruise missiles is discussed later in this chapter.

23. The expectation that Jindalee would have a capacity to detect and track shipping was raised by Dr J. L. Farrands (Australia's former Chief Defence Scientist) in his address to the National Press Club on 6 October 1976.
    > Imagine how many [conventional radars] would be needed to cover the Australian coastline and imagine the increased difficulty of locating ships out to the margin of the [320 km] economic zone.

    Cited in "Out of Sight Radar! Whee!", *Australian*, 7 October 1976, p. 11.

24. It is worth noting that OTH-B radar operation in regions subject to auroral disturbances can cause significant problems. This has been a major difficulty in the U.S. 414L OTH-B programme. See James R. Schlesinger (Secretary of Defence), *Annual Defense Department Report FY1976 and FY197T* (Washington, DC: Department of Defense, 1976), pp. 11-44.

25. The possible employment of OTH-B radar for the vectoring of aircraft defences is discussed by Ball, "Jindalee — Over-the-Horizon Radar in the Defence of Australia", pp. 17 ff.

26. This requirement for OTH-B radar and AWACs interaction is suggested by Philip J. Klass, "HF Radar Detects Soviet ICBMs", *Aviation Week and Space Technology* 95, no. 23 (6 December 1971): 40.

27. Ibid., loc. cit.

28. General Gould is quoted by Klass, in ibid., loc. cit.

29. Dr Desmond Ball suggests that the OTH radar transmitter could be shut down completely for periods of up to thirty minutes, if this were necessary. See Desmond J. Ball, "Some Further Thoughts on Jindalee", *Pacific Defence Reporter* 3, no. 11 (May 1977): 57.

30. This concept is outlined in *Aviation Week and Space Technology* 105, no. 8 (23 August 1976): 61. See also the testimony of Dr G. H. Heilmeier, former Director of DARPA, before the Research and Development Subcommittee of the Committee on Armed Services, U. S. Senate, *Fiscal Year 1977 Authorization for Military Procurement, Research and Development, and Active Duty, Selected Reserve and Civilian Personnel Strengths*, Part 11, 9 March 1976, pp. 5898-99. Dr Heilmeier is also quoted on this subject in *Aviation Week and Space Technology* 106, no. 10 (7 March 1977): 171.

31. The possibility of employing mobile OTH radar receivers is raised by Ball, "Some Further Thoughts on Jindalee", p. 57.

32. "USSR Develops Anti-B-1 Radar?", *Flight International* 111, no. 3539 (8 January 1977): 50.

33. Dr J. L. Farrands, Australia's former Chief Defence Scientist, indicated that he expected the total development cost (excluding final system installation costs) of Jindalee to be about $A20m; *Australian*, 7 October 1976, p. 11. This contrasts markedly with the U.S. expenditure levels at approximately $US50m by 1976. See testimony of Secretary Donald H. Rumsfeld, *Annual Department of Defense Report for FY 1977* (Washington, DC: U.S. Department of Defense, 1976), p. 90. One of the major reasons for this disparity was cited by the Minister for Defence, the Hon. D. J. Killen, "Costs have been kept down by borrowing special electronic equipment from the United States", Australia. House of Representatives *Debates*, Thirtieth Parliament, 4 June 1976, p. 3115. However, a second and possibly equally important reason is that the Australian programme has not had to solve the difficult problem of auroral interference. See *DMS Intelligence* 5, no. 5 (January 1977): 3-4.

34. For background on AWACS, see D. Boyle and R. D. M. Furlong, "NATO AWACS — Now or Never?", *International Defense Review* 10, no. 1 (February 1977): 43 ff.; and R. D. M. Furlong, "Can NATO Afford AWACS?"; N.

Cherikow, "Moss — AWACS with a Red Star"; and J. P. Geddes, "Airborne Early Warning for the US Navy"; all in *International Defense Review* 8, no. 5 (October 1975): 667-82; and also "Grumman Still Pushing E-2C in Europe", *Flight International* 111, no. 3559 (28 May 1977): 1474-75.

35. Testimony before the Research and Development Subcommittee of the Committee on Armed Services, U.S. Senate, *Fiscal Year 1977 Authorization for Military Procurement, Research and Development, and Active Duty, Selected Reserve and Civilian Personnel Strengths*, Part 11, 11 March 1976, p. 5747.

36. These developments are described at length in Larry L. Booda, "ASW — Challenges and Bold Solutions", *Sea Technology* 14, no. 11 (November 1973): 24-27.

37. Vice-Admiral D. Murphy, Director of U.S. Antisubmarine Warfare and Ocean Surveillance Programs, gave a clear indication of the sophistication and sensitivity of these systems when replying to a congressional question concerning their vulnerability to decoys:

> Decoys such as you have described [deleted] however, the more experienced the operator and the more sophisticated the sonar, the less effective the decoy becomes. Exact duplication of the target is not possible due to cost and size considerations — difficult tradeoffs are involved. This is an area where intelligence is a key factor. How sophisticated a system do you design against? Likewise, intelligence on decoys assists the operator in distinguishing between real and false targets.

See Hearings of the Research and Development Subcommittee of the Committee on Armed Services, U.S. Senate, *Fiscal Year 1977 Authorization for Military Procurement, Research and Development, and Active Duty, Selected Reserve and Civilian Personnel Strengths*, Part 4, 11 December 1975, p. 2015.

38. It is possible that the HALO satellite sensor programme will expand greatly U.S. capacities to detect, classify and track small tactical objects on the earth's surface. Dr G. H. Heilmeier, the former Director of DARPA, expressed the hope that this programme would "achieve the sensitivity to detect dim targets from high altitudes". See this cited by Miller, "Aircraft Detection System Advances", p. 23.

39. See, for example, the account of the Difar sonobouy's capabilities in Larry L. Booda, "Restocking the ASW Arsenal", *Undersea Technology* 13, no. 11 (November 1972): 20.

40. See the testimony of Mr G. Cann from the Office of the U.S. Defence Research and Engineer, Ocean Control, before the Research and Development Subcommittee of the Committee on Armed Services, U.S. Senate, *Fiscal Year 1977 Authorization for Military Procurement, Research and Development, and Active Duty, Selected Reserve and Civilian Personnel Strengths*, Part 4, 11 December 1975, p. 2005. For details of the very advanced Micropuffs system being developed for the Royal Australian Navy's Oberon-class submarines, see J. P. Geddes, "Advanced Fire Control for Oberon Submarines", *International Defense Review* 10, no. 2 (April 1977): 296-99.

41. For details of this system, see *Aviation Week and Space Technology* 106, no. 10 (10 March 1976): 17.

42. See the testimony of Dr G. H. Heilmeier, former Director of DARPA, before the Research and Development Subcommittee of the Committee on Armed Services, U.S. Senate, *Fiscal Year 1977 Authorization for Military Procurement, Research and Development, and Active Duty, Selected Reserve and Civilian Personnel Strengths*, Part 11, 9 March 1976, p. 5898.

43. This was the description of the powerful AN/SQ553 hull-borne sonar given by the crew of the *USS Forster*, the second of the new Spruance-class destroyers to be built. See J. P. Geddes, "Operational Assessment of a Spruance Class

Destroyer", *International Defense Review* 9, no. 6 (December 1976): 944.
44. Ibid., loc. cit.
45. Towed-array ocean surveillance conducted from rigid airships is discussed by B. Levitt, "The Rigid Airship in the Sea Control Mission", *US Naval Institute Proceedings* 103/1/887 (January 1977): 114.
46. See the testimony of Major-General P. R. Feir, Assistant Deputy Chief of Staff for Research, Development and Acquisition, before a Subcommittee of the Committee on Appropriations, U.S. House of Representatives, *Department of Defense Appropriations for 1977*, Part 5, 10 March 1976, p. 1074.
47. Ibid., loc. cit.
48. Ibid., p. 1080.
49. Ibid., p. 1083. The unit cost of this system was $US9917 in March 1976.
50. The shorter-range figure is given by General Feir in his testimony, ibid., p. 1083. However, earlier in his testimony, p. 1079, he stated that that same nightsight would:
    ... give [deleted] metres for TOW and enable us to take full advantage of TOW's range capability at night. We consider this a tremendous breakthrough and a tremendous tactical advantage for our side.
Tow's maximum range capability is 3750 metres. The cost for this particular night-sight was given as $US5180 in March 1976.
51. Ibid., p. 1083. The unit cost for this system was given as $US39 726 in March 1976.
52. The possible employment of infra-red scanning systems to replace radar installations in tactical fighter aircraft is discussed by Stefan J. Geisenheyner and Mark E. Berent, "Tactical Fighter for Tomorrow (Part Two)", *Aerospace International* 13, no. 2 (March-April 1977): 12.
53. For example, General Electric have developed a miniature phased array radar with six operating modes under the hostile weapons location system (HOWLS) programme. This programme has also been known as ULTRA (ultra lightweight transmissive array). See *Flight International* 111, no. 3538 (1 January 1977): 15.
54. Testimony before the Research and Development Subcommittee of the Committee on Armed Services, U.S. Senate, *Fiscal Year 1977 Authorization for Military Procurement, Research and Development, and Active Duty, Selected Reserve and Civilian Personnel Strengths*, Part 4, 5 February 1976, p. 2044.
55. Ibid., p. 2299.
56. Ibid., Part 11, 11 March 1976, p. 5772.
57. Ibid., p. 5773.
58. See the testimony of Mr A. Pennington of the Office of the Assistant Secretary of Defense, Program Analysis and Evaluation, before the Research and Development Subcommittee of the Committee on Armed Services, ibid., Part 4, 11 December 1975, pp. 1996, 1997.
59. Testimony before the Research and Development Subcommittee of the Committee on Armed Services, ibid., Part 4, 10 December 1975, p. 1945.
60. See Larry L. Booda, "Navy Approaches Ideal Goal in Ocean Surveillance", *Sea Technology* 16, no. 8 (August 1975): 43.
61. Statement before the Research and Development Subcommittee of the Committee on Armed Services, U.S. Senate, *Fiscal Year 1977 Authorization for Military Procurement, Research and Development, and Active Duty, Selected Reserve and Civilian Personnel Strengths*, Part 4, 5 February 1976, p. 2046.
62. This system will play a central role in reducing time-lag and other problems likely to be experienced in the operational employment of cannon-launched guided projectiles (Copperheads—CLGPs). See statement of Dr Currie before

the Research and Development Subcommittee of the Committee on Armed Services, ibid., Part 4, 5 February 1976, p. 2164.
63. Quoted in Paul Dickson, *The Electronic Battlefield* (Ontario: Fitzhenry & Whiteside, 1976), p. 171.
64. For details, see Philip J. Klass, "Advanced Weaponry Research Intensifies", *Aviation Week and Space Technology* 103, no. 2 (18 August 1975): 35-36.
65. For details of these difficulties, see Philip J. Klass, "Pentagon Seeks to Channel Research", *Aviation Week and Space Technology* 103, no. 9 (1 September 1975): 54. However, early in 1977, Dr Kumar Patel, the inventor of the high-energy carbon monoxide laser, was reported as saying that:
   ... with recent technology, his laser had the potential size, efficiency and power to be packaged in a transport aircraft from which it could knock other aircraft from the sky "at long ranges".
   See Drew Middleton, "Powerful Lasers Reported Bound for American and Soviet Arsenals", *New York Times*, 16 February 1977, p. 2.
66. This system is described in detail and illustrated with photographs by Philip J. Klass, "Current Systems Still More Cost-effective", *Aviation Week and Space Technology* 103, no. 10 (8 September 1975): 55.
67. For details, see *Flight International* 110, no. 3525 (2 October 1976): 1016; and also *Aviation Week and Space Technology* 105, no. 7 (23 August 1976): 9.
68. For details, see Commander L. J. Holt, "SWATH", *US Naval Institute Proceedings* 101, no. 3/865 (March 1975): 26 ff.
69. For details of the development of Chobham armour, see *International Defense Review* 9, no. 4 (August 1976): 641.
70. Ibid., loc. cit.
71. There is a secondary development in armour technology that is of some significance. This concerns the employment of thick ballistic blankets woven from commercially produced synthetic fibres. This type of flexible armour can be used inside conventional light armoured vehicles (APCs, MICVs, etc.) to greatly reduce the damage that can be caused by small metal splinters when such vehicles are penetrated by medium and large calibre projectiles. Alternatively, it can be used to protect personnel, weapon teams or objects of military significance in the open from the majority of shell fragments and small calibre direct-fire projectiles. For details, see Survivability Office, U.S. Army Material Systems Analysis Activity, Aberdeen Proving Ground, Maryland, *Survivability Primer* (Alexandria, Virginia: U.S. Army Material and Readiness Command, 1976), pp. 37-46.

An Introductory Note to Appendixes C and D: Approaching Current Problems in Australian Security Planning

One conclusion that has been emphasized on numerous occasions in this book is that in the future, the quality of Australia's security will be much more dependent upon the scale and character of its independent efforts. Perhaps the most vital element of this greatly enhanced requirement for self-sufficiency is the need to develop an indigenous capability to plan resource allocation coherently, to satisfy efficiently derived and clearly defined national security priorities.

However, the task of independently planning Australia's security in the future is of quite a different character to that of the forward defence era. As has been discussed in Chapter 4, the security planning system inherited from the past now appears to be deficient in several important respects. As a consequence, new conceptual processes must be found that provide a capacity to derive, evaluate, select and implement original solutions to satisfy Australia's unique security requirements. Only when clearly defined national security objectives, strategies, structures, doctrines and operational procedures are deduced in a coherent fashion in an unconstrained evaluative process can optimality be approached in the determination of priorities and the allocation of resources.

It may be recalled that the question of redirecting Australia's current processes of security planning was raised in Chapter 7. The nature and most important deficiencies of the current security planning concept were elaborated and a series of criteria for evaluating alternative concepts, strategies and structures were detailed and discussed. In a sense, this brief analysis raised more questions than it answered. For instance, in practical terms, exactly how could a series of properly representative scenarios be derived for planning purposes? How could this new type of planning structure be integrated as a whole? Could such a planning system be evolved within the bureaucratic structure that already exists? How might such a system work in practice?

Unfortunately, any serious attempt to answer these questions requires entry into an area of analysis that is inherently complex. But despite the difficulties of dealing with Australia's security planning processes, their central importance to considerations of the nation's future security necessitates that they be discussed in some detail in this volume.

Thus Appendices C and D introduce a number of conceptual techniques and tools that conceivably might be employed to overcome some of Australia's current security planning difficulties. Appendix C addresses the question of managing, for planning purposes, the vast array of conceivable pressures and threats. This discussion is followed, in Appendix D, by an analysis of a progression of planning concepts that might provide a feasible means of selecting strategies and force structures to optimize security capacity for a given financial outlay.

Appendix C

Managing an Uncertain Threat Environment: Deriving Representative Scenarios

As a consequence of Australia's changed strategic environment, it appears that, in the future, Australia's security will be much more dependent upon its indigenous capacity to meet the demands of a wide range of pressures and threats. But as was discussed in Chapters 3 and 7, the uncertain nature of Australia's strategic environment, with its innumerable theoretically conceivable pressures and threats, has complicated greatly the task of coherent security planning. If high levels of efficiency in resource allocation are to be approached, it is essential that the vast array of possible contingencies be reduced into a more manageable form.

What is required in these circumstances is a refining process, to elaborate, test and select a series of contingencies that, in terms of their security planning requirements, would be representative of the full range of pressure and threat possibilities. As was briefly described in Chapter 7 and is elaborated in much greater detail in Appendix D, the range of representative scenarios that might be produced by such a process would be well suited to play a central role in the processes of security planning as one of the four basic design and evaluation criteria.

The discussion in this appendix represents an attempt to derive a conceptual progression that might be effective in performing the contingency refinement function. The total process involves twelve steps. These are best understood by progressive reference to Figure 6, in addition to the main text.

Stage 1

The first stage involves a detailed analysis of the global and regional environment, with a view to highlighting the more significant developing trends. It is generally recognized that this function can be performed very effectively by the present type of Strategic Basis document. For instance, Sir Arthur Tange, former Secretary of the Department of Defence, has written:

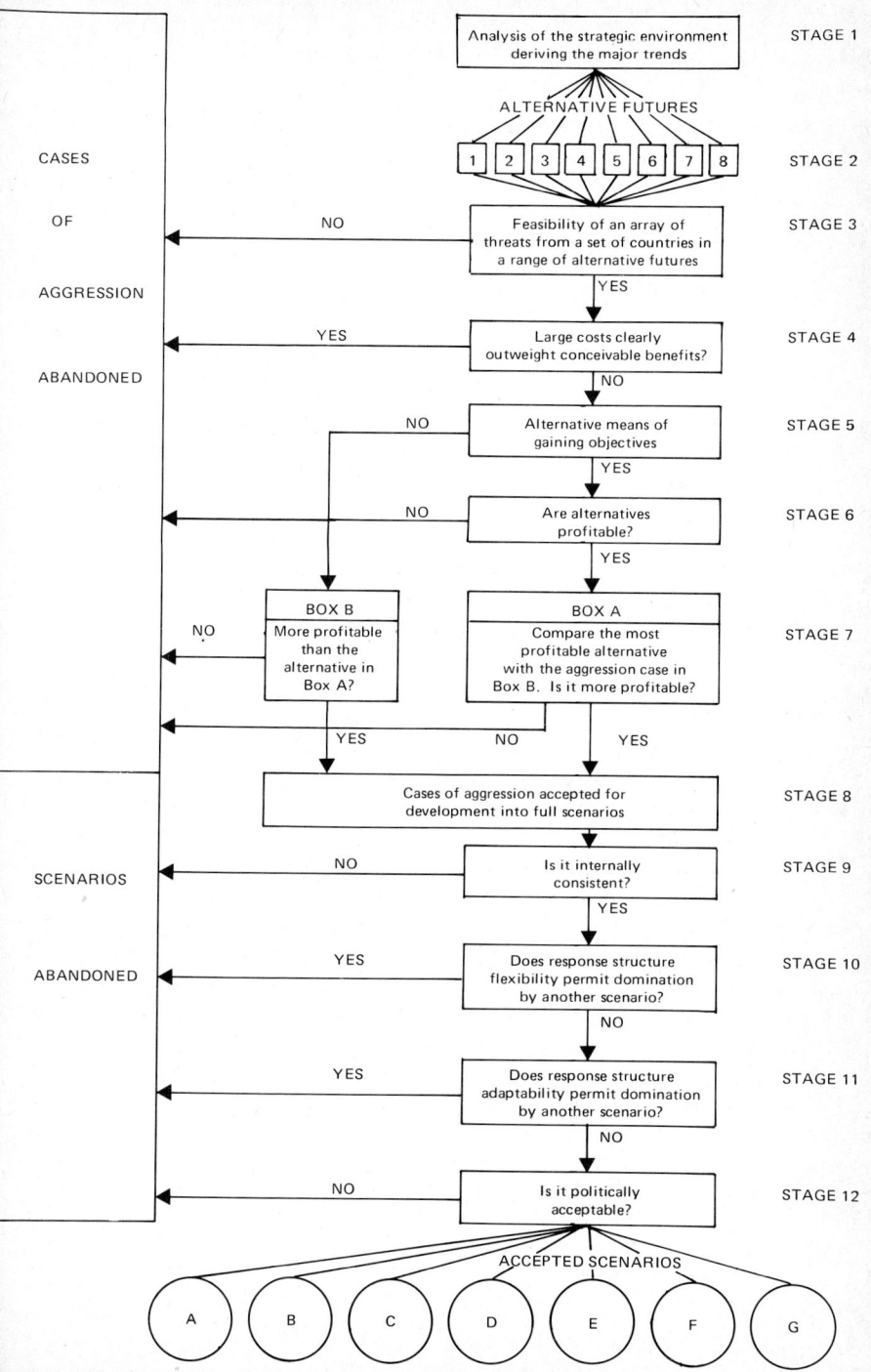

Fig. 6. Diagrammatic presentation of a means of deriving representative scenarios.

To assess Australia's strategic outlook for the purpose of defence decisions, we must distinguish between tides and eddies. There are types of violent events which, like eddies, are sometimes not predictable. They may well be injurious to others, but they will not necessarily be a threat to the security of this country. Events of this kind — outbreaks of religious violence, border disputes and the like — might contingently impose on Australia an obligation to contribute to a United Nations collective action; but experience suggests that this uncertain prospect, in itself, should not be a determinant of this country's defence effort . . .

But if we can ignore the eddies, or at least not over-react to them, we must study the tides of international movements; and such things as the changes in the distribution of military and economic power in the world, and in the political power of groups of countries, and in their objectives towards countries in Australia's position. These I believe are the tides which, in their ebb and flow, increase or decrease the vulnerability of Australia to threats of real consequence. They do not flow regularly. Their movement is, however, discernible and their implications for our future security can, I believe, be estimated. This is what the periodic Strategic Surveys by the Defence Committee set out to do for the Government.[1]

Ideally for the threat management structure being proposed, this basic environmental analysis would be reviewed and updated on a regular cycle, such as at 1, 1¼ or 2½ yearly intervals.[2]

Stage 2

By extrapolating from the developing trends identified in Stage 1, a series of alternative futures could be constructed for a period fifteen years hence.[3] Each of these possible future environments would describe a complete and coherent global and regional situation. For example, they might range from an environment fifteen years hence that was very similar to that of the present, through to situations with regional conflict close by, regional conflicts at distant locations, significant resource shortages, serious instability in the super-power balance, limited or unlimited super-power conflict, etc. The primary intention would be to derive a broad and reasonably representative range of possible futures without proliferating them in unmanageable numbers.[4]

Stage 3

The next step would be to draw upon the environmental analysis in Stage 1, to identify a number of international actors that, because of their present or potential intentions or capabilities, could conceivably present a threat to Australia in the time-span fifteen to twenty years hence.[5] Then by drawing upon a relatively large number of Australians who are experts concerning these countries[6] (in a process elaborated later in this appendix), judgements would be made upon the likely actions of these countries in the context of each of the alternative futures outlined in Stage 2. In order to make this process as explicit as possible, a series of threat types (perhaps similar to those outlined in Chapter 3)[7] would be introduced into the analysis at this stage. The experts then would be asked to pass judgement on whether Country A, when placed in Environment 1, might perceive aggression Type p as a reasonable means of attaining its higher regional or global political objectives. What would be the possible benefits to be gained by Country A in the circumstances? Then these same questions would be asked concerning Country A in Environment 1, but concerning aggression Type q, etc. (This process is depicted diagrammatically in Figure 7.)

By an extended process of placing the selected countries in the full range of hypothetical alternative futures, the experts would make judgements concerning the complete set of accepted aggression possibilities. Eventually, all the possible combinations of country, environment and threat would be evaluated. Those combinations judged to be unreasonable propositions (probably the majority) would be abandoned.

In order to facilitate further evaluation by the experts, the remaining combinations would be elaborated into descriptive cases of aggression. These would simply trace the type of international situation that would give rise to the threat, the general preparations and precautions that the foreign actor would require and the form of aggressive action that might be employed.

Stage 4

The next step would involve a generalized evaluation by the experts of the likely profitability of each case of aggression as it is likely to be perceived by the foreign actors. The first question might ask for an assessment of the likely perceived opportunity costs of undertaking the action against Australia. How profitable might alternative resource applications be when compared with the option of pressuring Australia? How much would the external actor's security in other spheres be reduced by mobilizing and applying the resources involved against Australia?

A separate but related function to that of opportunity cost would be an estimation of risk costs. What would be the perceived risks of other external actors intervening? To what extent might the external actor fear that the resources calculated as necessary to achieve the objective against Australia might be understated? What would

	COUNTRY A	COUNTRY B
Alternative Future 1	Feasibility of pressure or threat Type .... a? .... b? .... c? .... d? .... e? .... f? .... g? What possible benefits?	Feasibility of pressure or threat Type .... a? .... b? .... c? .... d? .... e? .... f? .... g? What possible benefits?
Alternative Future 2	Feasibility of pressure or threat Type .... a? .... b? .... c? .... d? .... e? .... f? .... g? What possible benefits?	Feasibility of pressure or threat Type .... a? .... b? .... c? .... d? .... e? .... f? .... g? What possible benefits?

Fig. 7. Diagrammatic presentation of the threat evaluation process in Stage 3.

be the perceived risks to the external actor of other undesirable consequences — for example, increased tension with other actors, super-powers, allies, neighbours, etc?

In addition, it would be necessary to attempt to evaluate the constraining force of perceived political costs, both domestically and abroad.

The other side of the profitability equation would involve an estimation of the foreign actor's anticipated gains from the aggressive action. Questions asked here would include a rough evaluation of the foreign actor's perceived value of any physical resources expected to be gained by the aggression, the foreign actor's likely perceived value of any strategic positions or strategic advantages won in relation to its competitors, etc. Estimations of likely perceptions regarding the value of economic and both international and domestic political advantages also would need to be made.[8]

Clearly, no matter how well-qualified the experts, the judgements required of them in this field could not be expected to take any precise mathematical form. However, in order to gain a very generalized view of a foreign actor's likely perceptions in a given situation, basic order-of-magnitude evaluations would be sufficient. What is really required from this balancing of the likely perceived costs and benefits is a simple and relatively reliable means of culling out those cases of aggression that would clearly be unprofitable from the external actor's point of view. The remaining cases of aggression would progress to Stage 5.

Stage 5

The next step would be for the experts to evaluate the cases of aggression in the context of their appropriate future environment and assess whether or not the foreign actor might have alternative means of attaining its overall politico-strategic goals with or without threatening Australia. If, in fact, there do appear to be alternative methods, these would be elaborated in the form of generalized cases of action and passed to Stage 6. (There may be more than one alternative option for each case of aggression.) On the other hand, if there are no alternative methods of foreign actor goal achievement apparent, the case of aggression would be transferred directly to Stage 7.

Stage 6

At this stage, the possible alternative foreign actor strategies would be evaluated for their cost-effectiveness, using the same criteria and methodology that were applied to the original cases of aggression in Stage 4. Those alternatives the experts judge to be clearly unprofitable would be abandoned. The remainder would progress to Stage 7.

Stage 7

Where multiple alternatives to an original case of aggression progress to Stage 7, the experts concerned would be asked to pass judgement on which would be most likely to be perceived by the foreign actor as the most profitable. This most profitable alternative would then be compared to the original case of aggression against Australia from which the alternative was derived in Stage 5. If the profitability of the aggression against Australia appears to be equal to, or better than, the best alternative, it progresses to Stage 8. On the other hand, if the most cost-effective alternative actions clearly appear to be more profitable for the external actor in the light of the postulated future environment, that case of aggression would be discarded from subsequent analysis.

Stage 8

The cases of aggression that progress to this level of analysis would then be elaborated into full-scale scenarios. The actual process of describing the scenarios would be very important. While brevity would be essential, at the same time, it would be vital to transmit clearly the information needed by the security planners, who, in the final analysis, would base much of their work upon those scenarios selected at the end of this threat-managing process.

Essentially, a scenario is a description of a hypothetical chain of events, commencing with the development of circumstances that serve to generate the external actor's aggressive intentions and terminating with the final features of the plan of attack or pressure. They probably would be best described in three distinct stages.[9] The first, conflict phase would deal with the chain of international developments that lead to a situation where the conflict is imminent. The second, aggression stage would analyse whether it would be necessary or expedient for the foreign actor to move against third parties in the international environment, before it could pressure or attack Australia. If this were judged to be likely or probable, steps would be identified in the foreign actor's activity and these would be clearly outlined. At each of these points, the descriptions of the situation would include an account of the actor's current estimation of the profitability (gains versus risks) of the intended action.[10]

The third, attack phase of the scenario would describe the main features of the aggressor's plan of attack or means of applying pressure.[11] To simplify this process, it would need to be assumed that the external actor designed its aggression to impact upon the Australian security structure and the nation as a whole, as it existed at the time the analysis was undertaken.[12]

Stage 9

The newly completed scenarios would now be referred back to the experts, to check that the various hypothetical actions and moves of the participating international actors are in general accord with their expressed doctrines as outlined in the strategic analysis of Stage 1. It would be essential for objectives, methods and means of all the actors to be consistent with their current and/or anticipated patterns of behaviour. In those scenarios where there are found to be inconsistencies of a relatively minor nature, it may be possible to make corrections in such a manner that the established form of the scenario remains unchanged. However, where this proves to be impossible, because the inconsistencies are of a more fundamental nature, the scenario would need to be abandoned.

Stage 10

At this point, the scenarios would be considered from the viewpoint of one of the major users of the end product, the force structure planner. From his point of view, it would be necessary to limit the finally approved number of scenarios to a manageable level (perhaps, ideally, between five and fifteen). One primary means of reducing the numbers of scenarios remaining, without affecting significantly the value of the few that comprise the final product, would be to test them for response overlap.

It would not be very difficult for strategic planners to determine, in general terms, the types and levels of forces that might be required to meet most effectively the scenarios that reach Stage 10.[13] In respect of their requirements for an Australian response, some of the scenarios are likely to dominate others. For example, a limited assault mounted by country A may require a very similar Australian response to an assault mounted by country B. If such were the case, one of these scenarios could be discarded. In addition, it is also possible that one scenario may dominate another of a quite different type, in terms of the response structure required. While the optimized response structures of the two scenarios concerned may differ in minor respects, it may be determined that the built-in flexibility[14] of one of the optimized responses would be sufficient for it to meet effectively the demands of the other scenario. Thus culling again may be possible. If this process of scenario discrimination is undertaken efficiently, it would be reasonable to assume that if a theoretical defence structure were designed and prepared to meet all of the remaining scenarios, it also should have a capacity to meet any type of scenario with which Australia may be confronted within the fifteen-year time limits of the planning structure. So, in summary, in terms of their response requirements, a wide range of scenario types is likely to remain for further consideration at the end of Stage 10.

Stage 11

At this stage, experts and strategic planners would attempt to determine, in a conservative manner, the minimum defence preparation time that Australian security planners could expect to receive in the circumstances of each scenario. In other words, judgements would be made concerning the point of time in each scenario at which it could be expected with a high degree of probability that the Australian government would authorize full-scale security force mobilization to meet the threat as it would then be perceived. From this judgement, it would be possible to determine, in general terms, the length of time likely to be available for changes to be made in the security structure before the external actor moves against Australia (i.e. the length of defence preparation time). In some scenarios, this time for structural alteration is likely to be zero, but in others it may be in the order of months or even years.

The hypothetical and generalized optimized scenario response structures of Stage 10 would now be resurrected, to perform another function. The optimized response structure of those scenarios where the minimum length of defence preparation time is judged to be relatively long would be compared to the optimized response structure of those scenarios where the minimum defence preparation time is judged to be zero or relatively short. It may be found that between these two categories there are optimized response structures that are fairly closely related. Where this is so, analysis would be undertaken, to determine the length of time that would be required to adapt the security structure optimized for the low minimum defence preparation time scenario to approximate the structure that is optimized for the scenario with relatively long minimum defence preparation time. Where this time period is found to be shorter than the difference between the defence preparation times for the two scenarios, the scenario with the relatively long minimum defence preparation time could be safely abandoned. By using this process and making explicit and realistic assumptions about the defence preparation time adaptability of particular security structures, it would be possible for individual scenarios with low minimum defence preparation times to cancel more than one other scenario at this stage. However, it must be remembered that, as a result of these processes, it may be necessary to secure structural adaptability as a goal in its own right. This would need to be expressed explicitly in the additional requirements of national policy.[15]

Stage 12

The final stage of the scenario culling process would be undertaken by politicians, probably by the Cabinet on the recommendation of the Minister for Defence. However, it should be noted that it would be highly advantageous if a politically bipartisan approach was adopted concerning the criteria employed in this process. Basically, judgement would have to be exercised as to the political acceptability of the final set of scenarios. It is here that politicians would be expected to make explicit judgements if they felt that the security forces should not be designed to meet specific types of pressure or threat. For example, it may be decided that in the case of a particular type of scenario, Australia's security forces, no matter what their strength, would be incapable of influencing international developments or even affecting significantly their impact upon Australia. In these circumstances, it might be decided that consideration of this type of scenario in the planning and design of Australia's security capacity would imply a misallocation of resources. By way of illustration, the politicians might decide to abandon consideration of scenarios involving heavy nuclear, biological or chemical attacks by the super-powers upon Australia's population centres in the design of the country's security capacity.[16]

In total, this scenario-refining process represents a serious attempt to devise a means of managing the high levels of uncertainty that currently bedevil Australia's processes of security planning. The conceptual progression that has been outlined largely avoids the dangers inherent in intuitive decision-making, which is undertaken in the context of a very large number of highly dynamic and poorly defined variables. It systematizes the processes of scenario evaluation into a logical sequence. It also demands that most judgements be made in an explicit manner on the basis of a clearly stated information source and in the light of coherently expressed criteria and assumptions. In addition, it provides well-delineated roles for system administration, experts with specialized knowledge of the countries concerned, security planners and politicians.

Finally, and perhaps most importantly, this type of uncertainty managing process provides a basis for marshalling a high level of specialized expertise to make intuitive judgements when these are unavoidable. Implicit in Stages 3-7, 9 and 11 are a series of judgements on likely foreign actor reactions to a range of hypothetical environments.[17] Obviously these evaluations would be susceptible to all of the problems of subjectivism. Yet these difficulties could be reduced to manageable proportions if a relatively large number of people were engaged for the task, each of whom possessed a high level of expertise concerning at least one of the foreign actors concerned. In practical terms, this probably could be done most effectively by employing some type of participatory polling technique.[18] Where it is considered that it might be beneficial, some of the questionnaire results might also be tested in carefully constructed simulation games.[19]

It is important to realize that all of these techniques are, of course, imperfect means of prediction. A range of assumptions accepted in the process — extrapolated international trends, the absence of unforeseen dramatic happenings and foreign actor rationality, to name just a few — cannot be justified in absolute terms. *As a consequence, it is fortunate that the major function of this type of system is not to predict the future. Rather, it is designed to provide a limited number of inherently consistent threat possibilities that, in terms of their non-time sensitive response requirements, would be representative of a much wider range of hypothetical, but clearly feasible, pressures and threats.* The overriding aim of the exercise would be to provide a very useful and generally accepted tool to assist in the management of threat uncertainty for the processes of long-term security planning.

Notes and References

1. See Sir Arthur Tange, "Defence Policy Making in Australia", in John Birman, ed., *Australia's Defence* (Perth: Extension Service, University of Western Australia, 1976), pp. 6-7.
2. This timing has been selected so that the strategic assessment would fit easily into the long-range planning phasing, which is elaborated in detail in Appendix D.
3. The selection of this time-span might be justified by a variety of arguments, but here the prime motivation was to obtain compatibility with the proposed processes of long-term security planning outlined in Appendix D. A point fifteen years hence is particularly appropriate as a long-range planning objective because it is sufficiently remote to make significant structural alterations feasible, but at the same time is sufficiently immediate to make detailed proposals realistic.
4. An appropriate number might be somewhere between ten and twenty alternative futures. A number smaller than this would probably not provide sufficient scope for the analysis and a sufficiently broad range of possible alternative developments. A number larger than twenty would tend to become unmanageable because of the proliferation of paper work it would cause in the subsequent stages of analysis.
5. In this context, the time-span is broadened from the initial fifteen years to permit hypothetical pressures or threats to be developed over the time period that would be required for them to eventuate.

6. These experts might be drawn both from within government service and from academic and business circles beyond. There are a number of precedents for the employment of external personnel for the provision of specialized expertise. Apart from the engagement of individual consultants from time to time, the Department of Defence, on occasions, has worked with specialized groups of academics in extended consultations with senior government officials. For details, see *Strategic and Defence Studies Centre* (information booklet prepared in Canberra for the Research School of Pacific Studies, Australian National University, 1971), p. 3.
7. The types of pressure and threat employed might include the following:
    (a) low-level pressures of peace, i.e. those consistent with a peaceful environment;
    (b) pressures resulting from a regional or global resource crisis;
    (c) pressures resulting from a regional or global conflict in which Australia is not a combatant;
    (d) demands and threats supported by political, military and/or economic measures;
    (e) economic warfare against Australia;
    (f) surprise assault with a limited objective;
    (g) full-scale invasion;
    (h) Australian involvement in a global or regional nuclear, biological or chemical exchange.
8. Attempting to gauge the likely perceptions of foreign actors in hypothetical situations is obviously a highly speculative process. The employment of such estimations in this system of scenario refinement is not to imply that similar considerations necessarily occupy the minds of major actors in real-life situations. Calculations concerning the profitability of a given action are frequently made in only a shallow manner, if they are considered at all. The question of employing such calculations in a theoretical framework is discussed by Kevin J. Foley, "Selecting an Australian Tactical Fighter Force: Marginal Strategies, Rationality and the Australian Aircraft Industry", in, *The Future of Tactical Airpower in the Defence of Australia*, ed. Desmond Ball (Canberra: Strategic and Defence Studies Centre, Australian National University, 1977), pp. 132-36.
9. This method of expression is employed successfully in Sweden. See Ministry of Defence, *The Defence Planning System — The Goal-setting Procedure* (Stockholm: Ministry of Defence, 1970), Publication 4/1970, p. 16.
10. This consideration would facilitate subsequent analyses concerning alternative methods of deterring, deferring, defeating or otherwise preventing the development of pressures and threats before they can be actively directed against Australia.
11. It is interesting to note that the Swedish defence planners have found by experience that in their situation the best method of scenario construction (as opposed to expression) is not chronological. In order to achieve a high level of internal consistency, they start by defining the international situation at the end of the conflict phase. From there, the entire aggression stage is designed. Only then is the conflict phase constructed and this is done by working backwards from the start of the aggression phase. When both of these processes are complete, the attack phase is designed and delineated in detail. For details, see Ministry of Defence, *Defence Planning System*, p. 17.
12. This implicit assumption would be made in order to simplify the experts' evaluations of foreign actors' perceptions of Australia's reaction capacity. However, there may also be scope here to test the sensitivity of various cases of aggression to explicit changes in Australia's security structure. It may be possi-

ble, by a process of submitting further detailed questions to the experts, to evaluate likely alterations to a foreign actor's profitability analyses resulting from changes to Australia's security capacity. However, this would be an aid to security planning rather than a means of assisting the management of uncertainty *per se*.

13. In any coherent and rigorous security planning system, there is a need for a group of specialist strategic planners. As is discussed in Appendix D, one of their most important functions would be to elaborate and test alternative concepts and force structures in order to determine their functional effectiveness in meeting national security requirements in given situations. Because of the nature of their normal work, the elaboration of generalized force structures that would most effectively meet the requirements of the scenarios reaching Stage 10 would most probably not be very difficult.
14. Flexibility is defined here to mean a structure's capacity to meet uncertainty (or a non-design optimized threat) where the length of advance warning is insufficient to make structural alterations possible (i.e. defence preparation time is zero).
15. The additional requirements of national policy are discussed in Chapter 7 and depicted in Figure 2 in that chapter.
16. It would clearly be important for politicians to command a high level of knowledge and expertise in order to make these judgements. Potential means of improving their capacity in this area are discussed in Chapter 6.
17. Judgements are also required of security planners concerning the nature of optimal security structures designed in response to specific pressures and threats (Stages 10 and 11), likely warning and defence preparation times (Stage 11) and the periods likely to be required to adapt optimal security response structures to approximate others (also in Stage 11). Finally, explicit judgements are required of politicians (Stage 12).
18. These techniques are discussed at length by H. Sackman, *Toward More Effective Use of Expert Opinion: Preliminary Investigation of Participatory Polling for Long-range Planning*, (Santa Monica: Rand Corporation, 1976), P-5570.
19. The potential utility of simulation techniques is discussed by Anatol Rapoport in *Strategy and Conscience* (New York: Schocken Books, 1969), pp. 125 ff. It is also important to note at this stage that a scenario derivation process, such as that outlined in this appendix, would need to be employed regularly if the end product is to be expected to retain its relevance. Changes in the international environment may alter considerably the scope for scenario construction. In addition, progressive changes to Australia's response capacity may have a significant impact upon the experts' evaluations of foreign actors' profitability calculations. Neither of these considerations can be expected to remain static for extended periods. As a consequence, a cyclical process of regular environment and threat reassessment is likely to be justified.

    This requirement is not to imply that each time the system is activated a completely new range of scenarios can be expected to emerge. Hopefully, this level of change would not be encouraged. In order to create as large a degree of conceptual stability as possible in the planning processes, scenarios may be refined from time to time and individual scenarios might be abandoned or replaced. However, unless it is made necessary by dramatic changes in the international or domestic environment, wholesale variations to the total set of scenarios ideally would be avoided as far as possible.

Appendix D

Towards Coherent Security Planning

An underlying assumption and basic foundation for much of the discussion in the later chapters of this book is that the processes of Australian security planning should be directed to determining the means of allocating national resources to maximize clearly stated national security objectives. Possible methods for deriving the four categories of planning criteria have been described in Chapter 7 and Appendix C. Once these are established, it should be possible to commence the processes of detailed security planning.

The four planning criteria would provide a conceptual basis for the detailed testing and evaluation of a wide range of alternative strategic concepts and force structures in realistic circumstances. As was discussed in Chapter 7, options could be tested for their capacity to maximize doctrinal goals in the circumstances of the selected scenarios while satisfying the additional requirements of national policy and not transgressing the bounds set by the elaborated constraints. However, because of the heavy constraining influence of the structures and concepts that already exist, this process would not provide an effective means of directly undertaking short-term planning. In order to provide the concept and structure designers with sufficient freedom to search for optimal solutions, it would be important, in the early stages of the planning process, for them to be given scope to start with virtually a "clean sheet". In order to make this possible, alternative structures would best be designed for complete implementation at a point in time sufficiently distant to make significant alterations feasible, but at the same time, sufficiently immediate to make detailed proposals realistic. For the purposes of this discussion, the long-term planning period is assumed to be fifteen years.

Constructing and Testing Alternative Structural Options

Within the context of these considerations, the first theoretical security structures could be constructed, each containing a selected mix of nuclear, conventional, territorial, economic, civilian resistance, civil and psychological defence elements. Initially, each structure would best be designed to optimize response capacity in the circumstances of only one of the accepted scenarios. The nature of the concepts and force structures derived by this process thus could be expected to vary considerably. However, it might be anticipated that, in practice, many of the structures would contain common elements in different proportions and linked in different manners.

For the purposes of their subsequent analysis, the alternative structures ideally would be described in three distinct sections. The first would outline the major operational principles and concepts of the structure, the type of strategy and the type of manpower to be employed, the levels of technology required and an assessment of the structure's flexibility and adaptability.

The second section of each alternative structure proposal would elaborate the objectives of the structure's major component programmes. The programmes themselves would need to be defined in purely functional terms, e.g. long-range surveillance, maritime strike, interdiction strike, air defence, ground attrition, ground strike, command and control, economic defence, etc. Goals for each of these programmes would best be expressed in terms of generalized performance capabilities in specific situations drawn from the accepted scenarios. Finally, in the second section, the minimum level of budgetary expenditure required to meet fully the response requirements of the specific scenario under consideration would be determined and an attempt would be made to distribute this hypothetical financial allocation between the programmes contained within the proposal.

The third major section of each alternative structure description would postulate characteristics for the essential programme components or projects. This would be the most speculative part of the proposal, for in fact it would involve detailing a generalized force structure or order of battle. By drawing upon the budget allocation in section two, each programme would be defined in terms of numbers and types of manpower, equipment, technology and support. An account of the assumed capabilities of the major individual project systems — ships, aircraft, vehicles, etc. — would also be included. Finally, the structure designers would express their expectations concerning the effectiveness of each programme structure to meet the requirements imposed by the scenario (or scenarios) that dominated the structure's design.[1]

When a broad range of alternative structures has been designed, they could be tested for flexibility. As was discussed briefly in Stage 10 of Appendix C, in order to meet uncertainty, it is desirable that a security structure possesses a capacity to satisfy effectively the demands of a wide range of future possibilities. When a threat arises for which the security structure has not been designed, if the advance warning is insufficient to make structural alterations possible (i.e. defence preparation time is zero), the basic structure's capacity to respond immediately is defined as flexibility.

For illustrative purposes, let us assume that a security structure has been designed to maximize efficiency in meeting the basic doctrinal objectives in the circumstances of each of the scenarios described in Appendix C, i.e. scenarios (A - G). It is further supposed that each structure's efficiency can be measured in generalized terms on a scale from 1 to 10 (with 10 being highly efficient). It should now be possible to plot diagrammatically the relative efficiency of the structural alternatives in the circumstances of each scenario.

Table 8. Efficiency of specialized force structures.

Alternative structures	Accepted scenarios						
	A	B	C	D	E	F	G
1	10	5	0	0	0	0	0
2	2	10	3	0	0	0	0
3	0	4	10	2	0	0	0
4	0	0	3	10	4	0	0
5	0	0	0	2	10	5	0
6	0	0	0	1	3	10	2
7	0	0	0	0	0	2	10

As can be seen from Table 8, each of the alternative structures is highly specialized in its performance. While each structure is very efficient in meeting the requirements of its specialized scenario, structural flexibility in meeting other scenarios is at best marginal and in most cases virtually non-existent. Because of uncertainty about the type of pressure or threat with which Australia may be confronted in the future, it would be extremely difficult to choose one of these seven structures to provide an overall capability. The consequences of preparing for the wrong type of threat could be disastrous. Clearly a much greater degree of structural flexibility is required.

As can be seen from structures 8-11 depicted in Table 9, it is possible to re-design specialized alternatives to provide a more generalized response capability. Two factors that are implicit in this

Table 9. Efficiency of less-specialized force structures.

Alternative structures	Accepted scenarios						
	A	B	C	D	E	F	G
8	9	8	6	4	3	3	1
9	6	8	7	5	4	2	2
10	4	5	7	7	5	3	3
11	2	3	4	6	7	8	6

process should be noted at this stage. Firstly, a large degree of flexibility usually means a loss of specialized performance. Secondly, the higher the levels of flexibility that are required, the more expensive the security bill is likely to be.

The second process of structural testing and modification is related to the first. As was briefly discussed in Stage 11 of Appendix C, structural adaptability is relevant where the length of advance warning received prior to the onset of a threat is sufficient to permit structural changes (i.e. defence preparation time is greater than zero). This point can be illustrated by reference to Table 9. In a situation where Australia possessed structure 9 and was suddenly confronted by scenario G, its response capacity would be limited by its marginal flexibility. However, if Australia receives sufficient advance warning of scenario G, there may be time to develop additional capabilities that would increase greatly the country's capacity to meet the demands of that threat. It may be possible, for instance, to boost rapidly the initial structural efficiency from 2 to 5 or 6, or perhaps even higher.

It is, in fact, possible to build a high level of adaptability into response structures by designing and constructing them in such a manner as to exploit defence preparation time fully and to minimize impediments to rapid structural change. In practical terms, these factors would imply the construction of an intelligence warning system of the highest efficiency and of a defence organization and structure prepared and practised in speedy adaptations. But inculcating an entire security structure with the necessity for rapid adaptability could not be expected to be inexpensive or easy. It would, for instance, indicate a requirement for a very high level of interest and expertise in strategic affairs at the key levels of political and bureaucratic decision-making. It would also imply a requirement for an advanced standard of technical and analytical research and development, so that the detailed knowledge in those areas that would be needed to make rapid and efficient adaptations possible could be provided with a minimum of delay. In addition, in order to provide the equipment and hardware requirements of rapid structural change, defence industries of many types would have to be maintained at a high technical standard and at an advanced state of readiness, to facilitate rapid starts, increases or changes of production.[2]

Clearly the acquisition of high levels of structural flexibility and adaptability would be extremely expensive. Consequently, as was mentioned in Chapter 7, it would be necessary for the government to lay down explicit guidelines in the context of the additional requirements of national policy for security structure design.

Relating Financial Input to National Security Output

As a result of the processes so far described, a series of hypothetical response structures would be on hand, each of which would fulfil, to a greater or lesser extent, the planning design criteria. Every one of the structures would possess a reasonable degree of flexibility and adaptability to meet a range of the accepted scenarios and they also would satisfy the additional requirements of national policy and be feasible in terms of the non-financial constraints of the real world. However, the alternative response structures could be expected to differ markedly in terms of their projected costs and also in terms of the types of scenario for which they would be optimized. What is really required in this situation is a means of relating the more capable response structures not only to the more demanding scenarios for which they were designed but also to the levels of financial input that would be required for their procurement. This is attempted in Figure 8.[3] The hierarchy of scenarios (A-G) is illustrated in the far right-hand column in the decreasing order of their response requirements. Adjacent to these are the alternative structures (22-28), which, in each case, have been designed primarily to optimize response capacity in the circumstances of the scenario that appears opposite. The alternative force structures (22-28) are depicted in a decreasing order of overall capability and total procurement cost. In addition, a time-scale has been introduced on the horizontal axis. This makes it possible to plot alternative financial decision paths from the commencement of the fifteen-year long-term planning period right through to its end, with the completion of an alternative security structure at year 15. It is also possible to plot the relative adaptability of the structures at year 15 in the circumstances of receiving an effective defence preparation time of two years. As can be seen from the relationships depicted between the structures (22-28) at year 15 and the scenarios (A-G) at year 17, the adaptability of all structures tends to be limited in meeting those scenarios that are more demanding of security resources than in meeting those scenarios for which the structures were optimized in design. Thus if at year 15 Australia were equipped with security structure 25 and it received two years effective warning of scenario A or B, it would not possess sufficient adaptability to effectively meet that threat. Alternatively, if on the other hand, Australia possessed security structure 23 at year 15, it could effectively adapt within a two-year period to meet any scenario. In other words, Figure 8 illustrates the obvious point that it is always much easier to adapt a security structure to meet the requirements of scenarios that are less demanding than to meet the requirements of scenarios that are more demanding. In simple visual terms on Figure 8, adaptability upwards is much more difficult than adaptability down.

It is also possible to draw meaningful conclusions by studying the implications of the budgetary choices at the decision-points (I-V) between years 0 and 12. By analysing the options at each of these decision-points, it can be seen that if the Australian government decided to spend large amounts of money throughout the early parts of the planning period and was spending budget level 1 or 2 at decision-point (DP) V, it would have the choice at that stage of acquiring structures 22, 23 or 24 by year 15. Hence it would be quite feasible to proceed to a structure that would have a capacity to meet satisfactorily the requirements of all the accepted scenarios at year 17.

On the other hand, if the Australian government decided to spend only moderate levels of expenditure on national security to year 12 and at DP V was spending budget level 4, the choice of year 15 structures would be limited to 24, 25 and 26 and it would not be possible to meet effectively the requirements of scenario A at year 17, no matter how much money was injected at that late stage. But if it were decided to proceed to structure 24, it would be possible to adapt to meet the requirements of scenarios B-G.

Alternatively, if the government takes a low or fluctuating spending path to financial level 6 at DP V, it would be impossible at that stage to procure a structure with a capacity to meet scenarios A, B or C by year 17. It would only be possible to develop a capacity to meet scenarios D-G. Moreover, if expenditure remained at comparable levels to that at DP V during the subsequent three years, the most effective structural option that would be financially feasible would be number 27. This would only possess an effective capacity to meet scenarios E, F and G.

At decision-points I and II, judgements would need to be made concerning the types and numbers of high-technology captial equipments required in the security structure at year 15. If it were decided

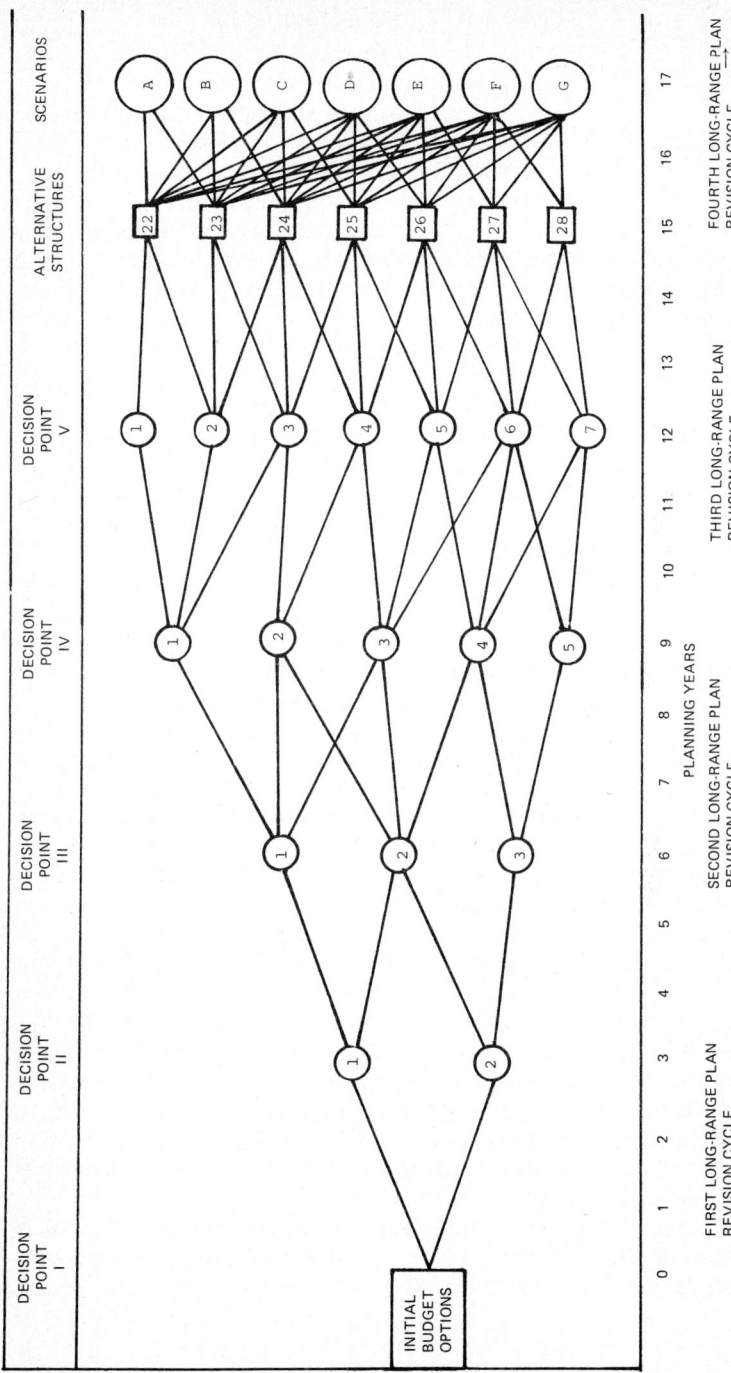

Fig. 8. Relating short-term financial input to long-term national security output.

at this stage that Australia should definitely possess a capacity to meet effectively all of the scenarios at the end of the planning period, it would be necessary to aim to provide structure 22 or 23. In order to retain the option of procuring structure 22, it would be necessary to pass through financial level I at DPs II and III. An essential part of structural options 22 and 23 most probably would be heavy expenditure on major items of capital equipment. At DP I, decisions would be required on exactly those types of systems that would be required and research and development funded where this is appropriate. At DP II, orders for advanced technology aircraft, ships and heavy armoured vehicles would have to be placed. Research and development into items with medium or short production lead times could continue.

However, it should be noted that, if at DP I the international environment appears to be relatively sanguine and a choice is made to spend at low levels for the first years of the plan, it can be seen that by moving to financial level 2 at DP II, the option of acquiring structure 22 by year 15 is already foreclosed. This is simply because a start must be made on the heavy capital equipment requirements of structure 22 at DP I, if they are to be operational in time. However, if at DP II the government feels less certain about the future, it could opt to move to financial level 2 at DP III.[4] This would leave open the structural options 23-28, in the hope that by year 6 clearer choices could be made. At financial level 2 at DP III, a firm decision would be required about whether structure 23 should be retained as an option for year 15. If it is to be retained, national security expenditure would need to be raised to level 2 at DP IV. On the other hand, if the government felt that it could not justify this type of expenditure, a choice would be necessary between financial levels 3 or 4 at DP IV. Financial level 3, at that stage, would retain the option of structure 24 at year 15, but financial level 4 would not.

The reason why it is impossible to move from financial level 3 at DP IV to structure 22 or 23, or from financial level 4 at DP IV to structures 22, 23 and 24, is that in the six years remaining in the plan, it would be impossible to procure the long lead-time capabilities those structures require. As a consequence of these factors, if Australia's security expenditure at DP IV is at level 4, even if a worsening security environment stimulated the government to accelerate national security expenditure rapidly at every decision-point from then onwards, at year 15 the country would still require two years' active defence preparation time in order to be able to meet the requirements of scenario C. The onset of more demanding scenarios of types A or B would find Australia's security response wanting. In this type of situation, the possession of only part of a required capacity is unlikely to provide an effective basis for the achievement of the government's national security objectives.

A rapid expansion, such as that postulated above, from financial level 4 at DP IV to achieve structure 25 within 6 years, would involve cutting quite a few corners. Structure 25, for instance, might include an x level maritime strike capability. In the originally conceived structural plan, it might have been decided that the most cost-effective method of obtaining this x level of maritime strike capacity was to procure P strike fighters, Q submarines and R ground-launched cruise missile systems. However, at DP IV and financial level 4, early preparations might have been put in train for only $\frac{P}{2}$ strike fighters, $\frac{Q}{2}$ submarines and $\frac{R}{2}$ ground-launched cruise missiles. Thus when at DP IV a decision is made to procure structure 25 by year 15, short lead-time substitutes would need to be found to provide the additional capability required. By refurbishing and re-arming old equipment already held or procurable overseas, some of the gap could be bridged. However, in the final structure at year 15, the required capability is likely to be provided by a different combination of component systems to that originally judged to be the most cost-effective. In other words, the final maritime strike structure might take the form of $\frac{3}{2}P$ strike fighters, $\frac{Q}{2}$ submarines and $3R$ ground-launched cruise missiles. It should be noted, in addition, that the basic inefficiency of this type of hasty expansion would be evidenced by the fact that the total costs of the completed structure always would be significantly greater than those that would be incurred by steady progress over the total planning period towards the ultimate structural goal.[5] Moreover, although it is not discussed here, this type of rapid expansion also might necessitate the adoption of unusual security concepts, doctrines and operational procedures.[6] An even more important consideration is that, as the decision paths and adaptability functions in Figure 8 display, the scope for this type of hasty alteration of structural design and size will always remain relatively limited and be directly proportional to the amount of active defence preparation time received.

One of the most significant aspects of this type of long-range security planning concept is that it effectively relates, in an explicit manner, the capacity of the force structure to meet the full range of potential pressures and threats to the government's decisions on budgetary inputs. In the simplest of terms, it ties firmly the level of budgetary input with the level of security output, expressed in terms of national capacity to meet the demands of the accepted scenarios. The higher the budgetary input, the more numerous the scenarios the security structure will have a capacity to meet effectively at the terminal stages of the planning period.

Detailed Planning:
Determining an Optimal Mix of Programme Components

How might such a long-range planning system operate in the real world? In practice, in year 0, once the non-financial planning criteria are established, the direction of the long-range plan most probably would be dependent upon the level of security expenditure that had been determined for that year and the government's expressed intentions for expenditure in the following four years. If the government expressed an intention to expend large amounts on national security up to and beyond DP II, the more expensive (and capable) alternative structures could be studied as a basis for planning (structures 22-25). If, on the other hand, the government expresses an intention to expend relatively low levels on national security during the course of the forthcoming five years, structures of less ccapability could be adopted for detailed long-range planning (structures 25-28). The emphasis at this stage would be on that which would be financially feasible within the government's budgetary expectations.

The alternative structures that are adopted at this stage for the processes of detailed planning already would be described in terms of their major programme characteristics and even their generalized orders of battle.[7] The major programmes of the accepted structures now would need to be analysed and tested in much greater detail, to determine the optimal project[8] system mix to maximize programme efficiency and then total structure capability within the determined financial constraints.

As was discussed earlier in this appendix, programmes would best be defined in broad functional categories to permit an open analysis of a wide range of alternative project possibilities. A simplified array of options for the maritime strike and air defence programmes is illustrated in Figure 9.

For a given programme budget, hypothetical project mixes could now be tested for their effectiveness in the context of the scenarios for which the adopted planning structures have relevance. This could be done by an extensive process of simulated war-games. When it is possible to quantify, in generalized terms, the optimal project mix for all of the structures' programmes, they could be tested for cross-interaction. This process would determine whether or not there may be total capability gains by trading inter-programme project allocations against each other. It would also permit informed judgements on whether funds allocated to specialized programme capacities might not be better re-allocated to projects that would provide a useful capacity in several programme functions. For instance, it can be seen from Figure 9 that strike fighters are an

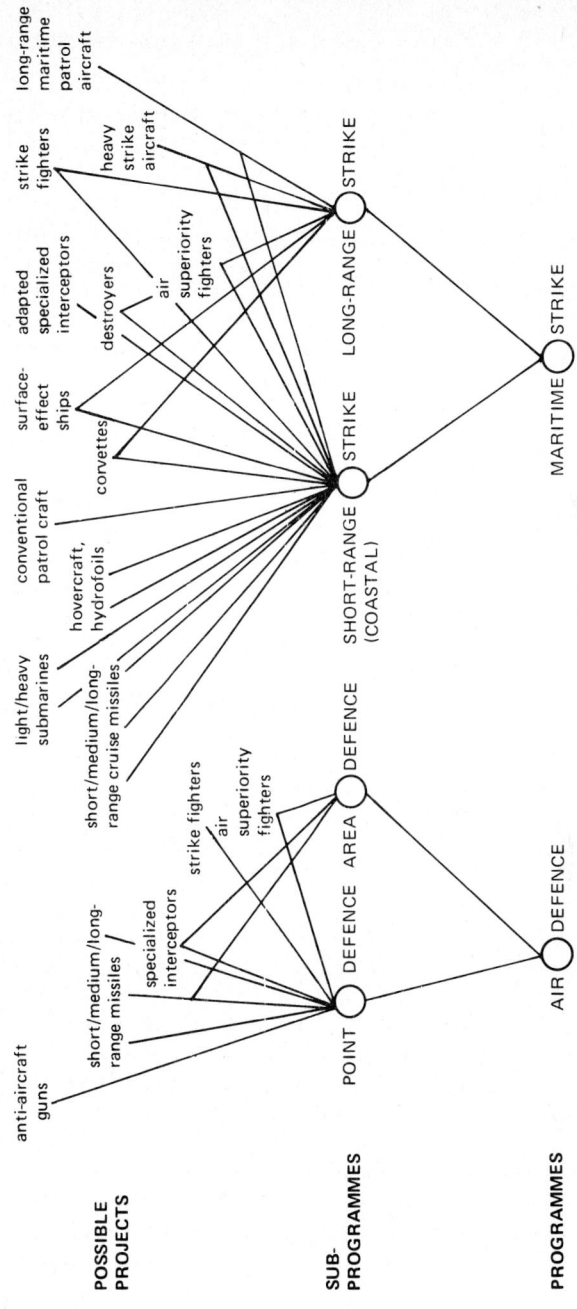

Fig. 9. Programme and project relationship.

optional project system for both the air defence and maritime strike programmes. Although not illustrated in this diagram, it is conceivable that strike fighters may also be an option in the interdiction strike, reconaissance and close air-support programmes. Obviously, if strike fighters were to be a viable option in all of these programmes, great advantages could be won by reallocating resources away from programme-specialized projects to enhance multi-programme capacity. Economies of scale would be evident in procurement, production, servicing, training and many other fields. An important additional bonus would be greatly increased operational and basing flexibility. Clearly there would be limits to the advantages that could be won by this type of trade-off. In some types of programme, highly specialized projects would be required. Appropriate programme balances could be expected to emerge from processes of intensive gaming.

There would be an important additional value in undertaking these detailed evaluations of programme and, indeed, total structure effectiveness. By thoroughly testing a wide range of structural possibilities in the context of clearly defined national security objectives, one is approaching a viable means of measuring national security output. In this context, this would be measurable in terms of a structure's potential efficiency in meeting the hypothetical, but accepted, range of pressure and threat possibilities. However, as Dr K.J. Foley has pointed out, this type of output analysis is vulnerable to a series of weaknesses resulting from the arbitrary assumptions that are implicit in the techniques of simulation.[9] For instance, the peacetime utilities that security forces can provide could not be taken into adequate consideration, nor could goal achievement be quantified with precision. However, because this type of analysis is designed to provide a basis for alternative structural choices and relative structural effectiveness, it could be expected to provide consistent information relating to preferred options. As a consequence, it could be well suited to perform the major function of input-output analysis in the Australian national security structure, that of providing a framework for the rational allocation of marginal resource inputs.

Integrating Long- and Short-term Planning Requirements

There remains a major conceptual difficulty with this type of planning system as it has been outlined thus far. In practice, no current defence establishment commences planning in year 0 without a defence structure in being and with a national security budget allocation, the sole purpose of which is to maximize national security goals in the time period 15+ years hence. In reality, Australia has a national security capacity of some significance already in existence. Large numbers of highly skilled personnel and great quantities of specialized equipment are currently deployed in operational and support units. Even if the processes of long-term planning determined that significant sections of the current structure were inappropriate to the needs of the future, the extensive investments already existing could not be abandoned arbitrarily. Serious consideration would have to be given to the maintenance of a significant and efficient national security capacity during the processes of structural transition. A great deal of skill would be required to determine the most appropriate allocation of national security resources between the three main areas of investment.

1. The first area of spending concerns maintenance of the current structure, including the retention and training of personnel in traditionally accepted roles, the maintenance, overhaul and upgrading of capital equipment already held in stock and the exercise of the total security structure in performing its priority functions.

2. The second area of expenditure involves procurement of supporting capital items that can be delivered within the current five-year defence programme (FYDP) for the development of the existing force structure.[10] This category includes the training of personnel and the provision of new capital equipment to complete the development of partially acquired capabilities.[11]

3. The third area involves investment in research and development and in long lead-time capital equipment that cannot be delivered within the time-span of the FYDP.

In the preceding discussion, most of the year 0 decision-making that has been discussed has been that concerning structural optimization for year 15 and beyond. While long-range structural planning clearly should have a central role to play, it has yet to be explained adequately how the transformation could be made from the inherited security structure to approach the planned optimum several years hence, for a given financial input. How could appropriate levels of investment in areas 1 and 2 be determined?

Basically, the processes of force structure transformation would need to be undertaken progressively. This would be aided by the fact that, by their very nature, national security structures are rarely static in their characteristics or capabilities. The major capital equipment items — aircraft, ships, armoured vehicles, etc. — gradually age, become more expensive to maintain and are relatively less effective when compared with other nations' holdings. In general terms, these processes of obsolescence are predictable. Thus in the present Australian structure, a need for replacement or substitute equipments is usually recognized at an early stage by the parent service and this is structured into the FYDP with justification drawn from the Strategic Basis document and the service capabilities papers, as appropriate. There is, in addition, restricted scope for the services to bargain for the introduction of new capabilities to the FYDP.

However, in the type of coherent planning system being discussed here, it most probably would be necessary to adopt new, and possibly controversial, methods of determining FYDP input. In this type of system, the main initiators of procurement programmes would not be the services directly, but rather the organization that performs the long-range planning function.[12] In practice, this would mean that when major pieces of equipment approach obsolescence or when additional financial resources become available, competing demands for new equipment would need to be examined carefully in the light of the requirements of the adopted long-range structural plan. As was discussed earlier, decisions in this area also would need to include considerations of the ongoing capacity of the security forces during the processes of structural transformation. In some areas, compromises in the long-range planning structure may be necessary, in order to lower the risks of unexpected conflict arising during the period of structural change.

Where there no longer exists a requirement for the original function of ageing equipment to be performed, financial resources could be freed for reallocation into areas where the long-range plan indicates that new or increased capabilities are required. Where the original function of ageing equipments remains an important requirement, the resources made available for the performance of this task could be allocated to those project systems that, in combination, are judged to provide the most cost-effective functional performance. Thus by a gradual process of reassessing functions in the light of the requirements of the long-range plan as major capital equipment items approach obsolescence, some would simply be replaced by better but comparable systems, others would be replaced by a more efficient mix of systems and still others would not be replaced at all, but instead would provide resources for reallocation into new areas of priority investment.

Once priorities are clearly established for project inputs, they could be incorporated into the FYDP in much the same manner as at present, so as to minimize financial peaks and troughs. However, in contrast to the present system, it would be most appropriate for projects, once introduced into the FYDP, to be relatively immune to dislodgement unless a significant change in the international situation or in levels of government funding altered the nature of the long-range plan.

The services would have the task of studying the projects introduced into the FYDP and making a selection from the brand-name contenders on the basis of the established project criteria. The timing of this decision-making and the subsequent processes of procurement, personnel training and service introduction would best be determined by the phasing of the FYDP.

Co-ordination of the long-range plan (LRP) and the five-year rolling programme (FYRP) would be vitally important to the efficiency of the total national security planning structure.[13] Probably the most effective means of achieving this objective in the Australian Department of Defence would be for the FYRP system and structure to be retained in a modified form. The LRP probably would best operate in phase with the FYRP on its five-year cycle. This would mean that the LRP cycle would begin every fifth year with the development of a strategic assessment. This would be the first step in LRP construction or revision. In brief summary, the following sequence of functions represents an outline of what conceivably might be undertaken in the subsequent months.

Firstly, from the completed strategic assessment via the processes outlined in Appendix C, the scenarios could be reviewed and refined. At that stage, the government might be expected to express its opinion concerning the acceptability of particular categories of scenario and also to outline and/or review the goals for national security doctrine and the additional requirements of national policy. At about the same time, a statement of internal constraints would be forthcoming from the Department of Defence, for governmental approval. Alternative long-term structures then could be conceptually constructed, tested and modified. Final structural options could be derived for particular levels of financial input and response capacity and, in their light, the government might be asked to indicate anticipated levels of funding for the forthcoming FYDP period. With this information at hand, decisions could be made concerning the most effective structure that could feasibly be procured. Once this choice was made, detailed project planning would be possible and this, in turn, would provide inputs for the annual cycles of the FYRP during the subsequent long-range planning period.

An illustrative example may assist in demonstrating this ongoing process. If we assume that in year 0, the LRP process begins with the derivation of a strategic assessment, the final project mix for the selected structure should be available by year 3. By carefully trading-off the requirements of the LRP that are concerned primarily with capacities judged to be desirable for years 15 and onwards against the short- and medium-range requirements of years 5-14, it would be possible to determine the procurement priorities for years 5-9. In years 3 and 4, analyses of the lead-time requirements and financial implications of the projects to be procured in years 5-9 could be completed and this would facilitate the construction of a properly phased FYDP for the next five-year period (years 5-9). This in turn would mean that the services could make final brand-name choices, according to the stipulated project criteria, for those systems that are to be procured during year 5.

During the course of year 5, the first procurement and structural choices forthcoming from the planning processes in years 0-4 would be translated into procurement decisions. At the same time, the processes of LRP revision would have commenced once more in the new five-year cycle, starting with the derivation of a new strategic assessment.[14]

It should be noted that in practice some of the present "rolling" nature of the FYRP would be removed in this system. At the beginning of year 5, for example, a full five years of FYDP would be decided and structured within the system. However, in year 6, only four years' definite decision-making regarding structural implementation would remain. In year 7, this would shrink again to three, in year 8 to two, and in year 9, theoretically only one year's detailed decisions regarding planning implementation would remain.[15] This would be because the results of the current five-year long-range planning cycle probably would not be available until year 8. As a consequence, the year 5 FYDP, in fact, would be run down until the new requirements derived from the LRP revision became clear. It would then be possible to structure in detail the FYDP for the years 10-14 in years 8 and 9. Thus in practice, the FYDPs would be changed (and hence "roll") only once every five years.[16]

An obvious result of this system would be to raise gradually the level of procurement uncertainty until the results of the LRP are available in the fourth year of each cycle. However, it is doubtful that this would cause any serious problem within the Department in practice, because continual internal exchanges of information could be expected to take place and a minimum of two years always would be provided for the services to make brand-name decisions. In the case of major equipments that are phased into the later years of a FYDP, the services could be given between five and seven years to make final brand-name decisions.

A second and not insignificant consequence of reducing the "rolling" nature of the FYDP would be to cut drastically the requirement for FYRP construction, management and review. The workload required for these functions would be concentrated heavily in the final two years of the LRP cycle and in overall terms could be expected to be reduced greatly.

By far the most important potential benefit to be gained from this type of integrated planning concept would be the approach to an optimization of national security goals for a given resource input. Total resource allocation could be made highly efficient and, in a relative sense, it could be measurable through input-output analysis. The importance of long-term considerations would be increased greatly. In addition, nearly all intuitive judgements could be made on the basis of an extensive information resource base and at the conclusion of a process of detailed gaming and testing. In normal peacetime circumstances, the scope for *ad hoc* decision-making could be reduced significantly.

Because of the systematic nature of the processes that would be involved in this type of security-planning concept, clear guidelines could be provided automatically for a large number of supporting elements. For example, for those tasked with the responsibility for detailed manpower planning, the structure of the LRP itself would provide a brief discussion of manpower types and numbers.[17] Important additional manpower planning processes, such as those to determine the types of training and skills required to maximize structural flexibility and adaptability, would be assisted greatly by the governmental statement on these matters in the additionally stated planning requirements and also by the conceptual framework provided by the analysis of alternative structural options.

Further, because an integral part of this type of planning structure would be a clear elaboration of a set of accepted scenarios, response structures and concepts, the services would be provided with precise guidance concerning the types of situation they are expected to meet. As a consequence, strategy, tactics and doctrine could be developed in a cohesive, integrated and harmonious fashion by all sectors of the security structure.

Thus, in summary, it would appear that this general type of conceptual planning sequence could provide clear direction and cohesion to the entire national security system. Unambiguous guidance could be derived for the development of strategy, structures, equipment priorities, manpower and training systems, doctrines, operational procedures, research and development programmes, defence-related industries and a wide range of other security system components. Objectives could be defined with precision, alternatives could be tested thoroughly and a sound basis could be provided for the maximization of national security capacity for a given financial input.

The coherent and co-ordinated development of the Australian defence structure is clearly an area requiring much greater attention.

The security planning system that Australia currently possesses has been inherited from the forward defence era and has not been designed to perform satisfactorily the functions it is now required to undertake. In operation, the current force-in-being/core force/terminal force planning rationale is an effective means of retaining most security response options open indefinitely. But this cannot be done without substantial costs. Attempting to maximize structural flexibility and adaptability, in practice, has encouraged weak planning criteria, induced indecision and militated against the development and retention of strong immediate response and surge capacities.

To some degree, these weaknesses were tolerable in the forward defence era. In that environment, combat deployments were rarely time-urgent and they were made almost exclusively to supplement the much larger capacities of major-power allies. However, in the new strategic environment, with Australia's security dependent primarily upon its indigenous capacities, the loose planning concepts of the past appear to be grossly inadequate.

With the requirements of meaningful change becoming increasingly obvious, the processes of Australian security policy formulation are likely to be the subject of much closer political, bureaucratic, academic and public attention. The alternative planning concepts discussed in Chapter 7, and in Appendices C and D, may broaden the scope of the debate and stimulate a more intense search for practical solutions.

Notes and References

1. The structure designers and those who might work in this type of long-range planning system clearly would need to be very highly skilled and largely divorced from service rivalries and prejudices. Ideally, an organization tasked to perform these functions would contain a mix of personnel from all three services, as well as civilian analysts.
2. The means of incorporating the high levels of structural adaptability mentioned in this paragraph are elaborated in greater length in Chapters 4 and 7.
3. A "decision-tree" analysis, which is related in basic concept to that of Figure 8, is elaborated in W. K. M. Brauers, *Systems Analysis, Planning and Decision Models* (Amsterdam: Elsevier, 1976), pp. 13-22.
4. In practice, the budgetary decisions of governments relating to national security expenditure in any one year frequently bear little relationship to perceptions of the probability of long-term pressures or threats. Short-term political considerations, the state of the economy, the competing demands of other categories of government expenditure, etc. frequently override simple national security considerations. However, this does not undermine seriously the discussion relating to Figure 8. Whatever reasons are used to determine the levels of the national security budget, the practical effect, in terms of options retained or foreclosed, remains the same and can be illustrated by this analysis.

5. The basic inefficiency and greatly increased costs that are associated with rapid force expansion are not effectively portrayed in Figure 8. For instance, it would appear that in procuring structure 25, it would be less costly to move through financial level 3 at DP III, rather than financial level 2. However, in reality, the rapid force expansion required from financial level 3 at DP III to achieve structure 25 by year 15 would imply the adoption of programme structures that are less cost-effective and, in total structural terms, more expensive than those that would be procured by passage through financial level 2 at DP III.
6. The varying surge capacities of alternative force structure concepts are discussed at some length in Chapter 9.
7. The processes of deriving these generalized alternative structures were described earlier in this appendix.
8. The term "project" is used here in a sense that is almost synonymous with the generally used term "defence system". The programme/project relationship is illustrated clearly in Figure 9.
9. See K. J. Foley, " A Methodological Prescription for Examining the Question of Changing the Organizational Structure of the Australian Defence Force: A Systems Approach" (unpublished Ph.D. thesis, Department of International Relations, Australian National University, Canberra, 1972), p. 235.
10. The FYDP is a statement of the major equipment and other priorities for the forthcoming five-year period. Its structure permits the sequence of annual expenditure to be phased over the five-year period so as to reduce the severity of budgetary peaks and troughs. See this elaborated in W. L. Morrison, "The Role of the Minister in the Making of Australian Defence Policy since the Reorganisation of the Department of Defence", in *The Defence of Australia: Fundamental New Aspects*, ed. Robert O'Neill (Canberra: Strategic and Defence Studies Centre, Australian National University, 1977), p. 87.
11. This category might include the procurement of final equipment items for long lead-time heavy equipments already delivered or close to delivery (e.g. weapons systems for already procured aircraft, ships, etc.) or it might include the procurement of additional equipment to complete the construction of effective units (e.g. the procurement of additional fire units to complete a SAM battery or the procurement of additional aircraft to offset an unusually high wastage rate, etc.).
12. It is re-emphasized at this point that it would be desirable for the organization that performs the long-range planning function to be composed of civilian analysts and a mix of military personnel from all three services. As a consequence, there would be ample scope for the direct expression of service views at every level of the planning structure.
13. The FYRP is the system by which the FYDP is updated. Each year, a programme for the pending twelve-month period is taken from the FYDP for implementation and a new year's programme is added at the other end, for tentative implementation five years hence. For details, see D. H. Eltringham, "Defence Procurement in Australia", *Defence Force Journal*, no. 4 (May-June 1977): 34.
14. The government may judge that, because of broader intelligence requirements, strategic assessments need to be produced more frequently than the LRP five-year cycle provides. If this is the case, the ideal timing of the strategic assessments would be at 1, 1¼ or 2½ yearly intervals. Phasing at these periods would ensure that a new or revised strategic assessment would always be available at the commencement of the planning cycle.
15. In practice, by the latter half of year 8 and during the course of year 9, it would be possible for status reports to be made available detailing developing trends

in the LRP. These could be expected to provide sufficient information to facilitate meaningful but tentative planning.
16. In a figurative sense, it could be said that, the current system "rolls" like a "pentagonal cylinder". By contrast, the type of planning system described in this appendix would be prised up like a "flat slab of concrete" and dropped down again, its own width away, every five years.
17. This would be derived from the detailed description of the alternative structure that is adopted to form the basis of the LRP.

Select Bibliography

Government Publications

Andrén, Nils, Bergquist, Mats, and Hellman, Sven, *The International Development — Prospects Towards the 1990s* (Stockholm: Secretariat for National Security Policy and Long-range Defence Planning, Ministry of Defence, 1974).
Agranat Commission of Inquiry into Yom Kippur War, Partial Report (Israel Government Press Office, 2 April 1974).
Australian Bureau of Statistics, *Official Yearbook of Australia 1974* (Canberra: Australian Government Publishing Service, 1975).
Australian Defence, a White Paper presented to Parliament by the Minister for Defence, the Hon. D. J. Killen, November 1976 (Canberra: Australian Government Publishing Service, 1976).
The Australian Army, Report from the Senate Standing Committee on Foreign Affairs and Defence (Canberra: Australian Government Publishing Service, 1974).
Bergquist, Mats, *War and Surrogate War* (Stockholm: Secretariat for National Security Policy and Long-range Defence Planning, Ministry of Defence, 1976).
Brodin, Katarina, *Surprise Attack — Problems and Issues* (Stockholm: Secretariat for National Security Policy and Long-range Defence Planning, Ministry of Defence, 1975).
Civil Emergency Planning in Norway (Oslo: Directorate of Civil Defence and Emergency Planning, 1974).
Committee of Inquiry into the Citizen Military Forces Report (Millar Report), (Canberra: Australian Government Publishing Service, 1974).
Commonwealth Directorate of Civil Defence, *Australian Civil Defence Handbook: General Information* (Canberra: Australian Government Publishing Service, 1972).
Commonwealth of Australia, *Parliamentary Debates. Senate Standing Committee on Foreign Affairs and Defence, Reference: The Australian Army 1973-74*, Official Hansard Report (Canberra: Australian Government Publishing Service, 1974).
Department of Defence, *Defence Report 1965* (Canberra: Commonwealth Government Publishing Service, 1965).
―――――, *Defence Report 1967* (Canberra: Commonwealth Government Publishing Service, 1967).
―――――, *Defence Report 1968* (Canberra: Commonwealth Government Publishing Service, 1968).
―――――, *Defence Report 1970* (Canberra: Commonwealth Government Publishing Service, 1970).
―――――, *Defence Report 1975* (Canberra: Australian Government Publishing Service, 1975).
―――――, *Defence Report 1976* (Canberra: Australian Government Publishing Service, 1976).

—————, *Defence Report 1978* (Canberra: Australian Government Publishing Service, 1978).

—————, *The FYRP System New Major Equipment Component* (Canberra, June 1975).

Ek, Kurt, *Civil Defence to Protect and Save Lives* (Stockholm: Swedish Civil Defence Administration, 1970).

Federal Republic of Germany. Force Structure Commission, *The Force Structure in the Federal Republic of Germany: Analysis and Options* (Bonn: Force Structure Commission, in concurrence with the Federal Government, 1972-73).

Franzén, Göran, *The Role of Research in Swedish Defence Planning* (Stockholm: Swedish National Defence Research Institute, Department 1, Planning and Operations Research, n.d.).

Hellman, Sven, *On the Use and Usefulness of International Strategic Studies* (Stockholm: Secretariat for National Security Policy and Long-range Defence Planning, Ministry of Defence, 1975).

Industrial Support for Defence Needs and Allied Matters, Interim Report of the Joint (Parliamentary) Committee on Foreign Affairs and Defence (Canberra: Parliament of Australia, June 1977).

Industries Assistance Commission, *Aerospace Industry* (Canberra: Australian Government Publishing Service, 1975).

Policies for Development of Manufacturing Industry (Jackson Committee Report), Green Paper (Canberra: Australian Government Publishing Service, 1975), vol. 1.

Population and Australia: A Demographic Analysis and Projection (Borrie Report), (Canberra: Australian Government Publishing Service, 1975).

Report on Use of the Army Reserve (Canberra: Government Members Foreign Affairs and Defence Committee, 1977).

Roberts, Adam, *Total Defence and Civil Resistance: Problems of Sweden's Security Policy* (Stockholm: The Research Institute of Swedish National Defence, 1972).

Royal Commission on Australian Government Administration Report (Coombs Report), (Canberra: Australian Government Publishing Service, 1976).

Schwarz, Brita, *Some Conceptual Problems in Long-range Planning* (Stockholm: Secretariat for National Security Policy and Long-range Defence Planning, Ministry of Defence, 1976).

Shelters in Norway (Oslo: Directorate for Civil Defence and Emergency Planning, 1975).

Sköld, Major-General Nils, *Defence Policy for the 1970s and 80s* (Stockholm: Secretariat for National Security Policy and Long-range Defence Planning, Ministry of Defence, 1974).

Sweden. Ministry of Defence, *The Defence Planning System — Summary of the New Planning, Programming and Budgeting System* (Stockholm, 1970), Publication 1/1970.

—————, *The Defence Planning System — The Execution Process* (Stockholm, 1970), Publication 2/1970.

—————, *The Defence Planning System — Planning and Planning Documents* (Stockholm, 1970), Publication 3/1970.

—————, *The Defence Planning System — The Goal-setting Procedure* (Stockholm, 1970), Publication 4/1970.

Tange, Sir Arthur, *Australian Defence: Report on the Reorganization of the Defence Group of Departments*, presented to the Minister for Defence, November 1973.

Third Report of the Royal Commission on Intelligence and Security: Abridged Findings and Recommendations (April 1977, tabled in the House of Representatives by the Prime Minister, Mr Fraser, on 5 May 1977).

United States. House of Representatives. House Armed Services Committee, *Reserve*

Authorization Hearings Before Subcommittee Two, House Armed Services Committee, 14 July 1973.
United States. House of Representatives. Committee on Appropriations, Subcommittee of the Committee on Appropriations, *Department of Defense Appropriations for 1977*, Part 1, February 1976.
―――――, *Department of Defense Appropriations for 1977*, Part 5, March 1976.
United States. Senate. Committee on Armed Services, *Disapprove Construction Projects on the Island of Diego Garcia*, June 1975.
―――――, *Fiscal Year 1977 Authorization for Military Procurement, Research and Development, and Active Duty, Selected Reserve and Civilian Personnel Strengths*, Part 2, February 1976.
United States. Senate. Committee on Armed Services, Subcommittee on Manpower and Personnel, *Fiscal Year 1977 Authorization for Military Procurement, Research and Development, and Active Duty, Selected Reserve and Civilian Personnal Strengths*, Part 7, March 1976.
United States. Senate. Committee on Armed Services, Subcommittee on Research and Development, *Fiscal Year 1977 Authorization for Military Procurement, Research and Development, and Active Duty, Selected Reserve and Civilian Personnel Strengths*, Part 4, February 1976.
―――――, *Fiscal Year 1977 Authorization for Military Procurement, Research and Development, and Active Duty, Selected Reserve and Civilian Personnel Strengths*, Part 5, December 1975.
―――――, *Fiscal Year 1977 Authorization for Military Procurement, Research and Development, and Active Duty, Selected Reserve and Civilian Personnel Strengths*, Part 6, February 1976.
―――――, *Fiscal Year 1977 Authorization for Military Procurement, Research and Development, and Active Duty, Selected Reserve and Civilian Personnel Strengths*, Part 11, March 1976.
―――――, *Fiscal Year 1977 Authorization for Military Procurement, Research and Development, and Active Duty, Selected Reserve and Civilian Personnel Strengths*, Part 12, April 1976.
United States. Senate. Committee on Armed Services, Subcommittee on Tactical Air Power, *Fiscal Year 1977 Authorization for Military Procurement, Research and Development, and Active Duty, Selected Reserve and Civilian Personnel Strengths*, Part 9, March 1976.
―――――, *Fiscal Year 1977 Authorization for Military Procurement, Research and Development, and Active Duty, Selected Reserve and Civilian Personnel Strengths*, Part 10, March 1976.

Books and Monographs

Albinski, Henry S., *Politics and Foreign Policy in Australia: The Impact of Vietnam and Conscription* (Durham, N.C.: Duke University Press, 1970).
Allison, Graham T., *Essence of Decision: Explaining the Nuclear Missile Crisis* (Boston: Little, Brown & Co., 1971).
Babbage, R. E., Ball, D. J., Langtry, J. O., and O'Neill, R. J., *The Future Operational Requirement and Officer Development* (Canberra: Strategic and Defence Studies Centre, Australian National University, 1977).
Ball, Desmond, ed., *The Future of Tactical Airpower in the Defence of Australia* (Canberra: Strategic and Defence Studies Centre, Australian National University, 1977).

Beaufre, André, *Strategy for Tomorrow* (London: Macdonald & Jane's, 1974).
Beaumont, Roger A., *Military Elites* (London: Robert Hale, 1976).
Bellany, Ian, *Australia in the Nuclear Age: National Defence and National Development* (Sydney: Sydney University Press, 1972).
Binkin, Martin, *US Reserve Forces: The Problem of the Weekend Warrior* (Washington, DC: Brookings Institution, 1974).
Birman, J., ed., *Australia's Defence* (Perth: Extension Service, University of Western Australia, 1976).
Boserup, Anders, and Mack, Andrew, *War Without Weapons: Non-violence in National Defence* (London: Frances Pinter, 1974).
Brown, Leslie H., *American Security Policy in Asia* (London: International Institute for Strategic Studies, 1977), Adelphi Paper 132.
Brown, William M., *Limiting Damage from Nuclear War* (Santa Monica: Rand Corporation, 1969), RM-6043-PR.
Burt, Richard, *New Weapons Technologies: Debate and Directions* (London: International Institute for Strategic Studies, 1977), Adelphi Paper 126.
Butlin, S. J., *War Economy 1939-42* (Canberra: Australian War Memorial, 1955).
Canby, Steven L., *The Alliance and Europe, Part IV: Military Doctrine and Technology* (London: International Institute for Strategic Studies, 1975), Adelphi Paper 109.
Clark, Claire, ed., *Australian Foreign Policy: Towards a Reassessment* (Melbourne: Cassell, 1973).
The Defence Forces of Switzerland (Tavistock, U.K.: Army Quarterly and Defence Journal, 1974); supplementary booklet.
Dickson, Paul, *The Electronic Battlefield* (Ontario: Fitzhenry & Whiteside, 1976).
Digby, James F., *Precision-guided Munitions: Capabilities and Consequences* (Santa Monica: Rand Corporation, 1974), P-5257.
————, *Precision-guided Weapons* (Santa Monica: Rand Corporation, 1975), P-5353.
————, *Precision-guided Weapons: New Chances to Deal with Old Dangers* (Santa Monica: Rand Corporation, 1975), P-5384.
————, *Precision Weapons: Lowering the Risks with Aimed Shots and Aimed Tactics* (Santa Monica: Rand Corporation, 1975), P-5495.
Dorfer, Ingemar, *System 37 Viggen — Arms, Technology and the Domestication of Glory* (Oslo: Universitetsforlaget, 1973).
Douglas-Home, C., *Britain's Reserve Forces* (London: Royal United Services Institute, 1971).
Dudzinsky, S. J., jun., and Digby, James, *Qualitative Constraints on Conventional Armaments: An Emerging Issue* (Santa Monica: Rand Corporation, 1976), R-1957.
Elliott-Bateman, Michael, *Defeat in the East: The Mark of Mao Tse-tung on War* (London: Oxford University Press, 1967).
Emy, H. V., *Public Policy: Problems and Paradoxes* (Melbourne: Macmillan, 1976).
Feigl, H., *The Impact of New Maritime Technologies* (London: International Institute for Strategic Studies, 1976), Adelphi Paper 122.
Forward, Roy, and Reece, Bob, eds, *Conscription in Australia* (St Lucia: University of Queensland Press, 1968).
Foster, James L., *The Future of Conventional Arms Control* (Santa Monica: Rand Corporation, 1975), P-5489.
Gelb, Norman, *Enemy in the Shadows: The World of Spies and Spying* (London: William Luscombe, 1976).
Gelber, H. G., *The Australian-American Alliance: Costs and Benefits* (Ringwood, Vic.: Penguin, 1968).
————, ed., *Problems of Australian Defence* (Melbourne: Oxford University Press, 1970).

———, ed., *The Strategic Nuclear Balance 1975*, Proceedings of a Conference organized by the Strategic and Defence Studies Centre, Australian National University, June 1975 (Hobart: Department of Political Science, University of Tasmania, 1976).

Graham, W. B., *A Look to the Future* (Santa Monica: Rand Corporation, 1974), P-5251; examines new developments in military technologies.

Grant, Bruce, *The Crisis of Loyalty: A Study of Australian Foreign Policy* (Sydney: Angus & Robertson, in association with Australian Institute of International Affairs, 1972).

Greenwood, Ted, Rathjens, George W., and Ruina, Jack, *Nuclear Power and Weapons Proliferation* (London: International Institute for Strategic Studies, 1976), Adelphi Paper 130.

Häckel, Erwin, *Military Manpower and Political Purpose* (London: International Institute for Strategic Studies, 1970), Adelphi Paper 72.

Halperin, Morton H., *National Security Policy-making* (Lexington; Mass.: Lexington Books, 1975).

Hazlehurst, Cameron, and Nethercote, J. R., eds, *Reforming Australian Government: The Coombs Report and Beyond* (Canberra: Royal Institute of Public Administration (A.C.T.), in association with Australian National University Press, 1977).

Hunt, Kenneth, *The Alliance and Europe, Part II: Defence with Fewer Men* (London: International Institute for Strategic Studies, 1973), Adelphi Paper 98.

Janowitz, Morris, *The Professional Soldier: A Social and Political Portrait* (Glencoe, Ill.: Free Press of Glencoe, 1960).

Kemp, Geoffrey, *Nuclear Forces for Medium Powers* (London: International Institute for Strategic Studies, 1974), Adelphi Papers 106 and 107, pts 1-3.

———, Pfaltzgraff, Robert L., jun., Ra'anan, Uri, eds, *The Other Arms Race: New Technologies and Non-Nuclear Conflict* (Lexington, Mass.: Lexington Books, 1975).

Klass, P. J., *Secret Sentries in Space* (New York: Random House, 1971).

Komer, R. W., *Bureaucracy Does Its Thing: Institutional Constraints on US-GVN Performance in Vietnam* (Santa Monica: Rand Corporaton, 1973), R-967-ARPA.

Liddell Hart, B. H., *Strategy: The Indirect Approach* (London: Faber & Faber, 1967).

Long, Gavin, *The Six Years War: A Concise History of Australia in the 1939-45 War* (Canberra: Australian War Memorial and Australian Government Publishing Service, 1973).

———, *To Benghazi* (Canberra: Australian War Memorial, 1952).

McGaurr, Darcy, *Conscription and Australian Military Capability* (Canberra: Strategic and Defence Studies Centre, Australian National University, 1971).

Mendershausen, Horst, *Territorial Defense in NATO and Non-NATO Europe* (Santa Monica: Rand Corporation, 1973), R-1184.

Millar, T. B., *Australia's Defence* (Melbourne: Melbourne University Press, 2nd edn, 1969).

O'Neill, Robert, ed., *The Defence of Australia: Fundamental New Aspects* (Canberra: Strategic and Defence Studies Centre, Australian National University, 1977).

———, ed., *The Strategic Nuclear Balance: An Australian Perspective* (Canberra: Strategic and Defence Studies Centre, Australian National University, 1975).

Pauker, G. J., Canby, S., Ross Johnson, A., and Quandt, W. B., *In Search of Self-reliance: U.S. Security Assistance to the Third World Under the Nixon Doctrine* (Santa Monica: Rand Corporation, June 1973), R-1092-ARPA.

Paul, R. A., *American Military Commitments Abroad* (New Brunswick, N.J.: Rutgers University Press, 1973).

Pressman, J. L., and Wildavsky, A. B., *Implementation: How Great Expectations in Washington are Dashed in Oakland; or, Why It's Amazing that Federal Programs*

Work at All, This Being a Saga of the Economic Development Administration as Told by Two Sympathetic Observers Who Seek to Build Morals on a Foundation of Ruined Hopes (Berkeley, Calif.: University of California Press, 1973).
Rapoport, Anatol, *Strategy and Conscience* (New York: Schocken Books, 1969).
Roberts, Adam, ed., *Civilian Resistance as a National Defence* (Harmondsworth: Penguin, 1969).
———, *Nations in Arms: The Theory and Practice of Territorial Defence* (London: Chatto & Windus, for International Institute for Strategic Studies, 1976).
Rowen, Henry, *Implications of Technologies of Precision for Japanese Security* (Santa Monica: Rand Corporation, Seminar on Arms Control and Foreign Policy, July 1975), Discussion Paper 52.
Sackman, H., *Toward More Effective Use of Expert Opinion: Preliminary Investigation of Participatory Polling for Long-range Planning* (Santa Monica: Rand Corporation, 1976), P-5570.
Stockfisch, J. A., *Models, Data and War: A Critique of the Study of Conventional Forces* (Santa Monica: Rand Corporation, March 1975), R-1526-PR.
Taber, Robert, *The War of the Flea: A Study of Guerilla Warfare Theory and Practice* (London: Paladin, 1970).
Teichmann, Max, ed., *New Directions in Australian Foreign Policy* (Ringwood, Vic.: Penguin, 1969).
United Service Institution of the Australian Capital Territory, *An Australian Nuclear Weapons Capability* (Canberra, 1975); published reports of syndicate deliberations on this subject.
———, *The Defence Capability of Australian Industry* (Canberra, 1977).
———, *The United States/Australia Alliance — Problems and Prospects*, Syndicate Research Reports (Canberra, 1976).
White, William D., *U.S. Tactical Air Power: Missions Forces and Costs* (Washington, DC: Brookings Institution, 1974).
Wohlstetter, Roberta, *Pearl Harbor: Warning and Decision* (Stanford, Calif.: Stanford University Press, 1962).

Unpublished Papers and Theses

Australian Parliamentary Library. Defence, Science and Technology Group, "The Purchase of the American FFG-7 Frigate in the Context of Future Equipment Policy for the Royal Australian Navy" (Canberra, 1976).
Babbage, Ross E., "A Strategy for the Continental Defence of Australia" (M.Ec. thesis, University of Sydney, 1974).
Ball, Desmond J., "The Politics of Australian Defence Decision-making" (Canberra: Strategic and Defence Studies Centre, Australian National University, 1977).
———, "The Politics of Australian Defence Decision-making — Ministerial Assistance and Defence Decision-making" (Canberra: Strategic and Defence Studies Centre, Australian National University, 1977).
———, "the Politics of Defence Decision-making in Australia — The Mirage Replacement" (Canberra: Strategic and Defence Studies Centre, Australian National University, 1975).
———, "The Politics of Defence Decision-making in Australia — The Reorganization of the Defence Group of Departments" (Canberra: Strategic and Defence Studies Centre, Australian National University, 1975).
———, "Some Notes on the Decision-making Process in the Australian Defence

Establishment" (Canberra: Strategic and Defence Studies Centre, Australian National University, 1975).
Ben-Zvi, A., "Surprise Attacks: Theoretical Aspects" (paper delivered to Conference on Strategic Issues, Leonard Davis Institute for International Relations, Hebrew University of Jerusalem, 7-9 April 1975).
Foley, K. J., "A Methodological Prescription for Examining the Question of Changing the Organizational Structure of the Australian Defence Force: A Systems Approach" (Ph.D. thesis, Department of International Relations, Australian National University, Canberra, 1972).
Indyk, Martin, "Detente and the Politics of Patronage: The October Middle East War Revisited" (Canberra: Department of International Relations, Australian National University, 1976).
McGaurr, A. D., "Defence Procurement — In Search of Optimality" (paper delivered to Conference on Armed Forces and Australian Society, Royal Military College, Duntroon, Canberra, 20-22 May 1977).
Mench, Paul, "Education and Officers: Changing Concepts of Officer Education" (paper delivered to Conference on Armed Forces and Australian Society, Royal Military College, Duntroon, Canberra, 20-22 May 1977).
Muggleton, T. P., "An Evaluation of the Analytical Infra-structure for Force Structure Decision-making in the Australian Defence Department" (B.A. (Hons) thesis, Department of Economics, Faculty of Military Studies, University of New South Wales, Royal Military College, Duntroon, 1976).
O'Neill, Robert, "Changes Required in the International Environment for the Development of Extreme Threats to Australia" (paper prepared for seminar entitled "The Potential for Extreme Threats in the International Environment and Australia's Response Options", held by Strategic and Defence Studies Centre, Australian National University, Canberra, 3-4 March 1977).
_____, "Future Goals for Australian Defence Policy" (Canberra: Strategic and Defence Studies Centre, Australian National University, 1976).
_____, "The Influence of Recent Developments in Conventional Weapons Technology on Strategic and Tactical Doctrine: Consequences for Australia" (paper presented to United Service Institution of Australian Capital Territory, Canberra, 5 May 1976).
Rosen, S. J., "Military Geography and Military Balance in the Arab-Israel Conflict" (seminar paper presented at Strategic and Defence Studies Centre, Australian National University, Canberra, 22 April 1976).
Schaetzel, S. S., "The Coastal Protection Problem" (paper presented at "Australian Symposium on Light Aircraft", University of New South Wales, 2-3 November 1976).
Smith, Admiral Sir Victor, "Military and Civilian Inputs into Defence Policy" (paper delivered to Conference on Armed Forces and Australian Society, Royal Military College, Duntroon, Canberra, 20-22 May 1977).
Smith, W. H., "The Determinants of Defence Policy" (paper delivered to Conference on Armed Forces and Australian Society, Royal Military College, Duntroon, Canberra, 20-22 May 1977)
Stretton, Major-General A. B., "The Role of the Natural Disasters Organization" (paper delivered to 1977 Industrial Mobilization Course, Mount Macedon, Vic., 24 May 1977).
Townsend, Air Vice-Marshal W. E., "Overseas Developments in Civil Defence" (paper presented to National Emergency Services College, Mount Macedon, Vic., 24 May 1977).

Index

Acheson, Dean, perimeter strategy of, 9, 19 n.16
adaptability and flexibility in Australian security planning. *See* planning, Australian security
Aegis system, American, 32
aerospace industry, Industries Assistance Commission's inquiry into, 79. *See also* industry
aircraft: airborne aircraft carrier concept, 251; AWACS, 30, 40, 235-36, 238, 242, 244, 250; Canberra bomber (B-20), 221-22; Caribou (DHC-4), 222; F-15, 127; F-111, 20 n.28, 160, 222-23; fighters and fighter-bombers, 28, 30, 40, 251; HIMAT, 251; helicopters, 218, 222, 239; Hercules (C-130), 222; Mirage III, 127, 222; multi-purpose, 25; oblique wing, 251; Orion (P-3), 20 n.28; role in warfare, 29; Skyhawk (A-4), 219; tactics of combat aircraft, 27-28; tanker, 21 n.28, 160; Tracker (S-2), 219-20; transport, 25, 250; V/STOL, 25, 32, 239, 251; Winjeel (CA-25), 222; x-wing, 251. *See also* airships; close air support; interdiction strike; propulsion systems; remotely piloted vehicles; surveillance
aircraft carriers, 29, 30, 42, 130, 220. See also *Kiev*
air defence systems. *See* artillery; missiles
airships, 239, 250
Albinski, Henry, 112
allies: as intelligence partners, 90-92; role in Australian security policy, xix, 4-5, 209-10, 222. *See also* ANZUS; United States

Allison, Graham T., 128
America. *See* United States
Antarctic, 34
anti-ballistic missile systems (ABMs). *See* missiles
anti-ship missiles. *See* missiles; ships, vulnerability of
anti-submarine warfare, 21 n.29, 220, 223, 233, 236-39, 244-46. *See also* countermeasures; night vision systems; radar; sensors; sensor weapons; sonar systems; surveillance; target acquisition
anti-tank weapons. *See* missiles; warheads
ANZUS: Australian perceptions of, 3; global strategic implications of, 14-17; regional co-operation under, xx; text of Treaty, 8-9; value of, 8-17, 18 n.9, 210, 224 n.2. *See also* allies; United States
armour, vehicle: Chobham "special", 35, 253; costs of special, 253; flexible, 259 n.71; plating, 34-35; spaced, 35. *See also* tanks
armoured personnel carriers (APCs), 34, 218. *See also* mechanized infantry combat vehicles (MICVs); tanks
arms control, 119, 120, 174
arms-sales policy, President Carter's, 119
army, 81, 85-87, 92-93, 129-30, 184-85, 195, 217-18, 223; aviation element of, 217-18; size needed to meet particular threats, 87, 218. *See also* Citizen Military Forces; Defence Force
Army In-flight Data Transmission System (AIDATS), 241

Army Reserve. *See* Citizen Military Forces
artillery: anti-aircraft, 27, 34, 218; guns, 28, 34, 65, 218; rockets, 28. *See also* Copperhead; missiles
Atlantic Ocean, 34, 224 n.2
attacks, limited, 66-68. *See also* threats
attrition of military forces: active, 26, 33, 36, 69, 164; passive, 27, 29, 33, 36, 164
Australia: conditions in north of, 67-69; mapping and charting of, 105 n.53
Australians: attitudes to conscription of, 113-16, 166, 195-97, 206-7; attitudes to defence spending of, 116-17, 124 n.28, 124 n.29, 166; changing social attitudes of, 114, 197; fears of, 74 n.8; interest and support for defence by, 112-16, 123 n.23, 212; mass preparations for war by, 166; national will of, 61, 62, 177; perceptions of United States, 3-4; physical concentration of in urban centres, 167, 174; public debate on defence issues by, 113, 142-43; views on nuclear weapon option, 160; vulnerability to physical attack of, 60-71, 99, 174
Australia's Defence, White Paper on. *See* White Paper on Australia's Defence
AWACS. *See* aircraft

Ball, Desmond J., 42, 79, 117, 127, 128, 140, 142, 187
Battery Computer System (BCS), 246
Beaumont, Roger A., 129, 133
Bennett, Jeremy, 180 n.25
B-52 aircraft, ocean control missions by, 20 n.28
Binkin, Martin, 188
biological weapons, 44; threat to Australia from, 70
blockades, 64-66. *See also* threats
Bloodhound system, 130
bombs: glide, 25, 42, 243, 248; runway penetration, 35. *See also* precision-guided munitions; warheads
Booda, Larry, 245
Borrie Report, 111

Boyd, Robin, 4
Britain as an ally, xix, 5
budgets, defence: attitudes of Australians to, 116-17, 124 n.28, 124 n.29, 166; in other countries, 185, 187, 199-200; large size as a bureaucratic goal, 131; projections of as a planning tool, 276; proportion for capital equipment and facilities, 185-87, 200-201; proportion for manpower, 185-88, 200-201; size in Australia, 117-18, 120, 185, 217. *See also* costs
Bundy, McGeorge, 10
bureaucracies: career incentives in, 135, 139, 141-42; conservatism by military in, 129-30, 132-33, 212; encouraging adaptation in, 137-43, 278-79; external review of, 136, 139, 142, 151, 204, 212-13; implementation of programmes in, 134, 140; ministerial control of, 134-35, 138; problems of, 91, 125-46, 151, 212; resistance to change in, 46, 129-37, 142-43, 151, 162, 212, 223; secrecy in, 137, 142, 145 n.36. *See also* bureaucratic actors; Coombs Report
bureaucratic actors: alliances between, 127-28; competition between, 125-31; differing perceptions of goals by, 126-27, 129-31, 135, 209; studies as a ploy of, 133-34; sub-optimization by, 127, 130, 149; training of, 138, 141, 146 n.47. *See also* bureaucracies

Cabinet, federal, 86-87, 271
cadre units, potential in Australia. *See* Defence Force
camouflage. *See* stealth technologies and techniques
Canberra bomber (B-20). *See* aircraft
Canby, Steven, 200
Caribou aircraft (DHC-4). *See* aircraft
Carter, President, 119
chemical weapons, 44; threat to Australia from, 70. *See also* threats; warheads
Chief of the Defence Force Staff (CDFS), 77, 125

China, People's Republic of: as a threat, 8. *See also* threats
Chobham armour. *See* armour
Citizen Military Forces (CMF), 184-185, 217; combat readiness of, 185. *See also* Millar Report
civil defence, 173-77, 195; costs of shelters in, 175; dispersal of population in, 175; rescue element of, 176; state of network in Australia, 174-75, 182 n.39; suitability of part-time manpower in, 176, 201-2; warning systems in, 176
civilian resistance, 168-71, 195; historical use of, 169. *See also* deterrence
Clark Air Base, 21 n.28
close air support operations, 28, 34, 47 n.9, 49 n.39. *See also* aircraft
close-in weapons systems for naval vessels, 31-33. *See also* Phalanx
cluster weapons. *See* warheads
Cocos Island, 63
combined arms tactics, 34
Committee of Inquiry into the Citizen Military Forces. *See* Millar Report
communications, Command and Control (C^3): new demands on, 37, 40, 46, 92-94; new developments in, 24, 241, 243-47. *See also* Defence Force, command structure of; fibres, optical
communications intelligence (COMINT), 21 n.29, 246
concentration. *See* dispersal/concentration
Condor, 243
confrontation strategy, 61-63. *See also* threats
Congress, United States, 11. *See also* War Powers Resolution
conscription, 187, 194-98; attitudes of Australians to, 113-16, 166, 195-97, 206-7; costs of, 195-97; exemption from, 195-96, 207 n.30; military utility of, 196; National Service Training Scheme 1951-57, 195; reserved personnel in, 191; selective form of, 197-98; universal form of, 194-97; use in mobilization, 86-90. *See also* mobilization; personnel, part-time
Constitution as a constraint on security policy, 144 n.16

contingencies. *See* planning, Australian security: scenario selection in
conventional military systems, 162-65, 195, 198; costs of, 163, 185, 188-89, 201-3; vulnerability to adverse force ratios, 164-65. *See also* Defence Force; deterrence
Coombs, H.C., 135, 136
Coombs Report, 135-36, 138-39, 141. *See also* bureaucracies; bureaucratic actors
Copperhead, 230. *See also* precision-guided munitions
core force concept, 85-86, 102 n.33, 149-50. *See also* force expansion concepts
costs: of alternative force structures, 81, 279; of civil defence shelters, 175; of conventional military units, 163, 185, 188-89, 201-3; of economic defence measures, 173; of military equipments, 42-43; of nuclear weapons options, 159-60; of part-time units, 188-89, 198-99; of remotely piloted vehicles (RPVs), 252; of satellites, 176, 182 n.49; of selective conscription, 197; of "special" armour, 253; of universal conscription, 195-96. *See also* budgets, defence
countermeasures, 25, 229-30, 242; airborne systems, 28; counter, 31, 230; decoys, 48 n.22, 237-38, 257 n.37; ship-borne systems, 30-32. *See also* stealth technologies and techniques
cruise missiles. *See* missiles
Currie, Malcolm, 32, 45, 139, 179 n.15, 243-44, 246
Curtin, John, xix
Cyprus: NATO intelligence facilities on, 16; Turkish invasion of, 16

DARPA (United States Defence Advanced Research Projects Agency), 236. *See also* research and development
Darwin, 11-12. *See also* Australia, conditions in north of
decoys. *See* countermeasures
defence capacity: immediate response potential of, 150, 218; independent potential of, xx, xxi n.2, 5, 9, 53, 70, 94, 97-98, 149, 158, 203-4, 209-10, 217-24; limit-

ed size of, 70-71, 149-50, 217-24. *See also* Defence Force; mobilization
Defence Committee, 264. *See also* Department of Defence
Defence Force: command structure of, 92-94; defensive operations by, 65-69; limited capacity of, xx, xxi n.2, 12, 70, 87, 150, 217-24; overseas deployments of, xix-xx, 5, 12, 53, 76, 85, 184, 204; potential of cadre units in, 185, 199-204; regional offensive operations by, 63, 67-68, 104 n.44; requirements for adaptation of, 84-85. *See also* army; defence capacity; force structure options; mobilization; personnel, full-time; personnel, part-time; RAAF; RAN; training and education
defence infrastructure, 67-68, 117, 191-94; planning of, 173; vulnerability of, 25, 39-43, 45, 62, 221. *See also* industry; logistics concepts
defence preparation time, 86-89, 90, 103 n.40, 151, 185, 223, 270, 277, 278. *See also* force expansion concepts
De Gaulle, Charles, 160
Department of Defence: authority and decision-making processes in, 77-83, 125-31, 142, 149-50, 154, 289-90; bureaucratic inertia in, 134-37; manpower structure of, 193; re-organization of, 82-83, 93, 125, 141; Secretary of, 83, 125, 262. *See also* bureaucracies; Chief of the Defence Force Staff; defence capacity; Defence Committee; Defence Force; intelligence organizations; Minister for Defence; security planning
destroyers, 220. *See also* patrol frigates
deterrence: capacity of adapted conventional forces, 163, 202; capacity of civilian resistance, 170, 202; capacity of territorial defence, 166, 202; criteria for effectiveness of, 12, 101 n.29; as a general concept, 66, 70, 99, 117; as a goal in security planning, 83; potential of nuclear weapons, 159; by proxy, 9, 14; regional, 44-45, 58-59
Diego Garcia, 21 n.28
Digby, James, 42
diplomatic resources, 55-56, 58, 60-61, 70-71
dispersal/concentration: of forces, 29, 36-37, 39-42, 46, 70, 94-95, 161, 168, 175; of populations in civil defence, 175
disproportionate response, 62, 63, 89, 104 n.43. *See also* deterrence
Doppler principle, 234
Dudzinsky, S.J., 42

economic defence, 95, 171-73; costs of, 173; stockpiling for, 95, 172
economic measures, 56, 58-60, 62-66; applied by multinationals, 56-58. *See also* threats
education. *See* training and education
electronic countermeasures and counter-countermeasures (ECM and ECCM). *See* countermeasures
electronic intelligence (ELINT), 246
engines. *See* propulsion systems
experts in defence matters, 113, 123 n.23, 265-72, 273 n.6

Farrands, J.L., 256 n.23
fibres, optical, 243-44
fighter and fighter-bomber aircraft. *See* aircraft
Finland, 165, 167
Fleet Air Arm. *See* RAN
flexibility and adaptability in Australian security planning. *See* planning, Australian security
Foley, K.J., 81-82, 286
F-111 aircraft. *See* aircraft
force expansion concepts. *See* core force concept; defence capacity; Defence Force; defence preparation time; force-in-being concept; mobilization capacity; terminal force concept; warning time
force-in-being concept, 149-51. *See also* force expansion concepts
force structure options, 153, 158-78, 269, 275-79; component programmes in, 276, 284-86; evaluation of, 153-58, 177-78, 212, 275-86. *See also* civil defence; civilian resistance; conventional

military systems; economic defence; forward defence; nuclear weapons; planning, Australian security; psychological defence; territorial defence; total defence
Forrestal, James, 137
forward defence concept, xix-xx, 5, 7, 12, 53, 85, 149, 151, 158, 184, 203-4, 212, 222-23, 292. *See also* Defence Force, overseas deployments of
Fraser, Malcolm, 4
fuel-air explosives. *See* warheads

Galbraith, J.K., 213
gas turbines. *See* propulsion systems
Germany, West: Force Structure Commission in, 185, 187, 199-200; proportion of defence budget expended on capital equipment in, 185, 187
Gould, Gordon T., 235
Greville, P.J., 109
Guam, 6, 21, n.28
Guam Doctrine, 6-7, 9-13. *See also* United States
guerrilla warfare, 165
guidance systems. *See* navigation systems; sensors; sensor weapons

Häckel, Erwin, 192, 208 n.46
Halperin, Morton, 126, 129, 131, 134
harassments, 61-62, 66, 151. *See also* threats
Heilmeier, G.H., 23, 236-37, 244-45
helicopters. *See* aircraft
Hercules aircraft (C-130). *See* aircraft
Herzog, Chaim, 29
high-low (technology) mix, 43, 95
HIMAG vehicles. *See* tanks
Hope Report, Justice, 90
hovercraft. *See* surface-effect ships
Hunt, Kenneth, 199
hydrofoils, 231, 252

Indian Ocean, 20-21, 34
Indonesia: as a target for Australian attack, 12; as a threat to Australia, 12. *See also* Indonesian confrontation
Indonesian confrontation, 54
industry: contribution to self-reliance, 94-98, 172-73, 203-4, 210; South-East Asian competition to, 110; state of, 109-11, 120, 203; support capacity of, 94-98, 109-11, 203-4. *See also* Aerospace industry; Jackson Committee Report; mobilization capacity
input-output analysis. *See* planning, Australian security
Integrated Battlefield Control System (ICBS), 247
intelligence organizations, 78, 86, 90-92; collection capacity of, 90-91; Joint Intelligence Organization, 78; over-the-horizon radar potential for, 235; warning system of, 176, 278. *See also* Australia, mapping and charting; communications intelligence (COMINT); electronic intelligence (ELINT); Hope Report; surveillance; United States
intercontinental ballistic missiles. *See* missiles
interdiction strike, 28, 67. *See also* aircraft
invasion, 68-69. *See also* threats

Jackson Committee Report 110, 114, 116. *See also* industry
jamming. *See* countermeasures
Japan, Sea of, 34
joint tactical information distribution system (JTIDS), 244

KC-135, 21 n.28. *See also* aircraft
Kiev, 32
Killen, D.J. 152. *See also* Department of Defence; Minister for Defence
Klass, Philip J., 235
Komer, R.W., 131-32, 136
Korean War, 54, 60

Laird, Melvin, 188
laser: designation of targets by, 226, 230, 240; gyros, 60, 228; high energy, 25, 33, 249-50
latent forces. *See* manpower, defence; personnel, part-time
logistics concepts, 38-39, 46

McGaurr, Darcy, 127, 130, 152
McLennan, Ian, 110
Malaysia, RAAF presence in, 222
manpower, defence: current struc-

ture of, 184, 191-94, 217-18; new goals for, 187-88; planning of, 85-90, 111-12, 184-204; weaknesses of current structure, 85-90, 150-51, 184-88, 192-94, 204, 218. *See also* conscription; personnel, full-time; personnel, part-time; training and education
maps and charts. *See* Australia
maritime surveillance. *See* surveillance
mass media: coverage of defence issues, 113, 142; coverage of international events, 112-13; survival of in crisis situations, 177
mechanized infantry combat vehicles (MICVs), 34. *See also* armoured personnel carriers (APCs); tanks
Mediansky, F.A., 78
Mendershausen, Horst, 189-90
Middle East War, October 1973, 29, 34
militarism, 144 n.13
Millar, T.B., 11, 18 n.9, 212. *See also* Millar Report
Millar Report, 184-85. *See also* Citizen Military Forces
mines and counter-mine warfare, 65, 220-21, 232, 249. *See also* sensor weapons
Minister for Defence, 125, 138, 152, 271; advisers to, 138. *See also* Killen, D.J., Morrison, W.L., bureaucracies, ministerial control of
Mirage III aircraft. *See* aircraft
missiles: Aegis, 32; air-to-ground, 226; anti-ballistic systems (ABMs), 40; anti-radiation, 48 n.21, 227; anti-ship, 30-33, 161; anti-tank, 34-35, 226, 230, 248; Bloodhound, 130; Condor, 243; cruise (long-range), 25, 40, 49 n.41, 50 n.42, 160-61, 176, 228, 231, 247; cruise (short/medium-range), 161; ground-to-air, 25, 27-28, 34, 130, 230; intercontinental ballistic (ICBMs), 40, 160, 176; medium-range ballistic (MRBMs), 130; sea-to-air, 30-33; Sea Wolf, 32-33; SS-N-12, 32; submarine-launched ballistic (SLBMs), 160, 176. *See also* bombs; navigation systems; propulsion systems; sensors; sensor weapons; warheads

mobilization (surge) capacity, 85-90, 102 n.34, 150-51, 184-85, 187-88, 199-204, 218, 223; industry's role in, 96-98, 203-4, 210, 279; structuring to improve, 89-90, 184-88, 199-204. *See also* force expansion concepts
modular concepts in military systems. *See* technological advance
Morrison, W.L., 77, 81-82
Muggleton, T.P., 79-80, 82
munitions. *See* warheads
Murphy, Daniel, 245, 257 n.37
Mutual assured destruction doctrine (MAD), 15. *See also* deterrence; nuclear war

National Service. *See* conscription
NATO, 224 n.2; facilities on Cyprus, 16
Naval Air Power and Tactical Air Weapons System Study (NAP/TAWS), 80, 82. *See also* RAN
navigation systems, 225; distance-measuring equipment (DME), 229; inertial, 228; laser gyros, 160, 228; Loran, 229; magnetic contour-matching (MAGCOM), 160; microwave radiometric (MICRAD), 160, 228; Navstar global positioning satellite system, 160, 229; Omega, 229; scene-matching area correlation (SMEAC), 228; Tacan, 229; terrain contour-matching (TERCOM), 160, 228; Vor, 229. *See also* sensors
Navstar global positioning satellite system. *See* navigation systems
New Zealand, 8. *See also* ANZUS
night vision systems, 38, 226-27, 240-41. *See also* sensors, infrared; surveillance
Nixon, Richard M., 6, 9
North West Cape, 15
Norton Sound, USS, 32
nuclear war: Australia as a potential target in, 22 n.29; Australian vulnerability in, 69-70, 161, 174; implications for Australia of, 69-70; probability of, 15. *See also* deterrence; mutual assured destruction (MAD) doctrine
nuclear weapons, 44; acquisition of

as an Australian strategic option, 159-61; costs of, 159, 160; limited battlefield utility of, 159-61. *See also* deterrence; missiles
Nurrungar space support facility, 15

oil crisis, 1973-74, 54
Omega. *See* navigation systems
O'Neill, Robert, 45, 54, 66, 78, 89, 84, 93
optical fibres. *See* fibres, optical
Orion (P-3). *See* aircraft
Osborne, John, 137

Pacific Ocean, 20-21, 224 n.2
Papua New Guinea: contingencies in requiring the presence of Australian forces, xix n.2; defence and security forces of, xxi n.2
participatory polling, 272
Patel, Kumar, 259 n.65
patrol boats, 65, 220-21
patrol frigates (FFG-7), 21 n.29
Pave Tack, 240
personnel, full-time: recruitment of, 89-90, 111-12, 115-16, 121, 187-88. *See also* conscription; manpower; training and education
personnel, part-time: battlefield potential of, 189-90; limits to employment of, 191; mobilization capacity of, 191; pay for, 188-89, 198-99; rationale for, 188-204; recruitment of, 112. *See also* Citizen Military Forces; civil defence; conscription; manpower; territorial defence
Phalanx, 32-33
Pickering, William H., 29
Pine Gap, space support facility, 15
planning, Australian security: communicating priorities to community, 93, 177; criteria for independence in, 152-54, 260, 262, 275; current processes of, xxi n.2, 77-83, 149-51, 260, 287-88, 292; economies of scale in, 150, 286; flexibility and adaptability in, 53, 211, 270, 276-80; goals of, 83-84, 99, 101 n.28, 149, 151-55; independent capacity in, 260; industry's role in, 96-98, 171-73, 210; input-output analysis in, 81-82, 155, 261, 279-86, 291; long-term, 155, 157, 212, 275-92; replacement complex in, 130; scenario selection in, 152-53, 261-72; self-sufficiency in, 13-14, 53, 77, 85, 91, 149, 177, 260; short-term, 286-91; "state of the art" rationale in, 150, 163, 187; towards an optimum model in, 154-57, 177-78, 212, 260-72, 275-92; uncertainty in, 9, 11-12, 53, 150-52, 262-72, 276-83, 290; utilization of civil facilities in, 210-11, 213 n.1, 213 n.2, 223. *See also* force expansion concepts; force structure options; strategic guidance and assessments
population. *See* Australians; Borrie Report
precision-guided munitions, 23, 36, 42-44, 161, 222, 225-31, 240. *See also* bombs, glide; Copperhead; countermeasures; mines; missiles; sensors, sensor weapons; torpedoes; warheads
pre-emptive strike, 30, 67-69. *See also* deterrence; surprise attack
Pressman, J.L., 140
propulsion systems, 24, 231-32; Brayton gas turbines, 231; ceramic components in, 231; integral rocket-ramjets, 33, 231; propellants, high density, 231; Stirling engine, 231; turbo/fan-jet, 231; Walter engine, 231
psychological defence, 177
public opinion. *See* Australians

RAAF, 81, 91-93, 127, 129, 130, 221-24; air defence capacity of, 222-23; presence in Malaysia of, 222; reserves in, 189-90, 198. *See also* Defence Force
radar: airborne, 241; ground-based, 241-42; over-the-horizon backscatter (OTH-B), 21 n.29, 38, 40, 176, 234-36, 238, 242; sanctuary (bistatic) concepts in, 235-36; ship-borne, 30, 32. *See also* aircraft, AWACS; Army In-flight Data Transmission System; countermeasures; stand-off target-acquisition system
raids, 25, 61-62, 87, 89, 103 n.37, 151; manpower requirements to

defend against, 87, 151. *See also* threats
RAN, 81, 92-93, 127, 129-30, 218-21, 223; convoying capacity of, 220; Fleet Air Arm in, 220; reserves in, 189-90. *See also* Defence Force; Naval Air Power and Tactical Air Weapons System Study (NAP/TAWS); ships
Rand Corporation, 165
Reed, Wilson, 247
regional powers as a potential threat. *See* threats
remotely emplaced battlefield sensor system (REMBASS), 241. *See also* sensors
remotely piloted vehicles (RPVs), 25, 37, 42, 65, 241-43, 248, 251-52; costs of, 252. *See also* sensor weapons
replacement complex. *See* planning, Australian security
research and development, 37, 278. *See also* DARPA; United States, defence science co-operation with
resource crises, likely level of U.S. assistance in, 13
Roberts, Adam, 167, 170, 190
rockets. *See* missiles; precision-guided munitions; propulsion systems
Royal Australian Air Force. *See* RAAF
Royal Australian Navy. *See* RAN
Rumsfeld, Donald, 20 n.25
Russia. *See* Soviet Union

satellites. *See* space systems
scenario selection. *See* planning, Australian security
Schaffer, Bernard, 117
Seaguard system, 237, 244. *See also* target acquisition
SEATO, 6
Sea Wolf system. *See* missiles
Second World War, 87, 98-99, 203
secrecy. *See* bureaucracies
self-sufficiency, economic, 56, 64, 171-72. *See also* economic defence; planning, Australian security
semi-submerged hull systems, 231, 252-53
sensors: infra-red, 38, 48 n.21, 227, 240-41, 245; remote, 38, 241. *See also* navigation systems; night vision systems; precision-guided munitions; radar; sensor weapons; sonar systems; space systems; surveillance; target acquisition
sensor weapons, 25, 248-49. *See also* mines; remotely piloted vehicles
ships, surface: hydrographic research, 221; landing, 130, 221; tug-area general ocean surveillance (T-AGOS), 237; vulnerability of, 29-34, 49 n.21. *See also* aircraft carriers; attrition, passive; destroyers; hydrofoils; *Norton Sound*; patrol boats; patrol frigates; propulsion systems; semi-submerged hull systems; submarines; surface-effect ships
simulation games in defence planning, 272, 284, 286
Siracusa, J.M., 3
Skodvin, Magne, 180 n.25
Skyhawk aircraft (A4). *See* aircraft
Smith, W.H., 112-13
sonar systems: air-delivered buoys, 238; Caesar programme, 237; hull-borne, 238-39; long-range passive seabed arrays, 21 n.29, 65, 237, 242, 244-45; moored surveillance system (MSS), 237; sonar surveillance system (SOSUS), 237; surveillance towed-array sensor system (SURTASS), 237; tactical towed-array sensor (TACTAS), 21 n.29, 239; towed arrays, general, 65; towed-array surveillance system (TASS), 237; tug-area general ocean surveillance (T-AGOS), 237. *See also* sensors; surveillance; target acquisition
Soviet Union, 8, 22 n.29, 224 n.2. *See also* threats
space systems, 15-16, 20 n.25, 40, 65, 233-34, 238, 250; costs of, 176, 192 n.49; high-altitude large optics (HALO) technology in, 182 n.48. *See also* sensors
SS-N-12. *See* missiles
stability, strategic, 15. *See also* deterrence
stand-off target-acquisition system (SOTAS), 241
"state of the art" rationale. *See* planning, Australian security

stealth technologies and techniques, 24, 37, 229-30, 242, 253; use in aircraft, cruise missile and RPV design, 40, 50 n.42, 251-52. *See also* countermeasures

stockpiling. *See* economic defence

strategic guidance and assessments, 76-85, 149-50, 153, 262-64, 288-89

strategic studies, study of in Australia, 123 n.23

Stretton, A.B., 175

submarine-launched ballistic missiles (SLBMs). *See* missiles

submarines, 30-31, 33-34, 220; new technology in, 239, 242, 253; vulnerability of, 33-34, 245. *See also* anti-submarine warfare; propulsion systems

surface-effect ships, 25, 231, 252

surge capacity. *See* mobilization capacity

surprise attack, 41-42, 46, 67-69, 166. *See also* deterrence; pre-emptive strike

surveillance: long-range, general, 24-26, 38, 43; long-range in air environment, 40-41, 233-36; long-range in ground environment, 233-36; long-range in sea environment, 233-38; maritime, general, 20 n.28, 59-60, 62, 65, 105 n.54, 223; short-range, 24, 38, 238-42. *See also* Australia, mapping and charting of; night vision systems; radar; sensors; sonar systems; space systems; target acquisition

SWATH. *See* semi-submerged hull systems

Sweden, 165, 167; population shelter programme in, 175-76

Switzerland, 167

Synnot, Admiral Sir Anthony, 77

Tactical Operations Systems (TOS), 246

Tange, Sir Arthur, 83, 262. *See also* Tange Report

Tange Report, 82-83, 125

tanks, 25, 34-36, 42, 218, 247, 253; ammunition for, 25, 35, 242, 253; HIMAG, 253; tactics of, 34, 253. *See also* armour; armoured personnel carriers; mechanized infantry combat vehicles

target acquisition: long-range, general, 24-26, 38, 41, 43; long-range in air environment, 40, 233-36; long-range in ground environment, 28, 39, 233-36; long-range in sea environment, 233-38; short-range, 24, 38, 238-42. *See also* night vision systems; radar; sensors. sonar systems; surveillance

task force concept: bureaucratic, 140-41; long-range aerial, 21 n.28

Taylor, Maxwell, 140

technological advance, military: capacity to change established ideas, 16-17, 22 n.29, 23, 45-47; ease of transfer to other states, 89, 119; impact on warning times, 89; implications for Australia of, xx, xxi, 25-26, 45-47, 96, 174; implications for military doctrine of, 15, 23, 26-47; modular concepts in, 248. *See also* countermeasures; laser; threats; precision-guided munitions

terminal force concept, 150. *See also* force expansion concepts

territorial defence, 165-68, 195, 198, 203-4; counter-offensive capacity of, 168; suitability for part-time manpower of, 166, 201-3. *See also* deterrence

terrorism, 43-44, 61-62, 66; manpower requirements to defend against, 87. *See also* threats

Thompson, James, 134

threats: Australia's stimulation of, 120; from chemical and biological warfare, 70; from China, 8; illegal activities in coastal zone, 58; from Indonesia, 12; peace-time pressures, 54-58; perceptions of, 86-88, 112, 152, 212, 264-72, 273 n.8; pressures of international aggression, 54, 60-70, 87-90; pressures of international crises, 54, 58-60, 70; probability of, 54-55, 70, 174; from regional powers, 16, 66, 88-89; from Soviet Union, 8, 22 n.29, 224 n.2; technologies providing new capacities for, 25, 63; timing of, 54-55, 85-90; uncertain form of, 53, 71, 77, 104,

n.42, 150, 152, 164, 210-11, 262, 271-72. *See also* attacks; blockades; confrontation strategy; economic measures; harassments; invasion; nuclear war; pre-emptive strikes; raids; surprise attack; terrorism
Tindal, airfield at, 12
torpedoes, 25, 30-31, 33. *See also* mines; sensor weapons
Torres Strait, 63
total defence (concept), 42, 71, 98-99, 210-11, 213 n.1, 213 n.2, 223. *See also* planning, Australian security, utilization of civil facilities in
towed-array sonars. *See* sonar systems
tracker aircraft (S-2). *See* aircraft
training and education: under aegis of ANZUS, 14; of bureaucrats, 139, 141, 146 n.47; as defence aid, xx, 11 n.2; new requirements for, 37; of part-time personnel, 189-91, 195-99; in strategic studies, 123 n.23
trucks, production lead times of, 97
Tweeddale, J.A., 97

uncertainty, management of in planning. *See* planning, Australian security
United Nations 56, 63; peace-keeping operations of, xx, 264
United Service Institution report on ANZUS, 8
United States: as an ally, xix-xx, 7-13; Australians' perceptions of, 3-4; capacities and intentions to assist Australia, xx, 11-17, 53, 224 n.2; co-operation in developing tactical doctrine, 14; co-operation in military operations and training, 14, 120; defence facilities in Australia, 15-16, 21 n.28, 63, 69; defence science co-operation, 14; economic relationship with Australia, 3; equipment compatability with, 162-63, 184; force withdrawal from Asia, xix, 6, 18 n.7; impact of Vietnam War on, 5-6, 17 n.6; intelligence co-operation with, 14, 21 n.29, 90-92; perceptions of Australia, 3-4, 10, 16, 21 n.28; security policy, direction of, 6. *See also* allies; ANZUS; Guam Doctrine; War Powers Resolution
United States Air Force, 21, 28, 190; reserves of, 190
United States Air National Guard, 190. *See also* United States Air Force
United States Army, 190
United States Marines, 190
United States Navy, 21, 190
urban centres, Australians' concentration in, 167, 174
U.S.S.R. *See* Soviet Union

Vietnam War, 140
V/STOL concepts. *See* aircraft

warheads: cluster, 24, 35, 232, 248; conventional, general, 232-33; fuel-air explosives, 24, 32, 36, 41, 232, 248; ground penetrator, 232, 248; runway penetration, 35; self-forming forged fragmentation, 35; shaped charge, 35, 232; submunition, 161. *See also* bombs; precision-guided munitions
warning time, 85-89, 91, 103 n.40, 176, 280; impact of technological advance upon, 89. *See also* force expansion concepts; intelligence organizations
War Powers Resolution, 19 n.18
White Paper on Australia's Defence 1976, 8, 82
Wildavsky, A.B., 140
Winjeel aircraft (CA-25). *See* aircraft
Withers, Glenn, 111
Woolner, Derek, 82

Yugoslavia, 165, 167